Wide as the World

Wide as the World

Cosmopolitan Identity, Integral Politics, and Democratic Dialogue

Jack Crittenden

LEXINGTON BOOKS
A division of
ROWMAN & LITTLEFIELD PUBLISHERS, INC.
Lanham • Boulder • New York • Toronto • Plymouth, UK

Published by Lexington Books
A wholly owned subsidiary of The Rowman & Littlefield Publishing Group, Inc.
4501 Forbes Boulevard, Suite 200, Lanham, Maryland 20706
http://www.lexingtonbooks.com

Estover Road, Plymouth PL6 7PY, United Kingdom

British Library Cataloguing in Publication Information Available

Library of Congress Cataloging-in-Publication Data

Crittenden, Jack.
  Wide as the world : cosmopolitan identity, integral politics, and democratic dialogue / Jack Crittenden.
    p. cm.
  Includes bibliographical references.
  ISBN 978-0-7391-4854-9 (cloth : alk. paper)
  1. Cosmopolitanism. 2. Democracy. 3. Dialogues. I. Title.
  JZ1310.C75 2011
  306.2—dc22
                                                                2010051796

☉™ The paper used in this publication meets the minimum requirements of American National Standard for Information Sciences—Permanence of Paper for Printed Library Materials, ANSI/NISO Z39.48-1992.

Printed in the United States of America

Ubi bene, ibi patria

("Where something is good,
There is my fatherland")

Table of Contents

Acknowledgments

If I were a maiden tied to the tracks of orthodoxy with the fetters of my own intellectual work, fearing the onrushing train of scholarly opinion, I would not expect to be rescued by Lexington Books of Rowman & Littlefield. But I have been. Twice. The first time they took a chance on *Democracy's Midwife,* when other presses had decided that as a hybrid of political theory, educational theory, and educational practice the manuscript had every characteristic of failure.

Even I recognized the edgy nature of *Wide as the World,* written as a dialogue between two fictional characters for whom I've invented a fair amount of "back story." Once again, Lexington took a chance when editors at other presses had declared it "a hard sell," "riskily unorthodox," and "for academics, full of red flags." Lexington saw that the book wasn't written just or even primarily for academics. Like me, they thought this a grace of the book, not a problem.

So I'd like to thank, first, those intrepid rescuers at Lexington with whom I've worked. Thanks to Jon Sisk at Rowman & Littlefield for sending word along the tracks; and thanks to those at Lexington who untied me: Joseph Parry, Abagail Graber, Erin Walpole, and Lynsey Weston.

Some friends and former students (and former student who are now friends) shouted encouragement along the way. Thanks to Michael Morrell, Alisa Kessel, Ryan Davis, Eddie Genna, and Keally McBridge. They didn't help untie me; sensing danger, they wisely kept their distance. Thanks, also, go to two undergraduate researchers, my two Junior Fellows Jenny Reich and Louie Weimar, who devised an experiment to test my method of democratic dialogue. Special thanks to Debi Campbell and Shannon Wheatley who helped me clear the path, but, typically, did more watching than clearing.

I'd also like to thank Arizona State University for providing two sabbatical semesters used for research on this book. That research, like a Trans-Siberian Railway line, stretched from the beginning of my first sabbatical in 2001 across seven years to the completion of the manuscript at the end of my second sabbatical. Each sabbatical, therefore, is a terminus: One marks the beginning of the research; the other represents the end of the journey. My good friend and the Director of ASU's School of Politics and Global Studies, Pat Kenney, was the conductor and engineer in the process of securing my sabbaticals. Now he won't return my calls. Such a smart man.

I also thank here for his inspiration, friendship, love, and usually unreliable advice my great friend Ken Wilber. Over the many years of our friendship, he has repeatedly shown through his judgment of my work that even I am not dumb enough to be wrong 100 percent of the time, despite what he claims are my best efforts.

Finally and as always my deepest thanks and appreciation go to my partner in all endeavors and the best editor I know, Pat Crittenden. When Pat finished editing the manuscript, she called me a "cosmotopian." I still don't know whether she did so as praise or in disgust. Regardless, it is an apt description, and I bear it proudly. Know that however bumpy you may find the ride when reading this book, the journey would have required Dramamine and tightened seat belts if not for her keen eye.

Introduction

Some men see things as they are and say, why? I dream of things that never were and say, why not?—Robert Kennedy

In 2007 Douglas Roche, four-time member of the Canadian Parliament and former Chairman of the UN's Disarmament Committee, wrote a book exploring the emerging ethos that he called "global conscience." Romeo Dallaire, whom I cite later in this text, wrote in the foreword to Roche's book that the emergence of this conscience is "palpable."

Although I, too, sense that a global conscience is emerging, I am not convinced, in spite of Roche's evidence and Dallaire's sentiment, that it is palpable. After all, despite the one hundred ninety-two national signatories to the UN's doctrine of the right of all persons to be protected against massive violations of human rights, the UN and many individual nations lacked the will to intervene, or intervene quickly or effectively, in recent cases of genocide, ethnic cleansing, or crimes against humanity. More needs to be done, and done soon and well, in terms of generating cosmopolitan opinion- and will-formation, as Jurgen Habermas phrases it. This kind of generation rests on developing cosmopolitan identity through democratic dialogue, or so I argue.

Thus, I would like to think that my own text and the democratic dialogue described herein can push the "emergence" even faster and deeper into the realm of palpability. I hope that people holding to and using concepts such as global conscience, cosmopolitan identity, and democratic dialogue may work with writers, scholars, activists, and concerned Earthlings to mingle and integrate their views to point to, if not form and reflect, a planetary consciousness that will fulfill the visions of world comity and peace that inspired such cosmopolitan thinkers as Immanuel Kant and H. G. Wells, as well as Douglas Roche.

To move in that direction I think that we need to find ways of creating, establishing, and perpetuating a cosmopolitan identity. I agree with Kenneth

1

Boulding: "[T]he concept of global civic culture requires the acceptance at some level of a shared identity with other human beings" (1988, 56). To sacrifice on behalf of and to work in concert with people—strangers, even, from far-off lands—requires building a sense of a common good through a global civic culture. That depends, as Boulding says, on a shared identity, which is a cosmopolitan identity.

That might seem easy enough to do, given that we share a common humanity and thus should be able to perceive through that lens a common good. But the recognition of that shared humanity is often lost in the welter of divergent cultural practices; religious beliefs; political ideologies; and seared and searing histories, grudges, and misconceptions that keep us divided. We too often see only the seeming gulfs that keep us apart and not the similarities that make us a part of one humanity. We need, in short, to be "a part" of and not "apart" from one another's lives.

Identity links us and makes us a part of others' lives and makes them part of ours. Thus, this book is about the nature and creation of cosmopolitan identity, our identity with all of humanity. The development of my ideas on the subject arises in the context of prior moral and political theory about cosmopolitanism, but, if you know this growing body of literature, you will see that I do not add much new or significant to it. There is excellent work in moral, legal, and political theory on cosmopolitanism by scholars far smarter and better read than I. Indeed, it almost seems as if every prominent theorist has written something about cosmopolitanism. Consider this abbreviated, but nevertheless impressive, list of contributing scholars: Martha Nussbaum, Jurgen Habermas, Jeremy Waldron, Bruce Ackerman, Peter Singer, Anthony Appiah, Brian Berry, David Held, Charles Beitz, and Seyla Benhabib. You will find references to some of their pertinent works in the bibliography.

So the moral, legal, political, and philosophical aspects of cosmopolitanism seem well covered. But not enough scholars have looked in depth at cosmopolitan identity and its relation to politics. Indeed, my treatment of the moral and philosophical aspects of cosmopolitanism is really little more than a set-up for my approach and emphasis: How do some persons come not only to have strong feelings for the plight of fellow human beings, but also to identify with all human beings? Is that sense of identity something that we theorists and activists ought to pursue? What are its political implications, good and bad?

The other important context for the development of my ideas is, not surprisingly then, developmental psychology. I have combined developmental psychology and political theory before, in *Beyond Individualism* (1992). Unlike that book, in this manuscript I refer mainly to recent findings in adult development, especially about dialectical thinking, and to studies of meditative states and brain function that reflect the experience of feeling at one with the universe and thus with all of humankind. I also rely on the AQAL Model, developed by Ken Wilber's comparative studies of consciousness East and West, which maps individual growth in conjunction with collective growth. As you will see, constructing cosmopolitan identity requires both psychological and theoretical understanding of individuals and collectivities.

Why is a focus on political identity so important? Why not focus on international institutions to bring about cosmopolitanism or at least global solutions to vexing international problems? The straightforward answer is because identity is tied, however indirectly, to the will (because of thoughts about the effects on the will by the unconscious). Identity is paramount in what people are willing to do. In this regard, consider this comment by Debra Satz:

> At the moment, the international community does not appear to have the capacity to defend or secure even a minimal level of human functioning around the globe. Campaigns of ethnic cleansing and even genocide have proceeded largely unchecked. Moreover, even when the world has been able to intervene, it has lacked the will. Rich nations give less than half a percentage of the GDP to poor nations. In such a context, it is not surprising that so many democratic theorists have taken the transformation of international relationship off the agenda (1999, 78).

A shift in identity can transform relationships. Changes in education and democratic procedures, which I discuss in this book, can lead us toward the development of a cosmopolitan sensibility. So, too, can those changes lead even more expansively toward cosmopolitan identity. Therefore, a shift in identity toward cosmopolitanism, on a large enough scale, can transform international relationships. Otherwise, I do not see how democratic theorists or political practitioners will put cosmopolitan relationships at the international level back on the agenda.

Cosmopolitan identity is, for me, the key to global cooperation and global governance that we need today and the absence of which keeps us from the realization of global conscience. Here is economist Jeffrey Sachs's prediction for the future based on the economic challenges facing us—that is, protecting our environment, stabilizing the world's population, narrowing gaps between rich and poor, and ending extreme poverty: "Global cooperation will have to come to the fore. The very idea of competing nation-states that scramble for markets, power, and resources will become passé" (2008, 3).

Yes, global cooperation, as a manifestation of global conscience, must come to the fore, but will it? Are these economic challenges sufficient to bring us out of our national bunkers to cooperate globally, rather than fighting others for what we need and what we think we can get? Global leaders do not seem, right now, to recognize the outright need for cooperation on these issues. Perhaps the financial crisis coursing across the globe will do it, because the other challenges do not seem severe enough. Yet if the reason for ongoing competition and the paucity of cooperation is the level of severity, then we can imagine that severity can bring out fear, and fear, as we have seen in the financial crisis, brings panic. Panic then heightens demands for action, possession, control, power, and resources, the very sorts of competitive impulses that Sachs thinks are going to become passé. Did the poverty, hunger, crime, disease, and instability of the last century push people and their leaders toward cooperation or toward competition, domestically and internationally? Why when the issues are scarce food and water and polluted air will the push be any different? Why will the definition of "we" in "Let's assure that we have what we need" be global and not national? Global catastrophes might bring about global cooperation and global conscience, but they might not, and that is a major risk.

I think that we need to open another door toward global cooperation and conscience. That door opens onto cosmopolitan identity. In "Politics" Ralph Waldo Emerson wrote (1844), "governments have their origin in the moral identity of men." Global governance, then, though not necessarily global government, can come from a new moral identity, a cosmopolitan identity.

One way, and perhaps the best way, to achieve that identity is to institutionalize democratic dialogue built of dialectical thinking, or so I argue in the text. That can be done, I think, most easily at the local level in schools, factories, businesses, towns, clubs, and the like, and then, most promisingly at the state, national, and global levels. Institutionalizing democratic dialogue locally can be a means of exerting political and social pressure upward, toward the top, toward the national and international power brokers and established elites. This too, I argue in the text. Dialogue eventuates through the exchange of free and often discordant ideas and positions in what Kant called "enlarged mentality." That kind of mentality is not reason alone, but the combination of emotion and thought. This, too, is one of my themes.

So, Roche and Dallaire's rising "global conscience" and Sachs's predicted future seem to exist today in what might be called a "culture of hope." In a culture of hope persons see glimpses of humanitarian action and wish to glean from those glimpses the stirrings of real and growing global conscience. There are many examples of such action and thus of persons exhibiting global conscience, what my friend Shannon Wheatley calls "everyday cosmopolitan acts." But I think that we can move today beyond discrete acts and beyond a culture of hope and toward, if not into, a culture of global conscience itself. To describe it otherwise, this is a culture of cosmopolitanism. I think that this culture can come about through systematic democratic action. We can move toward a culture of cosmopolitanism first by establishing the essence of and the need for a new kind of thinking—dialectical thinking, which, as said, I discuss in this book. Second, we can move toward that culture by structuring on multiple levels—local, provincial, national, regional, and global—forums and even institutions built of democratic dialogue based on dialectical thinking. The hope of this book is to encourage people to step forward and begin that establishing and structuring. The purpose of the book is to tell people why and how to do it.

The book is a dialogue between two persons: Stan Pinzak and Emile Whyte. It is a dialogue in that the two are "thinking together," though they also discuss or "break apart" lots of theories and ideas. The dialogue of "thinking together" is artificial in that much of it comes out of my conversations with myself. William

Isaacs comments that dialogue, to be effective, must begin first with asking ourselves, "How successful am I at listening to and speaking with *myself?*" (1999, 79; emphasis in original). That success is difficult to measure, and thus the question is difficult, if not impossible, for me to answer. But the dialogue provides ample evidence for others to try.

Why a dialogue? To those who study the use of language and its many structured forms there are doubtless good reasons for writing dialogue. Here are my reasons for doing so. All of them point to making the text more accessible to readers:

1. Dialogue offers readers a change of pace, as it breaks up the narrative flow, visually and intellectually. Those breaks relax the pace, which makes the discussion less dense and therefore more inviting. The relaxed pace of the characters' talk, like a stroll in the woods, keeps the reader alert for sentences and ideas that are alive.

2. Dialogue also offers frequent breaks in switching from one character to another. The reader finds more areas in which to pause and to stop. This can encourage reflection.

3. Pauses permit the reader to see openings in the conversation, where a different question could well result in a different direction. Wanting to ask that question changes the reader from one who absorbs to one who interrogates. It also underscores that dialogues are open, rarely fixed, and never finished.

4. Dialogue in its dramatic form tells a story. My story involves two fictional characters, their backgrounds, and their developing relationship. Engaging the reader in these fictional characters might be a way of generating greater interest in their philosophical and political encounters by introducing aspects that are not purely intellectual.

5. Dialogue is more suitable to and quickly grasped as a dialectic—the back-and-forth, often through questions—that highlights conflicting ideas, positions, reasons, and arguments and attempts to yield understanding. Following Plato's lead, I think that dialogue draws readers into the discussion.

I invite you, as a reader, to ask questions better than mine and to draw insights deeper and broader than mine. In this sense, as Plato possibly envisioned for his students studying his dialogues, I want my readers to ask questions and to raise answers that I never thought of myself.

To be fully honest, however, I thought about the five reasons listed above after I had already decided to write a dialogue. They are, then, rationalizations. I wrote a dialogue because I thought it would be fun. I was right. The format allowed me to be playful, flexible, and free from the tightly controlled and sometimes lifeless scholarly, narrative voice in any other way. Creating and bringing Pinzak and Emile to life helped me mute some of my overly academic linguistic proclivities. Each encounter, or chapter, begins with some history of and exchanges between Pinzak and Emile that reveal something personal about one of them that may or may not be related directly to the intellectual conversation between the two that then follows. These relaxed exchanges at the outset of each encounter, as well as the tone of their exchanges, have a positive effect, I think, on the language the characters use in the subsequent intellectual exchanges that constitute the body of each encounter.

Plus, the fictionalized characters illustrate a casual yet intimate kind of storytelling important in democratic dialogue. That importance is discussed in the text. Here, then, are other important themes discussed in the "Encounters," which is my term for "Chapters":

I begin the First Encounter with a brief "potted" history of the idea of cosmopolitanism, tracing it forward from the Greek Cynic philosopher Diogenes, through the Roman Stoics, into the Renaissance (with some attention to critics of the concept), and then to Kant. At this point, I switch the focus to some of the philosophical and political aspects of cosmopolitanism, especially to Kant's idea of a federated republic of states. Here I introduce Kant's suggestion that "the people of the earth" at the close of the eighteenth century had entered "in varying degrees into a universal community." The evidence for this, according to Kant, was the development that a "violation of rights in *one* part of the world is felt *everywhere*" (emphasis in the original). This observation serves as a segue into the idea of a cosmopolitan identity and Martha Nussbaum's idea of identity as concentric circles. Her idea is that persons have identities that move from self to family to neighborhood or community to nation and, finally, she argues, to all of humanity. Persons are constantly pulling closer to the center those affiliations that once lay on the periphery. I explore the implications of this idea as well as some of the criticisms of it.

Nussbaum is a transition to the Second Encounter, as the issue of citizenship and national identity is one of the principal criticisms of her position. Her position is that those personal qualities that we hold dear, those with which we identify—for example, religion, ethnicity, gender, nationality—are not morally relevant to what we owe to and how we treat other persons. All such considerations are at best secondary, because our primary obligation or allegiance ought to be to all human beings regardless of where they live, how they worship, what they look like, or where they come from. I examine this obligation and identity, and I use David Miller as a proponent of obligations established through community and especially through ethical communities called nations.

I use this discussion as a way to move to a different perspective on nations: What holds nations together is not shared religion or language or history; it is not even a shared territory. I argue that what holds them together is shared principles. If that is so, then Nussbaum's cosmopolitan identity can be formed similarly through shared principles—what Nussbaum calls the "community of justice and reason." I end this second encounter by reviewing Nussbaum's point, central to her view of cosmopolitan identity, that cosmopolitanism is the recognition that we share an ineradicable bond with all humans on the basis of our shared humanity. But that bond is not a substitute for those particular attachments that persons find meaningful. What kind of commitment would it be to forsake our special others—family, friends, fellow citizens—as we encircled and embraced "all others"?

What is the psychology that lies behind and can buttress the idea of a cosmopolitan identity such as Nussbaum's? In the Third Encounter I introduce the idea of dialectical thinking and its importance in fostering a cosmopolitan identity. I begin by reviewing what we mean, can mean, or ought to mean by the term "identity." I use developmental psychology to explain the central differentiation in identity between the concept or construct of "I" and the construct of "me."

This differentiation changes depending on the level or stage of development, mostly cognitive development. There is, throughout identity development, a hierarchy or "series" of selves, not so much a concatenation of selves but an "evolution" of self. I move quickly, and without jargon, through the standard developmental views of these stages of self, using notable examples as illustrations, and end up at adult psychological development. This is a recent area of study for developmental psychologists. In this area we find the use among some adults—very few, in fact—of dialectical thinking, which, I argue, is both a cause and a consequence of cosmopolitan identity. At this level of thinking, and it is found almost exclusively in adults, the person pushes to the limits (and some say beyond) of formal operational thinking or what is more commonly known as hypothetical or propositional thinking. Dialectical thinkers can even push beyond these limits; beyond, that is, language and logic themselves.

Here in dialectical thinking arise the possibilities found in meditation as a way of knowing beyond logic and language, which I investigate toward the end of the encounter. Dialectical thinkers show the ability to handle ambiguity, divergent viewpoints, and contradictions, which formal operational thinkers can do as well. But dialectical thinkers also *embrace* ambiguity, divergent viewpoints, and contradictions in order to find the unity or connections underlying them, which formal operational thinkers cannot and will not do. Here lies the connection to cosmopolitan identity, as the person attempts to go beyond boundaries . . . of almost any kind. The dialectical thinker is preoccupied with finding a balance between feeling unique and seeing herself as a part, a tiny part, of a deeper, greater whole. All of this is documented through research in developmental psychology.

The Fourth Encounter looks into the possibilities for an integral politics. I use the term "integral," because dialectical thinkers, as I said above, seek out and embrace ambiguity, divergent viewpoints, and contradictions as a way of integrating them into the basis of a cosmopolitan identity. Is there a politics, a kind of democratic politics, that could and should accompany, exercise, and at the same time engender dialectical thinking; that is, a politics that is simultaneously a cause and consequence of dialectical thinking and that can encourage and reinforce cosmopolitan identity?

To pursue this question I examine and later make use of Ken Wilber's integrative model. This model shows us how dialectical thinking fits in with an overall scheme for understanding human and social development and how different levels of development fit together or integrate. What does this model tell us about politics? First, it reinforces the idea that persons are both agents (wholes) acting with autonomy and independence and simultaneously members or participants (parts) in communion or community with others. Identity always has these two poles of agency and community, even when it undergoes developmental changes. This means that when arguing about policy, political theorists and politicians must consider the character of our citizens as well as our social institutions and programs; that is, as Wilber's integrative or "four-quadrants" model shows, we must consider both the inside (psychology) and outside (behavior) of every person both as an individual and as a member of collectivities. As I argue, in integral politics the health of an individual cannot be considered separately from the health of the community and from the community's social, political, and cultural institutions. Similarly, an integral politics involves both changing people's consciousness and simultaneously changing people's social conditions.

As I discuss in the Third and Fourth Encounters, a combination of dialectical thinking and meditation offers the best possibility of engendering a cosmopolitan identity. This is not to say, of course, that people cannot be persuaded by the moral, philosophical, and political arguments underlying and surrounding cosmopolitanism. But to engender an identity as a cosmopolitan requires, I argue, more than that. In the Fifth Encounter I engage the scientific evidence on mysticism and meditation, what is now sometimes referred to as the "neuropsychology" of spiritual experience. This involves investigating a new kind of science that has emerged over the past few years, "the cognitive neuroscience of religion." Whereas researchers over the past thirty years have looked into the psychological and physiological benefits of meditation, only recently have they begun looking into how meditation changes brain structure and brain function. The findings support the contention found in Wilber's quadrants model that spiritual, mystical, or meditative experiences show a biological correlate.

More significant, these studies underscore the idea that spiritual or mystical experience can yield valid knowledge, as valid as knowledge from science and culture, because the knowledge gained in all three of those domains can be validated publicly. Indeed, as I argue in this encounter, knowledge in each domain is validated through the same epistemological process; only the tools used for "seeing" vary from domain to domain. I examine in detail this claim and the process in all three domains and relate them to cosmopolitan identity and politics.

Democratic dialogue is how we generate public knowledge. Public knowledge is what participants in dialogue and deliberation come to realize about the nature of social or political problems and policies and to realize about the effects of problems and policies on themselves, their fellow citizens, and their fellow human beings. When a participant hears a diversity of views, she begins to understand the extent of the problem and the possible consequences of different solutions. This kind of dialogue, therefore, must have dialectical thinking built in, so that participants, as far as possible, will be required to listen to and even echo the positions of others. It will require, in other words, the exercise of empathy as participants step in and out of others' specific perspectives.

The Sixth and Seventh Encounters are about the institutionalizing of democratic dialogue. In the Seventh Encounter I look, finally, at institutions and institutional reform. In the Sixth Encounter I begin to lay out in detail the essential elements of dialogue. The structure of democratic dialogue, as I argue, is more important than even the venues in which it takes place. But the structure of the dialogue links, of course, to the venues themselves and to possible institutional changes and innovations necessitated by introducing those structures, especially dialectical thinking.

One issue central to the structure of democratic dialogue is how to get participants to open up, to reflect, and to change their minds. Social context and expectations are, I argue, crucial in doing so. This emphasizes the structure of the procedures and underscores the importance of the three dialogical elements discussed in this encounter: storytelling; detailing multiple, and even discrepant, perspectives; and deliberating on these perspectives.

Storytelling, the first phase of dialogue, is essential to building trust and to generating mutual respect. It permits participants to say whatever they want in the way they want, without fear of censure or critique and without needing to conform to controlled rationality. Laying out perspectives is the second phase of the dialogue in which participants freely state and imagine options, ideas, positions, and possibilities related to the issue under consideration. It is not a time for criticism, which comes during the third phase, but is the opportunity for participants to share their views and reasons behind those views. Both of the first two phases require careful, active participant listening, since the goal is mutual understanding. That understanding can lead to changes in consciousness.

Phase Three, the stage of scrutinizing the different perspectives, rests on the respect and mutual trust built through the first two phases. Phase three is the stage of deliberation, which is the distinguishing characteristic of this phase. Deliberation is a necessary prelude to the final phase, phase four, during which participants seek to create a compound or integrated common good from the available perspectives.

Building a compound common good, the objective of phase four and the opening theme of the Seventh Encounter, does not mean that participants will not be critical of the multiple, and often conflicting, perspectives presented in the dialogue; indeed, there will be ample opportunity to offer critique. It means that as far as possible participants give a fair hearing to all perspectives before arguing or deciding what goes into the compound common policy or perspective. In short, participants try to integrate various viewpoints into one overarching viewpoint. This approach is surely in keeping with dialectical thinking and a cosmopolitan worldview.

The conversation in the Seventh Encounter between Emile and Pinzak begins with talk about the outcomes of some groups that use dialogue as the centerpiece of their proceedings. Included here are Native American Wisdom Councils and the National Issues Forums. The experiences of participants in such dialogues reinforce how integration within persons takes place and how integration among persons, or cosmopolitan identity, can happen. Dialogue offers the dual benefit of exposing more sides of an issue and of expanding the sense of connection among the participants. The dual benefit facilitates the creation of a compound or integrated common good, as it helps uncover or discover deeper solutions to problems.

The size of the deliberating groups and the number of different perspectives offered within a large group are problems in thinking about instituting democratic dialogue. "Legislative Juries" are one possible solution. Although Legislative Juries appear to be a viable option, as I argue in the text, institutionalization will require political orchestration, especially by or through already established institutions. Chief among these is the United Nations. Here I offer some tentative suggestions for reforming the UN—involving, for example, a chamber of multinational corporations and transnational civil-society networks—and for establishing a global federation of liberal democratic states. In both cases, universal human rights are the centerpiece of any reform or innovation.

There is, finally, an epilogue that brings the story of the encounters between Pinzak and Emile to a close. The intellectual focus of the epilogue is cosmopolitan education, but I leave that topic underdeveloped. Cosmopolitan education is really only an interlude between segments of Pinzak's thinking and the narrative of action. The epilogue is not intended to be a disquisition on possible forms of cosmopolitan education, but is, instead, only a way to bring the conversation, and the book, to an end and to stand as an opening to further, and future, dialogue.

I began this research in earnest several years ago, when I was startled to read in his essay "Perpetual Peace" Kant's declaration, already mentioned, that a sense of global community in his day prevailed to such an extent that "a transgression of rights in *one* place in the world is felt *everywhere*." I was struck by his emphasis on the word *everywhere*. Even more remarkable to me was his claim that people "felt" it. That startled me, for Kant claimed not simply that people everywhere recognized the transgression; he claimed that they actually *felt* it. Perhaps Kant, like Roche and Dallaire long after him, had misread as palpability the emerging, the very slow emerging, of global community. For at the end of the eighteenth century, when Kant wrote that essay, people did not feel the transgressions, not everywhere. Nor did people seem to feel them everywhere in the nineteenth or twentieth centuries. Do we today? The world declares the killing in Darfur to be genocide, and yet we do not vigorously intervene. Starvation and poverty continue throughout the world, and yet we in the affluent industrialized world, where we consume most of the world's resources, do little systematically to eliminate them.

Do we not feel these transgressions? Perhaps we do not feel them enough. What would "feeling them enough" look like? How would that feeling change the political landscape? More important, can people really feel such transgressions happening thousands of miles away? Should they? The United Nations Universal Declaration of Human Rights states in the first article that all human beings "should act towards one another in a spirit of brotherhood." We should, but we do not, or we do not always, or we do not often enough. I wrote this book to understand through exploring the nature and development of cosmopolitan identity what we might do about that.

First Encounter:

Cosmopolitanism

God, grant, that not only the Love of Liberty, but a thorough Knowledge of the Rights of Man, may pervade all the Nations of the Earth, so that a Philosopher may set his Foot anywhere on its surface, and say, "This is my Country."
—Benjamin Franklin in a letter to David Hartley, December 4, 1789

Pinzak needed coffee. Strong coffee. In a big cup. He exited Widener Library through the rear entrance, crossed Massachusetts Avenue at the light, and headed out of Harvard Square toward Bow Street and the Café Pamplona.[1] Inside, the café was dark. Pinzak waited for his eyes to adjust. The few tables were occupied, strangers' knees and elbows knocking into their neighbors'. But Pinzak was not thinking about atmosphere. He wanted strong coffee. Seven hours nonstop in the stacks in Widener left him needing a wallop.

He carried his three-shot cappuccino out to the patio and surveyed the tables. All were taken. All had more than one occupant . . . except for one table near the sidewalk. The table was half in sunlight, half in shade. Sunning himself was a small elderly man, dressed in a long camel hair overcoat, fully buttoned. An ebony walking stick with a silver handle rested across his thighs, and the man's hands lay folded in his lap. He wore a black beret, which did not seem at all out of place at Pamplona or on this man. His eyes were closed, and his slight smile revealed that he was not sleeping but resting, maybe even meditating.

Pinzak did not want to sit in the shade. This was one of those rare, late August polar air mass days with the sky starched fresh. He wanted to be in the sun, soaking up the warmth, just like this man. But the only available seat for the moment was at this table, in the shade. Pinzak approached the table and stood for a moment looking at the man, thinking that his presence might cause the man to stir. It did not. Pinzak sat down.

The old man, almost in slow motion, turned his head, opened the eye closer to Pinzak, and nodded slightly. The salutation was so casual, so relaxed, that Pinzak wondered whether the man knew him. Pinzak simply said, "Hello."

"What time is it?" the man asked.

"Three o'clock," Pinzak responded after a quick glance at his watch.

"I have been sitting here for almost forty minutes. It seems like only five." The man looked at Pinzak and smiled. "Is that not what Einstein meant by relativity?"

Pinzak smiled in return. "Exactly. He said, talk to a pretty girl for an hour, it feels like a minute; but sit on a hot stove for a minute, and it'll feel like an hour."

The man kept smiling as Pinzak talked, but kept his eyes closed, warming his face in the sun. The two sat in silence for a few minutes. To Pinzak it felt like a few minutes; he didn't know what the man felt. Pinzak really wanted to be sitting in the sun.

Abruptly and without turning his head the man said, "My name is Emile Whyte."

"Mine is Pinzak, Stan Pinzak." Pinzak stuck out his hand, and Emile, without opening his eyes or turning his body, raised his right hand from his lap and met Pinzak's dead on.

"Stanley David Pinzak?" the man, now Emile, asked.

Responded Pinzak, astonished, "Yes!"

Emile let go of his hand, opened his eyes, and turned and looked at Pinzak. "I have read your book on Rousseau, *Romancing the Self.* I thought it quite good; especially the section on Julie's Elysium, the walled garden in *La Nouvelle Eloise,* as a metaphor for how Rousseau envisioned the self. The garden appears as totally natural, wild, and unsullied by human intrusion. But it is actually manufactured to look and feel exactly that way, just like the selves that Rousseau wishes to create—selves shaped and controlled but who feel natural, independent, and free. That was clever."

Pinzak looked down and then away. He was never comfortable talking about his work. He told people that he followed Michel Foucault's view that he wrote about something so that he would not have to think about it anymore. Pinzak's attitude was "Write it down and move on." It was the only way that Pinzak could, as Nietzsche said, get rid of his thoughts.

But the truth was that Pinzak felt too self-conscious to talk about his work. It embarrassed him. Deep down, he knew coming out of high school that he had gotten into Harvard because of basketball. He doubted that he could have gotten in otherwise. Pinzak could never get over the feeling that he didn't quite measure up, that at Harvard he was faking it. He was always faking it, even now after publications and tenure. Did he still think of himself as a dumb jock instead of a scholar? As usual, he deflected the attention. "Do you know Rousseau's work?" he asked.

"Well," said Emile, "I have read it. I do not know that that constitutes knowing it."

"So you know that Rousseau wrote a treatise on education called *Emile.*"
Emile Whyte nodded. "I do." There was nothing sarcastic or caustic about how
Emile said this, but Pinzak felt suddenly self-conscious.

The two sat in silence, with Whyte sunning and Pinzak sipping.

"Do people call you Emile?"

"Yes. Everyone does. Do people call you Stan?"

"Everyone calls me Pinzak. I can't remember the last time someone called
me Stan."

"So, you call me Emile, and I shall call you Pinzak," said Emile Whyte without turning toward Pinzak or opening his eyes.

Pinzak observed his tablemate while Emile sunned his face. He looked to be
about sixty; Pinzak would have been surprised had Emile been younger than
that. Yet he could be seventy; Pinzak couldn't really tell. Emile was clean-
shaven and wore glasses, large frames but with almost no color. Pinzak reflected
that when Emile looked at him, even though he was sitting in the sun, he didn't
squint.

"Emile, are you an academic?"

"No," replied Emile. "I am a reader."

"What do you mean, you're a reader?" Emile looked at Pinzak and gave him
a here-and-gone smile. "I mean, I know what a reader DOES. But I don't know
what you mean when you say, 'I AM a reader.'"

"Perhaps I did overstate it . . . for dramatic effect." Here Emile lifted his arm
and waved his hand over his head. "I simply meant that I read. A lot. And all
sorts of things. Heaven for me would be an overstuffed chair, preferably leather,
with a strong lamp, a pile of books on my left, and a pile of periodicals and
newspapers on my right. The ottoman would be optional." Emile tilted his head
back and laughed. The sound was primordial. "That is exactly what I have right
now."

"Do you write?" asked Pinzak.

"No. I read and think. I used to say when I was a boy and someone asked me
what I wanted to do when I grew up that I wanted to be a thinker. They would
say, 'Oh, you want to be a journalist or a professor.' And I would say, 'No. I just
want to think about things. Maybe talk about them once in awhile.' Reading has
been the best way for me to find things to think about."

"Like the Scarecrow," smiled Pinzak. Emile gave him a quizzical look. "On
the way to Oz, Dorothy asks the Scarecrow what he wants from the Wizard. The
Scarecrow replies, 'A brain.' Dorothy then asks, 'What will you do with it?' The
Scarecrow answers, 'I'll think of things I never 'thunk' before, and then I'll sit
and think some more.'"

"Yes," said Emile, "like the Scarecrow." Then he looked away.

Pinzak finished his coffee and thought about having another. "I'm going for
another coffee. May I get you something?"

Emile looked down at his demitasse and said, "A glass of water, please. With
lemon."

When Pinzak returned with his coffee and the water, Emile had swung his legs under the table. His left hand, with the right hand on top, rested on its edge. "Thank you," he said as Pinzak placed the water in front of him. Pinzak sat and then stirred his coffee as Emile took a long drink of the water. "So, Pinzak, what are you working on," he asked.

Pinzak's deflective shield came down. "I'm on sabbatical for the semester, so I'm spending the fall in Cambridge. I love New England in the fall, and there's no better research library in the world than Widener."

Emile just smiled with a look that took a short but cascading ride through Pinzak's retina down into his limbic system. Emile asked, "What are you working on?"

Pinzak smiled, too, and the shield rolled up. The second triple cappuccino must be having some effect, he thought. He would talk to this man; what could it hurt? It was not as if the man were another academic set out to judge Pinzak's work, looking for any opening, any excuse, to attack. The guy's a thinker. And a reader. Reasoning with another is always better than trying to think everything through by oneself. In fact, reasoning is really a collaborative effort, a dialectic that produces insights that could not have originated by one's thinking alone. And so they began.

Pinzak: I'm finishing up some articles and just starting to work on a book on cosmopolitanism.

Emile: Ah, yes, *kosmou polites* or "citizen of the world." A phrase used, if not coined, by the Greek Cynic philosopher Diogenes.

Pinzak: So, you're familiar with the term and its philosophical use?

Emile: I am familiar more with its history.

Pinzak: Well, I've not looked at that. I'm interested in its, ah, normative and political import.

Emile: Of course! You are a political theorist! If you are interested, I can share with you the little that I know of the term's history. *(Pinzak nods his head in assent.)* I would not be surprised if our interests did not converge on Kant.

It seems that cosmopolitanism is one of the great themes in the history of Western political thought,[2] much like the Great Chain of Being. As I said, it was Diogenes who when anyone asked him where he came from said, "I am a citizen of the world." But there are hints of cosmopolitanism even in Plato. In the dialogue *Protagoras,* Hippias the Sophist says to those gathered at the house of Callias: "Gentlemen, I regard all of you here present as kinsmen, intimates, and fellow citizens by nature, not by convention. For like is akin to like by nature, but convention, which tyrannizes the human race, often constrains us contrary to nature" (337c7-d3). Of course, Plato has a Sophist saying this, and although Socrates refers to him as "wise Hippias," what Hippias says could be contrary to what Socrates would say and to what Plato thinks.

Diogenes, no great friend of Plato's, is telling anyone who will listen that his independent intellect and his philosophical bent lead him not to identify with Sinope, his colony, to which he owes no special obligations.

Pinzak: What did Diogenes identify with?

Emile: I am not sure we can answer that. It is possible, as a cynic, that Diogenes did not identify with any place or moral obligation at all. Of course, this may also be a begrudging comment in that Diogenes was banned from Sinope and thus saw his world citizenship as supplanting his "political" one, not complementing it.

Pinzak: So his use of the term "cosmopolitanism" could be, well, "cynical." Because there is and can be no such physical place as the cosmopolis, then Diogenes is safe from anyone holding him to or demanding from him any ethical behavior at all. Nobody owes him anything; he owes no one anything in return.

Emile: That *is* a cynical response, but consistent with the ancient Greek Cynics. When the Roman Stoics come along, however, the sense of identification becomes somewhat clearer. Seneca, for example, thought that persons could be loyal both to an existing city or state and to cosmopolitanism, to helping all human beings simply because they are human beings. For Seneca, one's existing community is an accident of birth; the other, or cosmopolitanism, is "a state" whose boundaries are measured not by geography, but by the path of the sun.

Pinzak: But how did the dual loyalties work in practice? If the dual loyalties clashed, then what was the person to do?

Emile: Presumably the cosmopolite would abandon his loyalty to the city-state, which was subordinate. Marcus Aurelius Antoninus saw no conflict between his allegiances. He wrote: "[M]y nature is both rational and social. As Antoninus, my city and country is Rome; as a human being, it is the world. So what benefits these cities is my only good."[3] Already we can see the problems with this perspective. Neither Seneca nor Marcus Aurelius has answered your question, because neither seems to acknowledge that there can be tensions within their commitments.

Perhaps we get the answer, or at least this acknowledgment, during the Renaissance. Erasmus and Montaigne both argued that humans were by nature sociable and harmonious in their interactions. Persons were united by and in their humanity over any differences that arose among territories or states.

Pinzak: This "bond" among persons seems especially thin. It is so abstract. Why couldn't one nation claim that some other nation was acting "unsociably" and therefore needed to be "set straight" through warfare?

Emile: You are right. Natural law theory of this kind is often associated with social contract theory, and social contract theory, as you know, provides justification for the founding of independent, sovereign nation-states.

Pinzak: In fact, Rousseau can be seen as sticking a pin in any cosmopolitan balloon. He questioned whether men (He was not talking about women.) could be loyal toward any social organization larger than a nation. To him the idea of a world city was merely *(Pinzak pulls a small notebook from his hip pocket, flips* *a few pages, and reads)* a dream of "those pretended cosmopolites, who, in justifying their love for the human race, boast of loving all the world in order to enjoy the privilege of loving no one."[4]

Emile: You raise an interesting point. It is one that Hannah Arendt raised, obviously not the first to do so, and one to which I hope we can return after this "potted history." The point is this: If one is to be a "citizen of the world," as Diogenes said, then does one not have to be "citizen"? Can one be a citizen without some sort of city or country or nation? If not, then does a cosmopolitan not need a world city or world republic or world community?

Certainly there were cosmopolites who thought so. When the Danish[5] astronomer Tycho Brahe was about to leave for Switzerland, the king of Denmark gave him the island of Hveen on which to build the Uraniborg Conservatory. There Brahe also built a "city of philosophers," a monastic retreat where men of letters could settle. Voltaire proposed something similar in Prussia, and for Voltaire one's passport to citizenship was solely the quality of one's thinking.

Pinzak: But Voltaire undermines the whole cosmopolitan principle or spirit! His city or whatever it was didn't reflect the attitude of Diogenes or other cosmopolites. Diogenes seems to be saying that he is at home everywhere. His connection is to all of humanity. Voltaire's view is a betrayal of that attitude. His fellow cosmopolites aren't all of humanity. They're the intellectual elite, a colony of philosophers. Voltaire and his ilk, they imply, would only be happy or at home in that colony and would only really be comfortable with, and perhaps only welcome, those like them. This would hardly be an environment hospitable to all of humankind.

Emile: You are right. Bear in mind that many of these philosophers and men of letters were trying, at least in their minds, to find a way to live where they did not have to battle the governments of their countries, many of which were censoring their written work. So these writers sought to create a "republic of letters," as Jefferson described the new nation of the United States. The British historian Edward Gibbon thought that philosophers, whose intellectual approach and interests transcended national boundaries, should consider Europe to be "one great Republic."[6]

Pinzak: Still, such a perspective doesn't advance cosmopolitanism. It is just elitist cant. Sure, such men of letters as Gibbon and Voltaire could think of themselves in the exclusive yet cosmopolitan company of fellow writers and identify with them as equal members of a kind of cosmopolitan club. But to have Europe be a cosmopolitan territory, to have Europe truly be "one great Republic," well, it would have to look considerably different.

Emile: It is true that for these men geography meant little.

Pinzak: It isn't just geography. It is how that geography is built upon, protected, governed, and cultivated. In 1787, for example, Benjamin Franklin sent a copy of the draft U.S. Constitution to Ferdinand, Grand Duke of Tuscany. In the letter Franklin floated the idea that Europe should create "one Grand Republic of all its different States and Kingdoms." Two years later Franklin wrote, *(Pinzak pulls another, slightly smaller, notebook from a side pocket in his jacket, flips* *through several pages, stops, and reads)* "God grant, that not only the Love of Liberty, but a thorough knowledge of the Rights of Man, may pervade all the Nations of the Earth, so that a Philosopher may set his Foot anywhere on its surface, and say, 'This is my country.'" Yes, Franklin expresses a cosmopolitanism, and although he uses the term "Philosopher," he extends it beyond the elitism of Voltaire or Gibbon. By talking of the Rights of Man, Franklin does bring us back to the cosmopolitan notion of identifying with all persons as persons, regardless of who they are, where they live, or what they do. Yet where in Franklin, or any of the others, is the hard work of explaining how Europe could become one Grand Republic?

Emile: You raise a crucial issue. No one really explains that. Even "Anarchsis" Cloots,[7] who argued for the abolition of all states and the construction of a single world state, never really explains how it could come about. He uses social contract theory to make the argument. *(Pinzak shrugs his shoulders.)* It goes something like this; be sure to correct me if I am wrong: Because everyone agrees to submit to the authority of a state that can enforce laws that provide security, then everyone should agree to having a single state that can guarantee security. All individuals, every individual in the world, would be protected in this state. This is to be preferred to the anarchic system of plural sovereign states that interact in a Hobbesian state of nature where every nation sees every other nation as a possible threat, and therefore every nation is itself a threat to every other. But Cloots does not really explain how this single state can come about.

So, perhaps, then, we ought to turn our attention to Kant, who, as I said earlier, might be where my "potted history" meets your normative and political concerns.

Kant

Pinzak: Are you suggesting, Emile, that Kant proposes building one grand republic or a single super state?

Emile: Of course not. As you well know, he was at best ambivalent on that notion.[8] In "Perpetual Peace" Kant argues for a federation of like-minded states; that is, states governed by certain republican principles, one of which will be to honor the human rights of all persons, citizen and stranger alike. A free federation of such states could achieve perpetual peace.

For Kant, all rational beings—therefore all of us, potentially—are members of one moral community. But it is not just through a set of timeless moral principles that Kant conceives his project for perpetual peace. Rather, it is also through a philosophy of history.

Pinzak *(allowing a little exasperation to creep into his tone):* In the First Definitive Article of that essay, Kant wrote that all states should be republican, by which he means, translating "republican" into today's terms, representative democracies with protected individual rights.[9] Well, if all states indeed become republican, then won't we really have a world republic, a world state? Surely you can see how Kant's logic tends in that direction?

Emile: This was Kant's fear. As states reform and become constitutional republics, they join the federation. At some point, as you suggest, one can imagine that all the states of the world are republics. It would seem, then, that cosmopolitan law pertaining to every state would supersede the laws of individual states. At that point the particular freedoms of citizens in the individual states could be lost, as well as those states' national sovereignty.

Pinzak: And yet, Emile, if the states truly have republican constitutions, and those constitutions are founded on principles of reason, such as Kant's categorical imperative, then how could any particular freedom be lost, unless that freedom violated the principle of right, as Kant called it? As for sovereignty, would not cosmopolitan law permit some level of sovereignty, a kind of conditioned sovereignty, just as the states in the United States have?

But let's hold these issues aside for the moment. I'm curious how a philosophy of history is going to show us how to build a cosmopolitan republic or a "free federation of republican states."

Emile *(with a slight, and knowing, smile):* It shows the importance of historical context. That context addresses your thoughts about the world republic. Kant looks at the state of the world, the states in that world, and the people in those states. He knows that a world-state at that time would have to begin through force and would eventually devolve into a universal monarchy. Such a state, such a monarchy, would be a "soulless despotism" and a "graveyard of freedom" (1970, 113-14) eliminating diversity and eventually dissolving into anarchy. To have a world-state would require, therefore, having coercive power to ensure that everyone behaved or else it would be ungovernable. Such a power would violate the rights of persons living within the world-state. To keep the peace such a world-state could trample on the rights of some.

But as you suggest, Kant seems to foresee a universal world republic. Once a state establishes a republican constitution, it will "unite with other neighboring states and even distant states to arrive at a lawful settlement of their differences by forming something analogous to a universal state" (1970, 123). From his perspective at the end of the eighteenth century, however, "the positive idea of a world republic cannot be realized" (105), if only because Kant knows that states will not surrender their national sovereignty. The next best option? What Kant calls "a negative substitute": a federation of republics by which Kant really means a federation of peoples (Hoffe 2006).

Pinzak: Okay, so, what would bring states together into a federated union? What holds them together once federated?

Emile: Kant thinks that it is commerce and self-interest that does so, coupled with an increasing unity of principles and the emergence, through expanding communication, of a single enlightened world culture.[10]

Pinzak: What is that self-interest?

Emile: Are you testing me, Pinzak? *(Both laugh.)* Nations, to Kant, cannot undertake constant war readiness while simultaneously providing commercially for the well-being of their peoples. In our contemporary parlance, he thinks that a nation cannot have both guns and butter. The federated union of states could make the idea of war unthinkable because of the unity and cooperation within the union and the power of it to those outside the federation. Otherwise, states can only establish their security and peace by constant war readiness; that is, by always preparing and being ready for war.

In addition, Kant proposes cosmopolitan law. While all persons have individual rights granted through the constitutions of their states—that is, constitutional law—and while all states as states follow international law, Kant introduces cosmopolitan law as a third set of laws that guarantee rights to all persons as "citizens of the earth" and not simply as citizens of particular states. These are rights that extend across national boundaries.

Pinzak: I grant all of that. But what really is the argument that this will work? Is it Kant's view that by simply pointing out to people that they can't have both guns and butter that world leaders will flock to this Federation of United Republican Nations?

Emile: Kant thinks that this federation is the only way to gain and maintain peace. He sees this federation as the only way to achieve the unity of morality and politics. As Kant says, "A federative association of states whose sole intention is to eliminate war is the only *lawful* [political] arrangement which can be reconciled with their *freedom* [morality]" (1970, 129, emphases in original). This is so because such a federation is freely joined and its founding principles are those of right, and transparent, reason. According to Kant, following principles of right leads ineluctably to the "absolutely imperative" duty to respect the rights of persons. This is nothing other than Kant's categorical imperative, which in the context of politics he calls the principles of freedom. In other words, we treat all persons as ends in themselves and not as means to another's end, and this in itself is a universalizable, and universalized, principle.

Because such a federation is, for Kant, the only way to assure peace and not simply the cessation of hostilities among nations, he is interested in the actual structure of this federation. He is also interested because he thinks that such a federation can actually happen; it is not simply a utopian fiction. Similar to what the founding fathers of this country thought about the Constitution, Kant thinks that institutions of the cosmopolitan federation must counteract the self-seeking inclinations of humans. The self-seeking proclivities of one person or group must be neutralized by the self-seeking proclivities of others. Here is Madison's notion of faction counteracting faction, as Kantian "unsocial sociability" plays itself out. As Kant phrased it, even if a person is not morally a good person, he or she will feel compelled to be a morally upstanding citizen through the laws and procedures of the federation. This means, as Kant claimed in a famous observation, that a good state can be established even by a nation of devils.[11]

Pinzak: So, through the establishment of such a constitution among states or within a state, Kant thought that people can attain a moral culture in which even "devils" would be compelled to be good citizens.

Emile: He did, because for Kant the power of a republic did not rest on the virtues of those within it. All that is required for persons to do is "create a good organisation for the state . . . and arrange it so that their self-seeking energies are opposed to one another, each thereby neutralising or eliminating the destructive effects of the rest" (1970, 112).[12]

Kant scanned history and thought that the time for such a federated republic had come. In "Theory and Practice" he observed that humans were making moral progress. He wrote: "[T]he human race is constantly progressing in cultural matters. . . .[I]t is also engaged in progressive improvement in relation to the moral end of its existence." He wrote later in the essay that "the human race has made considerable progress. . . .[W]e have reached a higher level of morality" (89).[13]

Pinzak: So Kant's notion of achieving perpetual peace through a free federation is therefore based both on a set of timeless moral principles and on a philosophy of history. History or progress brings this higher level of morality, which makes possible the federation of republican states that for us today would be liberal democracies.

Emile: That is correct, but, as Kant saw it, these republics or liberal democracies would have a decidedly restricted suffrage. So for Kant the moral culture among states will continue to develop through the federation's constitution as men come more and more to agree not just on practices but also on principles (1970, 114). That growing agreement assures peace. In Kant's estimation and view of history, all nations will come to see the correctness at the same time. Thus some nations will be outside the federation. Interaction between those nations and the federation will be guided by the Preliminary Articles that Kant includes at the beginning of "Perpetual Peace."

Pinzak: But what is the evidence of the progress to a higher level of morality?

Emile: Kant argues in his essay "Idea for a Universal History with a Cosmopolitan Purpose," that while we as a species are a long way from moral maturity, we are progressing in that direction.[14] This is true enough for Kant that in the Third Definitive Article of "Perpetual Peace" he wrote, "[t]he peoples of the earth have thus entered in varying degrees into a universal community" (107). What are the signs of this community? We have developed to the point, according to Kant, "where a violation of rights in *one* part of the world is felt *everywhere*" (108, emphases in the original).

Pinzak: The United Nations as such a community? It does represent the nations of the world, irrespective of their type of political regime—democratic, monarchical, or aristocratic. But for this reason the UN is certainly not a Kantian federation of republican states. In fact, the UN could never be a Kantian federation because it treats all regimes, even tyrannous states, as equally legitimate.

We do currently have globalized commerce; globalization is largely of capital and markets, of production and consumption, of information and technology. That does seem to bring a degree of greater cooperation among trading nations and perhaps a weak sense of community. Just look at China and the West. But globalization is not cosmopolitanism. Indeed, it might be its opposite. Global-ized and globalizing enterprises, whether capitalist or state-run, want to maxim-ize profits and minimize costs, and do so by trying to minimize pay to workers and even to shortchange the workers on working conditions, health benefits, and occupational safety. On the other hand, if cosmopolitanism means anything, it must have, as Kant said, a focus on guaranteeing to all human beings the rights they have by virtue simply of being human. Among such rights will be some kind of economic justice.[15]

So, I don't see that commerce is going to bring us to an appreciation of our cosmopolitan rights, even if we were clear on what those rights were. It might even have the opposite effect and bury concern about rights in a rush to assure a steady flow of commercial products for ever-ready consumers. And it certainly isn't evidence of a cosmopolitan culture or cosmopolitan community. Nor do I hold out much hope that commerce is going to bring about a cosmopolitan community, for commerce looks at persons solely as workers and consumers. At the least, a focus on commerce, global commerce, makes it much more difficult, if not impossible, for indigenous cultures to stay true to their traditions and rit-uals.

Emile: I quite agree that increased commerce brings greater cooperation, and that commerce is insufficient—necessary, but insufficient—for generating greater cooperation on cosmopolitan rights. To have that kind of cooperation, to have that kind of a community, will require some kind of cosmopolitan identity. Let us return to something I quoted from Kant. He wrote that one sign of our moral progress was that "a violation of rights in *one* part of the world is felt *ev-erywhere,*" with his emphasis on the words that I just emphasized. He is saying something here that also, I think, deserves emphasis. He should not have written "felt *everywhere.*" Instead, he should have written *"felt everywhere."*

Pinzak: Your emphasis on feeling reminds me of King Lear's comment to the Earl of Gloucester in Act IV when they meet on the heath: Though you have no eyes, Lear observes, still you "see how the world goes." Gloucester responds: "I see it feelingly."

Emile: Gloucester responds further: "A man may see how the world goes with no eyes." Would that we not lose our eyes to see and save the world. Recall Gloucester's earlier comment that when he had his eyes, "I stumbled when I saw." *(Emile takes a sip of water.)* Bear in mind, Pinzak, that we are not talking here about emotion superseding intellect. We are not talking Hume over Kant, passion over reason. We are talking about "feeling" as a deep resonance within the core of one's being. This is a cosmopolitan sensibility, a profound awareness of and receptivity toward the situations of others. Here affection and intellection are combined and integrated with one's sense of self. When this sensibility ex-pands over time and circumstance, when it steadies into a persistent level of consciousness, then we have a cosmopolitan consciousness or cosmopolitan identity.

Pinzak *(extracts a pen from his jacket pocket and jots down something):* Well, how much do people feel, in your sense, such violations as Kant describes? Does Kant mean "feel" as you suggest? I don't think so. People may feel these violations of people's rights, but are not moved to do anything about them; read Samantha Power's book, *A Problem from Hell: America in the Age of Genocide*. We hear about such violations, read about them, even see them on television, and yet we are not moved to press for intervention to stop them. *(Pinzak drinks from his cup.)* Or, if I make a concession to Kant, those who feel them do press for intervention, but there are too few of them to make any difference. So if we have too few to make a difference now, are we to think that we have regressed since the eighteenth century when Kant made his observations, that now we are a less moral society?

Emile: There is a reason why the Bush Administration sanitized the war in Iraq. There is a reason that the media could not show body bags and flag-draped coffins and maimed and dead Iraqis. If U.S. citizens saw all of that, as the Arab world did through their media outlets, what might the result have been? Might more people have called for withdrawal from Iraq and for a declaration by the President that we shall never invade another country unless that country attacks us first? If U.S. citizens felt those violations of Iraqis and felt for the men and women whom we have put in harm's way, would they not have lamented this intervention? Would they not want to put an end to the suffering and death for legitimate, compassionate reasons? Is not Kant's implication that a violation in one part of the world should be taken everywhere as if one has himself or herself been violated?

All of that might be right. My point, however, was not to go in that direction. My point was that Kant was onto something important. He was at least hinting at something about identity. The idea of feeling a violation of rights, regardless of where it takes place, whether next door or in the desert five thousand miles away, is a key to developing cosmopolitanism.

I think that Kant is describing here not what is but what ought to be or what might yet be. We as humans should feel in our bones the violations of others. But many of us do not. Yet I think that there are ways in which persons can come to feel this way, and I think that they should. Nothing is necessarily lost in doing so, and a great deal is to be gained. At least I want to argue that at some point. How persons can come to feel this way is not easy or guaranteed, but I think that it is important. It is the key to developing a cosmopolitan identity.

Nussbaum

Pinzak: But by and large, positions for cosmopolitanism seem to repose on moral arguments and not on proposals for inculcating cosmopolitan sensibilities. Take, for example, Martha Nussbaum's essay "Patriotism and Cosmopolitanism" in *For Love of Country.*

Emile: I read that essay in the *Boston Review.*[16]

Pinzak: Yes, that's where it originally appeared. As you've made clear in your "potted history," as you called it, for centuries men have held the idea, and the dream, of all persons identifying with all other persons as persons, on the basis of their humanity and nothing more—not place of birth, rank at birth, racial or ethnic makeup—nothing but the mere fact that we are all members of the family of humans. Nussbaum claims that persons should owe their first allegiance to the moral community of all human beings.[17] What can she mean by that? Well, it seems to be a marker. She means to point out that we ought to do nothing in our other communities or in our lives that we know to be immoral from the perspective of that community of all humanity.

Emile: Based on the questions that you asked me, Pinzak, and what I recall from her article, it does not seem that Nussbaum is going to give you much more evidence or argument than Kant did for *why* we should act this way. Is she saying that people will or ought to *feel* this way? How do we know what is immoral from the perspective of all humanity? Would that not imply universal moral principles? Do we know what they are or even that they exist?

Pinzak: I totally agree. Is what Nussbaum suggests at all a feasible and not just a philosophical possibility? Your statement about universal moral principles raises a fundamental concern with cosmopolitanism, one to which we shall have to return and discuss in detail. But for now I want to use Nussbaum to head in a different direction.

I understand her point this way: We ought not to deny to any person that person's dignity found in her capacity to reason and to choose morally. That does not mean that we always agree with her. It means that we meet her reason and choices with our own reasoning. We meet her decisions with the dignity of a response that is reasoned and reasonable. In this way, I think, Nussbaum wants to assure that no person is excluded from ethical concern.

Nussbaum is laying out a philosophical or normative position. She does not seem at this point interested in the political aspects or in the psychological aspects. I want to follow up on her philosophical position as a way of getting the political and psychological implications of her point that, I think, relate to what you were saying about Kant.

Emile: Fair enough. I have some time.

Pinzak: I'm sorry, Emile. I hadn't even thought about the time. Do you have to go?

Emile: No, not until you do.

Pinzak *(giving Emile a quizzical look before looking down at his watch):* Oka-a-y *(looking hard at Emile).* I've got to meet some friends in forty minutes. *(Emile gives a slight nod.)* Anyway, Nussbaum argues that each person lives in two communities—the community into which he or she is born and *(Pinzak reads from his notebook)* "the community of human argument and aspiration" (7). This second community is an "imagined community," to use Benedict Anderson's phrase (1991), but it is not a community of territory or physical boundaries. This community is the source of our moral obligations. All human beings should be thought of and treated as our neighbors on the basis that all humans deserve equal ethical concern and dignity.

Emile: She is following the Stoics here.

Pinzak: Yes, and Nussbaum acknowledges that. Let's go one step at a time. To Nussbaum, and presumably to the Stoics, where we are born and the circumstances into which we are born are accidents of birth. Had someone been born one mile south of Nogales, Arizona, then he would be born in Nogales, Mexico. Could that one mile make a significant difference in the life chances of that baby? It certainly makes a difference in that thousands of persons each year are not risking their lives and the lives of their children to cross the border from the United States into Mexico.[18]

Emile: That is because they do not have to risk their lives. There are plenty of visas for U.S. citizens wishing to live and work in Mexico.

Pinzak: That's true right now. But imagine if millions of U.S. citizens or residents needed jobs and that jobs were more plentiful in Mexico. The demand would soon outstrip available visas. Then those U.S. citizens and residents would replicate what Latin Americans are doing at the border right now.

Emile: Yes, the shoe would be on the other foot. It is hardship that drives people to risk their lives and the lives of their loved ones. Too many people focus on the situations at the borders and not on the causes of why people go to such extremes to cross those borders. That is, people ought to be concerned about what we ought to do *for* those crossing, not what we ought to do *to* them or *about* them. This reinforces Nussbaum's Stoical philosophical position, which also relates to Kant. Our first allegiance is not to place—state, region, community, or even clan—but to the moral community of all human beings. If we accept this, then we would have to take seriously Kant's injunction to treat all persons as ends and not as means. That is what Nussbaum is driving at when she says to treat the reasoning and moral choices of all persons with equal respect.

Pinzak: That's right. And she is not saying to treat with respect all of the reasons that a person gives us or all of her moral choices. Some of those reasons will be deeply flawed and some of the choices weird, even pernicious. But because we recognize that all persons have the capacity to exercise reason and to make choices, we respect them as persons when we treat them as capable of exercising that reason and making good moral choices. In short, we reason with them; we try to convince them; we argue with them. By doing so, we treat *(again, reading from his notebook)* "all human beings more like our fellow city-dwellers" (9).

Emile: This sounds as if Nussbaum wants city-dwellers elsewhere to become like our fellow city-dwellers, as if how we live in the city is how all should live in their cities. Or worse than this, she is saying that we can and should remake all cities and city-dwellers in the image of our own kind.

Pinzak: I don't think that Nussbaum intends this kind of parochialism. Instead, I think that she is saying that we should think about all human beings as we do those who live close to us. In short, hold in our thoughts and hearts all persons of the world as if they were our neighbors, as we were all New Yorkers on September 11, 2001, when the World Trade Center was attacked.

Emile: This strikes me as overly philosophical. As such, it takes me back to a tension found in the cosmopolitanism of the Enlightenment, especially of Kant. On the one hand, the Enlightenment philosophers recognized that we are all one, united in brotherhood as humans. On the other hand, only an elite has the background and learning to judge wisely, which meant morally, according to universal reason. Of course, the philosophers' ability to exercise universal reason provided the open-minded and tolerant perspective that permitted them to transcend identity with any particular place or group of people.

Let us look at cosmopolitanism from a different perspective. This one is also related to Kant and might bring us to the psychological aspect that you want to examine. Montaigne captures the emotional aspect of cosmopolitanism in the same way, I think, that Kant does with his idea of feeling violations of rights everywhere. This is also what Nussbaum is saying. For Montaigne cosmopolitanism was not a conclusion drawn through rumination. "[N]ot because Socrates said it, but because it is really by feeling, and perhaps excessively so, [that] I consider all men compatriots, and embrace a Pole as I do a Frenchman, setting the national bond after the universal and common one."[19]

Pinzak *(while scribbling in his notebook):* You are right, Emile. This does seem to be what both Kant and Nussbaum are suggesting. Notice that Montaigne does not say that cosmopolitanism replaces the national bond. He says only that the universal and common bond—that is, cosmopolitanism—comes before the national one. Nussbaum claims, again following the Stoics, that a cosmopolitan does not need to surrender particularistic affiliations or identifications. Rather, a cosmopolitan should think of identity as a series of concentric circles *(Pinzak here reads aloud from his notebook):*

> The first [circle] is drawn around the self; the next takes in one's immediate family; then follows the extended family; then, in order, one's neighbors or local group, one's fellow city-dwellers, one's fellow countrymen. . . . Beyond all these circles is the largest one, that of humanity as a whole. Our task as citizens of the world, and as educators who prepare people to be citizens of the world, will be to "draw the circles somehow toward the center," making all human beings like our fellow city-dwellers. In other words, we need not give up our special affections and affiliations and identifications, whether national or ethnic or religious; but we should work to make all human beings part of our community of dialogue and concern, showing respect for the human wherever it occurs, and allowing that respect to constrain our national and local politics (9).

Emile: Well, one can cheer the sentiment without accepting the position as valid. We might well agree in principle that we should take into account "all of humanity" when we make decisions that can affect people internationally. However, I withhold final judgment as to whether even that principle is sound. When Tennyson wrote in *Hands All Round,* "That man's the best Cosmopolite who loves his native country best," what could he have meant? Notwithstanding a possible confusion as to what the term "cosmopolite" meant, Tennyson seems to suggest that one who loves his native country best will want to see the whole world modeled after his native land. Then all states should look like my state. Is that not what the Nazis wanted?

This, in turn, brings us to Hannah Arendt's view that "no one can be a citizen of the world as he is the citizen of his country." To be a world citizen, one would have to be a member of a world state. We have seen that Kant rejected that idea in the eighteenth century, though we have not established that we ought not to have such a state today.

Pinzak: Again, I'd like to defer that discussion until later.

Emile: As would I. Nevertheless, Arendt gives us good reason for agreeing with Kant in this regard. "No matter what form a world government . . . might assume," Arendt continued, "the very notion of one sovereign force ruling the whole earth, holding the monopoly of all means of violence, unchecked and uncontrolled by other sovereign powers, is not only a forbidding nightmare of tyranny, it would be the end of all political life as we know it."[20]

So, there must be a world state or global government in order to have world citizenship. Moreover, according to Arendt, such an eventuality would be a disaster for anyone wishing to have a free political life.

Pinzak: There is something to be said for the idea that if a cosmopolitan is a citizen of the world, as the term connotes and denotes, then that cosmopolitan is a citizen everywhere, which means a real citizen nowhere. Yet cosmopolitanism can convey the idea not that one is a citizen everywhere or that there ought to be a global state of which one would thereby be a world citizen. Rather, cosmopolitanism conveys the view that one's commitment is to all humans and all of humanity when one considers moral and political positions. That is Nussbaum's idea: That our first commitment ought to be first to all of humanity.

Emile: This returns us to Nussbaum and her image of identity as concentric circles. Does she offer anything as evidence or support? Does she offer a metaphor?

Pinzak: She offers only a metaphor, but it is a powerful metaphor. Identity is like the concentric circles that ripple when a stone is cast into a pond. According to Nussbaum, our tightest, closest circle is our self, and moving out from there, our immediate family, then our extended family, our neighbors, our extended neighbors, our countrymen, and finally, she says, our fellow human beings. Nussbaum's wish is to draw that outermost circle closer to the center, so that it is a fundamental attachment, like our attachment to our extended neighbors.

Emile: What is especially interesting about that metaphor, aside from your making it a mixed metaphor *(Pinzak looks at him quizzically)*—circles on a pond "drawn toward the center"?—is that Nussbaum does not see a commitment to cosmopolitanism negating a commitment to one's family or friends, to one's neighbors or fellow citizens.

Pinzak: I'm not sure that that's so clear.

Emile: Oh?

Pinzak: Nussbaum also says that a cosmopolitan is one *(Pinzak reads from his notebook)* "who puts right before country and universal reason before the symbols of national belonging" (17). Are we talking about equal measures both for all humans and for fellow citizens? Is she saying that we must assure everyone's basic rights before offering special concern to our fellows? What are the balances here? Are there tradeoffs?

Emile: Presumably, she is arguing that when principles of right or morality are in conflict with the tenets or values of one's country, then a cosmopolitan must put principles ahead of country. When a nation's behavior violates or contradicts universal reason, then one must honor the commitment to reason first. I think, however, that her metaphor comes into play when a nation's values follow the principles of right and morality. Only when they conflict does a cosmopolitan favor those principles over the nation's values.

Pinzak: That makes sense, and that is also similar to what Amy Gutmann says in her commentary on Nussbaum's essay: We need to focus on the values central to human life: individual rights and *(Pinzak reads from a notebook)* "justice for [our] fellow citizens as well as [our] fellow human beings, who are citizens of other societies."[21] Her focus is on the values or principles, not on communities.

Emile: But can one be attached to principles in the same way and to the same depth that one is attached to or identified with a family or a community or even a country?

Pinzak: I think that one can, and I think that Gutmann and Nussbaum are right. When we join the armed services or take the oath of citizenship in this country, we swear allegiance to the U.S. Constitution. The basis of that document, as with the basis of the Declaration of Independence, another of this nation's defining documents, is principles. These particular documents are grounded by universal principles.

Emile: It could seem, then, from what you are saying, that nationalism, if understood as an emphasis on principles, can bring us much of what Nussbaum wants from and says of cosmopolitanism, but can do so in a more realistic way. Yet there seems a temptation, if not a tendency, in nationalism to claim relativistically that what is good for us here is good for us, while what is good for you there is good for you.[22] We have principles of equality and justice; you may have such principles as well, though you understand justice differently from us. So you honor what you honor, we honor what we honor, and we shall both tolerate our differences. So even if we agree to focus on the principles underlying nations, and even when those principles seem to be the same—liberty, justice, equality, brotherhood—different nations can understand those same principles in different ways. Therefore even an emphasis on principles cannot get us beyond the particular and into the universal.

Pinzak: As presented by Nussbaum, cosmopolitanism offers recognition of universal values that pertain to all persons in all places. The tolerance that permits us to honor the values found in different nations is itself a universal. So our nationalism, in that sense, rests on the universal principle of toleration. But that's because toleration is not peculiar to one country; it is because toleration underlies the peaceful acceptance of diverse if not divergent ways of life and values in life. Otherwise, I must honor the values found in Nazi Germany. The Nazis had a racist sense of justice, and a global justice at that, but that did not mean that I would have had to tolerate their justice simply because it was presented as a universal principle that all nations honor—that is, "justice."

Emile: I am not seeing your point, Pinzak. Does tolerance not mean precisely that you would have to tolerate Nazi justice? Maybe not honor Nazi justice, but tolerate it?

Pinzak: I would use the universal of tolerance to oppose Nazi justice. I would not tolerate Nazi practices because the Nazis called them just or because their justice "works for them." The Nazis showed intolerance toward any values but their own. While it is true that tolerance as a universal creates a context in which different values and nations with different values can peacefully coexist, tolerance as a universal also rests on another universal—the universal that persons are equal. In this way I oppose the racism of the Nazis and do all that I can to thwart its use and spread, even in Germany. Relative tolerance of their values means that I must permit and even approve their enforcement of those values. If they think that those values are right and that they must be disseminated even by force so that other countries will live according to those values, then relative tolerance merely allows me to acquiesce. Universal tolerance allows me to oppose intolerance. In other words, universal tolerance allows me, at times, to override relative tolerance, especially, as with the Nazis, when it manifests as intolerance.

Emile: But where does the idea come from that tolerance is a universal and not simply a particular value of certain Western advanced industrial democracies? Nussbaum may talk about the importance of universal reason and even about universal values. But what is the argument that there really are such universals? Indeed, it may be for Nussbaum that when one comes to recognize an allegiance to the human race more "fundamental" or "primary" than the one to any particular group or community, only then do we have a universal conception of justice.

But all of this is premature. To honor the principle of tolerance as you understand it is to impose that principle on others, even if those others are hideous to you, like Nazis. Nussbaum herself asserts that the essence of humans is our reasoning and our moral capacity. This is itself an imposition, for surely not everyone around the globe would accept that view. Some could well assert that the essence of humans is the capacity to obey the word of God and to adhere to the teachings of those who have been selected, by whatever means, to deliver that word to the people. So, obedience before reasoning. Others could well reject the idea of a human essence at all.

Pinzak: We need to address, then, Emile, what we mean by universal values and how such values are determined.

Emile: We do, but this has gotten us sidetracked in our conversation, though I agree that we have brought up at least two important ideas that must be discussed later. One is the idea of nationalism and what we owe to our fellow citizens.

Pinzak: Don't forget that the title of Nussbaum's essay touches on that— "Patriotism and Cosmopolitanism"—and that it appears in the book *For Love of Country?*

Emile *(smiling):* I have not forgotten. The second idea is values relativism. That is, whether there really are universal values and principles, or whether they are all manifestations of particular cultures at particular times. Attempts to make those particularities appear universal rest solely on power and ideological imposition.[23]

But we were talking about Nussbaum's metaphor of the concentric circles of allegiance and the need to recognize a commitment to all human beings. Nussbaum seems to be saying, as you have presented her position, that a cosmopolitan commitment to "the worldwide community of all human beings" is one that we ought to make. Yet what we ought to do is not what many of us actually do. Declaring that we are citizens of the world does not make us feel the commitment to all persons. Such a declaration does not make us cosmopolites if by "make" we mean "identify with" all humanity.

Pinzak: Okay, so there are two motivations for cosmopolitanism. The first is the moral argument. We ought to act as citizens of the world because of what all human beings share or ought to be seen to share, and that is usually described as human rights or equal capacities. That's the normative claim.

Emile: On that view do we simply reason our way to cosmopolitanism?

Pinzak: That doesn't sound compelling, because there might be plenty of people who can intellectualize a kind of cosmopolitanism without acting on it.

Emile: Having Kant's notion of violations being felt everywhere but without people doing much, if anything, about them.

Pinzak: Right. So, following your suggestions, there is a second motivation, and that one is the psychological. We act as citizens of the world because we feel an attachment. That attachment is part of our identity.

Emile: Absent that psychological motivation, are people going to act as cosmopolites? Can you have cosmopolitanism without both the philosophical or normative justifications and the psychological attachments?

Pinzak: In her reply to her critics, Nussbaum says about the non-Jews who saved Jews from the Nazis that *(reading from his notebook)* "somehow, against all odds, their imaginations had acquired a certain capacity to recognize and respond to the human, above and beyond the claims of nation, religion, and even family" (132). How was this possible?

Emile: Is not the point that it is possible, that it happens, but maybe not against all odds? *(Pinzak looks perplexed.)* Is Nussbaum not damning her own cosmopolitanism when she says that somehow, against all odds, these non-Jews came to have this kind of imagination? Well, perhaps she is right. Perhaps it is against all odds for one to imagine in this way. But there is a level of thinking available, so studies have shown, where recognition and response of this kind are not a matter of imagination but of awareness, of consciousness. This is a level where feeling and thinking involve attachment to all of humanity. This would be, then, a combination of your two motivations—philosophical and psychological.

Pinzak: That would be a cosmopolitan identity that would draw one's moral commitment closer to the center of one's sense of self, so that one identifies with the plight of humans everywhere.

Emile: And that would mean that one's deepest commitment, not simply, as Nussbaum says, one's first commitment or allegiance, is to all human beings. If that is so, then a cosmopolitan identity would have as its center the community of all human beings.

Pinzak *(glancing at his watch):* I'm sorry, Emile, I've got to go. I've got friends waiting for me. *(He pauses after rising, looking down at Emile.)* This has been a wonderful discussion, and I'd really like to continue it.

Emile: As would I. It has been . . . invigorating.

Pinzak: But I'll be away for the next several days, up to the White Mountains. How about meeting here a week from today?

Emile *(with a pleasing smile):* I shall be here. Your absence will give me some time to read Nussbaum and to review some of the psychological literature that points to cosmopolitan identity.

Pinzak: But can we first talk about nationalism and patriotism, two concerns of mine, before we move on to the totally foreign territory of psychology and consciousness?

Emile *(rising and shaking hands, Pinzak towering over Emile):* Pinzak, in these conversations, I am entirely at your disposal.

Notes

1. Visitors to and inquirers into the Café Pamplona in Harvard Square will find that it is not exactly as I describe it. Any discrepancy is due to poetic license, which is sometimes, as in my case, a simple cover for a faulty memory.

2. There could be an argument made that cosmopolitanism is not simply a Western idea (or ideal). Claude Levi-Strauss, in an article entitled "Cosmopolitanism and Schizophrenia" (in *The View from Afar* [Basic Books, 1985, 177-85]), describes the syncretic mythology of Native Americans living along the Pacific Northwest coast. In addition, Levi-Strauss claims that the first references to cosmopolitanism appear in Egypt at the time of Aknaton, pharaoh from 1375 to 1858 B.C.E.

3. *Meditations,* Book 7.44.2, 55. Marcus refers to the "human community" as brought together by Zeus (Bk. 11.8, 107) as the "dear city of Zeus" (Bk. 4.23, 28) and "highest City, of which all other cities are mere households" (Bk. 3.11.2, 21). He also refers to the universe as "that most venerable archetype of a governing state" (Bk. 2.16, 15) and "a kind of community" (Bk. 4.3.2, 24). Thus, he concludes, "the whole human race shares a common constitution. . . . From there, then, this common city, we take our very mind, our reason, our law. . . ." (Bk. 4.4, 24-25). "[W]herever you live," Marcus concludes, "take the world as your city" (Bk. 10.15, 99).

4. Jean-Jacques Rousseau, *Social Contract with Geneva Manuscript and Political Economy,* ed. Roger D. Masters, trans. Judith R. Masters (New York: St. Martin's Press, 1978), 162. Notice that Rousseau mentioned "pretended cosmopolites," as if it might be possible to be an authentic cosmopolite who might well love the world as an expression of loving everyone. In "A Discourse on the Origin of Inequality," Rousseau referred to "some great cosmopolitan spirits . . . breaking down the imaginary barriers that separate different peoples." Clearly Rousseau held the possibility that national boundaries could be broken down or transcended, if only because such boundaries are "imaginary barriers." Yet in his time, some forty years before the world situation apparently changed dramatically according to Kant, such transcendence would have to be reserved to "some great cosmopolitan spirits," thus insinuating that such work would be rare (1983, 90).

But Rousseau also commented in "Considerations on the Government of Poland" that it is education "that must give souls a national formation, and direct their opinions and tastes in such a way that they will be patriotic by inclination. . . . When first he opens his eyes, an infant ought to see the fatherland, and up to the day of his death he ought never to see anything else. . . . [H]e sees nothing but the fatherland, he lives for it alone; when he is solitary, he is nothing; when he has ceased to have a fatherland, he no longer exists; and if he is not dead, he is worse than dead" (1986, 176). So, too, he commented in "A Discourse on Political Economy" that "[I]t appears that the feeling of humanity evaporates and grows feeble in embracing all mankind. . . . [I]t is proper that our humanity should confine itself to our fellow-citizens. . . . It is certain that the greatest miracles of virtue have been produced by patriotism" (1983, 130).

Thus, Rousseau's position seems less than straightforward. All humans, on Rousseau's account, naturally feel sympathy for the plight of others. Indeed, in the state of nature, it is sympathy or compassion that prevents persons from harming others. But sympathy is enervated with the advent of society and civilization. With the right education, however, we can reinvigorate our capacity to feel sympathy, or pity, and do so by extending self-love beyond oneself to one's fellow men. In *Emile* the tutor goes so far as to say that he wants his student to come to "love all men" because "the love of mankind is nothing other than the love of justice. . . . [O]f all the virtues justice is the one that contributes most to the common good of men. For the sake of reason, for the sake of love of ourselves, we must have pity for our species still more than for our neighbor." See Jean-Jacques Rousseau, *Emile,* trans. Allan Bloom (New York: Basic Books, 1979) 226, 252-53. That necessitates, of course, coming to love even strangers. This form of cosmopolitanism, which I feel safe in calling it, depends for Rousseau on the kind of peculiar education dispensed by the tutor that will enable Emile to remain a natural man. Emile says, for example, "Rich or poor, I shall be free. I shall be free not merely in this country or in that; I shall be free in any part of the world" (472). Indeed, Emile spends two years choosing where to live, so he hardly has any ties, and certainly not patriotic ties, to any special territory or fatherland. Always Emile will be *in* society, but not *of* society; he will participate in civic activities, but he will also be free of them.

5. Tycho Brahe was born in Skane, which at the time was in Denmark but is now in Sweden.

6. Thomas J. Schelerth, *The Cosmopolitan Ideal in Enlightenment Thought* (Notre Dame, Ind.: University of Notre Dame Press, 1977), 48.

7. The name "Anarcharsis" often appears in quotation marks because Cloots, Jean-Baptiste du Val-de-Grace, baron de Cloots, adopted that name to honor Anarcharsis, the Scythian friend of Solon, who was Athens's great lawgiver.

8. Any ambivalence may lie not simply with Kant, but also among Kantian scholars. Consider this line from "Idea of a Universal History with a Cosmopolitan Purpose":

"[T]he highest purpose of nature [is] a universal *cosmopolitan existence"* (1970, 51, emphasis in original). A cosmopolitan existence might be achieved for everyone through the expansion of a federation of republics, even assuming that every nation were in the federation. In short, cosmopolitan existence does not assume the need for a world government or world state. Yet Ted Humphrey translates this quotation in a way that leaves no doubt as to what he thinks Kant was after: "[N]ature's supreme objective [is] a universal *cosmopolitan state. . . ." Perpetual Peace and Other Essays,* trans. Ted Humphrey (Indianapolis, Ind.: Hackett Publishing Company, 1983), 38, emphasis in original.

9. In "Perpetual Peace," Kant talks about the innate and inalienable rights belonging to all of humanity that are or must be protected as one essential element in a republic. He also discusses the need for a separation of powers between legislative and executive branches. But most important, Kant discusses the need for "the actual consent of state citizens," especially if a republic is considering going to war. Hence, as Otfried Hoffe suggests, republics are not simply democratic, but democratic "with a participatory character in an emphatic sense." (All quotations are from Hoffe 2006, 181; see also 218.) Therefore, one could conclude that Kant's notion of republicanism is even a stronger form of democracy than our own representative systems. This idea of a stronger kind of democracy will be taken up later in this text.

10. In 1716 Francois de Callieres observed in his book, *On the Manner of Negotiating with Princes,* that "we must think of states of which Europe is composed as being joined together by all kinds of necessary commerce, in such a way that they may be regarded as members of one Republic, and that no considerable change can take place in any one of them without affecting the condition, or disturbing the peace, of all the others (quoted in Held 1995, 19). Kant is echoing this common eighteenth-century view on the significance of trade in creating global connections.

11. I address in the Sixth Encounter the social-psychological literature showing the widespread influence of situations and social contexts on behavior.

12. 1970, 112. Kant goes so far as to say that "we cannot expect [peoples'] moral attitudes to produce a good constitution; on the contrary, it is only through the latter that the people can be expected to attain a good level of moral culture" (1970, 113).

13. See also his 1784 essay "Idea for a Universal History with a Cosmopolitan Purpose," in *Kant's Political Writings* (1970).

14. "We are *cultivated* to a high degree by art and science. We are *civilised* to the point of excess in all kinds of social courtesies and proprieties. But we are still a long way from the point where we could consider ourselves morally mature" (1970, 49, emphasis in original).

15. According the 1999 UN Report on Human Development, the combined wealth of the world's three richest families is greater than the annual income of 600 million people in the least developed countries. As another example of economic injustice, consider that the number of people living on less than one U.S. dollar per day is 1.3 billion people, which is slightly over 20 percent of the world's population. Clearly cosmopolitan politics will have something to say about economic justice and the impact of globalized markets and economic systems.

16. The October/November 1994 issue of *Boston Review* originally carried Nussbaum's article with responses from various pundits and academics. Her article, some of the responses, additional commentaries, and a Nussbaum reply were collected by editor Joshua Cohen in *For Love of Country?* (Boston, Mass.: Beacon Press, 1996).

17. Cohen, *For Love of Country?* 7. All quotations in parentheses in this section, unless otherwise specified, are from that work.

18. The difference in the life chances intimated here reduces to economics, which is, of course, no full measure of the kinds and quality of lives that people can and do live. Nevertheless, the economic disparities between the Mexican and American economies help explain why large numbers of Latin Americans are willing to risk their lives and the lives of their loved ones to cross illegally into the United States. As Stanford historian David Kennedy point out, "The income gap between the United States and Mexico is the largest between any two contiguous countries in the world" (quoted by Samuel Huntington, 2004, 3).

19. "Of Vanity," in *The Complete Works of Montaigne;* cited by Schlereth, 1977, xxii.

20. Hannah Arendt, *Men in Dark Times* (London: Jonathan Cape, 1970), 84.

21. Amy Gutmann, "Democratic Citizenship," in *For Love of Country?* ed. J. Cohen (Boston, Mass.: Beacon Press, 1996), 70.

22. Michael Walzer, criticized by Brian Barry as a theorist of "blood and soil" nationalism, "insists that if the members of a nation are living in accordance with their 'shared understandings,' they are in a condition of justice for them, so any external interference is unjust" (Brian Barry, "Statism and Nationalism: A Cosmopolitan Critique" *(NOMOS 61: Global Justice,* eds. Ian Shapiro and Lea Brilmayer 1999), 29, emphasis in the original). Barry goes even further by suggesting that given his stance, Walzer must equally insist that there can be no legitimate basis even for criticism from the outside. See Walzer's response to his critics in *Pluralism, Justice, and Equality,* eds. David Miller and Michael Walzer (New York: Oxford University Press, 1995), cdf.

23. The first idea will be taken up in the Second Encounter; the second idea— universalism and relativism—will be taken up in the Fifth Encounter.

Second Encounter:

Nationality and National Identity

I live my life in widening circles
That reach out across the world.
—Rainer Maria Rilke

Events the following week seemed an eerie copy of those of Pinzak's first encounter with Emile Whyte. Pinzak immediately saw Emile sitting at the same table, hands folded in his lap, cane under his hands, the camel hair coat buttoned up to his neck, beret on his head, eyes closed, and a slight smile on his face, which was turned up to the sun. A demitasse occupied the table.

Pinzak, with cappuccino in hand, walked over and was about to say "hello" when Whyte, without turning or opening his eyes, beat him to it. "Hello, Pinzak. Welcome back to Pamplona."

Pinzak sat down and said, "Hello, Emile. Holding my place for me?"

Emile smiled and nodded. "Of course." Silence ensued. Pinzak stirred his cappuccino, and Emile smiled that enigmatic smile. He turned his head toward Pinzak and said, "How were the White Mountains?"

"Fantastic," Pinzak responded without hesitation. "We hiked, canoed, talked, walked, ate, and slept. It was great to spend time with some of my Harvard teammates again and to be in the mountain air. We did have rain one day, but otherwise, I couldn't have asked for better weather." Pinzak sipped his coffee. "And you? How have you been?"

"I have been fine, Pinzak; thank you for asking." Emile continued, eyes closed, bathing his face in the sun.

"While I was away, Emile, I couldn't get you out of my mind."

"Oh?" asked Emile, cocking his head and opening his eyes as if startled by a friendly voice. "Why was that?"

"Well, for one: Think of the serendipity of our meeting. What are the odds of my sitting at a table where someone had actually read my book?"

"Do not underestimate your book. Do not underestimate the environment. This is the Café Pamplona in Harvard Square, the Agora in the Athens of America."

Both men laughed. Emile closed his eyes again. "For another reason, you are so . . ." Pinzak struggled to find the word. "You are so . . . erudite."

"Pinzak," Emile said, opening one eye, "I *am* a reader." They both laughed again.

"That might explain how well versed you are in the history of cosmopolitanism, but it doesn't explain how you can cite passages without referring to notes. I mean, you just pull them out of the air."

Emile now turned his head to Pinzak and shifted his body so that he faced him across the table. "Hardly out of the air. I pull them out of my memory."

"But that's fantastic. How do you do it?"

"Frankly, I do not know. I used to think that I had a photographic memory. But I researched this and discovered that my situation did not fit the case. I do not 'photograph' passages or pages or books. Instead, I have an ability to recall passages. It is as if I have edited out those quotations or passages that I want to store. Then, like looking at an index, when a word or phrase or name comes up, I recall a related or relevant passage."

"How do you know in advance what you want to store?"

"Again, I do not know. I do know that when I wish to recall something, it appears as a full quotation or passage. When nothing like that comes up, then I can usually remember where I saw something related to or about that. Then, of course, I have to go back and look it up. Once I have done that, I never forget it." Pinzak stared at Emile through this explanation. "I have stopped analyzing it. I am just thankful for the facility."

"I've never heard of such an ability. Ever." Pinzak had both hands around his cappuccino. "Do you know how much time it would save if I could sit down in front of my computer and write out pages and pages with all the quotations marching out of my head, without needing to look up anything?"

Emile smiled enigmatically. "I suppose it would."

They sat silently for a few minutes. Then Emile broke into Pinzak's reverie: "I have had a chance to read a bit since we last met. Shall we resume our discussion?"

Taking his notebook and pen out of his jacket pocket, Pinzak replied, "I've been looking forward to it."

Emile: We had decided to postpone any excursion into psychology until we had talked more about the philosophical or normative aspects of cosmopolitanism.

Pinzak: That's right, and especially how cosmopolitanism fits in, if at all, with nationalism and patriotism.

Emile: I have now read *For Love of Country?*[1] Although we talked about Nussbaum's positions, we did not really discuss her objective in her contributions. She wants to promote those societies in which "we should recognize, at whatever personal or social cost, that each human being is human and counts as the moral equal of every other" (Nussbaum 1996, 133). To take seriously this moral equality is to treat as morally irrelevant, says Nussbaum, one's nationality, ethnicity, race, class, religion, and gender (133).

Pinzak: Well, she can't mean that.

Emile: Why not?

Pinzak: Because that, I think, would be a betrayal of what she is trying to present in her concentric-circles metaphor. If it turned out that one's nation, group, neighborhood, or family were morally irrelevant, then our only moral obligation in her cosmopolitan society would be to all human beings as human beings. In that case, the circles that we have transcended in order to pull the outer circles closer would simply disappear, leaving only the outer circle, the cosmopolitan circle, next to our inner circle or our self.

Emile: You are right. Nussbaum is not making that point. Instead, she is saying that those personal qualities that we often hold dear—what religion we practice, what ethnic group we were born into, our gender—are not morally relevant to what we owe to and how we treat other persons. Those personal qualities in ourselves are no more relevant, morally speaking, than those same qualities in others.

Pinzak: So we don't owe allegiance to others because they practice our religion or belong to our socio-economic group, any more than we withhold allegiance from those who are of a different religion or ethnic group. Yet Nussbaum does acknowledge that we do have allegiances to our family, our extended family, our neighbors, our fellow citizens. So why are these allegiances morally relevant, whereas personal qualities are not, especially if our clan or neighborhood is an intentional community? What if one grows up in a Hasidic community in New York? Do we owe allegiance to that community, to those persons, not because they are fellow Jews but only because they are fellow human beings living next door?

Emile: For Nussbaum all of these considerations are at best secondary because our primary obligation or allegiance ought to be to all human beings regardless of where they live, how they worship, what they look like, or where they come from. For her the first obligation, our moral allegiance, is not to any group or nation or even to cosmopolitan citizens because they are cosmopolites. We owe a principal allegiance to justice, to doing what is right, whether that pertains to our fellow citizens or to all members of our species.

Pinzak: What I find appealing about Nussbaum's position is her metaphor of the concentric circles. That shows us that we don't have to lose our allegiances to our family, group, neighborhood, or country if we recognize a moral obligation to all human beings. Instead, these allegiances move around, slide up or down in importance.

Does anyone under attack think first of defending his neighborhood before defending his family? And if the family is safe, does anyone think of defending the city before defending the neighbors? This is not simply a prudential calculation, that defending the neighborhood is prudent in order to preserve our family.

Instead, persons risk their lives to defend neighbors with whom they identify and therefore value.

We seem to move in concentric circles from family to neighborhood, out to the country. We know that many are willing to die for their country. We also know of persons willing to die coming to the aid of strangers, but no one then suggests that that person's identity was wrapped up in "love of strangers" before love of family or community or country. Just so, why assume that "feelings for all humans" necessarily means that we negate feelings of identity with family or community or country.

The time to look for such identity is when there is tension between family and country, or country and community, or community and humanity. Then we would not be shocked by anyone's individual commitment to any one of these. One could die for one's family or country or community or humanity: Germans saving Jews; white Freedom Riders risking their lives to register Blacks in Mississippi; foreign volunteers fighting in the Spanish Civil War; persons drowning while working for Greenpeace. At no time do we say that those who died necessarily loved their causes more than they loved their families or friends or communities.

Emile: I agree. That is the power of Nussbaum's metaphor. Of course, family plays a significant role for many persons, even for cosmopolites. In response to Nussbaum's essay Nathan Glazer asks, "Do we not sense . . . whatever the inadequacy of our principled ethical arguments, that we owe more to our family members than to others" (63)? We answer simultaneously "of course" and "it depends." "Of course" because we are in that circle of identity, and family is primary for most people at most times. But that is not so for everybody or at all times; so, "it depends" on the situation. People will judge when they owe allegiance or obligations to others. That is an essential aspect of autonomy, of making choices that affect our lives and express who we are.

Henry Sidgwick argued that our obligations to help others differ depending on the nature of the relationship we have with those others: family, friend, neighbor, citizen, and so on.[2] Whatever that relationship, each person needs to decide what obligations the boundaries entail—either to give or to withhold. This means that the obligation, even a special obligation, might be implied by the context of the relationship. Most persons will sense that we owe obligations to our family, even special obligations.

Pinzak: And what constitutes a "special" obligation?

Emile: It could be described as an obligation that we have and acknowledge even when we do not want to follow through on it. And such an obligation implies reciprocity. That is, others can demand or claim or expect fulfillment of obligations from you, as you can from them.

Pinzak: But doesn't the nature of the familial relationships really determine whether we can and will fulfill those obligations? We can imagine a family situation so abusive that obligations that we might normally see operating among family members are suspended or canceled.

Emile: David Miller claims in his defense of nationality that "because I identify with my family, my college, or my local community, I properly acknowledge obligations to members of these groups as distinct from obligations I owe to people generally."[3] But your point is that if one does not identify with family, college, or community, if one were to find each of them repugnant, would that person still owe obligations to those groups?

Pinzak: Conversely, would Miller say that if I identify with people generally, then I therefore must properly acknowledge obligations to them?

Emile: To be consistent would he not have to say that? The overall point is that I owe obligations to family, college, or community because of the formative relationships that I had with them. Identifying with them may well determine how and whether I fulfill those obligations. It does not determine, however, whether I have them.

Pinzak: Likewise, identifying with all of humanity may well determine how I fulfill my obligations to all persons, not whether I have them. But it cannot possibly be that I can create or have *special* obligations to all humans because I alone identify with all of humanity.

Emile: Yet identity implies relationship. Those with whom I identify can expect from me responsibilities that I owe them, because of our association or interpersonal ties, which I do not owe non-associates. Our relationship may generate special obligations. As Sidgwick says, it depends on the context and the nature of that relationship. It depends on the depth of identity. Thus it is not surprising to find that we expect persons to perform special duties to members of their families or communities.

Pinzak: But I might identify with someone as a role model with whom I have no association—say, Michael Jordan or even Vincent Van Gogh, who is dead. Or I might have special obligations to persons with whom I do not identify—say, my family. Then it would seem to be the nature of that association, and the cultural norm within which the association exists, rather than identity, that determines special obligations and responsibilities. I may feel an obligation to Michael Jordan, but he, not knowing me, does not reciprocate. So this is an obligation, but not a special one.

Emile: Yet when I do identify with associates, then I not only owe them duties because of that association, but I also feel that I owe them special duties.

Pinzak: The special obligation rests on reciprocity, doesn't it? That's why my sister can expect me to donate a kidney to her before I'd donate a kidney to a stranger. She can even make a claim for my kidney on the moral grounds that I owe her a special obligation, though I might not honor her claim. So a special duty would be to save my family members first, to give a kidney to my sister before a stranger, to loan money to my college roommate when he needs it before giving it to a charity.

Emile: We owe special duties to those with whom we have intimate relationships—again, family or community—even when we do not identify with them. The special duties mean that we give those persons priority.

Pinzak: Do special duties then have priority over other duties or responsibilities?

Emile: I do not know that they must, but the person will feel that they do. If we owe duties to all human beings and special duties to our associates, then our associates will have our priority—of time or money or attention or whatever—over our non-associates.

Pinzak: So special duties do not necessarily trump regular duties. One is not exempt from meeting duties to all humans because the person feels special duties to associates. But when time or money or attention is limited, then who gets what first?

Emile: The person will feel a need to fulfill special duties first. Yet one could argue that we must meet regular duties before we attend to special duties. We would then meet our duties to see to the welfare of all the poor, including those who live in impoverished nations, before we focus help exclusively on those fellow citizens living in the United States. We would assume that all persons had met at least the threshold of what we take to be well-being. Only then would we move on to grant to our intimates more than the threshold.

Pinzak: That's certainly the opposite of Miller's position, who does not think that justice in most cases requires us to intervene to safeguard the basic rights of strangers or outsiders.[4] You're suggesting that we feed Africa before making sure, for example, that Social Security guarantees a maximum level of return.

Emile: That is the argument. Of course, we make sure that the level of return is sufficient to enable retirees to meet their basic needs, before we turn to issues of how to make our fellow citizens more comfortable.

We do not think, for example, that our children are intrinsically more important than or superior to other children. We regard the lives of other children to be as valuable as the lives of our own. But it is unrealistic to think that we have equal concern for other children. Our own children are more important in our eyes because they are our children. We do favor those with whom we are intimate and with whom we identify. I think that that is Nussbaum's point: Think of family before neighborhood. But sometimes the decision as to what we should do is agonizing, even a moral dilemma. If my child's leg is caught on a train track, and I can only save my child if I pull a lever that will send a trainload of children to their sure deaths, do I pull that lever? If we always think that our children are more important than other children, then sacrificing those others for the sake of our own children would not be much of a moral dilemma.

Cosmopolites do not lose their attachments to and affections for family members simply because they identify with and as citizens of the world. Likewise, friendships spawn special relationships and thus special duties to particular individuals. These special relationships and duties do not dissolve because of our identity as cosmopolites. I am still a family member, a member of this circle of friends, or a member of this club, temple, or association without any or all of them being the center of my identity.

Membership carries with it obligations to fellow members. Why? Because membership in a family or neighborhood or club brings with it an intimacy created and maintained through interactions and shared experiences. It seems to me that membership brings about a bond even when the members do not know each other. Through the commonalities found in membership comes the recognition of obligations.

Pinzak: But is that true of citizenship? Do I have special duties to fellow citizens? Okay, I might well feel a bond with a fellow citizen that I do not feel for a person from another culture. If I am traveling in Peru and meet a fellow citizen of the United States who has fallen on some hard luck, do I have a special obligation to help him? No, but I might be more willing to because he is a U.S. citizen, which makes a connection between us. I know him in a way that is not like knowing a Peruvian stranger who approaches me and asks for money.

Such a bond might even be stronger if the fellow U.S. citizen were from my home state, because now I might feel that I know even more abut him and, more important, that we share a valuable connection—a "commonality" beyond our mere humanity. So if the Peruvian and I shared something important between us, then I might be more inclined to help him, because he would no longer seem a stranger.

Emile: This is William Godwin's point: "[I]t is impossible we should not feel the strongest interest for those persons whom we know most intimately, and whose welfare and sympathies are united with our own."[5] For the cosmopolite the feeling of sharing something significant with others extends to all humans. What is shared is our humanness. That *is* our commonality. There is nothing "mere" about it. Thus cosmopolites feel a connection to all humans and feel an obligation to help those in need. The Peruvian would receive help just as the U.S. citizen would.

Pinzak: But where does that sense of obligation end? Does the cosmopolitan give all of her money to the Peruvian, to as many poor Peruvians as she can, to as many as she sees?

Emile: Now we are into the details and complications. The limit for an individual would be the same as that for a state: A state gives as much aid as it thinks reasonable and practical. The state would not give so much aid that it could not help its own citizens or that could bankrupt the state. Just so, an individual has and senses limits. The cosmopolite is not overwhelmed by feelings so that she loses her sense and all of her cents. *(Pinzak smiles to acknowledge the pun.)* The cosmopolite will also see that handing out money randomly to the poor will not help alleviate poverty in the lives of these particular recipients or of all the poor living in that country or around the world. The cosmopolite knows that the commitment to the poor requires organizations and people dedicated to eradicating poverty here, in this location, but also around the world. It is a commitment to the poor and not just the poor here or the poor there.

What has changed for the cosmopolite is what is now the center of her identity. What has changed is what is essential to us in being who we are. While family, friends, work, church, and community might still be described as special, they will not be the first essential in the cosmopolite's description of "who I am." Commitments to them are no less strong; duties are no less imperative. Yet what has changed is their place in one's orbit, one's concentric circles of identity. I identify with them, as I identify myself as a cosmopolite.[6] My identification as a cosmopolite means that my first consideration, as Nussbaum claims, is to all of humanity. That connection and the obligations that ensue define who I am, who I take myself to be. That definition, that identity, tells others where my priorities and obligations begin but not where they end. These priorities are not just thought to be my moral commitments. They are *felt,* because of what I identify *as.*

The cosmopolitan allegiance that Nussbaum is after is not to create an exclusive identity with all of humanity. She is not suggesting that to ally ourselves with all of humanity means that we lose our identities to other more particular groups as persons. We can have multiple identities or multiple loyalties. In fact, we have a hierarchy of them.

Nationality

Pinzak: David Miller, for one, also has a conception of human hierarchy. He sees citizenship as a special kind of political identity resting on membership and participation in a particular culture. By virtue of that identity citizens owe special obligations to fellow citizens that they do not owe to all human beings. To think of citizenship in a cosmopolitan context is to reduce that citizenship to a thin liberal conception consisting of the possession of certain rights but that says little if anything about duties (2000).

Emile: I have read some of Miller's work, and it seems that Miller thinks of citizenship as "either/or"—we are either citizens of particular communities or we have a cosmopolitan allegiance. Can we not have both?

Pinzak: Isn't Miller's point that we can't *be* both?

Emile: Miller does say that national identity "may properly be part of someone's identity."[7] Thus he must think that one's identity has or can have additional parts. But I do not think that we can be both at the same time, depending, as always, on what we mean by identity.

Pinzak: We can certainly identify both with our communities and with our ties to all fellow humans, right?

Emile: According to Miller's notion of political identity, the whole idea of having obligations to all human beings, obligations that one is morally required to act on, is untenable.

Pinzak: Well, he is clear that the requisite political identity is established at the national level. He writes: *(Pinzak reads from his notebook)* "The relevant communities are nations" (1989); otherwise, you cannot have any conception of citizenship that has any political meaning, let alone political force.

Emile: So, political identity in the modern world largely means citizenship, and citizenship rests on the concept of nation. *(Pinzak nods.)* Therefore, to Miller, citizenship is necessarily bound to a particular place. One could not be a cosmopolitan citizen.

Pinzak: For Miller what makes nations relevant is the sense of justice that arises out of mutual trust, which itself arises out of a shared identity found only in national communities.

Emile: Surely Miller recognizes that smaller-scale communities, say, city-states, could generate this kind of mutual trust.

Pinzak: He does, but he thinks that such communities have little power to shape their environment (1989).

Emile: They have little power to shape their environment if that environment is the modern world. My point is that in earlier times the shared identity arose out of communities that were not nation-states. When nation-states arose, they created a different kind of community and with that a different kind of political identity. This, in turn, generated different kinds of obligations. So, why cannot the post-modern era of a Kantian global federation generate cosmopolitan citizenship and concomitant obligations?

Pinzak: Excellent question, Emile. If we insist, as Miller does (1999), that national identity is crucial to citizenship, then we might also insist that citizenship is crucial to identity. That is the point that you are making. Citizenship brings forth and solidifies a specific kind of national identity, and if you modify or transform citizenship from the nation to the cosmopolis, then what ensues is a new kind of identity. That is significant, because what arises then is a new set or a broader set of rights and obligations. So, if we were to foster a new kind of citizenship, a global citizenship or global villager, then from it might come a new kind of identity. At issue, then, might simply be what is the best way to foster cosmopolitan identity, not whether it can be done and whether that identity can be meaningful.

Emile: Well, when consciousness changes, new creations will arise. One such creation would be a cosmopolis that would bring with it new rights and obligations. Miller himself seems to acknowledge this when he observes that "ideas of nationality are the conscious creations of bodies of people . . . [that are] created and sustained by active processes of thought and interchange" (1995, 6).

Pinzak: Then we might concede to Miller, and to Arendt, that if you have a functioning cosmopolitan citizenship, then such a citizenship could only exist in a real political space. Such a space could be a Kantian federation. In that setting rights and obligations would be enforceable and would have meaning.

Emile: Such rights and obligations would be concrete, but that is not necessarily what gives them meaning. I would not want to see us getting carried away with the literalness of what Arendt, for one, might suggest. To be a cosmopolite does not literally require a world state. To think so is, I believe, to misunderstand the historical use of the term "cosmopolitan." Diogenes was pointing to a way of life or attitude toward life. He was even talking about a level of identity. But none of those demands a requisite political entity, though a Kantian federation of layered sovereignty would be, as you suggest, an aid. National identity, of course, does require such an entity.

For Miller it is the common national identity that holds people together in the modern world. That relationship has got to embody or express something fundamentally important and recognizable to the people in it. Is citizenship such a relationship?

Pinzak: Well, if it is, then what would fellow citizens share? There are over three hundred million people in the United States. I have relationships with very few of them, so what's the basis of the common national identity?

Emile: Is not the basis that you share with all U.S. citizens the same principles and the practices that embody those principles?[8] In short, is not the relationship a combination of universalism—universal or universalizable principles—and particularism—their embodiment or expression in particular practices and institutions?

Pinzak: I can acknowledge that point, if we bear in mind that "universal" here means "pertaining to all members of this particular community." It is not universal in the sense that these values pertain to all persons throughout the globe.[9] But granting that, then I can have a similar relationship with fellow cosmopolites, especially if we refer to the establishment, which you evoked earlier, of an actual federation founded on certain cosmopolitan principles replete with the institutions and practices that embody those principles. If I share that identity with them, then, presumably according to Miller, I would even owe special obligations to my fellow cosmopolitans.

Emile: That seems right. Your perspective puts weight not on the idea of "nation" in "national community" but on the idea of "community." Here the term "community" stands for the nature of the relationships among persons and in particular what is shared among them. Who can say, certainly Miller cannot, that the boundaries of national community cannot be extended? The United States, for example, added the states of Alaska and Hawaii, and they were not even contiguous with the forty-eight states that they joined. Jurgen Habermas argues that national consciousness is a thoroughly modern construct, built on the idea of national history, which itself, he says, is "an academic construct made possible by historians, folklorists, linguists, and literary critics."[10]

Pinzak: It took almost a century to construct and solidify this idea of nation.

Emile: That is right. Habermas further pointed out that to do so the political principles embedded in national constitutions had to become embodied in the practices of the citizens. That is, the people had to see these principles played out in their own lives.

Pinzak: They couldn't remain abstract; they had to become concrete for people.

Emile: Yes. Habermas's phrase for this transformation: *"[I]dentification with the states* mutates into an *orientation to the constitution,"* (2006b, 8, emphases in original), by which he means constitutional principles.

Pinzak: This is what Habermas means by creating "solidarity among strangers" (2006b, 8).

Emile: So through a similar process could not something like this happen regionally or even globally? A cosmopolitan identity might well define a new kind of community, a new kind of "imagined community," as Nussbaum observed using Anderson's phrase (1991). It would signify the "uncoupling of the constitution from the state" (Habermas, 2006b, 79). How is the European Union any less a real community than is Belgium or France?[11]

Pinzak: That question demands an answer, which no one can definitively give at this moment. The EU is too new for us to understand just how it is and is not a community, especially with its diverse population—ethnically, historically, culturally. Although the EU has not passed an official constitution, some observers suggest that EU treaties themselves already create an unofficial constitution (Idem). To answer that question we would have to examine what it is that holds Europeans together.[12]

Miller is right that there is a national identity that holds fellow citizens together. But what is the foundation of that identity? Is it merely living within the boundaries of a geographical space? As we have said, it is more than that. It is a relationship based on sharing values and experiences and institutions and practices. It is a relationship based on sharing what Miller calls "a public culture" (1995, 68-70). The relationships are not always, or often, personal ones, but there is still commonality.

Emile: And of course allegiances to a global federation no more eliminate nations than nation-states wiped out cities and neighborhoods.

Pinzak: But what happens, Emile, when these allegiances clash? What happens when the obligations to one's fellow citizens clash with obligations to human beings elsewhere?

Emile: Well, what happens when family obligations clash with national obligations?

Pinzak: We generate exquisite moral dilemmas.

Emile: Indeed we do. Recall Sartre's famous example of the young man torn between fighting with the Resistance during World War II and staying at home to care for, and protect, his mother. As Alasdair MacIntyre pointed out, such situations are moral dilemmas because doing either one leaves undone what should also be done. One can be a cosmopolite and still feel these contrary pulls.

Pinzak: Wasn't it E. M. Forster who said that if his country asked him to betray his friend that he hoped he would have the courage to betray his country?

Emile: "The guts."

Pinzak: Excuse me?

Emile: Forster said that he hoped that he would have "the guts" to betray his country. It amounts to saying the same thing, but it has the informal vernacular quality of "oomph." Saying "courage" is too . . . abstract and proper. "Guts" conveys the sense of conviction.

Of course, Forster could not have been serious that he would always betray his country for his friend's sake. If he were serious, then he would not confront a moral dilemma. If, for example, his friend were providing Al Qaeda with information about troop movements, would he feel that way?

Pinzak: Or consider the brother who turned in Ted Kaczynski, the so-called Unabomber. Clearly he made a different choice and had the guts to betray his brother.

Emile: We have ventured slightly off course here. Let us recapitulate for a moment. David Miller's point is that persons in the modern world live, by and large, in ethical communities called nations. Doing so spawns and reinforces the idea of national identity. Having a national identity, claims Miller, means that one has obligations to fellow members of one's nation. By having such obligations it is possible to achieve social justice for more and more people, for a wider arena of persons. These obligations, however, are special at least in the sense that one does not owe them to other human beings. The source of these obligations is not having a personal relationship with all fellow citizens. That is impossible in today's nation-states. Rather, the source is sharing identity with these fellow citizens.

Pinzak: What if I am Jewish and a U.S. citizen, but I share identity in my mind with my brethren in Israel? If I tell my fellow citizens this, that my identity is with Israel, do they no longer owe me obligations?

Emile: My sense is that they do, because even though you do not share a national identity—and they might well wonder why you do not emigrate to Israel—you still share with them your citizenship. That citizenship is based not on knowing people personally or simply on where you live. It is based on sharing principles and practices, as we said. You do not have to identify with your fellow citizens, but when living in the same country you do continue to share principles and practices.

Pinzak: But, Emile, if my allegiance is to fellow citizens and is based on sharing principles and practices, then isn't my allegiance really to those principles and practices . . . and to those principles and practices wherever they are found? So if the United States suddenly betrayed those, then I would no longer have an allegiance to the nation, to my national identity, or to my fellow citizens.

Emile: Yes and no, I think. One might well abandon a national allegiance under those circumstances. But one might also, in a sense, renew that allegiance by trying to bring the nation back to the principles and practices that have been betrayed. One might, then, try to reorient the nation back to what it was or what one wants it to be. That reorienting could itself be an expression of obligation.

Pinzak: My allegiance, still, is to the principles underlying the nation and the practices that express those principles. If that is so, then I can have allegiance to those principles, to those that emblematize my nation, but also have allegiance to the principles and practices of cosmopolitanism, assuming that they do not contradict.

Emile *(nods his head in agreement, sips his coffee, and clears his throat):* We can see how certain political principles transcend, or can be used to transcend, political boundaries. As an example, we can see how a focus on social justice in the United Sates will require us to ensure that all citizens and, indeed, all residents are guaranteed their social, political, and economic rights. Yet the same principle of enacting or assuring social justice, if we are serious about it as a goal, does not stop at our border. Others throughout the world are denied social justice. If that is our motivating principle, it cannot be isolated to action in one country or in one region or on one continent. We might begin our activist work at home and then look abroad; we might begin abroad, where we think the political, social, and economic circumstances of some are even more dire than at home; or we might try to tackle these different venues all at once. Whatever our approach, issues of social justice spill over borders. Our commitment to such principles can know no borders.

Pride of Principle versus Pride of Place

As we have said, a nation itself is really not any one thing. In the modern world it is most often an amalgam of people of diverse tastes, wants, views, ideas, values, goals, and the like. Not even geographical boundaries are constant. What holds them all together? It is not always sharing history or language or religion.

Pinzak: It is sharing territory. It is sharing a place.

Emile: Is it? As we said in our Israel example, identity does not rest on place. Could a Jew not identify with other Jews and as a Jew before Israel was established? Is not what holds people together the sharing of principles and practices and not really place?

If the principles that hold the United States together are found in part in the Declaration of Independence, which existed prior to the Constitution, then it seems that our allegiance, our commitment, is to them.[13] Such thinking might then lead inexorably to Nussbaum's position: "If we really do believe that all human beings are created equal and endowed with certain inalienable rights, we are morally required to think about what that conception requires us to do with and for the rest of the world" (13).

Pinzak: This sounds like what Jurgen Habermas (1992, 1994) called "constitutional patriotism," in which identity forms around the principles in the democratic constitution and not around any specific territory or culture or ethnicity, let alone the state. I find this idea attractive and even powerful. It is what Nussbaum refers to as "the world community of justice and reason" (8). But is this really a community? I am still troubled by the idea of having allegiance to prin-

ciples and not to persons. Those principles are lived out in some particular place
by particular people and manifested through particular institutions and practices.

I can intellectually accept the idea that we share a common humanity and
that trying to specify what constitutes that commonality will result in talking
about sharing abstractions—human rights, human needs, principles of tolerance
and justice. Still, could a communist not argue that his ideology is truly cosmopolitan, that all persons should live under communist rule, in a Stalinist state in
particular, and thereby be fulfilled? He could argue that only communism recognizes the true nature of human beings and that only Marx understood that a
special kind of socio-political arrangement could condition humans to realize
their "species being" or human essence.

Emile: Your point is a good one. What saves us from such an ideologue, it
seems to me, is to hold your point in mind: The allegiances we are talking about
are to principles, but not to principles alone. They are always to principles *and*
to persons with whom we share those principles in practice. That is, we share
with these others something significant, something deeply, even profoundly,
meaningful. That something is principles that we apply or that are applied to
persons. So we owe allegiance to all human beings who constitute and thereby
share this principled or moral community.

Pinzak: But you have not really addressed my concern. For the totalitarian
ideologue a world-Stalinist state is the exemplification of a moral community.
So how is he different from a cosmopolitan?

Emile: For the cosmopolite it is not sharing any principles or practices that
join all humans together in a moral community. It is sharing certain principles
and practices. We are not going to be loyal to fascist regimes that strike down
the rights of ethnic minorities. Central here is the Kantian principle of respecting
all persons as ends and not means. With that principle come the liberal values of
tolerance; mutual respect; autonomy; and civil, political, social, and even economic rights. These are the principles or values that enable persons to live the
kinds of good lives that they cherish; to live them without interference from others; and to allow others to live their cherished lives, however odd, also without
interference. As you suggested, these principles are expressed in public—that is,
political—ways through institutions.

Pinzak: I can see that cosmopolitanism reposes on such principles and values. But how are these principles recognized and constructed? Aren't they imposed by those mediating social institutions that form so much of our identity—
family, school, temple, work, and the like?

Emile: Well, surely these institutions are integral to our identities. And
there will be clashes, political clashes, among persons holding different conceptions of the good life and what kinds of lives can and should be lived. The cosmopolitan principles that we are talking about exist on a level underneath those
clashes. They deal with the recognition of the need for meaning and identity
among all persons. Implicit, then, in these principles is the acknowledgment that
persons do want to live the life they think is good; that they want those good

lives respected; and that, as persons capable of living good lives, they want respect as persons. What values can we hold that enable us to live without interference lives that we think are good? That position itself—having respect for diverse and divergent conceptions of the good—operates within states only because it rests on a set of principles and values that themselves have been accepted as necessary for holding that position.

Bear in mind as well that the very clashes that we are talking about can and will occur *within* persons themselves. Central here is the idea, I think, of multiple allegiances resting on the existence of multiple groups. This is what John Rawls called the "social fact of pluralism." We are all participants in multiple groups and hold multiple allegiances. Cosmopolitanism rests on the insight that we all need these multiple groups and allegiances. What is a multicultural community if not a kind of cosmopolitan community? Uniting that community are principles underlying different modes of living, different conceptions of the good life. That is at the heart of cosmopolitanism—universal principles underlying different modes of life.

So, it is the principles that bring and hold us together. It is the principles that we all share. But our particular backgrounds—our nations and neighborhoods and families and histories—are also what help us understand ourselves.

Pinzak: Multiple groups and allegiances put flesh on the bones of our principles.

Emile *(with a slight smile):* Something like that. A cosmopolite sees that the same kinds of groups to which one is committed exist for others as well. What makes at least one strong connection to all others is the realization that all others share in and need the same kinds of memberships that we do, though of course they do not all share in precisely the same memberships.

Herein is a paradox that helps make cosmopolitanism special. To form a bond with all humans we come to see that the very commitments we have made to special others and special groups—family, friends, neighborhoods, fellow citizens—others have made as well. This is part of our shared human experience.

But the groups to which we are committed, and the persons to whom we are committed, are not the same. Indeed, the cosmopolite will not only recognize the rich diversity of human interactions, groups, and relationships, but will also relish this diversity. Kai Nielsen comments that the cosmopolitan will "wish to see all [such groups and relationships] flourish that are respectful of the rights of others, including, of course, alien others."[14]

Recognition of this diversity, however strange some practices or groups might be, is not a threat to one's identity. It is now a virtue of that identity. Nationalists can gather together the limited diversity of their collectivity under a corporate umbrella, but the diversity under the cosmopolitan canopy is worldwide. That diversity includes the diversity found among nation-states themselves. In other words, nation-states do not disappear when the cosmopolitanism conceived is one of levels in a hierarchy, in the moral order as Nussbaum conceives it.

Pinzak: Where we place the emphasis in all of this is important. Yes, our allegiance as cosmopolitans is to persons as having or being of equal moral worth. What underlies this is the distinction between being morally equal and being equally moral. Clearly all of the practices and principles that people adhere to are not beneficial to others or even sometimes to themselves; not all principles and practices are equally moral. But the person as a person, as a human being, is morally equal to all other human beings. She is wrong in her practice of selling heroin to schoolchildren on the principle that everyone should live in the orgasmic ecstasy of heroin, but she shares with all of us the commonality of her humanness. So, as Kant said, we honor the dignity of her reason and moral choice, but not necessarily all of the moral choices that she makes.

Emile: This is what Nussbaum stipulates as one of humanity's "fundamental ingredients . . . our moral capacity"—our capacity to reason about and to aim for justice and goodness (1996, 7, 8). The emphasis must be on certain principles and practices that permit persons to think about, choose, and live out their own conceptions of the good life.

Pinzak: But those conceptions vary from culture to culture and person to person. They even change over time.

Emile: Then we must be clear that what we promote, as I said earlier, are the principles underlying the manifestations of those different conceptions of the good. That is, we share the same human desire to live a life that one thinks is best. That is one principle. Another is that we permit people to live as they think best, even if it seems wrong or deleterious, provided that they do not preclude others from living as they see fit.

Pinzak: People will choose all sorts of different ways of life, but the principle underlying those choices is a right to autonomy. The public or political institutions will express or reflect that principle.

Emile: That is so. To understand and even appreciate the lives that people choose to live, even when or especially when such choices seem execrable, will require us to put ourselves in their shoes. This is the exercise of tolerance and mutual respect. They require us to use perspectivism in understanding people's choices.

In his response to Nussbaum's essay, Anthony Appiah wrote: "Nations matter morally for the same reason that football and opera matter—as things desired by autonomous agents" (2006, 28). This statement captures two essential points. First, one's attachment to or identification with a nation is a matter of choice. Second, as a matter of choice, and an important choice, national attachment is like any other kinds of important choices that persons make. It is, to Appiah's way of thinking, no more or less important than people choosing to identify with a football team or people who choose opera over jazz.

Pinzak: But this is just what concerns nationalists or communitarians. It reduces community to something like a commodity or a preference that one can easily change her mind about. But is that so? Are autonomous choices subject to categorizing? Are some more important than others? Communitarians fear that community is being reduced through cosmopolitan thinking like Appiah's to a level commensurate with football and opera—things that I like, things that I prefer. This is what sociologist Ulrich Beck in *Cosmopolitan Vision* calls "banal cosmopolitanism" (2006, 10 and 40ff). By thinking in this way you reduce national or community identity to one's emotional attachment to Manchester United or to the Red Sox. What moral obligations flow from a rabid attachment to them?

Emile: You are right to raise this issue, but it is possible that someone who identifies with Manchester United or with the Red Sox could think and feel that moral obligations do indeed flow from that attachment. We cannot gainsay such a strong attachment, though we ourselves might not understand it. Relationships central to identity do carry duties and responsibilities. That sort of attachment is what Nussbaum is suggesting by her metaphor of the circles, and we would like to think that identity as social and political would entail some level of reciprocity. Cosmopolites would strive to introduce institutions and procedures whereby their cosmopolitan concerns may be acted out and acted upon. In short, they strive to develop and to establish some level of reciprocity wherein there is some notion of give-and-take. Few, if any, Red Sox or Manchester United fans have that sort of relationship with the team.

The matter of choice in identity arises when the person can gain some critical perspective on the focus or center of identity. That critical perspective means, really, some critical distance from the center. At that point one can judge with what and with whom to identify. Cosmopolitanism is utopian, claims Gertrude Himmelfarb in her commentary on Nussbaum, because, among other reasons, it has an "unrealistic assumption about commonality of 'aims, aspirations, and values'" (76). But cosmopolitanism is not about what others aim at, aspire to, or value. It is about what *underlies* those aims, aspirations, and values. How do we come to hold those values, aims, and aspirations? Communitarians and nationalists think that these are ends given to us by our communal context. But we can step back from those ends and gain some critical perspective on them and evaluate them. Through that critical perspective we come to a commitment to certain values, say. If those commitments are to values such as justice, rights, democracy, autonomy, toleration, and equality, then we have an obligation to help others, regardless of where they live, to live out those values, provided that we do not forget the humanity of those we oppose. This is our cosmopolitan allegiance, which emanates from an allegiance to the values that underlie cosmopolitanism.

Pinzak: But all of this is bloodless and cold, Emile. It is all so abstract and detached. Do you really think that national attachment is, as Appiah says, no more or less important than choosing to identify with a football team? Would you say that to a stateless refugee, that national attachment does not really matter? Persons are literally dying to become citizens of nations other than their own. This is not on a level of choosing football over opera.

Emile: Of course, Pinzak, you are right. I did not mean to downplay national affiliation or attachment for those in crisis. It is paramount to them, even more so sometimes, than family or friends, which is why some can abandon both in order to find a new and better life somewhere else. But they seek to establish themselves as citizens in that new country and then to establish their family and friends there as well. But many times they cannot. National affiliation for such persons will always be a central issue in their identities. But for those focused foremost on the principles and practices that underlie national identity, the nation itself will be secondary. Then national attachment will not be paramount, but attachment to the underlying principles and practices will be.

Pinzak: People who love their parents and siblings and friends and neighbors are not thinking about principles and practices, about perspectivism. If the connection to human beings in cosmopolitanism is to and through sharing principles, then it might not ever develop beyond some kind of vague, even glib, intellectualism. Having allegiance to all of humanity is itself a vast abstraction. We need to keep in mind the Kantian notion on which much of our conversation is built—that is, violations of persons must be *felt* everywhere. That is or ought to be cosmopolitanism.

After the terrorist attacks of September 11, 2001, we saw an outpouring of support for our fellow citizens and for our country. Why, Nussbaum asks in another context *(Pinzak looks down and reads from his notebook),* "should these values, which instruct us to join hands across boundaries of ethnicity, class, gender, and race, lose steam when they get to the borders of the nation" (1996, 14)?

Perhaps they should not, but perhaps they do. One reason is not on the level of intellectual or cognitive awareness, where we recognize that we should join hands across boundaries. Rather it is in how we feel. Feelings are for our fellow citizens, those who have been attacked, those who have suffered losses, and those who remain who are now equally vulnerable. While the danger of terrorist attack may be just as great, even greater, for others in various locations around the globe, we feel for those in our own country. We feel the special concern that Nussbaum says is acceptable. I think it is natural. At times of stress, we move around in our circles of identity, we move down the levels to those that are primary and most basic. When they are secured, then we move back up the hierarchy to higher levels. Or is it that our level of emotion or affect is underdeveloped, that it does not match our cognitive skills?

Emile: Feelings on and after September 11, 2001, did not stop at the borders of our nation. The French newspaper *Le Monde* carried the headline that day: "We Are All Americans Now." Surely the editors of the paper were not suggesting that all the French wanted to be Americans. Instead, they were expressing their solidarity with Americans, showing the bond among all human beings, showing that all could feel the pain, the vulnerability, and the grief that Americans suffered from those attacks.

Around the world people felt the violation. But remember that Kant said that it is the violation of rights that must be felt everywhere.

Pinzak: That returns us to the abstract. We have not even established what human rights are. I do not know that we can do so to the extent that all persons will agree on what such universal rights are, or what basic needs are, or how we define fundamental values. Keep in mind that there were also many on September 11, 2001, who did not commiserate with America, who did not think "We are all Americans now." They saw the opposite—that Americans might now understand a bit of the life that others have lived and are living. They saw in those attacks an opening, perhaps in cosmopolitan terms, that "now Americans can understand how we live. Now they feel like us."

It is one thing to be persuaded intellectually and even morally of the correctness of cosmopolitanism. It is another to act on that persuasion and still another to feel cosmopolitanism. Much was made of the fact that many persons around the country knew people or knew people who knew someone killed or injured either at the Pentagon, in Pennsylvania, or at the World Trade Center. More than that, we think that we understood what they were going through, that we could identify with them. We know the kinds of people who were killed and injured. We know the kinds of families they came from, the kinds of neighborhoods and towns where they grew up and lived. Now can we extend that knowledge, that feeling, that grief outward toward others whom we do not know, whose families we will never meet, whose towns we will never visit? Can we extend our vision outward and identify with them and the lives that they have suffered for years and years?

Ironically, it turns out that many foreigners were killed on September 11, 2001. Are we less sympathetic and empathetic toward those of foreign birth or foreign citizenship, because we may not identify with their backgrounds and practices? Perhaps, maybe even probably. It is psychology again, not moral theory. It is what we feel, not what we think anyone else is owed.

Emile: When we come to talk about the psychological aspects of cosmopolitanism, and later when we look at the implications of those aspects for politics, then I think that we might make headway on that.

Pinzak: Shouldn't we do so now?

Emile: We should certainly do so when we next meet. For now, I want to consider the moral force of cosmopolitanism. Should we cultivate a cosmopolitan attitude or mentality? Is that necessarily a good thing?

Pinzak: It certainly would not be a good thing if it weakened or destroyed people's attachments to local communities, to family, friends, or nation. It does not destroy them, at least not as Nussbaum presents cosmopolitanism, but I am not convinced that it does not weaken them.

Emile: Cosmopolitanism is the recognition that we share an ineradicable bond with all humans on the basis of our shared humanity. It is not a substitute for those particular attachments that persons find meaningful. What kind of commitment would it be to forsake our special others—family, friends, fellow citizens—as we encircled and embraced "all others"? It is not to forsake the other—whether other persons or other commitments—but to bring those along as we spread wide our arms and include in our embrace the community of all human beings.

Pinzak: You are saying that there would be no costs in expanding identity that way?

Emile: No. I am saying that the cost would not be to lose attachment altogether to those things that we identify with as important to our lives. There would be the cost of losing our exclusive identity with certain attachments. We would form other attachments of equal or greater importance. At the same time, if we are committing to principles over place, then we must acknowledge that this adds a layer of complication.

Pinzak: How so?

Emile: We apply the principles to the persons within our concentric circles; that is, with whom we identify. This can make us critical of the very groups or neighborhoods or nations that we identify with. We hold or want to hold them to standards that before we might well have uncritically accepted but not thought about. We must discuss this when we go into the details at our next meeting.

Finally, there are pragmatic considerations, which are crucial. Speaking of costs, there would be far more money spent to address problems throughout the world. That money would come from the United States. But bear in mind that as cosmop-olites we would not begrudge the taxes or dollars required from each of us to address these global problems any more than we would to help a friend or neighbor or family member. With a cosmopolitan identity compassion springs spontaneously from within. It is not felt to be an imposition.

Additionally, as cosmopolites would we not need to take into account the plight and situations of persons around the globe when we come to make certain international political decisions? Would we not need to think about how what we do affects those in other parts of the globe? Today we face global problems that require global solutions—for example, AIDS and other epidemics, deforestation, nuclear proliferation, overpopulation, extreme hunger and poverty, water scarcity, rapid capital transfer undermining political stability, forced migration and the generation of refugees, the flow of illegal drugs, and combating terrorism. How do we arrive at the best solutions? Does each nation think only in terms of national interests? Is the common good what is good for those living within certain political boundaries, or is it what is good for all those living on Earth?

Pinzak: What you are describing is a contemporary version of Garrett Hardin's tragedy of the commons.

Emile: Precisely. When the sheep eat the grass on the village green faster than the grass can grow, suddenly there is a problem that involves all the villagers.

Pinzak: The whole village shares in the problem and must cooperate to solve it.

Emile: All the villagers are in this together. They must decide on an approach together. Villagers, like nations today or like citizens within nations, cannot think only of themselves as individuals or even of themselves as citizens of a particular country. They are also part of a greater whole to which they owe some responsibility.

Pinzak: Today the globe is the village writ large, the global village.

Emile: I do not know how apt that metaphor is, but in this context, you are right. The earliest meaning of *kosmos* was "village."[15] Cosmopolitanism is the attitude or moral commitment, even the identity, appropriate for confronting today's global problems. At the very least cosmopolitanism expresses two moral commitments. The first is taking into consideration those throughout the globe who may be affected by political decisions, especially with regard to solving global problems. The second commitment is to help all human beings to secure their basic human rights, central to which is the right to autonomy. Autonomy demands that persons be consulted when political decisions are about to be made or are soon to be made.

Pinzak: Autonomy is the right that lets people decide for themselves what life is best for them and that permits or perhaps requires that they act on their decisions.

Emile: That is right, but in the context of global problems and cosmopolitanism, people cannot think and act solely as individuals or solely as citizens of particular nations. They must recognize that they are part of that larger whole, the entire planet.

Pinzak: Isn't it ironic, Emile, that cosmopolitanism wants to secure for individuals the right to autonomy or self-determination, but may need to sacrifice self-determination for nations?

Emile: It might be ironic if that were so, but I do not know whether it is. Perhaps there are levels of sovereignty just as there are circles of identity. Some levels may be lost. But if the persons within those states are guaranteed their rights, guaranteed the right to have and to act on their rights, then how great a cost would those levels be?

Pinzak: The cosmopolitanism that I have in mind rests on the realization of an obligation to aid persons in need, regardless of where they reside, and to balance that aid with some appreciation for the situation of those to whom I also have special obligations to aid: family, friends, or fellow citizens. If a cosmopolitan identity can do that and can provide affirmative responses to your questions, then we ought to encourage it or to promote it or to pursue it, whatever the appropriate verb is. *(Pinzak here looks at his watch.)*

Emile: Time again intrudes. "And time which takes survey of all the world must have a stop."[16] *(Emile looks skyward.)* Let us call an end to this discussion for today.

Pinzak: And may we resume tomorrow? I am eager to learn about the psychology that you have alluded to in our conversations about cosmopolitan identity.

Emile: I think that identity is the key. Identity is plastic, and we can promote cosmopolitan identity without eliminating national identity, though not exactly the kind of national identity that David Miller espouses. I think that we shall be able to see from a certain psychological level that what we reason morally that we *ought* to owe to all human beings is what we actually think and feel that we *do* owe to all human beings. (*Emile smiles at Pinzak as he rises from his chair. Both shake hands as Emile says, "So, we shall take this up tomorrow.")*

Notes

1. J. Cohen, ed., *For Love of Country?* (Boston, Mass.: Beacon Press, 1996).

2. Henry Sidgwick, *The Method of Ethics* (Chicago, Ill.: University of Chicago Press, 1962).

3. David Miller, *On Nationality* (Oxford: Oxford University Press, 1995), 65.

4. See the discussion in Miller, 1995, 73-80. Bhikhu Parekh argues that "when we all are supposed to be responsible [for all human beings], no one feels a strong sense of personal responsibility and the well-being of those in need gets neglected" (2003, 7). Parekh then uses the example of children in general who receive "adequate attention" (Idem) only because their parents, or some other particular people, have primary responsibility for them. But we know that what Parekh argues is not true. There are plenty of children—homeless, runaways, orphans, victims of catastrophes—who receive aid and attention, even beyond "adequate attention," from strangers, from persons with no connections to them and no special obligations to them other than a connection and obligation based on their humanity. The point of this section, chapter, and entire book is, contrary to Parekh's view, that cosmopolitans do feel a strong sense of personal responsibility for the well-being of those in need.

5. William Godwin, *Memoirs of the Author of a Vindication of the Rights of Women,* chapter vi, 90; quoted in Singer, 2002, 159.

6. The distinction between identifying *with* and identifying *as* will be addressed in the Third Encounter.

7. 1995, 10, emphasis added. Miller also comments that "national identities are not all-embracing " (26). Indeed, he sees "national identity" as merely one constituent of one's "final identity" (45).

8. In *On Nationality* (1995, 70-73), Miller distinguishes between the rights and obligations of citizenship and the rights and obligations of nationality. According to Miller, the former rest on a shared participation in a practice from which the participants expect to benefit. The rights and obligations of nationality, on the other hand, emanate from a shared public culture that is the basis of personal identity. Whereas citizenship rights and obligations rest on reciprocity, those of nationality rest on identity that takes us far beyond the reciprocity demanded of citizenship. Though I do not wish to take up the problems with this distinction, since it does not affect the perspective I have developed here, I must say that I do not think that Miller can sustain this position. One reason for this is that citizenship and nationality are intimately intertwined to such a degree that I doubt whether most persons would separate the two when discussing their political identities. Indeed, Miller seemed to suggest such an entanglement when he wrote: "Political participation . . . [is] a way of expressing your commitment to the community. Because the citizen identifies with it, he or she wants to have a say in what it does. . . . Interesting-

ly, the status of citizen is rarely seen as marginal or remote; on the contrary, for the great majority of people it forms a core part of their identity." See David Miller, *Citizenship and National Identity* (Malden, Mass.: Polity Press/Blackwell, 2000), 84. Miller even goes so far as to say that nationality is a foundation for republican citizenship, the sort of citizenship that he applauds (2000, 87).

9. The issue of the construction of universal principles, which is not, as it may seem, contradictory, will be taken up in the Fifth Encounter.

10. Jurgen Habermas, *The Divided West* (Malden, Mass.: Polity Press, 2006b), 76.

11. In a historical example reminiscent of Nussbaum's idea of concentric circles, the German philosopher Fichte suggested a kind of "cosmopolitan patriotism," which sees nations as serving a significant but instrumental purpose. A nation, any nation for Fichte, is a transitional tool to be used to get us to the uniting of our species "into one single body." Nations are for him nothing but instruments for carrying out at a more local level "human perfection" that points and leads us toward human perfection as the universal goal: "Cosmopolitanism is the will that this purpose be attained first of all in that nation of which we are members, and the wish that this light may radiate from this nation over all mankind. . . ." All quotations from Fichte are found in Robert B. Louden, *The World We Want* (New York: Oxford University Press, 2007), 77-79.

12. In 1995 David Miller commented that "very few Europeans actually acknowledge" a personal identity as European "in preference to their traditional national identities" (160). Seven years later A. S. Byatt, in her unscientific survey of Europeans whom she queried, found that the European Union has not engendered much of a European identity. Yet she did find that some members, especially the Scandinavians, have found a sense of identity beyond national borders as fellow Scandinavians. Likewise, a Spanish ambassador had discovered loyalties to other Spanish-speaking countries as powerful as the loyalties he felt to Spain, just as some British felt "natural affinities with Anglophone countries." (See "What Is a European? *New York Times Magazine,* October 13, 2002: 48.) Thus Miller may have been too quick to conclude that "prospects for a North American identity, a pan-Arab identity, or an East Asian identity (to mention some of those most frequently canvassed) must remain extremely dim" (162) simply because there is not, or not yet, a trans-European national identity.

13. In his commentary on Nussbaum's essay in *For Love of Country,* Benjamin Barber quotes English colonial emigrant Frances Wright: "What is it to be an American? . . . They are Americans who have complied with the constitutional regulations of the United States . . . [and] wed the principles of America's declaration to their hearts" (32). Ironically, Barber is using Wright's quotation *against* Nussbaum's views on cosmopolitanism.

14. Kai Nielsen, "Cosmopolitan Nationalism," in *Nationalism and Ethnic Conflict: Philosophical Perspectives,* ed. Nenad Miscevic (Chicago, Ill.: Open Court, 2000), 300.

15. See Robert Pinsky's response to Martha Nussbaum, "Eros against Esperanto" in *For Love of Country* (1996, 85). *Kosmos* was also a term introduced by the Pythagoreans to mean an ordered pattern of all domains of existence, from matter to math to *theos.* So the term encompasses all domains, not simply the material universe.

16. William Shakespeare, *King Henry IV, Part 1,* Act 5, Scene 4.

Third Encounter:

Cosmopolitan Identity

Homo sum: humani nil a me alienum puto.
"I am human; nothing human is alien to me."
—Terence

Pinzak arrived early at the Café Pamplona. His intention was to be early enough to watch Emile come down the street. Somehow he thought that watching Emile walk and even the direction he came from were important for understanding who Emile was. If you had asked him, Pinzak would not have been able to say why.

Pinzak had already secured their now-usual corner table. He had purchased a cappuccino for himself and an espresso for Emile. His plan was simply to observe the sidewalks as pedestrians passed by or entered the café. Emile would soon be among them.

But Pinzak had gotten distracted by his pens. He turned to the last page of his notebook. With his two pens clenched in his right hand, he scribbled furiously on the last page like a cook beating eggs. Nothing appeared on the page but white scars incised by the ends of the pens. On occasion Pinzak would stop and stare at the ends of the pens as if willing ink to flow to their tips. Then he would scribble again. So he did not notice Emile arrive at the table. Gingerly, as if not to wake a sleeping child, Emile said, "Here, try this."

Pinzak looked up as if someone had shouted his name. In his extended hand, palm up, Emile held out to Pinzak an exquisite ebony pen with gold trim and finely etched red annular rings. Pinzak took it in his hand. "What is this?" he asked.

"It is a Conklin Endura Long Cap. Very rare. They made them only for one year, 1925. It was given to me by the Prince of Wales. It did not work especially well when I received it. Perhaps that is why he gave it to me." Emile's eyes smiled. "Anyway, I equipped it with a proper Toledo-stamped 14k nib and installed a fresh ink sac. It works beautifully now."

"What do you think it's worth?"

Emile sat down and watched Pinzak examining the pen. "I have no idea. I have never had it appraised. I do not know where the Prince got it. He never said." He smiled again. "But I am not planning on selling it. Ever."

Pinzak turned back to the front of his notebook, where he had left off after their last meeting. "Next time we meet I'm bringing my laptop. I've got all of my notes from you transcribed there, and all of my notes from my reading." Emile sipped his espresso as Pinzak wrote a heading and the date. Emile said, "Thank you for the coffee."

"You're most welcome," Pinzak replied. "Emile, how do you know the Prince of Wales, and what's he doing giving you a pen?"

"I drove him and the Princess of Wales around New England one summer."

Pinzak waited for additional information. None was forthcoming. Emile sipped his coffee. With feigned exasperation Pinzak asked, "Why were you driving them around?"

"It was my job." Pinzak took a couple of sips of coffee and waited . . . he could wait out Emile. With a slight smile, Emile continued: "I was a chauffeur—well, a driver really. No one but the Prince and Princess ever really called me a chauffeur. I was a driver for the president—actually, presidents—of Harvard. That was my fulltime job, and I did it for over thirty-five years. On occasion the president would loan me to dignitaries who needed a reliable driver." He smiled. "I came highly recommended. I knew all of the highways and roads and back roads of New England, to say nothing of every street and alley in Greater Boston."

"And you knew all of them from experience?"

"From experience, yes, but also from maps. I read maps, studied maps, loved maps because . . ."

Here Pinzak interrupted: ". . . because you are a reader."

"Precisely. I was an excellent driver, not only because I never got lost. But also because I was observant, diligent, stayed within the speed limits, and yet almost always managed to arrive early at my passengers' destinations."

"How did you manage that without speeding?"

"If one plans routes carefully, maps out not just roads but alternatives, and studies traffic patterns based on roads and time of day, then one need not speed to make good time."

"One needs to plan."

"That is right. And I always did." Emile took another sip. "I also was informative and helpful without being intrusive. Because I loved to read, I would study the history of wherever the president and I or the dignitaries and I were going. Thus I could provide stories and local color to make trips more enjoyable. But I could also sense when people were not interested or had had enough. I did not wish to be a windbag."

"So you also enjoyed 'reading' people."

"How droll, Pinzak, but also quite accurate."

"Did you enjoy driving?"

"Well, as I said, I did it for over thirty-five years. So there must have been something I liked about it." He sipped his espresso. "It was perfect for me, Pinzak. I had only three responsibilities: to drive, to keep the car immaculate, and to keep the car running smoothly. The presidents kept cars for only a couple of years. Many of them were 'loaner' cars given to Harvard for promotional benefit, though nothing official in that regard. The cars were always in the best condition; thus keeping them running was never an issue. Well, needless to say, there was a great deal of downtime and 'dead time' or waiting. What could be better for a reader? I drove three presidents—Pusey, Bok, and Rudenstine—plus numerous heads of state, government officials, business leaders, writers, judges, scholars, athletes, film and theater stars, and more. Harvard is one of the most well-known and most prestigious institutions in the world. People seemed to think that the president of Harvard would have only the best of everything, including the best driver. So, often at a grand event—dinner at the White House, an international conference, consultation with a head of state—Pusey or Bok or Rudenstine would sing my praises. As a result, I was somewhat in demand, and I therefore had the opportunity to travel the world—the Far East, the Middle East, Europe, Africa—either driving for Harvard or on loan driving dignitaries. I even drove Albert Einstein, right before his death in 1955. The conversations, to say the least, were eclectic and often electric."

Pinzak, looking wide-eyed, said with patent admiration, "Talk about getting an education."

"Indeed. Most of my 'charges' were eager to recommend titles of books, articles, plays, and films that related to whatever topic of conversation we had wandered onto. It was like having a college scholarship. I had access, however brief, to the best minds and most experienced persons on the planet, who willingly supplied impromptu course syllabi. Plus I got paid for driving them and conversing with them. Not once did I drive anyone who preferred silence to talking about his or her life and work." Emile studied Pinzak for a moment, like a doctor, a conscientious doctor, with a patient. Then he said, "Well, let us not get distracted by my past. We have topics of our own to consider."

Pinzak *(lurching in his chair, as if abruptly awakened from sleep, righted himself, and picking up Emile's pen, which he had inadvertently put down sometime during the conversation, said):* I have been thinking about what you said at the end of our conversation yesterday. I don't know that we really need a cosmopolitan identity. Why isn't it sufficient to hold out to people the power of moral obligation or moral imperative? We have a moral obligation to think of the effects on others before we act.

Emile: Is the moral imperative, the moral argument, enough to get people to put down their knives and forks at supper and do something? Charles Jones asks: "If we can sympathize with the plight of persons who are victims of torture in faraway lands, why can we not also sympathize with those far-off persons who lack access to basic nutritional requirements, adequate housing, education, and health care" (1999a, 162)?

Pinzak: I think that we can, but we often need to see it to feel it, to have such instances get under our skin. Why haven't we met the goals of the United Nations Millennium Declaration calling for halving global poverty and hunger by 2015, ensuring primary education for all of the world's children, and reversing the spread of HIV/AIDS, malaria, and other diseases? Peter Singer says that "[W]e should feel a greater sense of urgency to eliminate poverty," but we don't (2002, 193). Leaders of the industrialized world have made all the right statements, but where's the action?

Emile: You are making my case. The point is to feel it. It is not enough to be right intellectually. The urgency is to get people to take action. In 2005 the United Nations General Assembly approved a resolution that holds nations responsible for protecting their citizens from mass atrocities. When nations cannot or do not fulfill that responsibility, then, according to this resolution, international forces may step in to offer protection. But as of 2010 in Darfur, in what most observers consider a textbook example of a nation failing to protect its citizens, member states of the UN have failed to provide protection. Sudan may have failed to fulfill its responsibility, but so, too, have other states. Sudan did agree in 2007 to permit UN peacekeepers to enter Darfur, but only as a contingent of the forces of the African Union, which provided only a force of seven thousand persons. Sudan continues to block the entrance of more troops into Darfur.

Pinzak: Nor have the industrialized nations provided air cover or air surveillance or logistical support. So the UN resolution shows willingness in theory to acknowledge that something must be done, but where is the practice? Intellectually, UN representatives acknowledge the need for action, but fail to deliver it. They see the need, but do not feel the need. This is just like the massacres in Rwanda in 1994, when the UN and the Security Council did little to stop the genocide there.

Emile: Romeo Daillaire, the Canadian general in charge of the UN Assistance Mission in Rwanda, called for reinforcements, and the Security Council then cut the number of peacekeepers from 2,500 to 450. Samantha Power commented that Daillaire did more than anyone else to try to stop the genocide and yet felt the worst about it. Why? Because, as Power observes, "[t]he only way risky action is ever taken on behalf of mere principle is when moral feeling overpowers reasoned self-interest."[1] Power goes on to say that the man who does the most in the face of such horror always feels the worst, just as the man who feels the worst often does the most.

Pinzak: And I would think that the action doesn't even have to be "risky." People and states pursue their interests, and sometimes those interests involve strangers. For example, we saw an impressive outpouring of financial aid after the Indian Ocean earthquake and tsunami of December 2004.

Emile: Yes, we did. But do you not suppose that much of the aid offered by other countries, especially Western countries, came because there were tourists from those countries lost and killed? Those who gave aid could see themselves in the shoes of their fellow citizens. They could "feel" their plight.

Pinzak: They can feel where the other's shoe pinches. Moral imagination plays a significant role here. We cannot assume that those who put themselves in the shoes of others in India or Indonesia only did so for those who were already in some ways like them. That is, why should we assume that persons around the world didn't respond sympathetically just because fellow human beings were in need?[2]

Emile: Because, as we have been saying, people seem to respond only when confronted via the media to the horrors that others are facing. Has newspaper coverage of the tragedy in Darfur led to massive outpourings of charitable giving and of political outrage? Perhaps persons are more willing to provide aid to those who have suffered a natural disaster, not a political disaster. A natural disaster can happen to anyone; we can see ourselves in that circumstance. But a political persecution or ongoing violence might not receive as much attention and thus not elicit as much aid. Those living in longstanding democracies, like those in the West, do not readily see that any such persecution could happen to them. One might then think that those suffering in other places are somehow responsible for bringing these heinous consequences on themselves.

Pinzak: Such people don't see themselves in that kind of political position and thus are more reluctant to help?

Emile: Or less interested in helping because part of the position is the victims' fault. Perhaps. Do not look so shocked, Pinzak. It is just a possibility. You have to admit, the UN Summit passed this resolution in 2005. How often have the Western powers interceded to stop violence and to protect people's rights? We are trying to understand how people come to feel the cosmopolitan connection to all other human beings.

Pinzak: So we agree on the need of persons to put themselves in the shoes of others, and not just of their fellow citizens . . . a need by persons to take into consideration the experiences and perspectives of all others. Won't we need to do that before we take any action or enact any legislation that can affect persons in our country and throughout the globe? If so, then shouldn't we educate persons to take up various perspectives and deliberate before they make decisions?

Emile: Get them to ask themselves, "What would it be like to be in their position? To live this way? To feel this anger or fear or envy or compassion?" This is certainly what Martha Nussbaum had in mind when she recommended a cosmopolitan education (1996).

Pinzak: It seems clear that identity relates to moral sense and moral judgment. We feel the weight of our moral obligations to those with whom we identify. *(Pinzak flips back through his notebook and reads)* Let me slightly modify the quotation from David Miller that you cited at our last meeting: "Because I identify with my family, my college, or my local community . . . I [see] myself as a member, [and] I feel a loyalty to the group" (1995, 65). This results in one's giving special attention to the interests of the group's members. But changing persons' identities seems a daunting if not mysterious task.

Emile: Why mysterious?

Pinzak: Because I don't know whether we know how to change people's identities. Even if we do, even if it isn't mysterious, it is still daunting.

Emile: You may well be correct that it is daunting, but I do not think it is mysterious. First, I think that taking up and sharing perspectives as you suggest is a way of shifting identity. It may also be a way that leads to people taking action.

Pinzak: It is a kind of action in itself.

Emile *(smiling):* Spoken like a true theorist. It strikes me that philosophy can lay out for us our moral obligations, but we require psychology to understand how and why people act. Raphael Lemkin, a Polish Jew, linguist, and international lawyer, was the father of the Genocide Convention. In the spring of 1941, at an academic conference at Duke, Lemkin asked those gathered: "If women, children, and old people would be murdered a hundred miles from here, wouldn't you run to help? Then why do you stop this decision of your heart when the distance is three thousand miles instead of a hundred?"[3]

Pinzak: Is the reason that we stop distance or boundaries? Would we stop the decision if the three thousand miles in question separated New Yorkers and Californians?

Emile: Distance might be the problem in terms of practicality; could we travel three thousand miles fast enough to help? But you are getting at the issue that Lemkin is really pointing out: Nations are constructed boundaries, and we can destroy and reconstruct or redraw them to be more and more encompassing. At that point what would stop us would be physical distance and not psychological or emotional distance from someone across our boundaries.

Pinzak: So you follow Hume who wrote: "Morality . . . is more properly felt than judg'd of."[4]

Emile: Well, Hume is certainly placing the emphasis in morality on feelings, but he is not excluding reason altogether. For Hume reason does play a role, but reason alone cannot motivate moral action.[5] Indeed, Hume thought that the basis of moral judgment was a combination, if not an integration, of thought and feeling. Likewise, I think that we need to combine reason and emotion, the philosophical or intellectual with the psychological, what is felt with what is known. Otherwise, one can know about the suffering of others but not be moved to do anything about it.

Pinzak: People can feel another's pain but not know what to do about it. Likewise, without reflection or intellection one is unable to discern which feelings to act on and which to let go of or even oppose.

Emile: That is correct. We need to integrate emotion and reason so that the heart and mind know together. This integration is what I mean by "felt" identity. *(He pauses and takes a sip of coffee.)*

Pinzak: And we need politics in order to act out and act on those feelings and obligations.

Emile: Let us take up again what we said yesterday about Nussbaum's metaphor of extending obligations and attachments. This idea of "circles" of attachments and duties is not new to philosophy. Edmund Burke argued that persons operate in a kind of hierarchy of attachments: "To be attached to . . . the little platoon we belong to in society . . . is the first link in the series by which we proceed toward a love of our country and to mankind." (Quoted by McConnell, in Nussbaum, 79.) Similarly, in *Il Convivio* Dante described a pyramidal shape to life's spheres of intercourse: A person needs a family, a family needs a neighborhood, a neighborhood needs a city, and a city needs a country (for Dante, a kingdom).[6] But why stop there? And what do countries need as a context? An integrated global context? Does identity not move through these "concentric circles"?[7]

Pinzak: More recently, philosopher Henry Shue has opposed the view of those like Nussbaum. When he looks at duties from the perspective of a pebble dropped into a pond, Shue sees that *(Pinzak reads from his notebook)* "I am the pebble and the world is the pond I have dropped into. I am the center of a system of concentric ripples around the pebble: strongest at the center and rapidly diminishing towards the periphery" (1988, 691).

Emile: This seems like common sense. Our duties are strongest toward those closest to us and weakest, presumably, toward those most distant from us. Identity closes that distance. Those with a cosmopolitan identity may at times feel their strongest duties to those farthest from them. That is so because those farthest from them in time and space may be close to their hearts psychologically. The focus of one's attention, even and especially the attention of the cosmopolite, can shift. When one's compatriots, or co-nationals, are in trouble, when one's community is under siege, when a family member needs help, then we shift our attention to those most in need. Our duties to them come to the fore. It is not that we develop duties to these various persons or levels; it is that we feel them at different times. We always have them, but we do not feel them or need to act on them.

Pinzak: So these relationships only become issues for us when they conflict. Here, again, is Sartre's moral dilemma about the youth in France during World War II who is pulled in opposite directions—in one direction is his obligation to remain at home to help his mother; in the other, his sense of obligation to join the Resistance and fight the Nazis.

Emile: This is not a dilemma for a person who does not have conflicting obligations. It would seem for Shue that no such dilemmas would arise. But from another perspective, the one that we are exploring here, we are not like one pebble dropped into the water. We are the water into which pebbles representing different situations and circumstances and dilemmas are dropped, where the ripples, the circles of identity, are fluctuations of identity. Our identities can shift, and the duties most salient can also shift. But that does not mean that our other duties disappear. Another pebble has been dropped, our center of attention shifts to a circle that previously had been on the periphery. Now that circle is itself the center.

Pinzak: So it might be better to think of the pebbles as incidents that get our attention and bring into our awareness our circles of identity relative to any single incident. The water radiates our circles as the pebble or incident sinks into consciousness. The pebble or incident reflects what or who is in which circle radiating from the center.

Emile: Yes, and identity shifts occur all the time depending on the incident.

Pinzak: The image or metaphor has gotten cumbersome.

Emile: Perhaps Burke's hierarchy is a better image than Shue's pebble in the water (though, keep in mind, it is an *image* that Shue opposes), because we can move up and down the hierarchy. Its levels do not disappear, even when we are at the top.

Bear in mind that a shift to a cosmopolitan outlook does not mean that we cease to have relationships with and therefore duties toward our family or friends or neighbors. It means that we form a new kind of relationship toward others in full recognition that the cosmopolitan identity has introduced something heretofore not acknowledged. One now examines relationships in the context of a new relationship to all others, to all human beings. That requires negotiating personal relationships in light of a new and more expansive context.

Pinzak: So it goes like this: I cannot understand my personal relationships until I understand the context in which I have relationships. Indeed, I cannot understand myself until I understand that context because the context is part of me.

Emile: This would seem to be especially true of cosmopolites. Those with a cosmopolitan identity, or so I hope to argue, seek out conflict in order to understand themselves fully. They know that conflicting perspectives are essential to them for understanding themselves. Conflicting views represent views that are within them, that are part of them, but that they have left out or not considered. Thus the more they engage with ambiguity and multiplicity or diversity the more they learn about themselves.[8]

Pinzak: The conflicts and contradictions they encounter are really within them as well. Two values that seemingly contradict, or that are at least incompatible—say, patriotism and cosmopolitanism—are intrapersonal as well as interpersonal. One could be, then, both patriotic and cosmopolitan.

Emile: This is what we have been saying about the ripples in the water representing our obligations and relationships. The conflicts and contradictions are also within ourselves. We are all selves of complexity and multiplicity. Because we are all humans, whatever any other human experiences is part of my experience.

Pinzak: So I cannot understand my view or form my view until I have heard from my multiple selves, which often means until I have heard from others.

Emile: Cosmopolitan identity is the recognition that identity is constructed and reconstructed, negotiated and renegotiated on the basis of what one hears from others in the dialogue. This process is never-ending.

Pinzak: Because there are always new perspectives to entertain.

Emile: That is correct. One does not say, "Now I have finished listening. I am complete."

What Is Identity?

Pinzak: I need to hear more, Emile, to sort this out.

Emile: That is why we are in conversation, and you are not in the library. *(Both men drink from their cups.)* Let us begin with identity in general, which will help us understand the construction of cosmopolitan identity. Identity is how and by what we define ourselves. It consists of two essential aspects. First is agency or the organizer of identity; second is a self-definition or what is organized into an identity. So identity tells us what is of central importance to the person. But it also reveals the person's selfhood.

Pinzak: I am not quite following you.

Emile: Let me say it differently. What is at the center of describing ourselves is our self-definition—those things and relationships that we cherish, would die for, cannot live without; in short, those that give meaning to our lives.

Pinzak: Conversely, that meaning might be based on things and relationships that one detests, would kill for, and cannot live in the face of.

Emile: That may be true, though it seems questionable to me that someone could build a self-concept or self-definition around such negativity.

Pinzak: Why couldn't one build his whole life around, say, revenge, like Hamlet seeking to avenge the murder of his father?

Emile: It seems to me that built into that self-definition is some positive notion as well. Hamlet wants to be a good son, a son obedient to his father's ghost. I think that whatever the negative, there would also be, perhaps would need to be, some positive.

But in any event, we can say that the self-definition will vary, and vary greatly, from person to person or group to group, depending on the notion of agency in effect.

Pinzak: And the agency is?

Emile: Again, *agency* is the subjectivity that does the organizing and of which we cannot be conscious. *Agency* is what Ken Wilber calls the "observing self" or the "I," in contrast to the "observed self" or "me" (2000b, 33), similar to Kant's "transcendental ego" and his "empirical ego."[9]

Pinzak: We cannot be conscious of that by which we organize our self-definition?

Emile: Correct. Once we are conscious of our subjectivity, then we have made that subjectivity an object of our consciousness. Once we have done that, then we act on what previously we acted according to. This simply means that once we can take as an object of our awareness what used to be the subject, the subject has now become an object that we can act on and no longer act according to. *(Emile smiles at Pinzak's perplexed look.)*

It is really quite simple. When we identify with something, we find that something so important, so meaningful, that we define ourselves by it. But who is the self, what is the self that is doing the identifying? That self is the subject who is doing the identifying. The nature of that aspect of self is not itself something that we can identify with because it is the subject doing the identifying. We identify *with* something because we as agents identify *as* something. That "as something" we cannot ourselves see without rendering it an object of our attention and no longer the subject that attends. *(Emile begins to laugh.)*

Pinzak: Are you enjoying this?

Emile: Immensely. It is not that complicated. Wilber describes it this way: "During psychological development the 'I' at one stage becomes a 'me' at the next" (2000b, 34). To understand this notion of identity, of how people construct identities, we shall need to take up the perspective of developmental psychology.[10]

Pinzak: People construct their identities? Aren't identities discovered or inculcated?

Emile: Not according to the research in developmental psychology. Developmentalists, as I shall call them, propose that there are stages of identity. Self-development proceeds through stratified stages characterized by increasing complexity, integration, unity, and interaction. Indeed, developmental psychologists are virtually unanimous on the existence, emergence, and nature of these stages.

What they all describe in looking through the prism of development is a hierarchy of stages. They see not one self but a "series" of selves. The "series" is not so much a concatenation of selves as an "evolution" of self. At each later stage—marked, as I said, by increasing complexity, integration, unity, and interaction—there are characteristics available that did not exist at the prior stages. Thus at each stage identity changes as the self disappears to be replaced by a "higher-order" self. At each new level of identity all the basic structures that preceded that stage are integrated into the new identity.

Pinzak *(talking as he is writing):* So when the next later stage emerges, it unfolds some new characteristic not seen at the earlier stages, right? *(Emile nods.)* At the least, the presence of this new characteristic points to greater complexity.[11]

Emile: Right. Development is about change. This is not any kind of change. It is growth from a stage that is less complex and less open in perspective to one that is of greater complexity and increased perspective. In developmental psychological terms stages represent or form an invariant sequence moving from less complexity to greater and greater complexity. Thus developmentalists refer to stages as forming overall a hierarchy.[12]

As we have been using the term, *identity* refers to a self-system consisting of agency and self-definition or self-concept. In our current context it is also a composite term for the description of the self-system at different stages of maturation, which here means greater complexity and integration.[13]

Pinzak: Give me an example.

Emile: All right. Let us consider the work of Lawrence Kohlberg. Kohlberg studied the changes that occur in moral reasoning as people develop cognitively. He observed that persons move from pre-conventional moral reasoning, where everything is about them and their feelings—for example, fears of punishment or desires for rewards—to conventional morality . . .

Pinzak: . . . my country, right or wrong?

Emile: Yes, examples like that . . . to post-conventional morality, where persons are concerned about universal principles that pertain or ought to pertain to everyone equally. Each subsequent stage in the sequence is more encompassing and complex as moral views move from thinking of oneself to thinking of one's community or clan or nation to thinking of all others.

Pinzak: So when someone begins to think about his community, this does not mean that he stops thinking about himself. It means that he thinks about himself and his group, clan, or nation. He thinks about what is right and good and just for him and others in the group. And the new identity is more complex because what was agency or subjectivity at the prior stage is now an object of attention of the new "higher order" subject. What was once subject is now object and can be acted upon.[14] In other words, what can now be "objectified" can be integrated into the new identity.

Emile: Right again. When children establish "concrete operations of thought," as Piaget called them, they begin to apply rules and roles that create and maintain a stable worldview and a stable sense of self. Those rules and roles come out of or from the children's membership in a group. Able to operate with concepts and thus to learn the rules and roles of the group, children learn to construct and perceive a particular shared reality—that of the group or clan or tribe or society. Everyone who comes into contact with the children is a teacher describing the world and its operations, until finally the children learn the rules for making that world and its roles their own, perceiving it as described. This membership is reinforced as the children act according to the rules of the group, fulfill their assigned roles, and share the common reality through communication. As George Herbert Mead put it, the self is "socially constituted . . . and must extend as far as the social activity or approaches of social relations which constitute it extend" (1934, 223).

Pinzak: Okay, but that is not the self-system. What you have described is really only the self-definition aspect.

Emile: You are doing well, Pinzak. Agency for the self at this membership level is constituted by the rules and roles of the group, while the self-definition is constituted by the contents or the shared reality.

Pinzak: So if agency is subjectivity and thus what we act with but not on, then the children cannot reflect on the rules and roles by which they are creating and maintaining their group membership or identity. A child *is* the group; she cannot be separate from it.

Emile: At this stage that is correct. A child at this membership level or stage can choose among the accepted social roles, but the very range of what is acceptable is circumscribed and determined by membership. The child cannot see her own agency, and thus she cannot scrutinize "the obligations, expectations, satisfactions, purposes, or influences" (Kegan 1982, 97) of the group. Because she cannot scrutinize or reflect on the rules and roles of her shared worldview—that is, she can learn them but cannot question them—then the group rules.

Pinzak: So she is embedded in the rules and roles of the group and cannot step back reflectively from and thus see them.

Emile: Yes. At the next level of development, what Piaget called "formal operations of thought," the child will have the inner capacity to judge rules and roles because she will be able to step back reflectively from them.[15] At this formal operational level, sometimes called the level of autonomy, the person can be said to be self-governing or self-authoring because he or she is not embedded in the rules and roles. But at the membership level, having no critical distance from them, the child is captured by the viewpoints, opinions, and expectations of the group and conforms to them. Indeed, to quote Berger and Luckmann, "the child does not internalize the world of his significant others as one of many possible worlds. He internalizes it as the world, the only existent and only conceivable world" (1967, 135).

Pinzak: The need to conform will therefore be the central feature of the self-definition, one of the two essential aspects of identity.

Emile: Right. *(He pauses as Pinzak is frantically writing. "I see you are putting my pen to good use, Pinzak.")* Agency here is the child's membership, and of this she is unconscious because it forms her subjectivity—what she operates by, not on. The limit of the self, then, lies in its inability at this stage to consult itself about, or to separate from, the shared or group reality. That ability will unfold at the next level of development. And then identity will shift so that agency becomes the critical ability itself. At that level the membership self and its concrete world will be merely one instance of what are now seen as infinite possibilities.

Pinzak: So if I understand this idea of membership self or identity correctly, then it is not that the child identifies with the group rules and roles, as if she has made up her mind that these are correct and good rules and roles. Rather, what the group offers or shares as perceptions and a worldview is herself. Whatever the group is, the group is the child's self.

Emile: Yes. Because the group is the source of self, there is no self separate from the group and thus no self to bring to the group. As Kegan remarked, others do not speak for her; she is the others' speaking (1982, 64). There is no gap, no space, between self and group. She *is* the community standards, purposes, ideals, rules, and roles.

Pinzak: These are not internalized because, as her agency, they are unconscious operators.

Emile: Rather than taken within, or internalized, the framework is built up from the inside.

Pinzak: But we are talking about children here, so you are not suggesting that persons with this kind of identity are those whom we earlier described as loyal to their countries. You are not saying that people who love their countries are childlike in their identities, right?

Emile: I am not suggesting that . . . at least not in most cases of adult identity. Remember that we are examining identity as having two parts—agency, or subjectivity, and self-definition, or how the person describes himself. I am assuming for the moment that many adults are self-reflective agents capable of stepping back from the country's rules and roles to scrutinize them. These adults are not captured by or embedded in those rules and roles. As a result, loyal Americans, for example, would be those who have a feeling of attachment or allegiance to their country, which they have developed over time. In other words, they have bound themselves through commitment to serve their country. That means that they have a self that is separate from the country's rules and roles that they can bring into allegiance with that country.

Pinzak: And children are not capable at the level of membership to step back reflectively.

Emile: That is right. At the membership stage, or as a membership self, the person lacks the cognitive capacity to step back reflectively. That capacity comes with the unfolding of formal operational thinking.

Pinzak: So cognitive abilities are necessary for certain kinds of identity?

Emile: Cognitive abilities, or, more precisely, cognitive structures, are necessary but not sufficient for mental or psychological growth. They are necessary in that they lead, as it were, the development of other aspects of psychological growth. So a person can have the structure of formal operational thinking, which means being able to generate counterfactual thoughts, make hypotheses, and draw inferences—in short, to think propositionally or to think about thinking—but might not be willing or even able to step back reflectively from his moral behavior to analyze it.

Pinzak: I understand the "willing" part of what you just said. Someone is unwilling to call into question his loyalty to his nation. But surely that person, with formal operational thinking, is "able" to do that questioning.

Emile: Well, he has the *capacity* to do it but not the *ability. (Pinzak shrugs his shoulders.)* I mean, he has the cognitive capacity, but not an adequate development of his moral sense to do it. That is why I said that cognitive structures are necessary but not sufficient for psychological growth. Psychological development and psychological health involve more than cognitive structures. They involve psychosocial development, affective development, psychosexual development, moral development, spiritual development, and more.[16] These developments, which Wilber calls "lines," although they emerge in the same sequential way, are relatively independent and do not develop at the same pace. So a person might be "very advanced in some lines, medium in others, low in still others—all at the same time" (Wilber 2000c, 28). The person whom we are discussing may well have moral development lagging behind his cognitive development. As a result, for deep psychological reasons, he is unable to call into question his moral behavior.

Pinzak: If we look, for instance, at the behavior of those in the White House and of those associated with the Nixon Administration during Watergate, we see people clearly capable of propositional thinking. You are saying that these people would not examine their illegal activities during this time because they were not able to do so.

Emile: Well, some were; John Dean certainly did, which is why he testified against Erlichman, Haldeman, and Nixon. But I think that some others were incapable.

Pinzak: Why? Why would they be incapable?

Emile: Answering that would require getting them "on the couch." *(Pinzak laughs.)* No, I mean it. Only a psychiatrist or psychologist could get to the bottom of that dynamic. It is fair to say, I think, that their identities as self-definition were so wrapped up in who they were as reflected in what they were doing—the roles they held and the rules they played by—that they could not reflect on what was going on and how they were behaving.

Pinzak: Philip Zimbardo uses himself as an example of this phenomenon. During the famous, or infamous, Stanford Prison Experiment, Zimbardo served as the superintendent of the experimental prison. He got so wrapped up in his role as the superintendent that he could not step away from the experiment to see that he had become the very kind of person that he detested—an uncaring authoritarian. Nor could he see that his "volunteers" were really suffering. It took an outsider, one of his former graduate students who happened to be visiting, to point out that real damage was being done to real persons. And all of that damage transpired in the prison experiment over only the first five days![17]

Emile: Zimbardo may well be an example of how easily we can slide back into rule-role thinking, how easily we can lose perspective when the situation we are in is intense and all-consuming. In that situation Zimbardo could not separate himself from his role as the superintendent of an experimental, mock prison. He was caught up in how the superintendent must act and could not see how the psychologist running an experiment that had quickly turned vicious had to act.

Pinzak: And if you had asked the Nixon loyalists why they were committing crimes . . .

Emile: They would have rationalized their behavior. I do not think that they could entertain the idea that they were wrong in what they were doing. They might well recognize that something they did was illegal and wrong in that sense, but it was justified morally by some higher purpose—national security or loyalty to President Nixon, for example.

Pinzak: Let me try another example. When the terrorists on September 11, 2001, crashed the airliners into the Pentagon and the World Trade Center, some people wrote off those acts as acts of pure evil. It seems to me that this stops dead any conversation about why the terrorists may have acted this way. If we dismiss the acts as evil, then there is no need to investigate what might have caused the young Muslims to commit such heinous acts.

Some people who dismiss the acts as evil might well be unwilling to look at Islamic fundamentalist terrorism as anything but evil, because they think that to do so would be unpatriotic. They fear that to do so might acknowledge that the terrorists, however misguided, had reasons for doing what they did. But these terrorists were not psychotic. They were misguided, but they believed in their cause and their martyrdom.

Emile: As Nietzsche observed, by looking throughout world history, "There is no more really vital theme than the age-old tragedy of the martyrs who wanted to stir up the swamp."[18]

Pinzak: Nietzsche saw such acts by martyrs as heroic acts of freedom, even of morality. Yet to acknowledge any legitimacy to such acts, to acknowledge that we are a target because of what we represent to these terrorists, these martyrs could unravel some people's own commitment or loyalty to our nation, its goals, and its methods. Others, however, might be *unable* to look at that commitment because what our country represents or stands for, the values that we espouse and live by, even putatively, are their very selves.

Emile: Evil is in the eye of the beholder, Pinzak? "For these words of Good, Evil, and Contemptible, are ever used with relation to the person that uses them."[19] You, and Hobbes, might be right. Thirty years ago, Ayatollah Ruhollah Khomeini, the Shiite leader of Iran, referred to the United Sates as "the Great Satan." What we did around the world and in the Middle East, Khomeini and his followers saw as evil. Nietzsche also wrote: "When man possesses the feeling of power he feels and calls himself good: and it is precisely then that the others upon whom he has to discharge his power feel and call him evil."[20] Simply calling anyone or any act "evil" does seem a way of stopping analysis or investigation. It is the ultimate judgment.

With regard to the terrorists, it seems to be a way to avoid thinking about what led these men to act and, further, a way to avoid evaluating whether our own behavior needs to be scrutinized and even altered. But keep in mind that terrorists wish to do us great harm. They have to be stopped, just as Kamikaze pilots during World War II had to be stopped. Conversing with people willing to kill themselves in order to kill you seems a waste of time.

Pinzak: The conversation is not with the terrorists. It is between us and those who might become terrorists.

Anyway, the unfolding of formal operational thinking is not itself sufficient to get people to move identity from a membership self to some more self-reflective kind of identity.

Emile: That is right. Formal operations unfold around early adolescence, but those operations are certainly not fully established until late in one's teens or early twenties. So a teenaged boy who grows up in Little Rock, Arkansas, hating blacks and then moves to Madison, Wisconsin, and becomes an egalitarian is still seeking conformity (Kegan 1982). Though the perspectives are diametrically opposed, the mode of defining himself is exactly the same: conformity to one's peer group, expressing the need to fit in.

Pinzak: But having no self that is separate from the group, the boy does not perceive it in this way.

Emile: Also right. Bear in mind that membership identity like this is not necessarily a pernicious level. For adolescents it marks a step out of egocentrism and toward full perspectivism. The ability to take the roles of others, even if limited by membership, is crucial to meaning-making and to forming a coherent worldview. It enables persons to share viewpoints. Adolescents are presented with new options, ideals, roles, and rules, but in a limited and manageable way. As Erik Erikson pointed out, in the adolescent quest for identity, "there is a universal trend toward some form of uniformity (and sometimes to special uniforms or distinctive clothing) through which incomplete self-certainty . . . can hide in group certainty. . . . Even those who care to differ radically must evoke a certain uniformity of differing" (Erikson 1960, 71).

Pinzak: But why should self-certainty be incomplete?

Emile: Membership is a level of shared and certain reality and thus of shared and certain self. But later in adolescence, belonging and membership become desperate needs, because affiliation can become conscious. The unfolding of formal operations often brings the onset of doubt as the adolescent expands perspectivism beyond the group and as the agency of the membership self becomes an object of the new self's attention.

Pinzak: Okay, I see how that can happen. But what spurs on adults, or anyone else, who already thinks at the formal operational level but is unwilling to question the group's rules or roles? For Zimbardo, for example, it took the shock of a former student pointing out that Zimbardo himself was allowing real suffering to go on in a fake prison. Is that how this works?

Emile: It is how all growth occurs, according to developmentalists. When the organism, in this case a person, is confronted with something shocking, new, and even threatening in the environment, that organism can either fight or flee. Remember that for the adolescent the movement out of the clan or tribe or gang to consider the perspective of the nation, of the whole social system, can be a reaction to the confrontation with disparate viewpoints or values. Dr. Johnson's *Dictionary* defined "national" as "publick; general; not private; not particular." We can see in this definition that part of the idea of nation is to eclipse particularity—local customs or allegiances or sentiments. In other words, nations, which are particular, superseded more local particularities. Did it eliminate those? No, but it did offer, even demand, a kind of affiliation that in some in-stances—war, for example—took precedence over local attachments.

So the adolescent can regress to a prior level where the threat or problem is ignored or buried or dismissed. Or the adolescent can "fight" by dealing with the demands of a national perspective and thereby dissociate from identity with the clan, tribe, or gang. He can confront the problem or threat by calling attention to it.

Pinzak: The person pulls his cognitive hat down over his eyes, or else he examines the problem.

Emile: Yes. So when the environment throws something at the person that he or she cannot handle using the self's current organization, then the person regresses or progresses.

Pinzak: Something frustrates or disturbs the person's equilibrium or bal-ance, something like Watergate or Iran-Contra or . . .

Emile: My Lai or Abu Ghraib . . .

Pinzak: Or thinking that the administration lied about weapons of mass destruction in order to go to war.

Emile: We could go on and on. The threat or problem does not have to be one major issue. There could be a series of small but significant problems. Nor do they have to be political. They could also involve the values or beliefs or practices of your immediate group or clan. It could be anything that, as you said, disrupts one's equilibrium, that throws the self off balance.

Pinzak: And it is the unfolding of formal operations that enables the ado-lescent to separate from and thus act on the group and its standards. Persons embedded in those standards, who identify as those standards, would see civil disobedience as mere lawbreaking. Martin Luther King, Jr., and Henry David Thoreau were simply troublemakers. Such standards would be the breeding-ground for extremist movements like the fascists for whom duty and obedience to the state were the sole source of meaning and value. But with the unfolding of formal operations the adolescent is no longer those rules and roles; she now *has* rules and roles.

Emile: Exactly. Whereas meaning for the membership self derived from the group, the adolescent with formal operations can seek out or form groups around her own meaning. The individual is autonomous in that responsibility appears above all to be to the individual self. Responsibility is always and ultimately a response of self that defines the relationship to the source of obligation, whatev-er that source might be—authority, social pressure, conscience. The boundaries of the group—family, gang, clan, tribe, nation—are transcended.[21] Other people are known for the first time, for they can be known as independent, separate persons and not as representatives or members of a social group.

Pinzak: Social attachments and allegiances are not necessarily lost, though.

Emile: Kohlberg pointed out that there are two stages of what he called "conventional" morality. By "conventional morality" Kohlberg means the kind of moral reasoning that leads someone not only to conform to the interests, values, and expectations of the group, but also to be loyal or devoted to the group. At the first, and less mature, stage the person's loyalty is limited to personal relationships, those specific individuals found in the family, group, or clan. At the more mature second stage the person takes up the perspective of the entire social collectivity. In short, the person takes up the perspective of society as a whole. Likewise, identity shifts from conformity and loyalty to specific persons or groups of persons to conformity and loyalty to the network of rules and roles that constitutes society. But with formal operational thinking social attachments and allegiances can even be more profound.

Pinzak: Yes, because the individual is separate from the group. Those using concrete operations can reflect on their lives, but do so only from within the concrete events, places, and relationships that constitute those lives. On the other hand, one using formal operations can evaluate the effects, and therefore the importance, of a group's organization, purposes, ideals, and assumptions by stepping back from her life, as if above or outside of that life. Where the self was earlier derived from the community, now the self is autonomous and can bring itself, can commit itself, to that community.

Emile: Precisely the same is true for personal relationships. Relationships at the membership level define the self, for there is no self that is independent of them. But at the autonomous level relationships are the content, not the context, of the self. No longer constituting agency, relationships can be operated on and can form part of the self-definition.

Cosmopolitan Identity and Dialectical Thinking

Pinzak: Relationships are now freely entered and not compelled. They are *conscious* relationships. So there is no reason why one's commitments cannot be to one's nation and one's compatriots. There is also no reason why one's commitments cannot be first to all humans, to all of humanity. But if formal operations equally underlie both kinds of commitments, then how do we move identity from the nation to cosmopolitanism?

Emile: It is the particular that makes cosmopolitanism possible. If there were no particular cultures—and thus no particular beliefs, values, practices, and so on—then Salman Rushdie, for example, could not construct a cosmopolitan identity. A universal cosmopolitanism does not negate particular cultures or nations. Identity with them does not disappear. Indeed, identity with them can generate conflict and dilemmas where none existed before. Cosmopolitan identity takes up differences; it does not efface them.

You are right that formal operations bring the individual face-to-face with the relativism of her own self-definition. Now her world is one of open possibilities, and so, too, is her self-definition. She is now aware of the beliefs, values, rules, and roles that had constituted the self. She now asks, "Where do I stand?" and, of course, "Who am I?"

Pinzak: I think that you are making an important distinction here. Anyone can respond to the question "Who are you?" Membership selves will have an answer to that question that builds on the rules and roles of the group. But only the self-reflective person, exercising formal operations, will herself ask "Who am I?" So it sounds as if identity is now focused on agency—who I am—more than on self-definition—what I am.

Emile: When you press persons who identify through formal operations—that is, autonomous selves—you find that they quickly abandon discussions of self-concepts and self-definitions and resort to descriptions of the processes—the "how"—by which they come to self-definitions. Autonomous selves, then, are concerned with how they construct their individuality as much as and probably more than with what is constructed.

This psychological development heralds a shift from conceiving of oneself exclusively as a member of a particular group or order to a sense of membership in the human community. The bond of tribal membership, for example, as A. D. Smith points out, is "an exclusive and all-pervasive one" (1991, 62). The autonomous individual can now step outside of the tribe and take up the perspectives of those not affiliated with the tribe. He does so in full recognition that others can do so and are doing so as well. As James Mark Baldwin (1911) said, individuality is singular, but it is also universal—a property shared by all persons. So here we can see a move toward cosmopolitanism.

Pinzak: What is it, then, that constitutes agency at this stage? What is it that the subject is embedded in that he cannot be conscious of?

Emile: An excellent question, which deserves another espresso. Would you mind getting us another "round," if I pay for them?

Pinzak: No need; I will do both. After all, I am getting more than my money's worth even if I always buy the coffee.

Emile smiles and nods in appreciation. Pinzak soon returns with a demitasse for Emile and a cappuccino for himself. Emile is slightly startled out of a reverie as Pinzak takes his seat.

Emile: Thank you. I will return the favor next time.

Pinzak: Emile, as I said, our conversation more than makes up for whatever minor expense I incur in buying your coffee.

Emile *(taking a sip):* Conversations are two-way, Pinzak. In exchanging words and "dwelling together," however temporarily, we generate the possibility of *conversare,* which is to convert or turn each other around.

Pinzak: You are as generous in your viewpoint as you are in sharing your knowledge, but the "conversation" seems decidedly one-sided.

Emile *(smiling):* So far. *(He waits as Pinzak takes a sip.)* Now, back to your excellent questions: What is the autonomous person unconscious of? Put simply, he is unconscious of, well, rationality. He is unconscious of the very language and logic used to create a self-definition.

Pinzak: So he is embedded in language and logic and cannot see beyond them?

Emile: Yes. He can criticize language and logic; he can analyze rationality. But to do so he must use language and the logic of language. He cannot escape them. If this stage of identity is characterized by self-reflection, then we must ask ourselves what it is that we use when we so reflect. The person is the organizer or active subject of the constellation of concepts, traits, values, goals, and the like that constitute one's self-definition. That organization is accomplished through self-reflective thought that is made up of language and logic or rationality.

The self cannot, at any stage, step back from its own subjectivity. The subjectivity of the individual—that is, the self-reflective person—is not, however, embedded in any specific evaluation, but is instead embedded in the process of evaluation itself. The self at this stage is, therefore, not embedded in any specific vocabulary or conversation but in the structure and logic of language.

Pinzak: So the autonomous self can criticize any standpoint, including its own, and it is not therefore necessarily identified with any specific contingency. Yet the autonomous self is not without any particular identity. After all, language, which is the basis of the ability to critique, is itself a social particularity.

Emile: Another way to say that is to say that the self is not empty. Because agency is located within the self in this process, and not within social rules and roles, then the self is autonomous, free of these encumbrances and attachments.

Pinzak: But no longer embedded in them does not mean no longer identified with them.

Emile: That is correct. The person is no longer identified *as* them. He or she might well decide to identify *with* them. Now the self can relate to them; now selves can be in and have relationships rather than being found in or derived from them.

Pinzak: What is impossible, then, is to transcend agency; that is, to transcend language and logic.

Emile: That is the proper way to state it. Of course, one can avoid language by speaking gibberish. One can escape logic by regressing to a level of illogicality and irrationality. The dilemma for thinkers at the highest stage of formal operational thinking is that they can take language as an object—that is, they can study language, its parts, its uses—but to do so they must also use language as the tool of thought. They are not simply thinking about thinking, but thinking about the language in which thinking is thought. But transcending language and logic is a totally different matter.

Pinzak: And that is impossible.

Emile: I did not say that. It is impossible for the autonomous self as defined through formal operational thinking to do so. But it is possible to transcend both language and rationality, which will become a feature later as we move more fully into conversation about cosmopolitan identity.

Pinzak: I thought that we already were fully in conversation about cosmopolitan identity.

Emile *(laughing):* We are indeed. I think that by pushing to the very limits of formal operational thinking we can stimulate a cosmopolitan sensibility. Yet to move into it in the most profound and stable way may well involve the need for experience beyond language and rationality or logic. But we are not yet at the place in this conversation for that topic.

Pinzak: What remains to be said before we get to that place?

Emile: We need to consider how cosmopolitanism might be initiated through a new kind of thinking. There are two ways, it seems to me, to a cosmopolitan identity. One way, going beyond language and rationality, we shall consider a little later. The other lies at the edges of formal operational thinking. At the edges is a level of thinking identified by some developmental psychologists as a further cognitive structure found in some, but at this point a limited, number of adults. Called variously, for example, "post-conventional" thinking, "post-autonomous" thinking, "dialectical" thinking, or "vision-logic," this structure is characterized by, above all else, the ability to handle ambiguity, divergent viewpoints, and contradictions. In dialectical thinking, as we shall call it, the person not only recognizes the presence of ambiguity, divergences, and contradictions, which anyone using formal operations can do, but the person also wants to deal with them.[22] Indeed, the person wants to find the unity or connections underlying them.

Pinzak: When a person faces conflicting or even contradicting views, then he or she tries to reconcile them?

Emile: Yes. The dialectical thinker seeks to find the connection among or unity underlying them. Deirdre Kramer, in studying dialectical thinking, found two forms of such thought. One is called "dynamic relativism," which is relativist or contextualist thinking; the other is "dynamic dialecticism" or dialectical thought. By the way, Kramer points out that attempts to reconcile or transcend contradictions are rarely seen before adulthood. Dynamic relativism and dynamic dialecticism are the two highest forms of thinking that she identified. Both of them unfold after adolescence, and evidence shows that they rarely occur before middle age.

Pinzak: Well, isn't middle age really the time one develops wisdom? Isn't "wisdom" a term for encapsulating the ability to see connections or even the unity among disparate things? *(Emile nods assent to both questions.)* That is why my generation cherishes people like you, Emile. You have built up this storehouse of associations through a lifetime of experiences.

Emile *(puts his hand to his chest):* I am touched.

Pinzak *(smiles and then says):* Anyway, a relativist or a contextualist would simply observe that here is a contradiction.[23] Two statements or elements contradict, and they just exist side-by-side. There is no attempt to try to reconcile or transcend them.

Emile: Correct. *(Emile pauses as Pinzak is again writing furiously. "You know, Pinzak, you are getting more use out of that pen in one afternoon than I have in the many years I have had it." Both men laugh. "I'm not going to run* *out of ink, am I?" "No," replied Emile, "more likely you will wear out the nib.")* Through dynamic relativism persons see that different social systems are culturally and historically relative, but they also see that these systems are dynamic; that is, they change and are reconstructed over time. Yet such changes and reconstructions are unpredictable, and there is certainly no relationship or connection seen among such systems. Because "this context is in continual and random flux . . . there is no necessary order or direction to this flux" (Kramer 1989, 135).

On the other hand, prediction with regard to changes and reconstructions is possible, Kramer argues, with dynamic dialecticism. Change occurs systematically, not randomly. Change occurs "via the interplay of conflict and resolution, resulting in forward directional movement toward greater unity and coherence" (1989, 135-36). Contradiction is apparent and temporary and not, as for contextualists, real and permanent. Contradiction and conflict exhort the dialectical thinker to seek out "resolutions that expose the real unity underlying the apparent contradiction" (1989, 136). Indeed, contradictions within or among systems are seen as opportunities for transforming those systems.

Pinzak: How about a "for instance"?

Emile: Well, Beck and Cowan, basing their model of development on the work of psychologist Clare Graves, observe that people at this level of dynamic dialecticism, whom they refer to as 'Second Tier' thinkers characterized by the 'Yellow Meme' or, higher still, the 'Turquoise Meme,' "tolerate, and even enjoy, paradoxes and uncertainties" (1996, 276). At the turquoise stage they approach "complexity through paradoxes" (290). As examples of this approach they cite those who want to maximize individual liberties while also guaranteeing the common good of the whole community, those who want equality in education and yet also want to help the brightest shine and the most challenged to grow, and those who want to build a profitable company but also offer the best possible benefits to employees (1996, 290).[24]

Pinzak: I don't know that I would call these "contradictions."

Emile: You might well be right. They do not seem to be contradictions in the philosophical sense. Bear in mind that contradictions or paradoxes do not have to be solved. They serve as challenges that move dialectical thinkers toward the integration of contexts or systems into a more comprehensive and inclusive system—a meta-system, if you will.

Pinzak: Presumably the meta-system is not only more encompassing but also more stable.

Emile: It is. Greater stability enables the self at this level to engage with and to handle "data" that at an earlier stage would frustrate the person and throw off the self-system's equilibrium. This is not simply a matter of adding new information or more information to the system. Instead, as Cook-Greuter observed in a few of her own subjects, persistent discrepancies that cannot be accommodated by the "meaning system"—what we have been calling "the self-system"—

cause a transformation of the system "into a new, more expansive and inclusive" one (1999, 17).

Pinzak: Would the new self-system found at the level of dialectical thinking also be more stable because what defined subjectivity at the earlier stage has now been incorporated or integrated as part of the predicate or self-definition?

Emile: That would certainly be so if dialectical thinking heralded a shift beyond formal operational thought. But as we said, that is controversial. We can say that at this dialectical level there is also greater stability because multiplicity is embraced. Multiplicity is not a challenge to the organization of the self. Instead, it is now seen as part of the rich tapestry of the self itself.

Pinzak: So when the person confronts values that conflict with or even contradict her own, she does not try to deny them or bury them or crush them.

Emile: That is correct. One of the insights from dialectical thinking is that we construct our values and identities. We do not discover them, as if they were lying deep inside us. From the dialectical perspective seeing that another set of values is incompatible with our own leads us to rethink or refine or reconstruct those values in light of both sets. The idea that there is a core self or essential self is seen at the dialectical level, as Cook-Greuter found, as a self-narrative that itself needs constant revision. The core self then is itself more of a process than a product.

Pinzak: But in the self-system the agent is always putting together a self-concept or self-definition. The self is both process and product.

Emile: That is so, but at the dialectical level sensitivity to this is acute. Cook-Greuter refers to this level as the "construct-aware" stage. At this stage the person expresses and feels "the paradox of being a rational, separate, individual locus of consciousness while also feeling interconnected and part of a deeper, non-individualized, all-pervasive consciousness" (1999, 59).

Pinzak: Can you say that in a different way?

Emile: Yes, and it will bring out the cosmopolitan aspect of this stage of identity. The person is preoccupied with finding a balance between feeling unique and seeing herself as a part, a tiny part, of a deeper, greater whole.

Pinzak: And that whole is all of humanity?

Emile *(nodding):* Those at the "construct-aware" level—which we can call the cosmopolitan level—construct reality, others, and themselves in the context of an embrace of all humanity. They do so, writes Robert Kegan, because "they can do no other" (1994). Persons come to see that any abstraction, including their own individual identities, is a partial representation of the whole. This underscores their connection to, the commonality of, all human beings.

Pinzak: Okay, so research shows that there seems to be a higher or more mature level of formal operational thinking, so much so that some researchers suggest that this level might even be "post-formal"; that is, going beyond formal operations. *(Emile nods as he sips his coffee.)* What I am not quite clear on is what dialectical thinkers do or can do that other formal operational thinkers cannot or do not do. Both require taking up the perspectives of others, right? The

formal-operational thinker and the relativist, or contextualist, can both conceptualize different values and can recapitulate the perspectives of those holding
different, even divergent, values. So what am I missing?

Emile: The problem for those thinkers, unlike the dialectical thinker, is seeing relationships among or underneath those differing perspectives that connect
them. Formal operational thinkers can step back from their own perspectives and
thereby step reflectively into the positions of others. Relativist thinkers are open
enough to take up the perspectives of others and to consider them as their own.
But are persons in either group—and remember that all relativist thinkers are (at
least) formal-operational thinkers—open to the need, to the challenge, of changing their perspectives on the basis of those differing views? That is what dialectical thinkers do—reconstruct their own self-narratives in light of what they hear
from others. As Michael Basseches observes, dialectical thinking carries with it
a heavy emphasis on reciprocity. Dialectical thinkers are not simply open to
divergent positions possibly shaping their own identities and positions; they are
also by necessity shaped by those relationships (1984, 26).

Pinzak: All of this relates to what you were saying earlier. A dialectical
thinker as a cosmopolitan comes to see his connection to all other human beings.
He sees that perspectives held by others reflect perspectives that he himself
could hold. He sees the others' perspectives as part of his own perspective, because of his connection to and his identity with all human beings.

Emile: To say it in an even stronger way: She sees the other as part of her
own self. When the cosmopolite sees suffering around the world, she sees that
she bears responsibility for helping end the suffering of others. She takes steps
to end their suffering, because their suffering is her own. That is so because for
dialectical thinkers, seeing the connection to all others, "we find ourselves in
others and others in ourselves" (Souvaine et al. 1990, 257).

Kegan says this in even more dramatic terms: Confrontation with an opposing and even hostile perspective can effect the realization that the problem between the two viewpoints is not a matter of opposition. It is, instead, a realization of one's own incompleteness that is taken for completeness. "[T]he
Palestinian discovers her own Israeliness, the rich man discovers his poverty, the
woman discovers the man inside her" (1994, 321).

Pinzak: There is no problem, then, making commitments to others because
they are now seen as part of us.

Emile: Correct.

Pinzak: The dialectical thinker examines his own basic assumptions about
life, identity, others, and the world. He needs a context in which to examine and
to question those assumptions. One context is dialogue with others to hear their
perspectives.

Emile: That is the best context, because the dialectical thinker, if left to her
own devices, reposes on the extent of her imagination. Conversing with others
can be more challenging because the perspectives can be divergent and, as we
have noted, even contradictory.

Pinzak: The dialectical thinker holds them all in an embrace as she tries to reconcile these different views and take them up into a more encompassing or comprehensive perspective.

Emile: This kind of context is what Carol Gilligan refers to as "a polyphonic structure" in which participants can "sustain the different voices of justice and care" (Gilligan et al. 1990, 224).

Pinzak: To embrace and nurture contradiction rather than yield to or expel it.

Emile: But keep in mind that contradictions are not always reconciled or transcended. It is not the case that cosmopolites, characterized, as we have been saying, by dialectical thinking, will unify all opposites. At the least, however, cosmopolites will be stimulated to seek out reconciliation and transcendence as they try to generate a more comprehensive and unifying perspective. That is the foundation for what we might call "deliberative dialogue."[25]

Pinzak: Persons work together to engender, to construct, a more encompassing perspective. They deliberate together to construct just such a compound or integrative perspective. This is what Chickering and Turner call a "transpartisan" approach, one that goes beyond partisanship.[26] This sounds like a kind of democracy.

Emile *(smiling):* Yes, it does. I think that we could call it "integral democracy." But we must save its elaboration for a later conversation.

Pinzak: Well, how about a political example where we might see this idea of trying to create a more encompassing perspective? This could give us a hint as to how this approach to integrating positions might work.

Emile: First, let me say that the idea of generating a more encompassing perspective is one way of looking at why Barack Obama wanted a "team of rivals" in his Cabinet. As a concrete example, what about the concept of welfare? How might that involve multiple perspectives taken up into a more encompassing embrace?

Pinzak: Well, we may think that all citizens have a right to a basic or minimum level of welfare, a social safety net. But others argue that persons need to take responsibility for their lives; they cannot expect and do not deserve handouts for sitting around and avoiding work. Then we have to look at the social circumstances facing citizens who are relying on this welfare. Some cannot work because of disability or illness; some cannot work because they cannot afford to travel where the jobs are or cannot find adequate childcare; some because of poor education and training cannot find jobs that pay sufficiently to enable them to meet their living expenses.

Emile: So we have people who want to work, who want and are ready to take responsibility, but for the reasons you cite, and more, cannot find work or adequate work.

Pinzak: At that point we have to rethink and reconstruct our values. What is the purpose of a welfare system? Don't we need to analyze how people in this country work? What is the point of work? Why do some want to work while others avoid it? And we ask and answer these questions in the context of society's social, economic, and political circumstances. In the United States there are still segments of the population who live in dire conditions, whose neighborhoods are nests of crime, whose schools are the dregs, where unemployment is rampant and residents cannot find work without needing to commute. In those circumstances we need government to step in to provide incentives to bring jobs to these neighborhoods or to provide job training to help people find work. We need government or the private sector or both to step into these ramshackle schools and to make them better, top to bottom—to change not simply where children learn and what they learn, but also what they think of themselves.

Emile: In your "scenario," Pinzak, the reconstruction that takes place is a way of combining two values—rights and responsibilities. You do not come down on one side or the other. You incorporate both. Children in school and adults in the neighborhood need to learn to take responsibility for their lives, but they must have the willingness and the tools, the education and training, to act on that responsibility. That is, they must be able to act responsibly. The children have a right to a quality education, and the adults need help getting out of the circumstances that mire them in poverty, hopelessness, and physical degradation.

Pinzak: To do that requires bringing to bear on this problem not just the people who live in the ghettos and barrios and rural areas, whose participation is and must remain central to arriving at any possible solution, but also the private sector; local, state, and federal governments; the neighborhood institutions like the schools and churches and businesses; social and political activists; scholars who study social, psychological, educational, economic, and political issues. . . .

Emile: Plus urban geographers, urban planners, demographers, psychiatrists, physicians, psychologists, epidemiologists, social workers and experts on the family, social historians, even, dare I say it, philosophers and theorists. But, most important of all and never to be overlooked: We need to involve the people in these communities themselves. *(Pinzak nods his head vigorously.)* I know that you mentioned them, but to me it seems crucial that we have to understand the life of the community, of each and every community. We cannot simply assume that what defines one community necessarily defines all such communities. It is not just a matter of figuring out how a certain community fits into a grid or matrix generated by social scientists. We need to understand the values, habits, experiences, and history of the community and its traditions and not treat communities as if they are all alike.

Pinzak: I could not agree more. You always start with the people, the attitudes and circumstances and institutions that form and inform their lives, and the values, prejudices, choices, goals, habits, and relationships that ensue from but also affect those attitudes, circumstances, and institutions. The first step is always to understand and to involve the very people whose lives are being affected. That first step must involve listening to those in the community.

Emile *(sips his coffee):* Now, Pinzak, imagine that we are cosmopolites discussing this issue. Where does the "we" end in your scenario?

Pinzak: I see what you mean. We would not stop at the boundaries of any specific city or state or country. These same problems, and many of them far worse than what we have in the United States, exist around the globe. Don't we have the same obligation to "reconstruct" our values worldwide? But we cannot think or reconstruct for others. We can serve as useful examples for others, and we can encourage others to undertake their own systematic examinations of social and political problems. But we cannot assume that as cosmopolitans we can speak *for* others. We can only speak with them about problems that we feel, that we all feel, affected by, regardless of their locations. So mustn't we, can't we, begin at home and then, once begun, expand our actions to others around the globe?

Emile: That is one way to deal with "ripples of responsibility." That response will be adequate for some and inadequate for others, and both the "some" and the "others" can be cosmopolites. What does "home" mean here? What does it mean to you? What does it mean to me? *(Emile pauses as Pinzak writes. After a few moments, when Pinzak looks up, Emile resumes speaking.)* What you have described, Pinzak, is a dialectical approach to welfare, and it is an integral approach to politics.

Pinzak: Because I suggested integrating values?

Emile: Well, that is part of it. You also suggested integrating different approaches to the problem. You proposed, we both proposed, bringing in any number of experts from different fields to integrate, presumably, their insights into policy and a plan of action. At the same time, we emphasized involving the very people of the community themselves. It is, of course, their community. They will live there, and they must be the focal point for understanding how life in that community can be better. No experts can substitute for the people themselves in confronting political problems.[27] We must integrate the perspectives of both experts and residents, who are, of course, experts on their own communities.

Take as another example the problem of illegal immigration in this country. The issue of undocumented workers coming across the U.S.-Mexico border is a political concern to conservatives and liberals alike. What should we do about it? Partisans go back and forth on the issues involved: Do we need new laws to penalize undocumented workers and the employers who hire them? No, we must enforce the domestic laws that already exist against this hiring. We must build a wall to keep illegal immigrants out. No, walls can be breached. We need new immigration policies and guest-worker programs. Undocumented workers pay taxes. Some do or they do sometimes, but they take away jobs from American citizens, and they receive free education and take advantage of our welfare infrastructure.

Pinzak: Given only what you just said, Emile, let us look at how complicated addressing this issue *ought* to be. We need to involve politicians, lawyers, business owners, labor leaders, service and farm workers, economists, moral philosophers, tax experts, public-school officials, medical geographers, demographic experts, health-care professionals . . . at the least. But also consider this: Since NAFTA came into effect in January 1994, over 1.5 million Mexican farmers have lost their jobs or gone out of business. Because the United States, through this agreement, can dump their corn onto the Mexican market—corn subsidized by the U.S. government to the extent that it sells for less than it costs to grow it—and Mexican corn farmers cannot compete. So, what do they do? They come to the U.S. for work. Do they want to stay? Not necessarily, but with the border patrolled, if not militarized, they find it difficult to go back-and-forth to Mexico, which many want to do. They do not want to remain in the United States; they simply want jobs.

Emile: The issue becomes even more complicated. Why is there so much corn? These Mexican farmers could grow other crops. Why do they not? It is clear that there needs to be investment in the Mexican economy. The problem of undocumented workers crossing the border must also involve the Mexican government, politicians and officials focused on their farm policies and ours, and representatives from agribusiness and those who represent Mexican farmers. Yet, again, I ask: Why so much corn? If it is not subsidized, then we can imagine farmers not growing as much of it. But it is subsidized because it is profitable. Corn and especially corn syrup are used in virtually everything we eat, to say nothing of our biofuels program. Their widespread use is a contributing factor to the burgeoning obesity problem in our country for the presence of corn syrup and corn byproducts enables food manufacturers to produce high calories for less money. But the foods produced, while high in calories, are nutritionally bankrupt and harmful. Low-income families stock up on chips and other junk food because they are high in calories, thus are filling, and are relatively inexpensive—again, because of the subsidized "foodstuffs" within them. Yet this "food" is terrible for one's health, and people eat a lot of it because this food lacks the nutrients that the body craves and so the body is never satisfied.

So now the issue of illegal immigration has expanded to include agribusiness, farm policies, and agricultural subsidies in this country and abroad. We have to include experts on the Mexican and American workforces, on agricultural import/export policies, epidemiologists here because of the obesity problem, health educators and health-care professionals to look at our own dietary needs and habits, and environmentalists to examine soil erosion and pesticide use and runoffs.

Pinzak: Nor should we stop there. Shouldn't we look at our farm policies and their effects on other parts of the globe? Surely not just Mexico is affected.

Emile: All of this is part of integral politics, yet integral politics is more than this. But, again, let us discuss that at a subsequent meeting.

Right now, I want to go back to and reinforce what we have been saying about the link between dialectical thinking and cosmopolitan identity. Dialectical thinking enables and requires the person to see that any perspective is not one that may be mine, but one that is mine since we are members of the community of human beings.

Pinzak: As the Roman poet Terence wrote: "I am human; therefore nothing human can be foreign to me."[28] We would like to think that for each of us, nothing human will be foreign to me. I can understand it; I shall understand it. And this is so because of the openness of identity required of dialectical thinking—the person needs to hear multiple perspectives to achieve greater inclusiveness in his or her perspective.

Emile: Holding multiple perspectives and contradictions in tension allows one to see one's own view as partial and limited, while also enabling one to find what is valuable and true in the positions of others.

Pinzak: And if one cannot reconcile or transcend the contradictions?

Emile: Then one chooses a viewpoint, or a composite viewpoint, from within the context of the broadest and soundest understanding possible; namely, one in which disparate views and arguments are presented. Thus even if an integrative view is not possible, the context of choice, the range of choice, has been expanded.

Pinzak *(talking while slurping coffee and fanning through his notes):* By the way, this kind of thinking also shows one's nation and culture to be only a part of one's identity. It undercuts the perspective that our cultural identity provides the context within which we choose, but is not itself an object of choice. Such a perspective is true, but only for one stage of development of identity. We are born into a culture; we do not choose it. That is the membership identity. But with formal operations, cultural identity can become a choice, as we separate from our community's or society's rules and roles.

Emile: Yes, and the range of choice, the context of choice, that we are talking about with dialectical thinking is expanded as the person looks for the connections among perspectives and systems of perspectives, otherwise known as cultures. Dialectical thinkers become "fascinated with questions . . . of cultural conditioning," as Cook-Greuter observed (1999, 127), with how the part of systems fit together and how different systems themselves fit together. They want to construct a meaningful perspective from, they want to make meaning out of, the welter of diverse and incompatible and contradictory values and beliefs and behaviors (1999, 135).

Pinzak: So the more diverse the perspectives on offer, the better that meaningful perspective will be, because it will encompass more "data."

Emile: "The more developed a person is," concludes Cook-Greuter, "the broader the range of experience that can be integrated and made sense of" (17). We can say, as you have, that this "integrative perspective" is better because it manifests greater complexity, greater coherence, and higher-order integration. This is where we began the discussion of identity: Persons at later stages of development can deal in a coherent way with experiences and "data," to use your term, that those at earlier stages cannot or would not process.[29]

Pinzak: This kind of integration or integrative approach is not just an ability of dialectical thinkers; it is a necessity. *(Emile nods in agreement.)* It is this integrative approach that points toward cosmopolitanism, because the dialectical thinker, in order to embrace viewpoints, ideas, or attitudes that conflict with one's own, must have both an open mind and an open self-definition. He sees that every system or worldview, including and especially his own, is partial and leaves something out.

Emile: In needing to integrate viewpoints or perspectives the dialectical thinker attempts to construct with others an inclusive solution. Being open to all perspectives leads her to see that no boundary separates her from anyone else. We are not only tied to all others; but we are also like all others, and they are like us. Carmichael describes this as "the awkward embrace": the preservation and holding of "all available contradictory views and perspectives" and the attempt to generate from them one inclusive perspective (1966, 176).

From such thinking we can see how cosmopolitanism unfolds. Psychologist William Perry called this "the Trojan Horse phenomenon." Tempted from the fortress of her own worldview, frustrated by some stimuli or data that her current level of selfhood cannot handle, the person becomes curious about an intriguing figure (idea, proposal, viewpoint, and so on) that she has not considered or seen before. Suddenly the figure opens up and spread out before her an army of considerations, consequences, suggestions, and the like that break new ground.[30]

Pinzak: For the cosmopolitan this means that there may not be simply one Trojan horse but multiple Trojan horses. There are all sorts of perspectives that the dialectical thinker will want and need to consider. Cosmopolitans as dialectical thinkers will seek to embrace and resolve conflicts, discrepancies, and contradictions. But will dialectical thinkers all become cosmopolitans?

Emile: That is a good question. Without doubt dialectical thinkers are able to move toward if not into cosmopolitanism because of the openness of their self-definitions and their need to hear multiple points of view. They have or develop not only a respect and tolerance for divergent views but also a need to hear those views in order to construct, reveal, and reinforce the unity underneath those views. The focus on what Deirdre Kramer calls the "real unity" reinforces cosmopolitan identity, because the unity lies not only in the views but also in the identities of those holding the views.

Pinzak: Dialectical thinkers see connections among opposing viewpoints and unity with the identities of those holding those viewpoints.

Emile: That is right. As we claimed earlier, dialectical thinkers—may we call them dialecticians—*(Pinzak nods)*—honor reciprocity in the sense that "a change in any one part of the system [or unity] influences and in turn is influenced by a change in other parts of the system" (Kramer 1989, 140). The system or unity that we are speaking of here is the system or unity of constructing identities through the awkward embrace—the taking up and integrating of multiple perspectives.

Pinzak: We are all connected, all related. What affects those of us over here also affects those of us over there.

Emile: The system that we are talking about is the self-system, and the cosmopolite through dialectical thinking shares her self-system with all other human beings. When self-systems face opposition or conflict that seems irreconcilable, then the dialectician sees an opportunity to transform those systems, including her own self-definition, into a more integrative, stable, and differentiated system.

Pinzak: I am not clear on how a dialectician, who wants to integrate various perspectives into a more encompassing, complex, and stable perspective, will make the leap from considering multiple views to identifying with all other human beings.

Emile: That is done through reciprocity. The dialectician sees that identities are constructed. All human beings are related through undertaking this constructive process, even if most are not at the level of dialectical thought. Thus, any perspective and all perspectives are mine as much as yours because of the unity that connects us as meaning-making selves.

Pinzak: I just don't see the connection, Emile. I must not be a dialectical thinker.

Emile: I do not believe that you can come to that conclusion. It does seem the case that not all dialectical thinkers will transform to cosmopolitan identities. They might construct integrative self-definitions but not transform agency. Also, keep in mind that less than one-half of one percent of adults appear to reach the level of dialectical thought (Cook-Greuter 1999).[31]

Pinzak: But have societies really tried to induce that level? By requiring dialectical thinking in our social and political institutions we might induce or at least get closer to cosmopolitan identity. If, for instance, the "systems" we were discussing were nation-states, then couldn't conflicts, opposition, or divergence lead to cosmopolitan solutions or institutions?

Emile: Perhaps, and those who think dialectically could be drawing up the policies, proposals, and insights that could lead to or even express integral outcomes. A social and political context that honors and uses dialectical thinking in which multiplicity is embraced can foster cosmopolitanism. It can do so by offering perspectives that challenge one's current self-system, those that induce growth . . .

Pinzak: . . . rather than regression.

Emile: Yes. So, of course specific kinds of institutional processes are also essential to cosmopolitan identity and politics. Carol Gilligan found, for example, that persons who wrestled with real-life dilemmas used "cognitive structures other than those deriving solely from formal logic" (1990, 213). Those persons showed "more differentiated and dialectical understanding" (214). What are political issues but real-life problems or dilemmas? Getting citizens to deliberate in democratic dialogues, properly structured, on such issues could induce and exercise dialectical thinking. Democratic dialogue may thus hold out a promise of cosmopolitan identity or more cosmopolitan identity. But before we talk about that, we need to consider the second way of inducing that identity. Remember?

Cosmopolitan Identity and Mysticism

Pinzak: *(flipping back through his notes and then reading from them):* Ah, yes, the need for experience beyond language and logic; a way to transcend both language and rationality.

Emile: A general term for this kind of experience is *mysticism.* Indeed, I think that such experience is essential not simply for inducing cosmopolitanism but also for stabilizing it. Establishing a secure cosmopolitan identity may well require a realization or a continual taste of mystical or transcendental states. You can enlarge your mentality through dialectical thinking; you can deliberate about and assess conflicting and contradictory perspectives in a dialectical dialogue.[32] But certifying a cosmopolitan identity can come if one experiences the transcendence of the boundaries that separate self and others, even self and world.

Pinzak: If dialectical thinking is part of formal operational thought because agents, even at the dialectical level, are still embedded in language and logic, then the only way to transform agency beyond formal operations is mysticism.

Emile: First, I strongly suggest that a combination of mystical experience and the kinds of inducements that we have been talking about for fostering dialectical thinking would be the best way to move toward or into cosmopolitan identity. But, second, mysticism is not a radical break from developmental psychology. Psychologists Kohlberg and Ryncarz argue that the only way to answer satisfactorily the question "Why be moral?" is to adopt a cosmic perspective (1990, 192). From this cosmic perspective the person comes to identify with the whole of life and the universe. "I am moral because I am a part of a universal community of being. I am in an intimate relationship with the entire cosmos. How could I act unjustly toward that which is really myself?"

Pinzak: This cosmic perspective is what we have been calling a cosmopolitan perspective?

Emile: It is what Wilber calls a "worldcentric" perspective or a planetary perspective, but it may be beyond cosmopolitanism in that it takes into account not just human beings but all beings. Kohlberg and Ryncarz describe the cosmic perspective as one coming from an experience of transcendental, non-dual unity between the individual or self and the cosmos as a whole.

Pinzak: What effects or induces this perspective?

Emile: Kohlberg and Ryncarz do not really say. They do say that transcendental experiences, even when infrequent, "can create a type of disequilibrium which induces construction of a new world view [sic] based on adoption of a 'cosmic' rather than an individual perspective" (1990, 25).

Pinzak: This is what we have already covered as the standard view of developmental psychologists on how identity changes: Challenges arise that the person cannot handle or assimilate. He then transforms or develops to a level where new capacities enable him to accommodate the challenges. For Kohlberg and Ryncarz the transformation occurs through transcendental experience. But none of this tells us what brings that experience.

Emile: Well, it is fair to say, I think, that one cannot reason her way to a non-dual, transcendental experience. Can we understand the nature of thought by using thought itself? Or must we transcend thought, language, logic, in order to understand them? Transcending them must come through mysticism and some kind of contemplative practice.

Pinzak: So mystical experience can allow us to act on, and thus differentiate from, what was earlier our subjectivity—language and logic or thought itself.

Emile: In her work on the postautonomous self, what we have been calling the cosmopolitan self, Cook-Greuter divided Loevinger's highest stage of ego development, the Integrated Stage, into two stages: the Construct-Awareness Stage, which we have already touched on, and the rare Unitive Stage. Those at the Unitive Stage sense that their separate self is an illusion and that everyone and everything are connected. They sense "universal connectedness [and a] profound expression of self as part of a larger world, humankind, history, ongoing creation" (1999, 59-60). Persons realize that identity cannot be found through any process now used since those processes are not just used to construct identities but are part of the construct itself. Included here would be language, logic, reason, and self-reflection. The self as agent has differentiated from these and can now act on them to integrate them into a new self-concept or self-definition.

Pinzak: Mystical experience brings on this Unitive Stage?

Emile: Cook-Greuter is not clear on what brings that stage forward. She is describing what people at that stage are experiencing as identity. They manifest "an attitude of complete openness" without needing to have a solid, stable identity. They experience the self moment-to-moment as it rises, falls, changes, rises, falls, changes, but without the need to hold onto any moment. Who they are is itself the meditative experience. "Immersed in the immediate, ongoing flow of experience . . . they are witness to their own being-and-becoming" (1999, 49).

Pinzak: Are you kidding me? This is what is required for cosmopolitan identity?

Emile: I do not think that we have to get quite this cryptic or ethereal. But we can assume that mystical or meditative experience is one way to this kind of fluid, open, world-oriented identity.

If we think back to Nussbaum's idea of identity as concentric circles emanating from a central source or self, then we can see why mysticism might be an important way to induce cosmopolitan identity. Let me borrow a quotation from William James that might help make this clear. "The suggestion, stated very briefly, is that states of mystical intuition may be only very sudden and great extensions of the ordinary 'field of consciousness'. . . . [T]he extension itself would, if my view be correct, consist in an immense spreading of the margin of the field, so that knowledge ordinarily transmarginal would become included, and the ordinary margin would grow more central" (1980, 215).

Pinzak: So the peripheral circles in our pebble-in-the-water metaphor for identity become more central as the field of consciousness expands, and the field expands or extends, as James said, through mystical intuition. I see that James uses the term "intuition" as a kind of shorthand for some sort of method of knowledge that is beyond language and logic. But what is being intuited?

Emile: It is the direct experience of God, the Divine, Creative Intelligence, Emptiness, Transcendence, Unity, or the One. It goes by many names, but we use the term "mysticism" to encompass, however crudely, all such direct experiences.

Pinzak: So mystics see God. To attain the open, fluid identity I need to see God.

Emile: As I said, mystical experiences are variegated. Some speak in terms of God, the Creator, or the Divine, some in terms of Reality or Being, some in terms of Nothingness or Emptiness. What they experience may well turn on what kind of practice they undertake. Most mystics turn inward, but some look outward on the physical world.[33] Most sit in meditation—like Zen Buddhists or practitioners of Yoga or those in contemplative Christian prayer—but some move like the Sufi Dervishes. For some the mystical experience unfolds gradually after years of practice; for others, it comes suddenly after years of practice; for others still, it comes unannounced and even unwelcome.[34]

Pinzak: Is there always a religious connection to mysticism?

Emile: Bear in mind that mysticism is experientially based. It is about seeing or knowing intuitively. Mystics do not have to have religious connections or concerns. A mystic is one who wants to know beyond our senses, including beyond our rational minds. So a mystic could be concerned with knowing Ultimate Reality, however that is configured or understood; she could want to know Truth or understand Nature; she could want to find out whether anything lies beyond our senses. Finally, a mystic could be a total skeptic who wants to discover whether there is anything to meditation or contemplation or mystical experience itself.[35]

In the early 1970s Dr. Herbert Benson of the Harvard Medical School created a practice he called "the relaxation response." This is a totally secular relaxation technique derived from studying different meditation practices. Benson found that in the complete absence of any spiritual or religious overtones persons who used his relaxation technique could achieve a deep state of rest that brought strong physiological and emotional results, including reduction of tension and stress.[36]

Pinzak: Because the technique is based on Benson's studies of meditative practices and in many ways mimics them but without the spiritual invocations or trappings, the implication is that without knowing it, practitioners of the relaxation response might also induce mystical states?

Emile: That is certainly one possibility. Why not? Those experiences, however, are not the focus. Reduction of tension and stress is. But it is a secularized way, possibly, to similar states and experiences.

Pinzak: To go back to mystics for a moment: mystics seek to know God or Emptiness or Reality or whatever through some method beyond conception and beyond language. These experiences are translogical and translinguistic. So how does anyone know that they are not just daydreams or hallucinations or psychotic episodes? I am reminded of what Freud said at the beginning of *Civilization and Its Discontents.* The French poet and scholar Romaine Rolland wrote to Freud and described experiencing a sense of eternity through an "oceanic feeling" (1961, 11). Freud responded that he looked into himself and then admitted that he could not discover this "oceanic feeling" in himself. Therefore, he concluded, this feeling must be a sign that Rolland, or anyone else who has it, has regressed to an infantile stage where the boundary between ego and object does not exist. So who says that there is anything to this but a slide down the ladder of development?

Emile: Well, why should we believe Freud? Why do we think that he is right in his assessment? Just because he never experienced the "oceanic feeling" hardly means that it does not signify movement toward higher consciousness. Andrew Newberg, a radiologist at the University of Pennsylvania, has studied the brain activity of Buddhist monks and Franciscan nuns. He found that "the mind remembers mystical experience with the same degree of clarity and sense of reality that it bestows upon memories of 'real' past events. The same cannot be said of hallucinations, delusions, or dreams."[37]

Bear in mind, Pinzak, that no mystic is telling you to accept what he or she says. Mystics are not speculating on the nature of reality; they are not theorists. They are telling us what they experienced. If you want to know whether there is anything to this, then undertake a practice that might result in the same sort of experience. From the mystics' perspective it is inadequate to review one's past and conclude that since this has never happened to me, the "oceanic feeling" is suspect if not pathological.[38]

Pinzak: I still do not see how you can determine whether the experience is a sign of growth or of regression.

Emile: You have to ask the mystic. Evelyn Underhill comments that the awakening of the Self through a mystical experience is "a disturbance of the equilibrium of the self, which results in the shifting of the field of consciousness from lower to higher levels" (1911, 213). So remembering our earlier conversation about equilibrium, we can see that someone undergoing such an experience, especially if it is spontaneous, as William James suggests can happen, might flee to earlier levels of selfhood.

So, you have to observe the mystic's behavior and demeanor. What is the effect of this experience on the mystic? Remember that within all religions there is a history of mystical movements, so it is not as if there is no literature that serves as a record of what persons have experienced. In the end, you have to talk to the mystic. But to appreciate fully what the experience entails, you must undertake a practice yourself.

Pinzak: So you are not denying that some mystics might just be crazy.

Emile: Some might be. For the last ten years of his life, Nietzsche was certifiably insane. But he was also insightful, if not a genius. So are some of his writings crazy, but others ingenious? If so, which is which? I am not suggesting that Nietzsche was a mystic. But as with mystics, who are sometimes considered crazy, so too with Nietzsche. To begin to ascertain the quality or insanity of his insights one has to read his work, think about it, and discuss it with others who have read it as well. In fact, what we are talking about here is the backbone of how we establish epistemological validity in any area.

Pinzak: Including what is "higher" or "lower."

Emile: Including that. But we need to save discussion of that crucial topic for another day and return now to mystical experience.[39]

Pinzak: All right. So mystical experiences take us beyond language and logic, and somehow that results in a "world-centric" or cosmopolitan orientation?

Emile: Mystical experiences are first and foremost transpersonal. That does not mean that they are impersonal. It means, as Ken Wilber points out, that they are "personal *plus*" (2000a, 288). Underhill, who wrote the classic work on mysticism, says that the mystical experience is, at the same time, non-individualist. "It implies, indeed, the abolition of individuality; of that hard separateness, that 'I, Me, Mine' which makes of man a finite isolated thing. It is a movement . . . seeking to transcend the limitations of the individual standpoint and to surrender itself to ultimate Reality" (1911, 85).

Pinzak: How can these experiences be "personal plus" and yet "non-individualistic"?

Emile: The boundary of the personal as we understand it is transcended. To quote sociologist Philip Wexler in the context of the self, we see "a debounded and debounding self, rather than defended self, emerging from the innerworldy mystical traditions. . . ." (2000, 135)

Pinzak *(reacting with apparent horror):* He actually used the terms "debounded" and "debounding"?

Emile: Granted, the terms are not euphonious. He means simply that one's sense of self spreads beyond the conventional and even post-conventional boundaries of the self. Those boundaries that defined the person as an individual, as a self separate from and brought to relationships, are transcended. Wexler also points out that although mystical experience is innerworldly, it does not result in withdrawal from the world or from others. Indeed, it is a renewal of our relationships as our sense of self, of identity, expands. Through mystical experience we "enlarge the meaning of both world and self" (Ibid, 137). Self, society, the world, and other persons are now intimately involved with us in what Wexler calls "a dialogue of wholeness" (2000, 138). Wexler uses all sorts of evocative terms and phrases: "reunion," "reintegration," "revitalization," and, most salient, "a recreation or enlivenment of self/body and world" (139). All of this is by way of gesturing toward "the range of relations and dimensions" that are "broader and more dynamic" than what preceded mystical experience.

Pinzak: A lot of these terms and ideas relate to dialectical dynamism. One cannot attain this kind of reunion or revitalization through dialectical thinking?

Emile: It seems clear that one cannot think one's way to this kind of insight. Mystical experience is well beyond formal operational thought, whereas dialectical thought may not be. This is so because, to repeat, mystical experience is, by all accounts, beyond language and logic. When the mystical experience matures into an ongoing awareness of transcendence, then the person is said to be "witnessing" the flow of activities rather than being embedded in them. The person is then awake to "his real Self," which is his true nature beyond or transcendent to all language, symbol, logic, or activity. Although the individual ego—and all levels of mind [of thinking]—continues to function actively in [transcendent] consciousness, awareness is now primarily associated with the nonchanging (sic), silent Self at the source of all thought" (Alexander et al. 1990, 314).

Pinzak: And therefore. . . ?

Emile: Well, the people who experience the transcendent realm find it more satisfying, more balanced, and more integrated than the realms of the separate self (Miller and Cook-Greuter 1994, xxviii). This, of course, is how psychologists, and the people experiencing the transcendent, describe the later stages of development. With the mystical or transcendental experience the world and the person as the Self are one. This unity shows no boundaries between oneself and others. "Clearly the representational aspects of the ego as a separate construct end" (Ibid, xxvii). So the experience is not only trans-linguistic and trans-logical, but it is also post-conceptual, non-representative, and non-relative. Its qualities are ineffable; its nature, universal.

Pinzak: Yet these are individual experiences. The people having these experiences are few—How many mystics are there running around the planet—and even isolated. If so, then how does society transform into something encompassing cosmopolitanism?

Emile: Well, it certainly would not do so overnight. Wexler suggests that as postmodernism decentralized the sacred, so now, in an era of post-postmodernism, social transformation will not come through the rituals of our religious institutions, or even perhaps through our established political institutions. Most of these institutions, as we have already observed, lack the kind of dialectical dialogue that citizens need. Instead social transformation will come "more microcosmically" (2000, 140). That is, it will come "in the smaller movements between private mystical experience and socially shared revitalization" (140).

Pinzak: Is he talking about a tipping point at which the aggregation of individuals undergoing mystical experiences of this type suddenly move the society in a new, and in this case a revitalized, direction?

Emile: I do not know. But it seems to be more of a crashing of waves as persons interacting through and after their mystical experiences smash against the rigid boundaries, the walls, of current social institutions. Wexler's own preferred arena of social action is our educational system. What he wants to see is "an education of imagination; the capacity for cognitive reframing rather than cumulative information processing; ecological self-integration; and a reselfing reunion through connection to some transcendental [William] Jamesian 'More,' Kabbalistic 'Ein Sof,' or unboundedness" (2000, 141).

Pinzak: *(gripping the table with mock concern):* I am getting vertigo, Emile. This is just mystico-psycho-twaddle, and I mean "psycho" in the broadest sense of the term.

Emile *(laughing):* And "twaddle" in the narrowest sense? We do not have to follow Wexler in this direction to see what he is getting at. Education, even in its postmodern forms, continues to emphasize outcomes, performance, achievement, and the like. Postmodern education might place some focus on creating student-to-student or teacher-to-student partnerships and collaborations. It might introduce affective or emotional intelligence and its development to the curriculum. It might also open up boundaries between workplaces, schools, home, and neighborhoods. Yet the emphasis still remains on performance. Missing for Wexler is "an ethnography of being" (2000, 103).

Pinzak: Wexler means all of this to be helpful, right?

Emile: Of course. He sees and wants to see education as a transformative practice.

Pinzak: So what, he wants to introduce mystical experiences and altered states of consciousness as part of the curriculum?

Emile: Yes, he seems to want that, though it is not clear from what he writes that he is not simply laying out how those who study education ought to proceed (Wexler 2000, 107). This seems to be an overly generous interpretation of what he is after.

Pinzak: Well, if he is proposing a "curriculum of being" in education, then that cannot be appropriate for any level of schooling before college. Given what you have been saying about developmental levels, maturity and growth are contingent on passing through these unfolding levels. So before you can transcend a self-reflective ego, you must first establish a self-reflective ego. Mystical states and altered states of consciousness undermine that process, right?

Emile: I think that that is correct. Perhaps a curriculum predicated on an ethnography of being would be suitable only for those who have an autonomous self. What would you think of a college curriculum like that?

Pinzak: I imagine there would be outright resistance and hostility. Professors are paid to generate knowledge and to transmit it. This would shift the emphasis in the curriculum from epistemology to ontology.

Emile: Ontology is crucial to epistemological validity, which you professors take for granted. Anyway, that is a topic for a later conversation. At this point, bear in mind what Wexler said. He would expect resistance and hostility. They would be the waves crashing against the walls of institutions.

Pinzak: Actually you said that Emile.

Emile *(pondering for a moment):* So I did. Well, Wexler *did* say that social transformation will come "more microcosmically." A few colleges here and there with his "being curriculum" might help the transformational process.

Pinzak: I am all for experimentation and diversity. I would certainly like to see more of it in my department at Western.

Pinzak looks down at his watch. "Have we been at it for this long?" Emile nods, smiling. "I've got to stop; I'm exhausted. If we meet tomorrow . . . (Emile nods his agreement) then I'm bringing my laptop."

Just as Pinzak finishes this statement, Emile extends his hand palm up toward Pinzak and says, "Then you will not be in need of my pen." Pinzak replaces the screw-on cap and for a moment, turns the pen over in his hands.

"No, I won't need it, though I love using it."

Emile, taking the pen from Pinzak and placing it in the inside breast pocket of his overcoat, says, "Then let us return tomorrow to Pamplona and return to that social context of utmost importance to us: institutional structures and political change. Certainly this must be at the heart of any social transformation."

Pinzak smiles and they both rise from their chairs. Emile says, "Until tomorrow, then, Pinzak."

Notes

1. Samantha Power, "A Hero of Our Time," *New York Review of Books* 51, no. 18 (November, 2004): 10. On the same page Power also quotes from Czeslaw Milosz's *The Captive Mind:* Moral action "proceeded not from the functioning of the reasoning mind, but from a revolt of the stomach."

2. People and states around the world respond to crises. In January 2010, a devastating earthquake struck Haiti. Organizations and nations sent so much aid that it became difficult to deliver. Nevertheless, despite this outpouring, President Obama summarized well the attitudes of many nations: "Haiti must be a top priority for our departments and agencies right now. This is one of those moments that calls out for American leadership. We have no higher priority than the safety of American citizens, and we've airlifted injured Americans out of Haiti." Thus there is still a priority to favor one's own, rather than to tend immediately to those most in need, regardless of nationality. See The White House Press Release and "Remarks by the President on Recovery Efforts in Haiti," January 14, 2010.

3. Cited by Power 2002, 27-28. Peter Singer makes the same point in an equally powerful way: "[I]t makes no moral difference whether the person I help is a neighbor's child ten yards from me or a Bengali whose name I shall never know, ten thousand miles away." This quotation (2002, 283) is from Singer's article, "Famine, Affluence and Mo-

rality." To the quotation Singer adds this 2002 commentary: "As far as I am aware, no one has disputed this claim" (Idem). From a moral perspective distance does not matter. What does make a difference, though it is a different matter, is, as Singer points out, the degree of certainty that the aid one offers will get to the people who need it.

4. David Hume, *A Treatise of Human Nature,* Book III, (Oxford: Clarendon Press, 1968), Part i, Section 2.

5. It is "impossible," Hume wrote, "that the distinction betwixt moral good and evil, can be made by reason . . . since that distinction has an influence upon our actions, of which reason alone is incapable" (1968, 462). To complete more fully Hume's account of moral judgment, Sharon Krause looks at Hume's moral-sentiment model within the context of liberal democracy. At one point she observes that "the greater inclusiveness of the American polity over time is not the result of the public having become more rational and less passionate. Instead, it illustrates how the exercise of sympathetic imagination in the presence of political contestation has generated new moral sentiments and gradually transformed the public's horizon of concern—and with its laws. Our minds are changed when our hearts are engaged" (2008, 125).

6. And another example: "There is nothing to prevent individuals from identifying Flanders, Belgium, and Europe simultaneously, and displaying each allegiance in the appropriate context; or free feeling they are Yoruba, Nigerian and African, in concentric circles of loyalty and feeling" (A. D. Smith 1991, 175).

7. Did Montesquieu describe the evolutionary circles of identity when he wrote: "If I know of anything advantageous to my family but not to my country, I should try to forget it. If I know of anything advantageous to my country which was prejudicial to Europe and to the human race, I should look upon it as a crime"? (Baron Gaston de Montesquieu, *Pensées et Fragments Inedits de Montesquieu* 1, 1899): 15.

8. As a way of distinguishing cosmopolitanism from universalism, and as a way of supporting my point, David Hollinger states that "cosmopolitanism is defined by an additional element not essential to universalism: recognition, acceptance, and eager exploration of diversity. . . . For cosmopolitans, the diversity of humankind is a fact; for universalists, it is a potential problem" (2000, 84). From the perspective that I am developing in this chapter, I agree with Hollinger. But Hollinger does not really help that development, for he offers no argument for why cosmopolitanism is or must be defined this way or why multiplicity or diversity is itself, as he says, a fact. Introducing dialectical thinking, which I do in this Encounter, is one way to argue on behalf of Hollinger's point.

9. Thanks to Debi Campbell for pointing out this similarity.

10. Ken Wilber also describes this phenomenon as the "self syntonic" versus the "self distonic." The former is agency or the self one "looks through"; the latter is what one identifies with or "looks at" (2002, 383). For a detailed argument as to why developmental psychology is the best approach for understanding identity, see Crittenden 1992, especially pages 3-208.

11. In his study of the development of religious faith, James Fowler concludes that each stage of development "represents a widening of vision and valuing, correlated with a parallel increase in the certainty and depth of selfhood, making qualitative increases in intimacy with self-others-world" (1981, 274). This seems straightforward enough, though one ought to pause to contemplate what Fowler means by an "increase in the certainty . . . of selfhood. . . ."

12. For examples representative but by no means exhaustive of such developmental psychologists, see Piaget 1952; Kohlberg 1981; Kegan 1982; Loevinger 1976; and Cook-Greuter, 1999.

13. Originally the term "identity" meant "quality of being the same" *(Oxford Etymological Dictionary,* 459). It was used in conjunction with a philosophical issue: "Identity" was what was permanent underneath apparent change. In terms of individual identity, it meant that a person is perceived by himself and others to be the same person "again and again." It also pertains to individuals as members of a group who are seen to be the same in significant ways as are other members of the group, but different from others or those outside the group. By the eighteenth century "identity" had come to mean a distinctive, enduring subjective core. By the time we reach "identity politics," "identity" had come to mean self-definition.

14. See Crittenden 1992, especially "The Self as a Two-Track System," 34-37, and Chapter 2.

15. The existence of Piaget's formal operations is not in doubt, but the age at which they unfold and whether all adults develop to that stage are controversial.

16. For a discussion of the multiple lines of developments see Wilber 2000b, especially Chapter 2, "The Developmental Lines or Streams," and "Charts," 197-217.

17. Philip Zimbardo, a psychologist (now emeritus) at Stanford University, designed and ran the prison experiment at Stanford in 1971. Along with Stanley Milgram's "shocking" experiment in 1963, it is one of the most famous psychological experiments into human responses to stressful situations. For more on the prison experiment and Zimbardo's reflections on it some thirty-five years later, see *The Lucifer Effect* (2007). It is perhaps no coincidence that the damage suffered by the "prisoners" in Zimbardo's experiment is eerily similar to that suffered by prisoners at Abu Ghraib: sexual humiliation, forced nakedness, sleep deprivation, and hooded heads. Of course, under the intense stress of combat and war, far greater than that at the Stanford mock prison, we should not be surprised that the abuse at Abu Ghraib did not stop there.

18. Friedrich Nietzsche, *Daybreak,* ed. Maudemarie Clarke and Brian Leiter, trans. R. J. Hollingdale (Cambridge, U.K.: Cambridge University Press, 1997), 17 (aphorism 18), emphasis in the original.

19. Thomas Hobbes, *Leviathan,* ed. R. Tuck (Cambridge, U.K.: Cambridge University Press, 1991), 110.

20. Ibid, 111 (aphorism 189), emphasis in the original.

21. As Robert Kegan tells us, "The very expression of its vitality and integrity is the community's capacity to regulate its parts like a single living organism, to warn those constituents who are in danger of transgressing its limits and boundaries and to rescue those who step over the line. This is the real meaning of the 'ortho' in 'orthodox'; it refers not to rigidity or dogmatism but to the action of correcting or straightening (like 'orthodontia')" (1994, 104).

22. Some developmental psychologists refer to this kind of thinking as "postformal." See, for example, Gilligan, Murphy, and Tappan 1990; Kramer 1989; Blanchard-Fields 1989; and Benack and Basseches 1989. The clear implication here is that this level of thinking is beyond Piaget's formal operational thinking. According to these researchers, formal operational thinking involves seeing truth as independent of the subject, whereas in postformal thinking truth is seen as relative to the perspective through which one operates. Regardless of the site of truth, and I shall have more to say about relativism in a subsequent chapter, the method for finding, if not generating, truth, requires using language and logic. Because I see the autonomous self or subject as embedded in language and logic, I conclude that formal operational thinking, characterized by that embeddedness, is not transcended as those psychologists contend.

Moreover, because I see autonomy as having a social nature, I also question whether dialectical thinking is also characteristic of a move into "postautonomy"; see Cook-Greuter 1999. If, however, we think of autonomy in Kantian terms, then it is true that dialectical thinking moves the self away from the idea of a system of self-sufficiency toward one of openness to divergent views and a dialectic of contradiction and paradox. This is called "interpenetration" of systems. Of course, I disagree with Kant, for as Robert Kegan says, "deciding for oneself" is not the same as "deciding by oneself" (1994, 219). See also Crittenden 2002, especially 40-42, and Crittenden 1993.

I think that the debate about formal vs. postformal reasoning is really of an intramural variety. Little seems accomplished by arguing that dialectical thinking is or is not post-formal. Deirdre Kramer (1989) argues, for example, that a dialectical "logic" replaces the formal logic of formal operations. Yet what differentiates this logic as *beyond* formal logic remains murky. Indeed, Kramer herself acknowledges that "it is not at all clear that formal operations cannot account for . . . dialectical thought" (1989, 141). See also Kramer 1983. Of interest are 1) the characteristics of this mode of thinking; 2) whether and how it is a good and effective method; and 3) how we might induce it, if it is good. I do concede, as stated in this section, that dialectical thinking pushes the self to the very edges of formal operational thinking.

Ken Wilber, in his discussions of "visionlogic," claims that visionlogic permits the subject to see a network of logical connections or relationships in one encompassing, intuitive vision. (See, for example, Wilber 2000b, 21-27, and 167-69.) I concur that the process for seeing the connections and relationships is "translogical" and that this insight or vision is beyond formal operations. Yet is this kind of intuition available as a stage that arises only after formal operations? In other words, is this kind of intuition part of the invariant sequence that is the hallmark of unfolding stages of cognitive development, or is this intuition available at any stage? If available at any stage, then although the intuition at the center of visionlogic is transrational and translogical, it is not necessarily a sign of a later stage of cognitive development. Additional studies would help clarify these issues.

So, I would still argue, though I could be persuaded otherwise without complaint, that the logic in operation, in connection, is the same logic as formal operational thinking, though it is processed quite differently. If this process amounts to a new or postformal logic, then I can be persuaded. If you see or use logic in a new way, is it then a new logic? The confusion here might well amount to a distinction that needs to be made between the different ways in which one processes or "sees."

23. "Relativism" and "contextualism," although extremely close in meaning, are not exactly the same. Relativism is a topic that we shall consider in more detail in a subsequent chapter, but for now a simple rendition of it is to see it as the realization or acknowledgement that there is no absolute knowledge or truth. In the face of multiple viewpoints, practices, and diverse positions, the relativist argues that the truth of the matter at hand—and that might include, for example, certain cultural beliefs or moral principles or standards of evaluation—is relative to something else. One standard form that relativism takes is that the truth or goodness of some claim is relative to the context in which it appears. Meaning and truth are then seen as context dependent, and contexts are multiple and often divergent. Thus contextualism is often a basis for relativism.

24. For an example of the latter, see Dennis Bakke, *Joy at Work* (Seattle, Wash.: PVG, 2006).

25. Deliberation and dialogue are central themes of the Sixth and Seventh Encounters.

26. Chickering and Turner 2008. The authors see bipartisan action as compromise that splits the difference, whereas transpartisan action includes but transcends bipartisanship: Transpartisan involves bringing adversaries together, as well as citizens and government together, to solve mutual problems (2008, 3). Yet, there seems to be more to transpartisanship than the authors emphasize. Whereas bipartisanship seeks to include but transcend the positions taken by the two principal political parties in the United States—the Republican Party and the Democratic Party—transpartisanship implies including but transcending those positions as well as the positions of third parties and minor parties—e.g., Libertarian Party, Federalist National Party, Green Party, Labor Party, Natural Law Party, Constitution Party, Democratic Socialists of American, and the Communist Party, U.S.A.

27. As Saul Alinsky wrote in *Reveille for Radicals,* "It is impossible to overemphasize the enormous importance of people's doing things themselves. . . . What you get by your own effort is really yours. It is a part of you, bound and knit to you through the experiences that you have undergone in securing it" (1946, 76).

28. Terentius or Terence wrote: *Homo sum: humani nil a me alienum puto.*

29. See, for example, Piaget (1954); Kegan (1982) and (1994); Loevinger (1976); Cook-Greuter (1999); and Kohlberg (1981).

30. Kegan 1980, 379; see also Perry 1968.

31. Even more sobering, according to Robert Kegan, "at any given moment, around one-half to two-thirds of the adult population [in the United States] appear not to have fully reached the fourth order of consciousness"—that is, the identity predicated on formal operational thinking (1994, 188, 191).

32. Gilligan, Murphy, and Tappan (1990) argue along the lines of what I have been developing here: Dialectical thinking can expand identity through the integration of higher-order reasoning—formal operational thought—and affectivity or love and care. Such expansion occurs, in their view, through a full recognition of all competing perspectives.

33. See W. T. Stace, *The Teachings of the Mystics* (New York: New American Library, 1960), for discussion of the "introvertive" and "extrovertive" forms of mysticism.

34. One ought not to conclude that those undergoing a mystical experience are all "seeing" or experiencing the same things. What is experienced, even though transcendental, translogical, translinguistic, depends not only on the type of practice engaged in, but also on the level that one taps into. As Ken Wilber points out in *Sex, Ecology, Spirituality* (2000a), and in many of his other works, there are levels of mystical insight, just as there are levels of psychological development. Wilber distinguishes among several levels of transpersonal experience, which include in order of evolutionary unfolding the psychic, the subtle, and the causal. To delve into these levels and into issues related to them would take us too far afield. My interest here is not so much what is experienced as the effect mystical experience has on one's sense of self when life in the empirical world is resumed. For simplicity's sake, I am assuming that only the earliest transpersonal, postconceptual, and trans-linguistic level—described by Wilber as "psychic"—need be in play here.

35. W. T. Stace defines *mysticism* as "the apprehension of an ultimate nonsensuous unity in all things, a oneness or a One to which neither the sense nor the reason can penetrate" (1960, 14-15).

36. See Herbert Benson, *The Relaxation Response* (New York: Harper Torch, 1976), updated and expanded in 2000. For the description of Bensons' relaxation technique, go to www.relaxationresponse.org/steps/.

37. Quoted in Mario Beauregard and Denyse O'Leary, *The Spiritual Brain* (New York: Harper Collins, 2007), 259. Newberg's quotation can be found in his book *Why God Won't Go Away* (New York: Ballantine, 2001), though no page reference is given.

38. Again, see the Fifth Encounter.

39. I take up this discussion as well in the Fifth Encounter.

Fourth Encounter:

Integral Politics

My country is the world. My fellow citizens are humankind.
—Tom Paine, *Common Sense*

The rain kept Pinzak away from Café Pamplona for three days. He missed the conversations with Emile, but this gave him time to read some of the developmental psychology that he and Emile had discussed at their last meeting. Pinzak had read, among other books and articles, Robert Kegan's *The Evolving Self* and *In Over Our Heads,* not only because Kegan was a highly regarded psychologist but also because he taught at Harvard's Graduate School of Education. Pinzak thought that he might drop by to see Kegan, if questions of sufficient merit arose. Thirty years ago, had Pinzak been enrolled at Harvard, involved in this study, and not dreaming instead of recording "double-doubles" for Harvard's basketball team, he could have dropped by to see Kegan or Lawrence Kohlberg, Carol Gilligan, William Perry, James Fowler, or William Torbert. All were teaching at Harvard then, in something of a golden age of developmental psychology in Cambridge. But, Kegan aside, all were gone now, to other institutions or to the afterlife.

The skies had finally cleared. Pinzak headed into Harvard Square. The rain seemed to have driven off any remnants of summer. Early September was still summer in New England, but the air had turned into fall. Pinzak spotted Emile at the usual table, sitting in his usual position, keeping order in the universe: hands folded, walking stick, camel hair coat, beret, closed eyes, smile . . . all as before. But now there were two cups of coffee on the table. "How did Emile know whether or when I would be coming today?" thought Pinzak as he approached Emile's table.

"I have been expecting you," commented Emile, eyes still closed. "See whether your coffee has gotten cold."

Pinzak gave no hint of surprise at Emile's sensing his approach or at the statement that Emile had been expecting him. Why would Pinzak not come? The rain had stopped, the sun was out, and the air was cool. Certainly both men had expressed an interest in resuming their conversation. They usually met at around this time. Now Pinzak's forearms, which he had not realized felt tight, as if he were carrying fifteen-pound weights in both hands, began to relax. Indeed, his whole body began to relax, but Pinzak was perplexed. He could not quite figure out whether it was the sense that his behavior was predictable, or whether it was a kind of wonder bordering on awe about Emile. The old man seemed not-quite-real, like a powerful dream you awaken from and carry around for the rest of the day.

Having seated himself, unpacked his laptop, and sipped his coffee, Pinzak said to his meditative tablemate, "The coffee's fine. How long have you been sitting here?"

"Not long. A few minutes." Emile paused, with eyes still closed, as Pinzak turned on his computer. "This is about the time we meet, is it not?"

Pinzak noted to himself that this seemed like a logical explanation for Emile's behavior, but logical or not, this did not fully satisfy Pinzak, or fully relax his forearms. The problem was Emile's whole aura—his manner, his dress, the quotations, his history, his smile. Pinzak pondered each of these as he rotated his fists to relieve his forearms. Perhaps he was in the presence of a true mystic. If so, then with the exception of a Native American shaman, Emile would be Pinzak's first.

"Tell me, Emile, how did you come to the insights about mysticism? By following the trail of dialectical thinking through developmental psychology?"

"Quite the opposite. I came to developmental psychology through mysticism," he replied, reaching for his coffee. He sipped and replaced the cup. "I was on loan for a month one summer. I was driving a United States senator and his film-star wife around Europe. They were taking a three-day cruise down the Seine and had no need of my services. With three days off I decided to do some sightseeing of my own. I went to the usual places—the Louvre, Versailles. But I also wanted to see the Cathedral at Chartres. Chartres is considered one of the greatest examples of gothic cathedrals. Around the outside are these complicated flying buttresses. Stretching into the sky are its two contrasting spires—one, a plain pyramid and the other, a tall flamboyant-style spire built on top of a tower. Inside, the stained glass windows spread colors all over the floor. It is truly a magnificent building. But I had come as much for the labyrinth as for the architecture and stained glass.

I arrived at the cathedral on a Friday morning. I knew that on Fridays the chairs are cleared away so that 'pilgrims' can walk the labyrinth. On other days, because the labyrinth is in the middle of the nave of the church, chairs cover it so that services can be held. Are you familiar with labyrinths, Pinzak?"

"Well, I know what they are—elaborate mazes or puzzles. The point is to try to get to the center, and the labyrinth offers lots of false passages and traps."

"What you have described correctly is a maze. But labyrinths are different. There is no trick to getting to the center. The path you take—indeed, any path you take—leads you there. You cannot get lost in a labyrinth. In fact, the whole point is to 'find' yourself. While mazes are multi-cursal with dead ends and cul-de-sacs that are meant to deceive you, labyrinths are uni-cursal, which means simply that they provide a direct path, however tortuous, to the center. The purpose is to take a journey to the center, which is a metaphor for the spiritual journey to the center of one's true or deepest self. Having reached the center, the pilgrim then takes the same path back out into the world, presumably with a new or better understanding of oneself."

"So here is the connection to mysticism," stated Pinzak.

"Well, here is the connection to psychology. The mysticism came through my experience at Chartres, not through the history and architecture of labyrinths. Chartres's is an eleven-ring labyrinth placed near the entrance of the nave. The location symbolizes our first steps on a spiritual journey. During the Crusades pilgrims who could not travel to the Holy Land came to Chartres to walk the labyrinth, on their feet or on their knees, as a metaphor for 'going to the Center' or to God. In this way they were symbolically united with the Crusaders.

The labyrinth at Chartres is forty feet across and is set with dark blue and white stones. It consists of eleven concentric circles that contain a single path that twists and turns and eventually leads to the center stone, a rosette or rose petals. The rosette symbolizes Mother Mary. The path makes twenty-eight loops: seven on the left side toward the center, then seven on the right side toward the center, followed by seven on the left side away from the center, and finally seven on the right side away from the center. So one crosses four quadrants several times when walking, which will be important later in today's conversation. A pilgrim walks to the center and then retraces her steps to return to the world outside.

When I began walking, there were only a few, no more than a handful, of other people walking the labyrinth. As I walked I felt increasingly relaxed . . . nothing more than that. I would not call it being 'at peace' or 'at one with the universe.' I simply felt relaxed. But when I got to the center rosette, I was pulled down into a sitting position. No one literally pulled me, and I did not think to myself 'I want to sit down.' I simply HAD to sit down. When I did, sitting cross-legged at the center of this labyrinth, I felt this sudden surge of energy, like a window shade snapping open, shoot up my spine. It seemed to come from beneath me and then rocketed out of my head. I was then aware of having no sensation of sitting. There was no sense of hard ground or stone beneath me. I seemed to be suspended, floating. I was not frightened. The sensation was intense but pleas-ant. As I sat, amazed at this sensation, my sides began to fall away. I cannot describe this in any other way. I felt as if I had been living in a hollow tube or well, and the walls of that tube or well were simply falling away. My focus, however, was not on the walls falling but on the sense of expansiveness. As I breathed in and out, that expansiveness continued. I was unbounded. I had no boundaries."

"You were experiencing the 'unbounding' of the self that Wexler talked about?" asked Pinzak.

"I was. Soon I was . . . I was . . . well, weightless. I cannot really describe what was happening. I have rarely talked about this, and my words are clumsy. But my self was space. I was the space in which all things exist. I was this center, the cathedral, the space itself. I was the sky, the ocean, the mountains, the universe. I did not *feel* free; I was FREEDOM. There was no self present to feel anything. There was no 'I.' There was just this all-encompassing observing and this expansiveness. This was true Self. Not mine, but the nature, the true being, of all of us. This is what we truly are—not anything, but the timeless, limitless, joyous space in which anything takes place. It was the most natural of experiences. It was the opposite of an alien or foreign feeling. It was a total exhalation of all tension, anxiety, rancor, devotion, energy, thought. I simply WAS.

Then suddenly I was aware that I was sitting on stone. When the awareness registered as thought, immediately I was back to being 'me,' Emile. There was no reverse rushing of a collapsed sense of self, no rebuilding of walls of identity. I was just back at the center of the labyrinth, sitting on the center stone, back to being my enclosed, small self; back to being 'me.' I looked around. People had gathered around the labyrinth and were looking at me. A tall man with a broom was saying something to me in French and saying it with palpable exasperation. My blank stare indicated to someone in the gathered group that I did not understand this man. A young woman in the crowd said in English, 'Do you speak French?' I responded to her, while keeping my eyes on the man with the broom, 'No.' 'Well,' she said in English, 'It is seven o'clock and time to close the cathedral.' 'My God,' I thought to myself, 'I have been in here for over nine hours, and I've probably been sitting here for eight of those hours . . . and never noticed it.' I stretched out my legs and stood up. I was not even stiff. I was thinking, 'How can this be?' But it was so. I had been so still, so quiescent, so relaxed, that I had no stiffness at all. Indeed, I felt loose and energetic. I immediately headed for the door.

I had completed only half the 'pilgrimage,' but I did not want to take the time to resume my labyrinth walk, this time back to the outside world. I walked quickly, sensing not embarrassment but simply an urgency to leave, so as not to inconvenience people any further. I felt buoyant, even joyous. I was enjoying some kind of afterglow. I had no sense that any time had passed, let alone nine hours. When I got outside, I looked at my watch to verify what the young woman had said in the cathedral. I also looked at the people coming out of the cathedral walking past me, whispering and smiling and even pointing. Over eight hours, Pinzak; I had been in there for over eight hours, and it felt like one."

"Relativity, Emile, relativity. What exactly had happened to you?" Pinzak asked.

"That is precisely what I wanted to know. And so I began a quest for understanding what I had experienced. I began by reading about labyrinths in general and Chartres in particular. Apparently Celtic Druids created an underground shrine to the Black Madonna, who is sometimes associated with the Egyptian goddess Isis, at the same site where the cathedral now stands. The center of the Druid shrine was now the center of the labyrinth, which is often described as a vortex of energy. This led me to those cultures throughout history that have used labyrinths as a means of investigating human consciousness. I learned that labyrinths have been used by cultures throughout history and in every part of the globe to induce altered states of consciousness, especially spiritual states of consciousness."

"I know that the Hopi and Papago tribes in Arizona still use them in sacred ceremonies and in healing rituals," shared Pinzak.

"They are often used for healing and for quests for the sacred, just as pilgrims used the one at Chartres. Soon I was reading about altered and higher states of consciousness, spiritual experiences, mysticism, psychology, and Eastern philosophy. A whole new world of learning opened up. However, I wanted some grounding to that world, some continued contact with Western science and rationality."

"You did not want to drift off into the occult or into superstition."

"Exactly. That is when I found Ken Wilber's *Spectrum of Consciousness.* Here was a writer who not only made sense of these kinds of experiences and of higher states of consciousness, but also did so from within a framework that respected scholarship and the history of Western psychology and philosophy. In the book Wilber shows that the spectrum of consciousness runs from the states explored and emphasized by Western psychologists like Freud, Jung, Skinner, and Maslow, to the Eastern meditative traditions that explore states beyond language and logic."

"What we were discussing as mystical states," Pinzak said.

"Yes, let us resume our discussion," declared Emile.

Emile: In subsequent books, and there must be a dozen or so by now, Wilber elaborates on how these various states of consciousness East and West can be integrated into an overall model or intellectual whole. Wilber created the most comprehensive integrative model. This he calls the "AQAL" model, which stands for "All Quadrants All Levels."

Pinzak: This "AQAL" model is going to be helpful for understanding cosmopolitan identity?

Emile: Not only helpful for understanding its nature, but also helpful for understanding how to stimulate it. Wilber's model can show us how dialectical thinking fits in with an overall scheme for understanding human and social development.

Pinzak: Weren't we going to discuss political institutions today?

Emile: Well, we were. But you have us heading in a slightly different direction, one that is still germane, however, to our overall topic of cosmopolitanism.

Pinzak: This "detour" is fine with me, but before we get too far into it, let me see, by way of recapitulation, whether I have understood what you have been building up for me. The cosmopolitan identity is characterized, first and foremost, by dialectical thinking. It is, in a sense, a by-product of dialectical thinking, which is a system of thought whereby the person acknowledges, addresses, transcends, and/or accommodates as many perspectives as possible. This is especially so of perspectives that conflict or even contradict.

The dialectical thinker is one who looks for the unifying themes underlying conflict or contradiction within and among perspectives or even systems. For the dialectical thinker, and thus for the cosmopolitan, the truth of the matter, whatever "the matter" is, is constituted by a compound of multiple views. Integrating views, even more than entertaining ambiguity, is the goal and hallmark of dialectical thinking. The desire, if not the need, for integration is what opens up identity and leads to cosmopolitanism. The person comes to see that perspectives and the contexts in which they arise and on which they depend are infinite. He comes to see that every perspective reveals an aspect of one's own self, since selfhood is what one shares with all humans. All of this pushes identity or the self to the very edges of formal-operational thinking, if it does not itself herald a move into postformal operations.

Emile: A very good summary, Pinzak. Let me add a few additional points. The cosmopolitan identity that we are describing here is what psychologist Abraham Maslow termed "the authentic person" (1982, 11). The authentic person shows a level of moral imagination, which here is an integration of emotion and intellect . . .

Pinzak: . . . as in an integration of sympathy and empathy. . . .

Emile: That is correct. *Sympathy* is sharing one's feelings with another, as in the literal Greek meaning of "having a fellow-feeling," and *empathy* is being able to place oneself in the positions of others. It is the power of understanding things outside of ourselves. It is the heart in step with the mind. Cosmopolites, I think, want people to respond to evidence of, say, starvation in Africa. But we do not simply want an impassioned outpouring of money sent to corrupt governments that will block aid and squander the money. We need an exercise of reason along with the outpouring of feeling. We need to be moved enough not just to write a check, but to examine the causes that lie behind the starvation and the social and political context from which those causes arose and occurred. The causes and the context at some point must be addressed as well.

Pinzak: This is what you referred to the other day as "felt identity," a combination of emotion and reason.[1] *(Emile nods.)* Can we say that this integration is also of compassion and wisdom?

Emile: We can, provided we understand that compassion adds to sympathy the ingredient of seeing the feelings of others as suffering and wishing to relieve it. *Wisdom* in this case we might define as the combination of experience and insight or judgment. *(Pinzak types on his laptop as Emile speaks.)*

Thus Maslow's authentic person has moral imagination sufficient to detach one's self from one's own perspective and to take up accurately the divergent, and even hostile, perspectives of others. That detachment, and the moral imagination underlying it, is possible because the authentic person relies upon self-validation through internal standards. As a result, he or she does not need the approval of others, especially those within one's own society or culture. The authentic person is able, therefore, to transcend identification with his or her specific culture and identify instead with the human race. As Jenny Wade says, "[A]uthentic people evince a deep feeling of identification, sympathy and affection for others. They embrace the human condition with all its foibles. They are critical in the sense of being discerning and clear-sighted, but not condemning" (1996, 164).

Pinzak *(clicking rapidly on his keyboard):* So Maslow's "authentic" level is equivalent to Suzanne Cook-Greuter's "postautonomous" level? *(Emile nods.)* She claims, based on her study, that postautonomy is *(Pinzak reads from his laptop)* "a stage of transcendence where one is no longer the center of one's world construction." One is, rather, "just one 'other' in a network of interconnected beings or part of an infinite whole" (1999, 91, 93). That network of beings, that infinite whole, is the human race.

Emile: One is no more than one connection in that network. But one also sees that one *is* a connection in that network. That double insight is the basis of the cosmopolitan identity. One is a discrete, tangible individual, but one is also simply one part of a much greater whole. In Cook-Greuter's terms, this Integrated, Postautonomous Individual "sees and experiences himself and others as part of ongoing humanity." It is a "global or universal vision" (93) and therefore a global or universal identity.

Jenny Wade comments that such persons, such selves, can be "radical innovators" (1996, 165). Radical innovation comes out of the melding and enfolding and creating of unities out of the multiple perspectives. While such innovation is available through the cosmopolite's own imagination or invention, it comes out largely through conversation, where real alternative perspectives can be met, taken up, and integrated.

Pinzak: We are talking about a real ability to synthesize or integrate and to reflect, to think outside the system.

Emile: Yes. According to Wade, our cosmopolite, or the "Authentic" person, makes decisions that are not "ego-invested in a particular choice. If a decision later seems to be suboptimal, [then] another choice is made, and then another, as he constantly adapts to changing circumstances" and perspectives (167).

Pinzak: In this way parties to the conversation may arrive at settlements that each considers just and equitable. *(Emile nods as he sips his coffee.)*

Assuming as we have been that dialectical thinking is the most advanced stage of formal operations, then thinkers at lower-order formal operations cannot think dialectically.

Emile: Correct.

Pinzak: But dialectical thinkers can integrate all levels of formal operations and all the cognitive operations that precede that level.

Emile: Also correct.

Pinzak: Then can we not conclude that because of that integration, to say nothing of the multiple perspectives and contradictions that dialectical thinkers can integrate or transcend, that dialectical thinking is better and higher than the earlier levels of formal operational thinking?

Emile: I think that we can. For "dialecticians" every whole is really only a part of a greater whole when seen from the perspective of the next and higher level of development.

Pinzak: So as the person moves into dialectical thinking, he separates from the worldview that at the earlier level looks whole. Through dialectical thinking he now sees that the multiple worldviews, the multiple perspectives, need to be and can be integrated into a more comprehensive or encompassing understanding.

Emile: Yes, because dialectical thinking is oriented toward building analysis and constructs on the differing perspectives of others.

Pinzak: But through this process will dialectical thinking not undercut the reference points that enable us to make sense of our world, that provide intellectual coherence and thus social and political stability?

Emile: Dialectical thinking has, of course, its own patterns of coherence. The emphasis is placed on the process of change. Recall that the thinker dissociates from the earlier worldview *and* integrates the multiple perspectives into a new worldview, one that encompasses the earlier worldview as one part in the now greater whole. This process is not capricious. It results in its own stability and coherence, but at a higher level of integration. During the time between dissociation or differentiation and the new integration, the multiple perspectives that dialectical thinking recognizes and demands as parts of the new whole might look untethered and unstable. As Basseches comments, open-mindedness is freedom from intellectual limitation that might initially come at the expense of security (1984, 29).

Pinzak: Speaking of untethered and unstable, mysticism breaks down the boundaries of self so that one senses an identity with all humans, if not all of life.

Emile: As we said in our earlier discussion, dialectical thinking can lead to a cosmopolitan identity and concomitant with it, of course, a cosmopolitan worldview. But inducing such a shift or transformation is expedited by adding mystical experience. The two in combination are almost a guarantee.

Pinzak: Wilber's AQAL model shows us that?

Emile: Wilber's model reinforces the insights of developmental psychology, but he also integrates into developmental psychological models a developmental sequence for altered or higher spiritual states of consciousness. Thus one can readily see how dialectical thinking, even if it is the highest stage of formal operational thinking and not itself postformal, can combine with mystical experience to lead to a cosmopolitan identity.

In addition, Wilber sets these psychological insights and this new developmental integration in a context that includes the necessity of taking into account the social, cultural, and behavioral aspects of development as well.

Pinzak: You will have to be more specific for me, Emile.

Wilber's Four-Quadrants Model (AQAL)

Emile: Let us start at the beginning, at the "creation" of the Four-Quadrants, or AQAL (All Quadrants All Levels) model. In 1992, while living in his hillside home outside of Boulder, Colorado, Wilber, who, by the way, is an autodidactic philosopher and comparative psychologist with, as I mentioned, over fifteen books to his credit, had spread out on his living-room floor over two hundred developmental schemata written out on legal pads. They surrounded his executive chair like sharks encircling a lifeboat. Like such sharks, they had his full attention. For weeks he sat staring at, walking around, meditating over, and intently contemplating how these disparate schemata might fit together. While all were developmental hierarchies, they were also all diverse and divergent and of varying degrees of complexity. There were "the easy ones," as he called them, the schemata from the natural sciences with which every researcher agrees: hierarchies that run from atoms to molecules to cells to organisms.

Pinzak: Every researcher agrees because every one of them can see the same hierarchy by looking empirically.

Emile: Right. More challenging, however, but also compatible were the hierarchies of developmental psychologists. Their hierarchies, while different in certain specifics, were uniform on the basics: Cognition moves from sensation to perception to impulse to image to symbol to concept to rule. Nobody starts at image or concept; nobody develops to rule cognition and then moves back to images.

But, of course, unlike the schemata in the natural sciences, nobody can pull out an instrument to look directly at the psychological hierarchies. In several ways the two sets of hierarchies did not match up. As Wilber said, "It is not at all obvious how these hierarchies would—or even could—be related" (2000c, 39).

The problem of relationship was merely the early sign of the complexity. Moving past these "fairly easy hierarchies," Wilber considered less pliant varieties: hierarchies from linguistics, religious traditions, astronomy, cultural studies, technology, economics, phonetics. You name the discipline, and Wilber had a hierarchy from it on a legal pad in front (or beside or behind) him.

Pinzak: But somehow all of them suddenly fit together?

Emile: Not exactly. Wilber did not have the single Archimedean moment when he shouted "Eureka!" as all the pieces, or hierarchies, fell instantly into place in one architectonic, grand hierarchy. Gradually over time things began to jell. As he says, "Toward the end of [a] three-year period the whole thing started to become clear to me." "The whole thing," however, was one architectonic, grand hierarchy. It was the Four-Quadrants Model, or AQAL (All Quadrants All Levels). Wilber saw that some hierarchies were addressing individuals; others, collectivities. Some were addressing interior realities; others, exterior realities. If we hold in mind those four distinct realms or quadrants—individuals, collectivities, interior realities, and exterior realities—then all the hierarchies can be seen as fitting seamlessly into a four-quadrant model. It would take Wilber only the 850 pages of *Sex, Ecology, Spirituality* to lay out and argue for that model.

Pinzak: Should political theorists take seriously this architectonic hierarchy?

Emile: Theorists can ignore it or dismiss it out of hand, especially because, as we have been discussing, Wilber delves into mystical or spiritual states that might seem fanciful or even softheaded to a superficial reader. Yet the model involves much of what theorists take seriously: a model built on evidence and argument; a model that uses sociology, anthropology, psychology, feminism, philosophy, grand theory, moral development, sociobiology, religion, social theory, ecology, systems theory, political ideologies, along with other disciplines, subfields, and epistemological approaches. Theorists might well disagree vehemently with how Wilber uses any or all of these subjects and approaches. But, in order to be cogent, such disagreement requires that the theorists argue against Wilber, which means taking Wilber seriously.

If, for example, political theorists take seriously the political social philosophy of Hegel . . .

Pinzak: . . . which for the most part they do . . .

Emile: . . . then how does a political theorist dismiss out of hand a hierarchical schemata not unlike Hegel's? Indeed, Wilber's model, like Hegel's, describes the unfolding of Spirit *(Geist)*. Wilber makes significant use of Hegel's conception of *Aufheben,* as the stages of the quadrants' hierarchy show "sublation."

Pinzak: The Hegelian view, then, would be that a higher stage "negates but preserves" or "transcends but includes" the lower stages. This is what we were saying earlier: A dialectical thinker transcends identification as earlier selves but includes the cognitive skills found at those earlier levels. He can now integrate multiple viewpoints and transcend contradictions and thereby generate a more comprehensive and integrated understanding.

Emile *(nodding):* By *Aufheben* Hegel meant to convey a sense of hierarchy through sublation as something "is raised from a lower place to a higher one." The term derives from the Latin term *sublatus,* meaning "to take; to carry away; to lift up."[2] *Sublation* carries with it an ambiguity. It means both to negate and to preserve, to take up to a higher place and to store or put away.

Pinzak: This is a far more accurate term than "synthesis," which, of course, Hegel himself never used, for *synthesis* conveys the sense of two things merging rather than the properties of one thing being preserved at the same time as those properties are transcended with the introduction of new properties not found in the original thing.

One might think, for example, of moving from Newton's worldview to Einstein's. Newton's worldview was not rejected outright in favor of Einstein's. Instead, Newton's view and physics were seen to be correct but limited. Within its proper ambit Newton's physics works well to explain certain phenomena. So, Einstein's view makes use of Newton's physics—that is, "includes" Newton's physics—but also supplants it or "transcends" it, by introducing concepts and theories that go beyond what Newton presented and explained.[3]

Emile: Newtonian physics are still present in Einsteinian physics. Einstein can be seen to be offering a higher or better system in that Newton's physics are "preserved" but simultaneously "negated." Einstein adds new insights that explain or handle phenomena that go beyond what Newton's physics could deal with. As Hegel says in the *Phenomenology, Aufheben* is not merely "abstract negation," but is also a movement that "supersedes in such a way as to preserve and maintain what is superseded."[4]

One can see without much difficulty how this relates to Wilber's model. He offers a developmental hierarchy that lays out the stages of growth from lower to higher. Stages that come after preceding ones are higher in precisely the way Hegel uses *Aufheben:* They sublate, or transcend but include, the lower. The higher stages introduce new properties not found in previous stages, while also including or preserving those properties found earlier or below.

Pinzak: Again, this is precisely what we have been talking about in terms of developmental psychology leading to dialectical thinking and cosmopolitan identity.

Emile: It is. But just for a moment let us take a wider view of Wilber's model to gain more perspective on what he proposes.

Early in *Sex, Ecology, Spirituality,* Wilber asks whether there are what he calls "patterns of existence" or "tendencies of evolution" or "propensities of manifestation" that permit us to map how things grow in complexity over time. In short, he is asking whether we can map how things evolve. Are the patterns, tendencies, or propensities such that we can say that they "make this universe a genuine *uni-versum* ('one turn')? Are these the patterns that connect?" (2000a,

40).[5] If we return to Hegel for a moment, we might describe what Wilber is suggesting in Hegelian terms: When Spirit manifests, it does so always as and in the four quadrants. All manifestation is Spirit, and all manifestation is in the form of the quadrants.

Pinzak: I still do not know what specifically those quadrants are.

Emile: Patience, Pinzak. I am giving you the wider view, remember? So in Wilber's view, the universe—that *uni-versum*—is composed not of wholes and parts; it is composed of wholes/parts or *holons,* a term that Wilber borrows from Arthur Koestler.

Pinzak: Are holons, as wholes/parts, not the same as wholes and parts?

Emile: No, Wilber says, for they cannot be separated. Parts cannot be and are never separate from the wholes of which they are a part. Nor are the parts ever just parts. They are always wholes/parts. Reality is composed of simultaneous wholes/parts. Every whole is simply a part of a larger, more encompassing whole that takes up and preserves . . .

Pinzak: . . . sublates . . .

Emile *(pausing, then smiling):* . . . the essential properties of the whole-now-part. But the new whole adds something entirely new, something not available when the now-part was a whole. Thus parts—that is, what is seen from the perspective of the new whole—are wholes that exist in larger wholes.

Pinzak: And the point is?

Emile: The point is to avoid reductionism, to avoid giving pride of place to any thing or to any particular process—or process itself. To see the universe as composed of holons means that we must include both entities and processes, because all of them are holons. This position avoids seeing the world either as atomistic—all things are fundamentally separate or discrete—or as holistic—all things are merely parts or strands of the larger whole. Neither is correct. There are only whole/parts.

We can see the immediate benefit of this view in philosophy. The world is not based on idealism or materialism. It is not this or that. It is whole/parts. Any time you identify a whole and think, "There we are!" then in your next breath you must say, "What is this whole a part of?" Every whole is a part, endlessly.

Pinzak: We can also see the immediate benefit of this view in political theory, for it means that no one can now claim that his vision of the whole—of how the universe, society, and humankind work—should be taken as anything but partial. That vision must itself be part of a larger whole. What does this say about politics? First, it reinforces the idea that persons are both agents (wholes) acting with autonomy and independence and members or participants (parts) in communion or community with others.

Emile: Wilber says as much: Too much agency and one ends up in alienation and repression; too much communion and one gets fusion and dissociation (49).

Pinzak: Obviously, this wholes/parts observation is important, for it means that those theorists who claim that humans are by nature social or by nature individual are half-right and half-wrong. Identity has, then, two poles: agency and community. As we said in an earlier conversation, both poles change as identity changes. What we identify with as community changes—from family to group or clan to nation to humanity; what we identify as agency changes as well—from being embedded in rules and roles to being embedded in language and logic, even to transcending those through mysticism.

Emile: Wilber describes this as the difference between self-adaptation and self-transformation. When one fits into the community aspect, she finds herself a part of a larger whole and adapts to it by identifying with that whole. But self-transcendence is the shift in identity to another context, another whole. That is, the person becomes a new whole and the sense of community changes. Self-transcendence, this idea or phenomenon of becoming and thus being a new whole, is evolution. The inside, the subject or what one identifies as, now becomes the outside or the object of one's attention.

Pinzak: And the four quadrants?

Emile: We have really just outlined them. One way to examine and explain anything[6] is to accept that it has four dimensions. We might also call them, following Wilber, four distinctions,[7] four strands (2000a, 125 and 146—"four strands of evolution"), four major aspects (127), or four "forces." The four are 1) outside, 2) inside, 3) singular or individual, and 4) plural or community. Wilber advises us that in our approach to any subject or phenomenon we must take into account these four aspects or quadrants. Failure to do so means that we are leaving out of that account something significant.

For humans, those forces or quadrants are 1) our individual or singular outside—that is, our body and our behavior; 2) our individual or singular inside—that is, our mind and intention and psychology; 3) the social institutions of our context—that is, society/community; and 4) the worldview or ethos of our social context—our collective values, beliefs, and the like.

Pinzak: So the two quadrants associated with body-behavior and with mind represent agency; the two associated with social institutions and cultural beliefs and practices represent community. Is agency in tension with community?

Emile: Wilber says "yes." Agency wants more agency and thus less community; community wants more relationship and thus less independence or agency.

Pinzak: But the person has to establish some equilibrium or to achieve some balance, right?

Emile: Right. Otherwise too much agency begets alienation; too much community begets fusion. Keep in mind what we learned from other developmental models: It is the tension between organism and environment—or, in our terms, the individual and community—that propels development or evolution.

Balance and harmony among the quadrants is a sign of health. Too much agency or too much community—"inflating the self or losing the self in the others" (2000a, 306)—will throw off that balance and produce pathology. Thus it is important for healthy growth to balance or integrate the quadrants. Every level needs to be balanced, and therefore every level needs to have integrated quadrants.

Pinzak: Let us do a graph of Wilber's Four-Quadrants, or AQAL, model. (See Figure 1.)

Emile: All right, we can do that. *(Emile takes out his pen and begins sketching on a piece of paper that Pinzak hands him.)* The North-South axis in the model divides interior and exterior; the East-West axis divides the individual and the collective, as you can see here.

Upper-Left Quadrant (UL)	**Upper-Right Quadrant (UR)**
"I"	"IT"
Interior-Individual	Exterior-Individual
Intentional	Behavioral
Lower-Left Quadrant (LL)	**Lower-Right Quadrant (LR)**
"WE"	"ITS"
Interior-Collective	Exterior-Collective
Cultural	Social (Systems)

Figure 1. Wilber's Four-Quadrants (AQAL) Model

The four quadrants, then, are the Upper-Right, or empirical/behavioral; the Upper-Left, or psychological/intentional; the Lower-Right, or empirical/social; (that which can be seen, weighed, measured about society); and the Lower-Left, or cultural or worldview.

Pinzak: So, we've got the Upper-Right, or UR, and that's the "body" quadrant; the Upper-Left, or UL, and that's the "mind" quadrant; the Lower-Right, or LR, and that's the "social" quadrant; and the Lower-Left, or LL, and that's the "values" or "worldview" quadrant.[8]

Emile: The right half of the quadrants model can be described in "it" or objective language, since these quadrants refer to empirical phenomena. Those phenomena consist of what can be experienced through the five senses or their extensions. Persons investigating these quadrants, whether they study groups or individuals, are interested in form or surface, not interior; they focus on behaviors.

The entire left half of the model cannot be seen empirically. These quadrants are interior. As Wilber says, "Whereas the Right half can be seen, the Left half must be interpreted" (132). Whereas surfaces can be seen and measured, depths or interior must be interpreted. The key question asked by those studying interiors is, "What does this mean?"

Pinzak: Can't we see and examine empirically the "insides" of something—say, our brains?

Emile: Yes, but we cannot empirically examine an interior. You can cut open a human head and examine brain tissue. But interiors—what one is experiencing—must be interpreted. To examine something empirically is what Wilber calls "monological" examination, because one needs only a monologue and no dialogue. On the other hand, interiors must be interpreted, and interpretation requires talking or dialogue, which is to say that depth is dialogical (40).

Pinzak: If the right side is talked about in "it/its" language, then, presumably, the Upper-Left quadrant can be described in "I" or first-person language; the Lower Left, in "we" or third-person language.

Emile: Correct. This is not so strange, as Wilber points out (149), that something similar to the quadrants model is found in others' research. Karl Popper proposes three "Worlds"; World I is the objective world (or Wilber's UR), World II is the subjective world (or Wilber's UL), and World III is the cultural world (or Wilber's LL), which, Popper says, can also be embedded in material social institutions (or Wilber's LR).

Likewise, the quadrants model resembles Kant's three Critiques: the *Critique of Pure Reason* (theoretical or scientific reason), the *Critique of Practical Reason* (morality or intersubjective reason), and the *Critique of Aesthetic Judgment* (subjective or personal). These realms of "I, We, It" are also known as person, culture, and nature.

Pinzak: How about this as an example of understanding Wilber's three spheres of "I, We, and It": Galileo. Galileo famously showed us that the earth revolves around the sun, not vice versa. This scientific fact, this "it," removed us from the center of the universe. But on another level, or in another sphere, Earth is currently the center of the universe for the simple reason, now still a fact, that we are the only populated planet. So "we" are alone, but "we" are together. Finally, each of us looks out onto a landscape that is part of Earth and thus part of the universe. But this makes each person, each "I," the center of his/her world and universe. However much postmodernists might want us to "decenter," the fact remains—a fact that Galileo did not emphasize or did not emphasize sufficiently—that we are center. This brings with it, it seems to me, immense responsibility for our world, especially for making that world better, as microscopic as that "making" might be. This reinforces a kind of cosmopolitanism.

Emile: The dilemma for modernity, argues Wilber, is not that we have differentiated these three spheres—the "I," "We," and "It," or . . .

Pinzak: . . . person, culture, and nature . . .

Emile: . . . or art, morals, and science; even subjective, intersubjective, and objective. The dilemma is that we have failed to see how to integrate them, and that failure can be a problem for cosmopolitanism. Hence we leave the spheres separated and isolated, with pioneers and explorers in one sphere having little effect on, because little communication with, the other two.

Integrating these spheres, not merging them, is the goal of what Wilber calls "integral studies." Because the sphere of science had such breakthroughs using its methodology, it did not take long for scientific thinking to subordinate if not dominate the spheres of religion and morals, what Habermas calls "the colonization of the lifeworld." That is what Wilber is fighting, the absorption of two spheres into one. Wilber calls this "scientific materialism" or "flatland," where the notion of anything that cannot be measured or empirically tested disappears. Thus is lost all sense of interiority, as well as the ideas of higher and lower.

Pinzak *(stops typing and looks up):* It seems to me that the Upper-Left or mind quadrant is the most important. You can't very well get shared values or a communal worldview if people aren't "seeing" it; that is, if they aren't at the level of consciousness or awareness where such sight and sharing are possible. You can't build social institutions around that worldview if persons don't have the mental framework or consciousness to propose and carry out the proposals for such institutions.

Emile: That may be right, but Wilber insists on reminding readers that the interior quadrants do not precede the exterior quadrants, anymore than the exterior precede the interior. They arise together, and, as Wilber says, go together at every stage. Another way of saying the same thing is to see the connection in human relationships: We are always in contact with each domain or quadrant; we are always connected to "I, We, It," and they evolve together (150). The Left side and the Right side are mutually codetermining (fn. 43, 594). People cannot get to the next level, cannot raise consciousness to a level of cosmopolitanism, if they, and we, do not have the values and processes and social structures for transforming them, for moving and changing identities.

The paramount point is that the quadrants are interactive. Thus states of consciousness (UL) have correlates in parts and aspects of the brain (UR). Cultural meanings and practices (LL) can influence, if not mold, our perceptions

(UR). For example and this might be apocryphal, when indigenous persons in North America first saw men (Europeans) riding on horseback, they thought that horse and rider constituted a single beast. In addition, the economic and technological base of society (LR) helps determine how the world looks (LL) and whether, how, and for whom consciousness (UL) evolves (445). All four quadrants are important in the development of any individual.

The quadrants model gives us an outline of the kinds of significant transformations, internal and external, that humans go through. Transformation, however, is not a simple matter of rising through the levels, for, as Wilber points out (215ff), there are waves of consciousness (levels of consciousness), but also streams or lines of development. These lines stand for different aspects of individual development: cognitive, moral, psychosexual, affective, interpersonal, and the like. As we said during our previous conversation, one can be at one level of cognitive development but at a lower level of moral development.

Pinzak: I still think that the Upper-Left or individual consciousness quadrant is the most important. Unless you have someone experiencing dialectical thinking, or you have philosophers on the basis of their intellectual or personal experiences declaiming and arguing that they are "citizens of the world," then you don't even begin to think about social institutions that might reflect and foster those values. *(Pinzak pauses to sip his coffee and grimaces slightly, as it is beyond cold now.)*

So, the lower quadrants are the social and cultural holons through which and in the context of which a person develops. Worldviews, then, are the cognitive maps of the world that are created by each level (or wave) of consciousness.

Emile: Wilber finds, following some of the macro-historians of the social sciences such as Gerhard Lenski and Jean Gebser, that each order of consciousness (UL) carries with it a worldview (LL). Society is ordered, therefore, according to the basic patterns found in each order of consciousness. When a critical mass of persons in a society expresses a certain order of consciousness, then the central social organizing force of that society is that expressed order of consciousness. This is what Wilber calls the "collective center of social gravity" (fn. 9, 752).

Pinzak: So here is the crux: If more and more persons are expressing a new, or higher, order of consciousness, and if that order of consciousness is the predicted dialectical order, based on dialectical thinking, then is the forthcoming worldview associated with this level—the cosmopolitan level—going to unfold? According to the theory, the cosmopolitan . . .

Emile: Or what Wilber calls "planetary."

Pinzak: Okay, the cosmopolitan or planetary worldview is inherent to the dialectical order of consciousness. That is so because, according to the quadrants theory, every new order simultaneously expresses itself in each quadrant.

Emile: The worldview associated with Wilber's vision-logic level—or our level characterized by dialectical thinking—is, indeed, cosmopolitan. But for that worldview to be dominant in society, a critical mass of persons in that society would have to reflect the vision-logic or dialectical level of consciousness. At that point, the collective center of social gravity would shift, or transform, to the new level.

Pinzak: Yet we've seen, according to researchers like Cook-Greuter, that there are very few dialectical thinkers in our population. So planetary consciousness and cosmopolitan identity are not exactly around the next corner.

Emile: No, obviously they are not. But has any society tried installing, let alone integrating, dialectical thinking into its social systems? We are still operating at Wexler's "microcosmic" level of transformation. Thus any movement toward cosmopolitanism at this point will be small, incremental, and possibly "everyday."[9] Still, we can begin the steady process of introducing the powerful combination of dialectical thinking and mystical thinking that can alter individual consciousness and social institutions.

Pinzak *(typing and almost talking to himself):* Whatever the level of consciousness, and wherever we are in the social and political procession toward cosmopolitan identity, the upper or individual quadrants must be integrated with the lower or collective quadrants. Individuals need community or sociality, and societies are constituted by individuals with their own interiority; that is, persons are not just faceless ciphers to be manipulated for the sake of the state. Communities or society and individuals always go together. One does not precede and is thus not prior to the other.

Emile: The Four-Quadrants Model presents the view that you cannot have individuals without a community. Of course, individuals can leave a community, but they have had experience of one. No one, in other words, is born an independent individual. Likewise, you cannot have a community without individuals. As Wilber says, "You cannot have a population of cells with no cells at all" (90).

"In other words, the individual and the social are not two different coins, one being of a higher currency than the other, but rather the heads and tails of the same coin at every currency. They are two aspects of the same thing, not two fundamentally different things (or levels)" (90).

Pinzak: According to the model, we must consider and then integrate all quadrants. At our last meeting we talked about the need when changing welfare, for example, to consider both the character of our citizens and of our social institutions and programs. Politicians and policy experts, and the community members themselves, need to think about behavior and character; about the social, economic, and political environments in which they as citizens live; and about the kinds of attitudes and values they live by and espouse, as well as the kinds of customs and rituals they follow.

Emile: Can people get to work on time? That means, not just can they find adequate transportation, but do they also have the habits of getting up and getting ready early enough?

Pinzak: All of this points to the need for considering all quadrants: personal behavior (UR) and psychology (UL), as well as the physical (LR) and cultural (LL) environment in which people live and work.

Also, if we follow this model, we'll see growth or evolution from less complex levels of organization to more complex ones. This is precisely what we talked about with developmental psychology.

Emile: This is the basis of Wilber's model.

Pinzak: That's right. But evolution of individuals or humans requires not just psychological change, but also a change in environments and "sodalities" as persons develop and change.

Emile: What you are talking about are the organizing principles of societies. Tribes, for example, began by organizing their societies around kinship—one could trace his/her membership to a common ancestor. This kinship held the group together, and personal identity, if such a concept had any meaning then, developed through or as identification with that ancestral group.

With the rise of problems within the group that challenged its organization around kinship—problems such as unequal distribution of social wealth—groups began to experiment with a different kind of social integration. Hence arose the movement from kinship to politics and the movement from a common ancestor and bloodline as the glue of the group to a common ruler dispensing justice according to norms based on tradition. Here is the rise of conventional morality. What was needed, comments Wilber, "was not tribal but transtribal awareness" (175). Mythology and not magic provided the impetus and the organization for this new awareness, as a common mythological origin glues together various tribes.

Pinzak: Mythology permits different tribes with different bloodlines to be integrated or united, because they are linked not through kinship but by being descended from the same gods and goddesses.

Emile: Yes, holding people together through mythology requires not biology, but common gods and goddesses and thus common beliefs and rituals and values.

From mythology we can see how the next evolutionary step would be from common ruler to common rules or common law and then to the rise of postconventional morality.

Pinzak: From there we then go . . .

Emile: . . . to the common rules underlying and organizing the common law/rules—that is, common rules regulating common rules; in short, a metaperspective. Always the trajectory is toward greater complexity and a wider embrace.

Pinzak: Arriving at cosmopolitanism and a planetary worldview.

Emile: From Wilber's model we see every development as manifesting in all quadrants simultaneously. Thus "global problems demand global awareness" (525). The global problems that we see manifesting in the physical and social worlds—that is, the Upper-Right and Lower-Right quadrants—require recognition and solutions from the Upper-Left and Lower-Left quadrants. The condign global awareness, dialectical and cosmopolitan (or planetary), comes through the interior development of consciousness.

Pinzak: So, to back up for a moment, at the concrete operational level, the mythic worldview is supplanted by the move into formal operational thinking. There the characteristic worldview is the rational-scientific worldview. What remains of the mythic level is not the worldview but the elements that characterize concrete operational thinking—to wit, the operational structures themselves: the capacity to think about the forms, images, symbols, and concepts; the capacity to make and follow rules; and so on.

Yet the worldview of the mythic world is gone. That worldview was an exclusivist one; as an exclusive awareness it has been superseded by the rational worldview. One who identifies through formal operations cannot have a worldview that is part myth and part rationality. That is so because the structure of the world depends solely on the level of consciousness. When one has only concrete operational thought, one can structure only a mythic worldview.

Emile: One cannot have a worldview that is part myth and part rationality? What about religious worldviews? What about, say, Christianity? Is it not part myth—the virgin birth, for example—and part rationality?

Pinzak: Well, what's the rational part? If one accepts the birth, death, and resurrection of Jesus Christ, then one can plot and follow logical or rational deductions from these premises. But that reasoning, though rational, is no more than a concrete operation. We can see how confused the Fundamentalist Christian worldview is, for example, when Fundamentalists accept that Earth was created in six days only six thousand years ago, and yet they accept and rely upon Western medicine and science in much of their daily lives.

Emile *(smiles and takes a sip of his coffee):* At this point let us not get bogged down in religious dogma of any sort. Instead, let us examine how commitment now becomes important. Prior to the formal operational level there could be no commitment to community or neighborhood or tribe or family, for there was no self separate from any of these. So when one transcends to the formal operational level one does not cease to care about the community. On the contrary, one is able for the first time to commit. Yet that commitment is based on the ability to stand back reflectively from that community and to assess it in terms of formal operational thinking. That is, one assesses her community in terms that are rational and thus rest on universal principles that pertain to all humans in that community. Some would even think that these principles pertained to all persons in all communities at all times. But clearly principles here transcend place.

Pinzak: This is important to cosmopolitanism. The foundation of one's commitment to place reposes on the principles that undergird that place and not simply on the place itself. During the Vietnam War those who told protesters to

"Love America or Leave It" misunderstood the nature of both patriotism and protest. Indeed, some protesters argued that *they* were the true patriots. Their commitment was no longer to the place—America—"right or wrong." Their commitment was to the ideals and principles that continue as the foundation for the nation—those of liberty and justice; of transparency of actions and statements by our elected and appointed officials; of the rule of law and not of men; of deliberation on the causes and consequences and the course of the war.

Emile: The worldview at the formal-operational level is one of commitments made self-reflectively and rationally, based on principles that pertain to all. So an attitude of "my community or country, right or wrong" indicates the concrete-operational level. At the next level that attitude becomes "my community or country needs to get it right" according to rational principles, principles that some will think are universal.

Wilber categorizes those principles as the depth of reason and reason's "capacity for universal-pluralism, its insistence on universal tolerance, its grasp of global-planetary perspectivism, its insistence on universal benevolence and compassion" (259). Circumstances that require exceptions will themselves be based on reason.

Pinzak *(after draining his cappuccino):* Here is the value of the Wilberian model: If we are concerned about the health of a person, then we must also be concerned about the health of the community, the cultural and social holons, of which that person is a member.

Emile: We must include in any definition of health all four quadrants and all levels of consciousness and development. Failure to account for all of this and for harmony on each level and among the levels is to render any version of health both partial and problematic.

Pinzak: What happens, Emile, if we add in the mysticism that you've talked about? What happens when the self goes transpersonal?

Emile: At that point, Wilber says, "the worldcentric conception gives way to a direct worldcentric experience, a direct experience of the global Self/World, the Eco-Noetic Self, where each individual is seen as an expression of the same Self or [Emerson's] Over-Soul" (299, emphases in the original).

The shift is from the mutual understanding found at the worldcentric stage to the mutual identity found at the stage of Over-Soul (fn. 21, 640). This is our cosmopolitan identity. As we have been saying, the shift in identity might very well happen for some, perhaps for many, through a society-wide institutionalization of dialectical thinking.[10] That could result in this shift from conceptualization to experience and identity. As we discussed last time, mystical experience seems the direct path to realization of that identity. This is what Wilber refers to as "a direct experience . . . of a truly universal Self . . ." (301). We would get the best results, presumably, combining dialectical thinking and mystical experience.

The person at this level is not acting as if we are united with all others. Instead, the person experiences that unity immediately and directly. This experience, Wilber comments, is the "only source of true compassion" (301).[11] Moreover, the person at this level is free only if she takes the worldcentric or global perspective into account.

Pinzak: When Christ says, "Love thy neighbor as thy self," he is not saying, love your neighbor as much as you love yourself. He is saying, love your neighbor because he is your self. That is the message Wilber is conveying here, and it applies to all human beings: We are all only one Self. Then both our conception and our experience are cosmopolitan. So, too, will be our identity and our worldview.

Emile: At this level of identity there is no moral imperative, no moral injunction, to "treat all persons with love and respect." That kind of treatment is now simply the outcome of one's "unity" experience. Here is Hegel's authentic morality, the spontaneous action and expression of what one has come to realize within himself and not as the pawn of the categorical imperative. Experienced directly at this level is "the universal compassion through universal identity [as] the commonwealth of all beings: that I would see in an Other my own Self . . ." (300). This is exactly the kind of language we used when talking at our last meeting about cosmopolitan identity and dialectical thinking.

Pinzak: What happens if someone has a mystical experience prior to the establishment of dialectical thinking?

Emile: Wilber points out in virtually all of his works that mystical experiences are and have been available at all levels of psychological or consciousness development. Those who have these experiences prior to dialectical thinking, especially experiences that go beyond mere glimpses, "funnel the intuition into pre-rational structures, into egocentric or ethnocentric dispositions, which merely serve to reinforce the egocentricity or ethnocentricity; they, and they alone, now have God on their side, at which point they begin to suspect that there is no other God" (fn. 59, 653).

Without what Wilber calls "worldcentric rationality" (fn. 59, 653), what we have been calling dialectical thinking, no one can see that the insight or intuition about Self and God can be applied to all humans.

Pinzak: This is why the best way to induce cosmopolitan identity is through a combination of dialectical thinking and mystical experience. In that way those undergoing such experiences will be at a cognitive level where they can translate those experiences in worldcentric terms. They won't have the egocentric or ethnocentric predispositions, but will, instead, be able to see identity in cosmopolitan terms.

Then let's talk about how to structure conversations or decision-making to stimulate dialectical thinking.

Emile: Our goal is to achieve a dual outcome. We want to stimulate dialectical thinking as a way of inducing possible movement toward cosmopolitan identities among participants. Second, because dialectical thinking is higher-order thinking—because it can resolve, integrate, or transcend multiple and divergent viewpoints—we want to use it to arrive at decisions that persons can agree to. In short, we want to arrive at just outcomes acceptable to all.

Pinzak: We'll get both outcomes through the same process, right? We structure conversation around dialectical thinking. Requiring participants to think dialectically, to the best of their abilities, will get them thinking dialectically. By doing so, they must take up . . .

Emile: . . . and recapitulate . . .

Pinzak: . . . and recapitulate the perspectives of others. Doing so may get them to think about integrating or transcending any particular perspectives to create one common perspective acceptable to all. Now, they may not be able to generate this common perspective; in this particular instance such a perspective might not be possible. But through this process participants help create a just outcome and simultaneously open up their identities to the cosmopolitan perspective.

Emile: Will placing people in settings that require dialectical thinking induce them to think dialectically? If we treat people as if they are already dialectical thinkers, do we, can we, help them become dialectical thinkers? By adopting a dialectical attitude and approach, persons might gradually develop dialectical thinking as their default thinking. Attitude might then lead to identity.

Pinzak: Providing settings that require dialectical thinking enables persons to emerge from identities based on formal operations (or lower levels of formal operations). Then there is a further topic that we need to consider here: In what sorts of institutions should these kinds of structured conversations be held?

Emile: Before we move on to that, and I realize it is a conversation that we keep postponing, I think that we ought to consider what the term "integral politics" might mean.

Pinzak: You mean because Wilber's is an "integral" model? *(Emile nods while staring into his demitasse. He picks it up, looks at Pinzak, then looks back at his cup. "Perhaps another round first?" Pinzak, with mock exasperation, get up and removes both cups. He returns several minutes later with refills. He says, "Where were we?"*

Integral Politics

Emile: The politics that we are talking about, then, are those that both express and stimulate cosmopolitanism. An integral politics would involve both changing people's consciousness while simultaneously changing people's social conditions. Do we know what that could look like?

Pinzak: Marx claimed that we could not predict what a post-capitalist, or true socialist, politics would look like in any detail; he didn't want to propose recipes for the kitchens of the future. Indeed, one reason that Marx criticized the utopian socialists was that they offered blueprints of future society. Instead, all we can do, he said, is provide broad outlines, even orienting generalizations, of a post-capitalist politics.[12] Likewise, we cannot predict in detail what a cosmopolitan, integral politics would look like, because it depends so much on a shift in the center of collective consciousness into dialectical thinking. We could think together, however, about its broad outlines.

Emile: Let us, then, think together about one perspective on integral politics that precedes our own. That perspective comes from Greg Wilpert, who published an article, "Integral Politics: A Spiritual Way," in 2001.[13]

Wilpert wants to see how different political ideologies map onto Wilber's four-quadrants (AQAL) model, because integral politics must integrate personal behavior and psychology with the physical and cultural environment. One place to start thinking about integration, says Wilpert, is with political ideologies, which serve as examples of organizing principles for society.

So, using Wilber's model, Wilpert maps out in the quadrants where political ideologies lie based on whether an ideology "believes that internal or external factors shape us as individuals or as a society." Thus, for example, and according to Wilpert, conservatives tend to believe that personal lifestyles and individual values lead to poverty, whereas liberals believe that external forces such as unjust political policies produce poverty.

Pinzak: Already I have problems with what Wilpert says, which seems reductionistic, if not simplistic. But I'll play along to hear what else he has to say. So, you've mentioned the interior-exterior quadrants. And what about the north-south axis?

Emile: Wilpert uses that also. On that axis he maps the degree to which an ideology emphasizes the individual or the collective. So fascism, on his account, will be placed in the extreme "collective" category. According to Wilpert, "Fascism typically focuses on the collective and the internal. . . . [I]t is concerned with the internal motivations of people, their values or culture, and with the collective orderliness of society." On the other hand, leftist ideologies like socialism "see the primary causative forces as being external, usually in the form of the economy or the government."

Pinzak *(creating a graph of this mapping on his computer):* So libertarianism emphasizes individuals, and Wilpert would put them in the Upper Left extreme, while state socialism or communism emphasizes the collective and externalities and so would be placed in the Lower-Right extreme.

Emile: That is precisely where Wilpert places them.

Pinzak: And these distinctions are meant to do what?

Emile: They are meant, presumably, to show how an integral alternative will transcend but include these ideologies.

Pinzak: These renderings seem simplistic. They are almost caricatures. There is no political ideology, fascism included, that does not take into account as principal considerations both individuals and collectivities, as well as both internal and external forces. Wilpert's distinctions might hold if he were talking only about political ideologies as they appear or are used in current politics. That appearance or use should be contrasted with the underlying theories that constitute political ideologies. But Wilpert can't mean just political use, because he is talking about ideologies as belief systems. Those systems themselves rely upon and are justified by political theory.

Consider John Stuart Mill, the father of modern or welfare liberalism. Mill emphasizes all four of the quadrants. Indeed, if he did not, he could not have forwarded his arguments on behalf of balancing individual self-interest and the common good, which is the foundation of his liberalism

Emile *(taking a sip of coffee):* Say more about this, Pinzak.

Pinzak: In *Considerations on Representative Government,* Mill argues that the best kind of government is representative democracy, but he recognizes that many who can, and should, qualify for citizenship are ill-prepared to exercise their suffrage. So Mill proposes that those members of the learned professions and those with college educations should have additional or "plural" votes. In this way the educated can offset the votes of the many who are under-educated. The under-educated should still have the vote, but their votes would not count as heavily.

Emile: All citizens are equal, but some are more equal than others?

Pinzak: Yes, temporarily. Mill also proposed a national examination that any citizen could take. If he passed it, he then got plural votes. At some point, ostensibly through universal education, the need for plural voting would end. So Mill focused on individuals while holding in mind a concern for the whole, for the collectivity, for the common good. Mill wanted to assure that all citizens would participate in politics, because that was an excellent way to develop one's character. At the same time, however, Mill wanted to assure that selfish interests did not overwhelm the commonwealth. He thought that those who held the largest stake in society—the propertied—would be certain through plural voting to counteract the under-educated, who were more likely to follow their whims or to be hoodwinked by demagogues. But for Mill the under-educated are able to become educated. They are able to expand their views and increase their abilities. As a result, society through education and political participation—which Mill saw as a highly effective form of education—may help a citizen *(Pinzak clicks open and scrolls through a file on his laptop and begins to read:)* ". . . to feel part of the public and [to feel that] whatever is for their benefit is for his benefit" (1972, 255).

Something similar can be said for Mill's essay *On Liberty.* Here he argues for extending to all persons the greatest amount of freedom possible, provided that one's behavior does not impinge upon the freedom of others. At the same time, Mill argues that government has an obligation to help persons develop their "higher pleasures," as he called them. Such pleasures involve the development of intelligence of one's moral and spiritual capacities. Mill wanted all humans to extend the "largeness" of their "conceptions and sentiments." He wanted them to be introduced to a "range of ideas" that would lead to a development of intelligence quite beyond that of *(Pinzak again reads from his computer)* "those who have done nothing in their lives but drive a quill, or sell goods over a counter" (1972, 233). Clearly, Mill is talking, as a liberal, about internal individual development. Such development could come about most expeditiously through civic and political participation, which is about community.[14]

My point is that liberalism, as with any ideology, reflects an abiding concern with balancing the individual and the community, and a concern with when, and not whether, to look at the internal or the external.

Emile: Did Mill not think that character was simply a product of proper social engineering? Was it not for him a matter of setting up the right kinds of behavioral conditions? Would that not keep us in the exterior quadrants?

Pinzak: This might have been true of his father, James Mill, or true of Jeremy Bentham, but it was certainly not true of the later John Stuart Mill. He thought that his own mental breakdown was the result of too much emphasis on intellection and not enough on emotion. He saw the need to balance both mind and emotion, while his father and Bentham did not. For Mill the general or common good rests on a sense of duty, which itself, contrary to Kant, rests on moral feelings. Such a sense of duty for Mill can be cultivated by working on the interior, on the inside of oneself.[15]

John Stuart Mill also proposed as open an array of lifestyles as possible, which he called "experiments in living," which you're not going to get through extensive programs in social engineering. Furthermore, he proposed wide-open political discussions, arguments, debates, and campaigns as ways of disseminating ideas and improving citizens' reasoning. He also thought that all citizens, especially those without a lot of formal education, should serve on parish councils and on juries as means of expanding their minds. He did not suggest in any of these circumstances that only a certain set of ideas or rigid experimental conditions be presented or used as behavioral triggers. Indeed, he was talking about conversations and debates; he was talking about intersubjective interactions, which are found in the Lower-Left or interior-collective quadrant.

Finally, Mill discriminated between "barbarous" nations like China that lacked a development adequate for establishing representative democracy and those like Great Britain that had developed sufficiently. He did not think that the Chinese lacked the capacity for self-government, but at the time that he wrote *Considerations on Representative Government,* around the middle of the nineteenth century, he believed that they lacked the internal or character development for it.

Emile: This is an interesting and generous reading of Mill and liberalism. Yet surely modern liberalism, even Mill's variety, wants to keep the state from intruding into the souls, or psyches, of its citizens.

Pinzak: It does, but that doesn't mean that liberalism ignores or eschews the inner life of persons. Liberalism is a political ideology and as such has a great deal to say about how persons can, and even should, structure their relationships. But much of that is considered by liberals to be private, not to be decided by the state. Statecraft is not, as it is for traditional conservatives, soulcraft.

Emile: And you think, Pinzak, that *every* ideology shows a concern for balancing inner and outer, as well as the individual and the community? What about Marxism? Surely you acknowledge that it emphasizes the external or mode of production over the internal.

Pinzak: Well, every significant ideology as a theory shows the concern for balancing inner and outer. Even Marxism. Marx does see the organization of work as crucial to how societies operate and what social classes are generated. It is true that the superstructure—those values, beliefs, rituals, institutions, and the like, especially the religious and the political, that are necessary to support and perpetuate the social system—repose on the structure or mode of economic production. But, again, this is a limited rendition of Marxism. While it is true that Marx acknowledges technological breakthroughs as what galvanizes changes in the organization of work, it is the case that such breakthroughs cannot generate a new system of work, a new mode of production, without a superstructure. In short, structure and superstructure go hand-in-hand.

Emile: What about Marx's idea that "the nature of individuals thus depends on the material conditions determining their production"?[16] It is clear that he is saying that economics or the material forces of production determine the kinds of persons we are and can be.

Pinzak: Marx, who was a student of history, as well as of economics and philosophy, might well have thought so for earlier stages of history, up to the industrial age, as the age of individualism. Economics or the organization of work was a necessary means of survival. Economics provided a way of transforming life crises—such as, Where will we get enough food to live until tomorrow?—into manageable difficulties.[17] Of course, as Engels commented at Marx's gravesite, humankind "must first of all eat, drink, have shelter and clothing, before it can pursue politics, science, art, religion, and so on."

With the advent of machines, however, the nature of the crises facing people changed. Now people could easily produce more than enough for survival, but the mindset of capitalists denied workers the wherewithal to purchase the very products those workers were producing and kept them alienated from their work, their comrades, and their own selves. At this point the social relations of production became more salient than the material forces of production.

Emile: But we are still talking about materialism and Marx's "mode of production."

Pinzak: We are, but with a new emphasis. *(Emile shrugs his shoulders.)* With the advent of industrial machinery the superstructure for Marx becomes predominant *over* the structure. In Marx's imagined communism, machinery and mechanization don't change. Any aspect of work that can be mechanized will be mechanized, for under "true socialism," or "higher communism" as Marx called his final stage of history, increased mechanization translates into greater leisure time for citizens. What does change, however, is the workers' relationship to machines and mechanization. What does change is the workers' attitude toward or consciousness of mechanization or mechanized work.

Central to Marx's critique of capitalism, for example, is the concept of "false consciousness." In fact, only when members of the proletariat can step out of false consciousness to identify the roots of their oppression can a successful socialist revolution occur. Of course, a proletarian must live oppressed; he wouldn't be a proletarian if he weren't. And that proletarian is probably also out of work. These are both pressing social conditions. But recognition of one's situation and proper analysis of that situation—its causes and its consequences—is a matter of individual, internal development. It's a matter of change in consciousness.[18]

The rise of socialism is not predicated on a shift in technology. Socialism, for Marx, comes about through a raising of consciousness, not the invention of robots or infomercials. Indeed, for Marx the development to higher communism is all about consciousness and little about technology or the material forces of production. Any change in the mode of production is seen as a change in the social relations of production, as workers own and control the means of production. That is due, again, to a change in consciousness. Granted, there is an interaction in Marxist philosophy between the "objective" economic conditions—in this case, the economic crises of ever-intensifying recessions and depressions—and the "subjective" conditions of revolutionary class consciousness—the result of stepping out of false consciousness. This interaction precipitates the seizure of state power by the workers and then the "dictatorship of the proletariat."

When sufficient numbers of the proletariat have stepped out of false consciousness, then a socialist constitution can be written and the state, as Marx predicted, will wither away.[19] This is true, as Marx wrote, because the relations of production must be "appropriate to a given stage in the development of the forces of production."[20] But the forces of production at the end rest on a change in consciousness and not on technology or technique. That is what precipitates the change in who owns and controls the means of production and thus the ensuing social relations of production.

Emile: I agree that Marx might well warrant a closer examination, or at least a more open reading. But you cannot gainsay his overarching perspective that it is not "the consciousness of men that determines their existence, but their social existence that determines their consciousness" (Marx and Engels 1975, 28).

Pinzak: I wouldn't deny it. I would simply point out that, in the quotation from Marx you cited, he is not talking only about the Lower-Right quadrant, as many people suggest, but about the Lower-Left quadrant, or cultural existence, as well. It is a simplistic reading to take Marx to be a crude materialist. In fact, in his "Theses on Feuerbach" Marx criticizes the utopian socialist Robert Owen for arguing, as Engels himself seems to do after Marx's death, that human beings are simply products of their circumstances. If this were so, then Owen, himself a capitalist, would have exploited his workers to the fullest instead of seeking ways to humanize the workplace, their residences, and his "Village of Cooperation" at New Lanark. Nor would Marx have commented that "[t]he materialist doctrine that men are products of circumstances and upbringing, and that, therefore, changed men are products of other circumstances and changed upbringing, forgets that it is men that change circumstances."[21]

I concur with you that Marx did not have a full appreciation for what consciousness is and how it is determined, but he was not simply and only an economic determinist either. He did understand that the economic system or structure had to be analyzed in conjunction with the ideological superstructure.

Emile: Yes, but for Marx is this not a chicken-and-egg mystery? The superstructure rests on the structure, always. The structure is always about the organization of work.

Pinzak: That is so, but could Marx have really thought that a new technology could emerge without first having been in someone's head? Didn't he have to think that the technology first had to arise as an idea, an internal product and a result of development in the Upper-Left quadrant? Marx recognized that humans are actors in the world, and that they can act to change the world they perceive and to change themselves. Unlike Hegel, however, Marx argued that persons did this in the real world, the world of "work," and not just in thought. Humans do not just conceptualize a new worldview; they work and produce to transform the world physically. In this view, Marx's theory shows the necessity for interaction among all the quadrants—individual and collective "labor" and action mixed and matched with individual and collective thought. The result is, of course, new forms of production, but also new forms of social existence through social interaction.[22]

Emile: Interesting thoughts, Pinzak. Would you make similar arguments against Wilpert's mapping of other ideologies, say, conservatism?

Pinzak: I would. Traditional conservatives, who trace their lineage back to Edmund Burke, argue that the role of government is to assure that society raises the proper kind of citizens. To do so requires preservation, or conservation, of those social institutions that inculcate the requisite values. So both external or social institutions, which Burke called the "little platoons"—families, churches, schools, civic associations, and the like—and internal or individual development, as Wilpert points out, are central to conservatism.

Emile: This is why a staunch conservative like George Will can argue that a welfare system is necessary in any modern society.

Pinzak: Yes, because a conservative like Will, who is serious about assuring the development of virtuous citizens, sees that government has a significant role to play in guaranteeing, for example, the creation not only of the proper education or "virtue" curriculum, but also of the proper educational institutions.

My point is that any political ideology that has lasted for more than a few decades will take into account the four quadrants. It is not helpful to truncate ideologies as Wilpert does, because it elides significant elements that make and have made political ideologies long-lasting and powerful. Wilpert's mapping does have the benefit of showing us how real-world politics has modified, even bastardized, political ideologies.

Emile: So, Wilber tells us, using Rousseau and Nietzsche as two examples, that philosophy can be used, or misused, to bolster sinister strategies, policies, and regimes. Rousseau was used by the Jacobins during the French Revolution to justify the Terror and the execution of hundreds of those declared "state enemies, while Nietzsche's *Ubermensch* became a symbol of Aryan greatness and Nazi superiority."[23]

Pinzak: And those justifications rest on perfunctory and tendentious interpretations of the philosophies involved. Rousseau presented a view of a collective will, the general will, but it was never the expression of any particularistic will, say, of Robespierre or of the Jacobins themselves. Likewise, German fascists might parade under the banner of Nietzschean "supermen," but the kind of individual creativity that Nietzsche championed was aesthetic, philosophical, even artistic, not political and certainly not totalitarian.

Emile: Agreed, Pinzak. But politicians, you will concede, reduce in all sorts of ways the political ideological leanings of themselves and their constituents. Indeed, they may have to do so in order to accomplish certain political ends.

Pinzak: Yes . . . well, activists playing in the field of real-world politics may have to "dumb down" the ideology to appeal to where most members of the electorate currently are in their socio-political development; politicians to get elected in the first place must emphasize certain aspects of an ideology at the expense of introducing or elaborating on others.

Emile: Theoretical sophistication does not translate easily or well into election-time sound bites.

Pinzak: Right. So Wilpert does us a service by showing us how ideologies can be crudely used politically and chopped up strategically. But there's another problem with his mapping: it cheapens the alternative. It pretends that an Integral Politics does what other forms of politics cannot do, which may well not be the case. To map ideologies on a grid requires a deep respect for, manifested through deep learning about, those ideologies.

Emile: Wilpert is critical of those who propose a "third way" or alternative politics, because they often simply fall into a movement toward the center, which is a compromise of two, or more, dominant ideologies and not a transcending of them.

Pinzak: I think that he's right to point that out. But the danger is that in mapping ideologies so cavalierly or seemingly superficially, Wilpert may be guilty of creating "straw men" versions that permit him readily to create what looks like an alternative, when in fact the ideologies themselves point to the same methods and goals as does the alternative. If we're going to integrate political ideologies to create an integral politics, if we're going to transcend those limiting elements in these ideologies while honoring those insights from them essential to healthy collective life and individual growth, then we need to be sure that we properly understand the breadth and depth of those ideologies.

Emile: But is it not all right, then, to offer as Wilpert does broad generalizations about these ideologies?

Pinzak: Yes, provided that those broad generalizations do not excise significant aspects of the ideologies and thereby reduce them to a mere fraction, if not a fiction, of their importance and influence. Liberalism is thereby portrayed as excessive individualism, where persons are devoid of any personal responsibility, where McDonald's is at fault for burns from hot coffee, or a Twinkie diet leads to aggression and murder.

On the other hand, conservatism can be portrayed as placing complete responsibility on personal character, which reduces the complexity of issues and persons to simplistic insights. Thus we get, for example, the horrors of *Buck v. Bell,* the notorious case of Carrie Buck, a seventeen-year-old unwed mother who was declared mentally deficient and ordered by the court to undergo sterilization. On such readings, social circumstances have nothing to do with, say, crime and poverty. These are, instead, the outcome of deficient character. So in the 1920s twenty-nine states had laws forcing sterilization on prisoners, mental patients, and the poor. Outside the context of the quadrants, which both liberalism and conservatism acknowledge and, I would say, respect, ideological portraits become like these examples, distortions with often monstrous results.

Emile: Yet Wilpert does more than offer the quadrants. He also says, for example, that a fourth dimension of political ideologies is "direction of change." Some ideologies show a propensity for reform and others for revolution. Revolution, Wilpert says, is what Wilber means by transformation, moving to a higher level of development.

Pinzak: Can a revolution return us to an earlier level or type of organization? Technically that could also be a revolution. Originally the term was meant literally, as in a wheel's revolution. Thus Edmund Burke could support the American colonists in their War of Independence against the British, because he thought that their revolution was returning to the colonists what was originally theirs—that is, their rights as Englishmen. Notice the irony of a conservative supporting a revolution, but it was a revolving back to what was originally theirs.

Besides, reform versus revolution is not a probe into the direction of change. It is a probe into the manner of change. Every ideology, bar none, has a conception of freedom and, more important, a conception of greater freedom. The issue for the proponents of any ideology is how to achieve that greater freedom; that is, what does that greater freedom look like and what obstacles must be overcome to achieve it? *Every* ideology points in the direction of change for greater freedom. This is another reason that trying to map ideologies on the AQAL grid is a dicey proposition.

So what is it that Integral Politics in Wilpert's version offers that other ideologies do not? How does it transcend but include what other ideologies ignore or suppress? So far, I've not heard anything about that.

Emile: Wilpert does suggest another dimension of political ideology important to Integral Politics. That is the ideology's degree of inclusion or embrace. How far up the developmental hierarchy, in whichever quadrant, does the ideology go? To Wilpert an Integral Politics will recognize the importance of embracing as much of the hierarchy as possible.

Pinzak: Now we're getting somewhere. Think back to an earlier part of our conversation today. Could a Nazi be happy? On the AQAL model a Nazi could be "happy," from a perspective internal to Nazism, but such happiness must rest on being deprived of the higher levels of development. Fascism, and its racist cousin, Nazism, could not countenance a population of formal operational thinkers. The cradle-to-grave totalitarianism of fascism requires establishing a catechism to inculcate the proper conformist values. That catechism will not be questioned, and so fascism cannot brook criticism or the kind of self-reflection emblematic of formal operational thinkers. So that level of cognitive development and all the quadrants associated with it, including free and open democratic elections, are unacceptable. So, too, would be all levels above that, because they transcend but include formal operational thinking. So although there might be integration across the quadrants—that is, the integration of individuals into the collectivity so that the agent is inseparable from the group and vice versa—there cannot be vertical integration or the integration of higher levels of development. Any integration will be stunted.

Wilpert is right to suggest that this inclusion, or embrace, is a way to discriminate among ideologies. It is more than simply showing that some ideologies are limited in their view. This also shows that some are pernicious in that their elimination of levels of development is pathological.

Emile: Wilpert goes so far as to say that we can have "a politics that makes reference to this highest level of soul and spiritual truths/contexts."

Pinzak: That's not surprising, given that we ourselves have been talking about the potential of mystical experience for cosmopolitan identity.

Emile: He seems to be going beyond that. He says, "The practice of Integral Politics requires a spiritual orientation because it is a vision that lies beyond ordinary rationality."

Pinzak: *Requires* a spiritual orientation? One cannot espouse Integral Politics and be an atheist? One *must* be spiritual?

Emile: How could you embrace all of the developmental levels but eschew, or deny, spirituality?

Pinzak: Because politics might "stop" at a certain level. That is not to say that politics is inappropriate for a spiritual person. I'm not suggesting that. I'm saying instead that spirituality might not be required of politics. Indeed, the highest levels of spirituality are, I think, extraneous to institutions of politics, especially democratic politics. Your identity with all human beings, your one-ness with the universe, informs how you behave in and view the world, but democratic politics requires interaction with others, not Spirit dictating *to* others.

Emile: The most highly evolved spiritual persons cannot bring spirituality into politics?

Pinzak: I'm not saying that either. As citizens of their countries or citizens of the world, they are entitled to political participation in Integral Politics. The knowledge they gain through the highest spiritual realms may inform their ideas and ideals, which they can share. But the danger is that this knowledge, different from most peoples', will be construed as somehow more important than the knowledge gained through levels of rationality, empathy, and imagination. Reasoned discussion or dialogue is the heart and soul of democratic politics. Revelation, while important for helping people understand the nature of Reality or Being, is not an appropriate basis for politics. By thinking it is, we drift into crowning philosopher-kings with their "superior" insight to make decisions for us. We thereby lose the human capacity to reason together, to deliberate, to make collective decisions that affect us all.

Emile: So Plato was wrong? Would we not be better off having elites with special knowledge who know what is best for us?

Pinzak: First, Plato wasn't wrong, because I think that most of his positions on politics are metaphorical, even satirical. But if one insists that in *The Republic* Plato is advocating authoritarian rule by those Guardians who have become, because they have seen, the Good, then, yes, Plato was wrong. In that regard one ought to keep in mind Kant's comment that political power invariably corrupts reasonable judgment.[24]

To introduce spirituality as an essential aspect of Integral Politics is to fail, I think, to accept the nature of politics as collective decision-making. It is one thing for those who are enlightened—like Plato's "philosopher kings"—to see the ultimate Good for all. But then to impose conditions on people because those people lack the same insight is to denigrate persons and to deny them the experiences they need to grow, to realize the very Good that is the highest level. What is needed, instead, is the creation of democratic processes in which persons can function at their own level but that simultaneously frustrate them to spur them to grow or develop.

Second, an elite with special knowledge does not know what's best for us politically, because political decisions are best made by those people who will live with their effects. We legitimize those decisions by participating, actually or virtually, in them. A mystic may know about Absolute Being, but that doesn't mean that his experiences enable him to understand how to build bridges.

Emile *(sipping his coffee):* Certainly no bridge that I want to cross . . .

Pinzak *(smiling):* Right. As Aristotle pointed out, the kind of knowledge or judgment we need for politics is rationally based and practical, which, again, is Kant's point.[25] You don't need mystical states for that.

Emile: To show others genuine mutual respect, especially when their views are antithetical to your own, requires not just tolerance but also a willingness to embrace difference; indeed, even an appreciation of difference. Mutual respect also requires an ability to search through difference for commonality. This is part and parcel of a cosmopolitan identity, which can be educed through dialectical thinking and mysticism.

Pinzak: That is an important combination, but not necessarily essential.

Emile: You anticipate my conclusion: I agree with you that one can participate in Integral Democracy without necessarily having experienced higher states of consciousness. One can have a cosmopolitan identity without such experiences. But if we want the best chance of educing such an identity, then the combination seems our surest path.

Pinzak: Agreed. Mystical experience is important for helping expand peoples' identities or, in Mill's terms, their moral and mental horizons. In democratic deliberations, however, people have to translate those new horizons, those new insights, into positions that they can explain to and defend before others. If cosmopolitanism is a featured part of Integral Politics, if it really is simply another term for "Integral Politics" itself, then "a spiritual orientation" is not, as Wilpert states, required.

Emile: What Wilpert means by that is "an openness toward the nonordinary . . . toward the suprarational."

Pinzak: Okay, that's pretty innocuous. But I don't think a practitioner even needs that, unless Wilpert means simply that one ought to maintain an open mind. Even this is tricky, because how do persons, in the face of repugnant ideas, maintain an open mind . . . about those ideas and about their own? Does he talk about that?

Emile: No, but Wilpert does continue: "Integral Politics does not merely 'add' spirituality to politics. Instead, it finds a place for spirituality in politics and a place for politics in spirituality."

Pinzak: I don't even know what that means. It sounds facile. Do we have a bit of Jabberwocky as chiasmus here?

Democratic institutions can surely demand that participants follow procedures that are built on and that reflect dialectical thinking. We've already established that such thinking is a higher level and therefore a better way of thinking. But no such institution can demand that participants practice some sort of meditation or undergo mystical experiences. This is a category error.

Emile: What about the outcomes of such democratic deliberations? Would not elites, those who possess dialectical abilities, make better decisions for us than ordinary citizens who are struggling to participate in dialectical, deliberative procedures?

Pinzak: One of Madison's arguments in the *Federalist Papers* for adopting the United States Constitution was that only men of "fit character" would be elected to the newly created national offices. Well, it turned out that those men of fit character were driven by exactly the same kind of self-interest as the "common Herd of mankind," as John Adams called the *profanum vulgus,* the common or ordinary people.[26]

Emile: George Washington himself called ordinary farmers "the grazing multitude."[27] I do not think that he was being complimentary. So is your point that we would be hard pressed to find dialectical thinkers who also evince the proper cosmopolitan character?

Pinzak: The whole purpose of moving toward cosmopolitan identity is to help *all* people develop to a point where we can address and find just outcomes for the local, regional, national, and global problems that confront us. From the perspective of Integral Politics, cosmopolitan identity is the recognition that development toward worldcentric or planetary consciousness heralds greater health for the individual as well as the collectivity. Because each successive level integrates the qualities of the levels that precede it, then the cosmopolitan identity integrates concern for family, clan or tribe, community, and nation. The individual can incorporate all of these as he embraces the world. Part of the developmental path is having people participate and grow from their current levels to higher levels, while carrying forward these various concerns. Politics is an arena for such participation, perhaps the arena *par excellence.* To deny persons democratic participation because certain elites might think more dialectically is to condemn persons to truncated development.

Emile: Their development would not be truncated. They would not be denied further development. But it would mean that until they are ready, they would not participate in political decisions at certain levels. So this might delay their development, but it would not truncate it.

Pinzak: If by "certain levels" you mean that not all political decisions lend themselves to mass democratic participation, then I agree. We elect representatives to make important decisions when immediate action must be taken or when the complexity of an issue requires attention that most citizens cannot afford. Can you imagine if we had to pass military procurement bills every year through each state, let alone bodies of deliberating citizens? There is clearly a need for political leaders and leadership, and it would be best if those leaders were dialectical thinkers, or at least operated through procedures based on dialectical thinking, and had a cosmopolitan outlook so that they could understand circumstances from the highest to the lowest perspectives. However, in a democratic system can we require that those running for office, or those appointed to office, must be dialectical thinkers? How would someone demonstrate dialectical thinking? Would he or she need to take a test? If so, who would create, administer, and score such a test? And what offices would require such a test—local or state or national or global? What we can insist on is that *any* democratic procedure ought to be based on dialectical thinking.

Emile: Are you not generating the same problems? Who will create those procedures?

Pinzak: Well, we shall, you and I . . . in these discussions. *(Both laugh.)* We can devise procedures as best we can that reflect and encourage dialectical thinking. What we won't do is grade how dialectically someone is thinking.

In fact, all persons who are eligible to participate in the proceedings, however eligibility is determined or established, ought to be able to do so. It is the timing of the decision or the time required for the decision that dictates whether citizens can participate, not the level of development of the citizens or participants themselves. It is certainly not the requirement of attaining certain levels of cognitive operations that determines when and how they can participate. It seems to me that democratic procedures based on dialectical thinking can be a method for moving participants, whatever their levels of development, toward cosmopolitan identity.

Emile: You have reminded me of a quotation from Reinhold Niebuhr, the Protestant theologian. He wrote in *The Children of Light and the Children of Darkness,* "Man's capacity for justice makes democracy possible, but man's inclination to injustice makes democracy necessary."[28] It is democracy and not the Archons of virtue that will save us from injustice.

Pinzak: And here Niebuhr is echoing Aristotle who argued that it is the diners and not the chef who are the best judges of the meal. Those who must live with or under laws and policies—that is, those who have to "eat it"—are the ones who should decide those laws and policies.

Emile: So everyone has a say or can have a say? *Quod omnes tangit ab omnibus tractari et approbari debet*—the legal maxim from the private law of the Romans: "What touches all must be discussed and approved by all." By the beginning of the fourteenth century, kings all over Europe were summoning representative assemblies of their noblemen, clergy, and townsmen on the basis of *Quod omnes tangit:* "What touches all must be approved by all." This became part of the theoretical basis for parliament and for participatory democracy.

Pinzak: Perhaps the best statement describing Integral Politics is Marx and Engels's wish for communism from the *Communist Manifesto*—that the free development of each is the condition for the free development of all.[29] How do we attain that? We do so by setting development in a context of democratic dialogue in which what touches all must be discussed and approved by all. That is Integral Politics.

Emile: It is interesting that Wilpert sees the need in Integral Politics for cosmopolitanism. He wants to see an "expansion of human sympathy to cover the globe," but he never suggests how that might be done. Integral Democracy, —how I think of Integral Politics—requires participants to think dialectically, which may be one way to do so. Here participants must take up and seriously consider the perspectives of others. Participants must not only understand those different perspectives, but they must also seek commonalities among or underneath them as they seek to resolve or embrace or transcend differences. Wilpert recognizes this, since he calls for the democratization of power at all levels, from global to local.

Pinzak: Does he say what such democratization will look like in practice? *(Emile shakes his head.)* Then we can conclude, along with Kant, that this might work in theory but not in practice.

Emile: To conclude today's discussion, Pinzak, we agree that in Integral Politics we need to address and act to change both consciousness and, simultaneously, social conditions. With reference to Wilber's AQAL model, the individual quadrants interact with the collective; the interior quadrants, with the exterior ones. They interlock, as Wilber says, "in a rich network of values, degrees of consciousness, and qualitative distinctions" that are not exclusively physical or mental, empirical or ideational (428).

Common sense tells us that humans are individuals in need of sociality, that humans are born into families, communities, neighborhoods, villages. They are not born alone and independent. So humans are both individuals and social creatures. We need an ideology that does not just recognize, and thus build on, individuality and sociality or agency and community, because they all do. We need as well an ideology that integrates the quadrants.

Pinzak: Wilber's model lays out graphically, in both senses of the term, that, as Hegel wrote, humans can develop a sense of themselves only through sociality, and humans can learn to use and follow reasons only in the context of a language community.

Emile: How, for example, can laborers, assembly-line workers, or telemarketers develop a sense of themselves and find satisfaction and growth in their jobs? In what kinds of communities do workers live? Do those communities, and those workplaces, honor both individuality and collective change?

Pinzak: People need to be able to make self-reflective choices about how they want and need to live their lives. They want to live their lives from the inside out, but they also need to recognize the importance of the social, political, and economic contexts in which such choices are made. We can call this "autonomy in community," and it is a summary statement of Integral Politics.

Emile: Of course, one cannot argue cogently that what you have just described is a kind of neutrality. Choosing a good life is itself a value and a central value at that. It means that we need a society that is pluralistic to make choices among conceptions of the good life. We might go so far as to say, in honor of autonomy, that persons should not only be prepared and permitted to make such choices; but they should also be required to make such choices. Having and making such choices make the human being a certain kind of creature; that is, a meaning-seeking or meaning-making person.

That kind of person is a Kantian idea, one that presupposes a level of development that enables us to be able to hold and follow a conception of the good. Those who think that conceptions of the good are preordained by God or given by community will struggle with this view of politics. We cannot presuppose that level without missing the vital needs required of humans at the levels below the rational Kantian person. This is elucidated in and by the AQAL model.

Pinzak: People must be respected, regardless of their level of development. To presuppose a level of autonomy, without arguing for autonomy, would be like falling asleep on an elevator and waking on the eighth floor. We don't think about how we got there, what happened that enabled us, some of us, to get to the eighth floor. We just walk off and assume that this is what life is and where thinking about it begins.

Emile: So, first, an Integral Politics must pertain to persons at all levels of the developmental hierarchy and must relate to all quadrants in the model. Second, an Integral Politics must involve dialectical thinking—what we can refer to as democratic or deliberative dialogue—among as many perspectives as possible, however odious some of those perspectives may be.

Pinzak: Integral Politics, then, sounds more like an approach than a content.

Emile: Yes, but it must offer content as well. An Integral Politics is an approach or a process that generates political content. Part of what is integrated is not simply multiple perspectives through dialectical thinking, but also the levels and lines of development themselves. As we have commented, not everyone is going to be practicing Integral Politics from the level of dialectical thinking. Yet everyone is going to practice Integral Politics by participating in the process. Those at earlier levels of thinking will simply do the best they can.

Pinzak: Is every person in a country equally eligible to participate? If we go global with Integral Democracy, is every person in the world equally eligible to participate? On the face of it, that sounds unrealistic, if not disastrous.

Emile: Let us wait until we get into a discussion of Integral Political institutions before we address that topic.

Pinzak *(He closes his laptop, stands up, and stretches.):* I'll tell you, Emile, Integral Politics hangs on something that makes it significantly different from any other kind of politics, though I'm not suggesting that if you run most ideologies out to their near-teleological conclusions that you won't find something similar. Integral Politics rests on dialectical thinking and institutions that reflect and engender its use. You can already see in this the importance of the internal—the thinking and character of the individual participants—and the external or the institutionalization of the dialectical practice.

Emile: To establish that thinking and those institutions, I think you will agree, requires dialogue and deliberation. That involves individual participants in groups making collective decisions.

Pinzak: "Agents" and "communities."

Emile *(He stands and extends his hand to Pinzak.):* I have been thinking of this as "Integral Democracy." So, we are back to where we began or thought we were beginning—political institutions. Let us explore that next time.

Both men shake hands. Pinzak says, "Emile, did you ever have that mystical experience again?"

Looking up at Pinzak, Emile replies, "Well, I have never been back to Chartres, so I suppose not." Then he smiles, and the smile spreads across his face. Emile begins to laugh loudly as he turns and walks away. Pinzak watches him walk down the street. Emile is still laughing as Pinzak himself smiles and laughs, though he is not quite sure why.

Notes

1. For a discussion of this combination or integration from the emotional side, see Daniel Goleman, *Emotional Intelligence* (New York: Bantam Books, 1995). Goleman concludes: "In a very real sense we have two minds, one that thinks and one that feels. These two fundamentally different ways of knowing interact to construct our mental life. . . . These two minds, the emotional and the rational, operate in tight harmony *for the most part,* intertwining their very different ways of knowing to guide us through the world" (1995, 8-9, emphasis added). So, although these two minds are often in balance and "exquisitely coordinated" (Idem), they are "semi-independent" and thus their development and harmony or integration are not a foregone conclusion.

2. *Sublation* first appears in English in 1839 as a translation of the German *Aufhebung.* See the *Compact Edition of the Oxford English Dictionary,* 3122.

3. In *De Anima* Aristotle outlined a notion of a "higher grade." A grade or level is considered higher because it possesses the essentials of the lower, but not the incidentals of the lower, and adds essential and differentiating characteristics of its own that are not found in the lower.

4. See Hegel, *Phenomenology of Spirit,* trans. A. V. Miller (New York: Oxford University Press, 1979), "Self Consciousness," paragraphs 15-22 and 188.

5. All quotations in parentheses unless otherwise specified, are from *Sex, Ecology, Spirituality* (2000a).

6. Thus one should not be shocked by two of Wilber's titles: *A Brief History of Everything* and *A Theory of Everything.*

7. This is not to say that they have only four distinctions or dimensions; it is to say that they have *at least* four.

8. Wilber uses "social" both in a narrow and in a general way. The narrow way is used to describe the Lower-Right quadrant, since much of sociology examines the empirical world; the general sense refers to LR and LL quadrants as social, to distinguish them

from the individual or upper quadrants. Also, I refer to the LL quadrant as that of shared worldviews, which in Wilber's terms are "shared interior meanings" (131).

9. See Shannon Wheatley, "Everyday Cosmopolitical Practices in Contested Spaces: Moving Beyond the State of Cosmopolitanism," Ph.D. diss., Arizona State University, 2010.

10. See the Sixth and Seventh Encounters for discussion of such institutionalization.

11. The unity expressed here is with all sentient beings, including animals. Thus in the discussion that follows about compassion and treatment, this unity, though not stated, should be held in mind. See also Wilber 2002, 143-47.

12. One of Marx's claims, however, was that politics would end because conflict would end, and with no conflict and no politics, the state would "wither away." Nevertheless, government, something like the workers' democracy Marx saw in the Paris Commune of 1870, would remain to put into effect those collective decisions that the legislative-executive body (There would be no need for a liberal democratic separation of powers when the governing body is truly representative and responsive.) would make— e.g., where to put a new hospital, whether to build a new bridge, and the like.

13. Greg Wilpert, "Integral Politics: A Spiritual Third Way," *Tikkun* 17, no. 4 (2001): 44-49. Citations in my text refer to Wilpert's essay as it appears on the website http://www.Integralworld.com (accessed June, 2009).

14. See Crittenden, especially "Participation as Cultivation of Character," (1992), 97-100.

15. John Stuart Mill, *Utilitarianism, On Liberty, and Considerations on Representative Government* (London: Dent, 1972), especially Chapter 3: "Of the Ultimate Sanction of the Principle of Utility."

16. Karl Marx and Frederick Engels, *The German Ideology* (New York: Oxford University Press, 1977), 161.

17. Certainly at earlier stages in history, we can see that changes in technology contributed significantly to changes in identity. A case in point is the change from traditional or tribal identity to national identity. The creation of mechanical printing generated pools of information to be shared among people who were territorially apart. This development undercut the reliance on oral culture and enabled people living miles apart to find common elements that held them together. Thus, national identity was spawned in part through the mechanization of information and communication technologies. See Benedict Anderson, *Imagined Communities* (London: Verso, 1991).

18. Marx presented in his critique of capitalism what might be called a view of "capitalist consciousness." Marx thought that capitalism or our "capitalist consciousness" contained only two salient features: selfishness and indifference. Persons, according to Marx, pursue private interests with little if any regard for the interests, positions, or attitudes of others. They are willing to, and do, sacrifice the interests of others, if not the others themselves, for the sake of their own interests. Under capitalism, relationships are purely instrumental in that others are the means to one's own selfish ends. As Marx himself said in reference to Benthamite utilitarianism, the philosophy *par excellence,* in his view, of capitalism: "The only force bringing [people] together, and putting them in relation with each other, is the selfishness, the gain and the private interest of each. Each pays heed to himself only, and no one worries about the others." See Karl Marx, *Capital,* Vol. 1 (New York: Penguin, 1976), 280.

Of course, Marx thought that humans were by nature social and had been corrupted by capitalism. It was inconceivable to him, as it is to any reasonable person today, to think that humans could develop into individuals without society, relationships, and community. Even creativity, which Marx applauds as part of our "species being," is done within a social or communal context. One cannot become an artist except through social relationships; one cannot be an artist, however original or rebellious, without a social context against which to measure what the artist does. Furthermore, Marx did not suggest that individual interests would disappear or wither away, or that people would become altruistic, willing to sacrifice their own interests for the sake of the community and of others. Rather he thought that differences would remain but could be addressed and even resolved by persons meeting with mutual respect. When each person recognizes himself to be both an individual and a social being, a person always in relationships, then he would be willing to try settling disagreements without coercion and in a way that is just and fair.

19. See Karl Marx and Frederick Engels, "Critique of the Gotha Programme," in *Selected Works* (New York: Oxford University Press, 1975), 564-570.

20. Karl Marx, *A Contribution to the Critique of Political Economy* (New York: International Publishers, 1970), 161.

21. Karl Marx and Frederick Engels, "Theses on Feuerbach," as edited by Engels, in *Collected Works Volume Five* (New York: International Publishers, 1975), 7.

22. This "schematic" corresponds to Wilber's own outline of the process of cultural transformation: "[T]he overall movement . . . is from the Upper-Left of individual cognitive potential to the Lower-Left collective worldview, at first marginalized, but finally embedded in Lower-Right social institutions, at which point these basic institutions automatically help reproduce the worldview (LL) and socialize the individual (UL and UR) in succeeding generations, acting as 'pacers of transformation'—a transformation first started or begun in a moment of individual creative emergence and transcendence" (2000a, fn. 43, 607-08).

23. See the online version of "Integral Politics: A Summary of Essential Ingredients," 2007, 55.

24. Immanuel Kant, *Kant's Political Writings,* ed. Hans Reiss (Cambridge: Cambridge University Press, 1970) 115. Kant's entire quotation reads: "It is not to be expected that kings will philosophise or that philosophers will become kings; nor is it to be desired, however, since the possession of power inevitably corrupts the free judgement of reason." What democratic republican societies ought to do is to assure that the class of philosophers can speak publicly so as to share their insights. If philosophers remain philosophers and are not tempted into politics, then we can be certain, comments Kant, that they cannot be accused of propagandizing since philosophers are "by nature incapable of forming seditious factions or clubs."

25. This is what Aristotle called *phronesis* or practical judgment. See *The Nichomachean Ethics,* trans. David Ross, revised by J.L. Ackrill and J. O. Urmson (New York: Oxford University Press, 1998). For more discussion of its importance in democratic politics, see the Fifth Encounter.

26. For more on the composition and interests of the first Congress, see Gordon Wood, "Interests and Disinterestedness in the Making of the Constitution," in *Beyond Confederation,* ed. Richard Beeman, Stephen Botein, and Edward D. Carter II. (Chapel Hill, N.C.: University of North Carolina Press, 1987), 69-109; and Gordon Wood, "Knowledge, Power, and the First Congress," in *Knowledge, Power, and Congress,* ed. William H. Robinson and Clay H. Wellborn (Washington, D.C.: Congressional Quarter-

ly, Inc., 1987), 44-65. See also Jack N. Rakove, "The Structure of Politics at the Accession of George Washington," in *Beyond Confederation,* 261-94.

27. See Crittenden 2002: 14-20.

28. Reinhold Niebuhr, *The Children of Light and the Children of Darkness* (New York: Charles Scribner's Sons, 1960), xiii.

29. Similar ideas can be found in the history of Western political thought, though not stated as succinctly as Marx and Engels did. See, for example, Kant's essay "Idea for a Universal History with a Cosmopolitan Purpose" in which he argues that humankind's highest achievement is to create "a civil society which can administer justice universally." This requires that persons enter into states that will, by necessity, bind and discipline their freedom. Each person needs a just *"master* to break his self-will and force him to obey a universally valid will under which everyone can be free" (*Kant's Political Writings,* 1970, 46; emphasis in the original). Finding a just master is, as Kant suggests, "the hardest task of all" (46); nevertheless, history points toward a cosmopolitan constitution "within which all natural capacities of mankind can be developed completely" (50).

Fifth Encounter:

Integral Epistemology

All mankind is of one author, and is one volume . . . any man's death
diminishes me, because I am involved in mankind.
—John Donne, "Meditation 27"

Pinzak arrived at Pamplona a little past three o'clock. Emile was already waiting for him at the table, sipping coffee and casually looking about at the other patrons. A cup of cappuccino with a saucer on top marked Pinzak's place across from Emile. As he unpacked his laptop, Pinzak said, "Good afternoon, Emile." To this Emile replied, "And to you, Pinzak."

Pinzak said with a smile, "Emile, I realized last night when looking over my notes on the laptop that I'm going to have to spend a fair amount of time running down all those quotations you've given me."

As Pinzak finished this sentence, Emile pulled from the interior breast pocket of his camel hair overcoat several sheets of paper. "This should make your life easier. I have written down the citations for the quotations I have given you . . . at least the ones that I can remember." He handed the sheets to Pinzak and then placed both of his hands on his walking stick.

Pinzak took the sheets and looked them over. "Well, you've certainly remembered a lot of them."

"If you find any that I may have overlooked, just mention them to me in passing, and I shall give you the citations."

"Emile, I'm grateful that you spent the time doing this for me."

"Nonsense, Pinzak," replied Emile. "It gave me a chance to use my pen." Both men reached for their coffee. Each gave a small smile and a salute with their raised cups.

"Have you ever written anything, Emile, articles or books or pamphlets?"

"Not really," Emile replied. "On occasion I have tried my hand at something expository, but it was never very good. I also found that it interfered with my memorization. I do not know why, but I struggled to recall information when I was writing. I did not have the command. There was no natural, effortless flow."

"That's what Plato said makes writing a curse and not a benefit," responded Pinzak.

"Why is that, exactly?" queried Emile.

"Well, according to Plato, writing plants forgetfulness in men's souls. When we write, we stop exercising our memories because we rely on what we've written down. We know that it will not fade or go anywhere, that it is permanent."

"It is the section in the *Phaedrus* where Socrates tells the story of the Egyptian King Thamus talking to the god Theuth," commented Emile.

"See, you remembered." Pinzak smiled. "Rousseau wrote in the *Confessions* that something similar happened to him whenever he wrote something down. From that moment forward he ceased to remember it entirely." Then, after a brief pause, Pinzak asked, "What about creative writing? What about fiction?"

"I did not have the patience or imagination for it, and thus quickly lost the interest."

Pinzak sipped his coffee. Emile stared straight ahead, smiling. Pinzak waited to see whether Emile would continue. "Once I had a writing task of sorts," Emile said. Emile paused here and looked at his coffee. "Well, I think you could call it writing." Now Pinzak knew that Emile was being intentionally vague as a way of piquing Pinzak's curiosity. Pinzak wanted to remain nonchalant, but his interest was piqued, and he could not restrain himself. "Well, what happened?"

"One July I was driving President Bok and his wife . . ."

Pinzak interrupted, "Sissela Bok, the philosopher. I know her work on secrecy."

Emile continued, "I was driving them to a special, exclusive conference held in Gordes, in France. Gordes is a small mountain community in Provence. An ultra-rich French entrepreneur, philanthropist, and educational innovator, Jean-Louis Cosnard de Closet, bought and totally renovated the old castle there. He was holding a lavish conference for sixteen university presidents from around the world to discuss the future of higher education. Cosnard had decided that he would give gifts of $50 million to four of them, after he had met with and heard presentations from all sixteen presidents or chancellors.

I dropped off the Boks at the castle, which sits atop the mountain overlooking the hills of Luberon. They would remain there for three days and would be, by the look of things, cosseted and well entertained.

I headed back down the mountain and through the valley on my way up to Fontaine de Vaucluse and then over to Avignon. I had four days of sights to see. I had noticed storm clouds earlier, and now, as I drove a short distance outside of Gordes, the clouds looked black, strenuous, and minatory. It was only about seven in the evening, but it looked as dark as midnight. Suddenly began a torrential downpour. I had no visibility, even with the wipers going at full speed. I crept slowly along the road, peering through the windshield. I could see nothing but sheets of rain. I had to get off the road, so I pulled off onto a small road or driveway on my right.

A figure suddenly appeared, banging frantically on the passenger-side window. I was startled, but only for a moment. I unlocked the door, thinking that this person wanted to say something to me, and the figure jumped in. It was a man of about forty, dressed in a white cowl with what looked like a black apron over it. He was dripping wet. "Thank you," he said. "You are welcome," I replied with no hesitation but with little idea of what was happening. His English was excellent, but a very slight accent told me that it was not his first language. "Are you going to the Abbey?" he asked. I looked blankly at him. I knew about the Abbey of Senanque, also known as Notre-Dame de Senanque, because of my research for the trip, but I had no idea where it was or of visiting it, especially now. I replied, "No. I just turned off the road to wait out the storm." The monk—for what else could he have been—turned his head away from me and looked out the windshield. "There is no waiting out this storm. This will continue all night. We are famous here for such storms."

"I have to get to Avignon," I said.

"Well," he answered calmly, "not tonight." Now it was my turn to look out the windshield. He continued, "We shall be happy to put you up for the night. We are famous for that around here." At this comment we both smiled.

We drove in silence the short distance to the Abbey. I do not know whether the silence was induced by our concern about the heavy rain or the monk's preference for silence or both, but neither of us said a word. The monk pointed to a place where I could park, and both of us dashed for the door. Inside the monk led me down two or three corridors to a row of rooms with small doors. He opened one and waved his arm in a gesture of letting me inside. "You may stay here tonight. There is a bathroom down the hall on your left. If you wish, dry off a bit and follow this corridor to the left, past the bathroom, as far as it goes. There is a refectory at the end. You may have some dinner there."

I thanked the monk, turned to survey the room, and he was gone. I peered out of the door and both ways down the corridor; no sign of him. I returned to my survey. The room had a small window now closed and shuttered. The bed, with two pillows, sheets, and two blankets neatly folded at its foot, was under the window. Next to the bed was a small table. On it were a lamp and a Bible. A single crucifix decorated the walls. Only the light from the hallway lit the room, so I went over to the table and turned on a lamp. I sat for a moment on the bed. It felt surprisingly comfortable. The room was silent; I could barely hear the rain.

After visiting the bathroom I went to the refectory. There was no one there. On a massive wooden table, surrounded by maybe twenty chairs, was a place set for one. Laid out was a wonderful-looking meal, lit only by two candles, beautifully presented though the food was simple—a loaf of coarse bread, a bowl of broth of some kind, and a large salad bowl full of greens and teeming with vegetables. On top of the bread was a small sign that read 'for our guest.' I sat down and waited. For some reason I thought that someone else might come in. The room was completely silent, no footfalls, no sounds of movement or cleaning or washing. No sounds at all. I ate in silence, as was meant to be.

When I had all that I wanted, and I ate quite a lot, I took the bowl and plates into the kitchen. Again, no one was there. So I went to the sink, turned on the water, found some soap, and began washing the dishes. I recall thinking that I had not heard any sounds at all—not of monks and not even of the storm. Perhaps lost in these thoughts, I did not notice or hear my passenger-monk approach. But suddenly he was beside my right arm. "Please leave those," he said gently.

Startled, I replied, "Hello." I continued washing. "I do not mind doing them."

"You are our guest. We would prefer it if you did not do them."

"Fine," I answered. I stopped washing. I looked for a hand-towel. The monk opened a drawer, removed one, and handed it to me.

"Thank you."

The monk smiled. "Pas de quoi," he replied.

I dried my hands and turned to look for a place to put or hang the towel. I could see no suitable place. When I turned back, the monk was gone, as silently as he had come. I folded the towel and laid it by the sink. I headed back to my room.

I slept well in the total silence of the monastery. Again, I heard no sounds, not even the sounds of the rain. In the morning, after a brief washing up, I returned to the refectory. Once again, the table was laden with food—granola, milk, toast, honey (for which the Abbey is famous), and what looked like flax butter. Someone had placed the same tiny sign on one of the plates. No one was in or about the room. And I heard nothing but my own crunching.

After eating I walked about to the cloister, which is the heart of the Abbey. Four covered corridors with twelve arches each bordered the courtyard and gardens. While I was admiring the beauty of the architecture's simple lines, my passenger-monk approached me. "Our Abbot would like to see you in the calefactory." Historically, the calefactory was the only room in a monastery that had heat, which was required because the monks copied manuscripts there and needed to keep their hands warm for that task.

I followed the monk to the calefactory. He opened the door for me and let me pass into the room. He closed the door behind me. Inside this large room were two men sitting near the fireplace in two large chairs facing each other. There was a small fire burning, but the size of the conical chimney indicated that much larger, indeed massive, fires could be built inside it. Both men rose as I walked toward them.

They looked to be about the same age, early seventies possibly. Both were dressed in the white cowls with black aprons, which were the traditional dress of the Cistercian monks: a white habit and long black smock called a scapular cinched with a leather belt. Both smiled as I approached. "Hello, Traveler. I am

Father Romano, the Abbot here at Senanque. We are a Cistercian community, based on the rules of Saint Benedict. This Abbey belongs to the Cistercian Community of the Immaculate Conception. We have been here for over eight hundred fifty years. We would like to remain another eight hundred fifty . . . or more." He paused, looking at, almost studying, me. He then turned his hand, palm up, toward the other man.

"This is Dom Bernardo, the Abbot of Citeaux." I raised my eyebrows at that introduction. The Cistercian order began in the twelfth century at the monastery at Citeaux, which is the dominant monastery in the order. *Cistercium* is Latin for *Citeaux.* I was truly honored at having been invited to meet both men.

"Thank you, Father Romano, for your hospitality last night and this morning. I am truly grateful." Father Romano smiled at me and then at Dom Bernardo.

"Traveler," Father Romano said, "I might need to test how grateful you are. Please sit down." He indicated a small chair a few feet from their two chairs. I sat down. Father Romano said, "No, please, pull your chair near ours." As I did so, Father Romano and Dom Bernardo sat down. Then Father Romano said, "We need a favor from you. We need someone to transcribe a conversation between the two of us. Because of the nature of the topics that we shall discuss, we cannot have a monk perform that task. The task must be completed in the next three days, for reasons that I cannot go into with you. We have both prayed for guidance on this matter, and, then, last night, you arrived."

Dom Bernardo said, "It is Providential."

"Are you asking me to transcribe your conversation?" Both men nodded. "But you know nothing about me. You do not know who I am, where I am from, what I have done in my life, what I do. You are talking about subjects not suitable for monks, but somehow they are suitable for me? How can you entrust such a conversation to a stranger?"

"We live away from modern life. But that does not mean that we do not know people," Dom Bernardo said. "That does not mean that we do not know how to read hearts."

"But I cannot take dictation. I do not know shorthand. I cannot transcribe your words with speed and accuracy," I stammered.

Father Romano laughed. "Who said anything about speed?" Now both men laughed. I looked from one to the other. "We do need you to be accurate," Father Romano said, "but we do not care about speed."

"Do you have three days to devote to this task?" asked Dom Bernardo.

"Wait," I said, "you cannot possibly be serious. I have no training. You do not know me. You cannot really believe that I can, or should, do this job."

"Now you are simply repeating yourself," said Father Romano.

"We have already covered those arguments," commented Dom Bernardo. "Do you have three days to devote to this task?"

I was not expected to pick up the Boks for another three days, so I did have the time. "Yes, but . . ."

"And are you willing to undertake this task for us?" asked Father Romano.
"Of course, but . . ."

"Now you are repeating yourself again," said Dom Bernardo, and both men laughed.

I did not laugh; I felt ill. What on Earth was going on here?

Dom Bernardo then said, "You will be doing us, and posterity, a great service. We are fully appreciative of your willingness to help us."

"I will do it, but what if I do not get every word down? What if I do not get every word down accurately?"

Both men smiled at me. "First," said Dom Bernardo, "we shall dictate in English because that is your language. It is not our native tongue, so we shall have to think carefully about what we are saying. That will slow us down considerably."

"Nor do we expect you to copy down every word," said Father Romano, picking up the conversation. "I am not sure that we want you to. There are some English phrases that we may use that are better rendered idiomatically. We do not know those idioms; those you can add for us."

"We are asking you only to do the best that you can," commented Dom Bernardo, placing his hand on my shoulder.

I nodded but said nothing.

"So, Traveler, shall we get started?" asked Dom Bernardo.

"Now?" I said with some alarm.

Both nodded again. Father Romano motioned to a table and asked me to take my chair to it. It was not far from where we had all been sitting. On the table were a lamp, an inkwell, a couple of nondescript pens, and an open book. The book was the size of an account ledger, but the pages had no lines on them. I sat in my chair, turned on the lamp, picked up a pen, dipped it into the inkwell, filled its bladder, and looked at the two conversants. Both men had been watching me. When I looked at them, they turned to each other and then began the conversation."

Pinzak said, "Well, Emile, what did they talk about?"

"I am sorry to say, Pinzak, that that is not your business. Not that I do not wish to tell you, but I do not think that it would be appropriate. There was a reason that they did not want their monks to hear the conversation, and I think I understood that after only a few minutes of talk."

"But I'm not a monk, Emile." Emile shrugged his shoulders. Pinzak knew that Emile was not going to say anything about the conversation. "Did the Abbots tell you not to talk about what was said?"

"No. They never said anything about that. They were completely true to their word. They wanted me to transcribe what they said, to fill in or to alter grammar and syntax where I thought it appropriate, and to ask for clarification or repetition now and then. And they went slowly enough that I had plenty of time to get down with great accuracy what they were saying. I tried not to think about what they were saying, so that I could concentrate only on the words themselves. And I never read over anything that I wrote. Whenever we took a break or I finished for the day, they would ask me to start with a fresh page each time. So I never read anything that I was taking down. I am confident that single sentences and maybe complete paragraphs were sound. But whether the conversation held together over hours, let alone days, I cannot say."

Pinzak said, as a question, "So, they never gave any advice or instructions about what to say or not to say?"

"No. They left that to my discretion. My discretion is to be silent. Besides, I could not give an accurate account of what they said, even immediately after completing my services. To say anything about that conversation without one hundred percent accuracy would be a disservice to them."

"Why did they want the conversation transcribed at all?"

"I do not know why, and I do not know what they did with the transcription. They never said anything on either topic."

After a few moments, Pinzak said, "Well, that's not really writing, Emile."

Emile smiled. "No, it is not. But I said that it was writing of a sort."

"And what did you tell the Boks?"

"They asked me how I had spent my few days. I told them that I had simply relaxed. That was true. Although I was concentrating heavily for three days, I found the experience relaxing, not taxing in any way. In fact, I felt totally relaxed and at peace when I left the monastery."

Pinzak and Emile sat for a few minutes in silence. Pinzak sensed that he wouldn't be hearing any more about this experience. Then he said, "Speaking of religion, Emile, and to return to the topic of our own conversation, I have to tell you that I'm not comfortable resting cosmopolitanism on some kind of mystical mumbo-jumbo."[1]

Emile *(smiling and sipping his coffee):* Well, as we said last meeting, mysticism is only part of the way, and maybe not the best way, to cosmopolitan identity. Dialectical thinking, the heart of that way, has strong evidence behind it. Mysticism might as well.

Pinzak: Mysticism has evidence behind it? Are you serious?

Emile *(continues smiling):* You should be skeptical, Pinzak, but skepticism, from the Greek *skeptikos,* means "inquiring and reflective." Skeptical is also open-minded.

Pinzak: I'm definitely skeptical, and I'll try to remain open-minded. But it seems that with mysticism we enter a realm of pure subjectivity, where one person's unbounded self is another person's psychotic episode.

Emile: Well, I am not sure that there is anything such as pure subjectivity, as if what one person experiences or feels or thinks is somehow unique. Be that as it may, hear me out before you infer, or assume, anything. There are two approaches that we ought to consider. The first approach consists of some scientific studies that are worth investigating. The second is an epistemological approach, and Ken Wilber has some important things to say about that.

Pinzak (*putting his elbows on the table, resting his chin in his hands, and staring straight at Emile*): I'm all ears, Emile.

Emile (*not smiling*): First, let us recall that our religious traditions are all based on somebody's spiritual or mystical experience.

Pinzak: You mean the founder's experience.

Emile: Usually, and every religion has some tradition of mysticism within it—for example, the Kabala of Judaism, Sufism in Islam, and the Prayer of the Heart in the Eastern Orthodox Christian Church. In the East these mystical aspects are the principal focus of the religions, so much so that we might describe Eastern religions as developmental psychologies. They examine systematically the realms of being and becoming that all humans are capable of experiencing, that all humans can grow into. These religious psychologies offer meditative techniques or practices to induce and stabilize those experiences.

Now, if we follow the AQAL model that we used last meeting, then we should expect evidence of these mystical or meditative experiences in the Upper-Left quadrant, the individual-interior or psychological quadrant, and some sort of correlates to those experiences in the Upper-Right quadrant . . .

Pinzak (*now typing and not looking up*): That's the individual-exterior or physiological quadrant.

Emile: That is correct. Western science has been looking at the psychological and physiological benefits of meditation for over thirty years.[2] Over the past few years, as scientists have begun investigating changes through meditation in brain structure and function, a new kind of science has emerged, which some are calling "the cognitive neuroscience of religion."[3] For example, Andrew Newberg at the University of Pennsylvania—the head of Penn's new Center for Spirituality and the Mind—has been using a brain-scanning machine on meditators to measure what happens in the brain during spiritual experiences and meditative practices.

Pinzak: You mean he is using an MRI scan? The subjects have to lie down and endure endless clanking and banging! What about claustrophobia? How can anyone meditate in that environment?

Emile: Actually, he uses single-photon-emission computed tomography, or HMPAO-SPECT imaging. He injects a radioactive tracer into the meditators as they are meditating. The active parts of the brain absorb the tracer. At that point the meditators enter the scanner, which can show where in the brain the tracer has settled.[4]

Pinzak: And what has he found? Little angels skipping through regions of the brain?

Emile: That is beneath you, Pinzak. Be open-minded and skeptical, but not cynical.

Pinzak (*with feigned exasperation*): Fine. What did he find?

Emile: Newberg's findings are preliminary, but he found that meditators' brains showed heightened activity in their frontal lobes, which relates to focused attention or increased concentration, and decreased activity toward the back of the brain, the area of space and time orientation. The findings are significant in at least one regard: Newberg concludes that spiritual experiences have "a biological correlate to them, so there is something that is physiologically happening."[5] This supports Wilber's idea in the AQAL model that there are physiological correlates to the psychological or interior experiences of persons. Religious or spiritual experiences should not be any different. Indeed, the increased activity in the frontal lobes and the concomitant decreased activity in the parietal lobes correlate with the meditators' saying that they experience unity with everything and everyone.[6]

Pinzak: So such spiritual or mystical experiences can now be explored scientifically.[7]

Emile: They can be studied, and, as I have said, they are being studied. In another study Mario Beauregard and his doctoral student Vincent Paquette used functional magnetic resonance imaging (fMRI) and quantitative electroencephalography (QEEG) to record the brain states of fifteen Carmelite nuns during their prayers.[8] Collectively, Beauregard writes, the fifteen nuns spent about 210,000 hours in prayer (2007, 263). Beauregard and Paquette found that mystical experience is not located solely in the temporal lobes, but involves many brain areas, including the inferior parietal lobule, the visual cortex, the caudate nucleus, and the left brain stem. Such regions of the brain are associated with perception, cognition, emotion, body representation, and self-consciousness. Finally, they found an "abundance of theta activity during the mystical condition" (275), the same kind of activity found in Zen Buddhist meditators and practitioners of Sahaja Yoga. This theta brain-wave activity demonstrates a marked shift in consciousness.

Additionally, Richard Davidson and his colleagues at the University of Wisconsin used both EEG and MRI scans to examine the brain functions of highly trained Tibetan Buddhist meditators. In a paper in 2004 they concluded that long-term meditation can lead to measurable improvement in attention. Their meditating subjects showed the highest level of synchronization among neurons ever reported for healthy humans—"the highest reported in the literature in a non-pathological context."[9] They also found high activity in the prefrontal cortex, which equates with feelings of happiness, compassion, and joy.

Pinzak: Shouldn't we take notice of the fact that the subjects in these studies were "highly trained" meditators, in one case, and nuns well practiced in their praying, in the other? Wouldn't it be better, if we are talking about the combination of meditation and dialectical thinking, to use casual meditators; you know, the kind that we find in the United States who meditate for thirty to forty minutes per day?

Emile: Extensive research has been done on just such meditators with the Transcendental Meditation movement that has been in this country since the ear-

ly 1970s.[10] Also, Sara Lazar and her co-authors looked at subjects who meditated six hours per week. They found that even among these "casual meditators,"
as you call them, there are some important findings. One is that these meditators,
in comparison with a control group, had thicker brain regions associated with attention and sensory processing. This cortical thickness was most pronounced in
the older meditators, which suggests that the cortical thinning associated with
aging may be reduced through meditation. Cortical thinning is implicated in the
slowing of emotional and cognitive processes.[11]

Pinzak: So we know that something physical or physiological is happening
to meditators, in addition to what they are experiencing psychologically. But
people in the religious traditions where you find these meditation techniques
don't usually undertake them simply to relax, feel better, and improve their
health. They are after, and claim to find, higher states of consciousness, mystical
awareness, a sense of oneness with the universe and all in it.[12] That's the connection you were making to dialectical thinking and cosmopolitan identity, and I
don't see that the connection can be made or that those claims can be verified by
"the cognitive neuroscience of religion."

Emile: You do not see it, nor should you expect to. Science can investigate
the physiological or even behavioral aspects of meditation. It cannot investigate
claims for which there is no empirical evidence. A neuroscientist can correlate a
meditator's claim of experiencing the oneness of all of life with certain brain
changes or activities in that meditator. Yet if that same neuroscientist looks at
pictures of changes and activities in the meditator's brain, she cannot predict
what that meditator is experiencing or has experienced. It is like knowing that
two persons are talking on the telephone—we see that the phones have been ac-
tivated and are working—but we have no idea what the persons are talking
about just by looking at the phone activity.

Pinzak: So of course we cannot predict from brain activity that persons are
having a mystical experience of God or that they are thinking dialectically.

Emile: No, we cannot. To ascertain that we would have to ask them. That is
precisely why I said at the outset of today's conversation that there is another
line of inquiry, the epistemological line, we must also examine.

Pinzak: Which we'll do now.

Emile *(taking a sip of coffee):* Precisely. Let us set mysticism in an overarching context of epistemological validation. That is, let us see whether we can
treat mysticism in the same way that we treat any prospective domain of knowledge.

Pinzak: And how do we do that?

Emile: We begin with a map of knowledge—what we can know and how
we come to know it—divided into what philosopher Charles Taylor *(Sources of
the Self,* 1989) calls three domains: religion, science, and culture.

Pinzak: What we referred to, following Wilber, as the subjective or "I"
realm, the objective or "it" realm, and the intersubjective or "we" realm *(Sex,
Ecology* 2000a).

Emile: Very good, Pinzak; you have done your homework.

Pinzak *(giving a slight and slow head nod):* But Taylor points out that each of these three domains is in tension with the other two (1989, 409).

Emile: That need not detain us.

Pinzak: Well, why not? Taylor is a philosopher of some renown.

Emile: Yes, he is. But the framework within which he was working is quite different from ours. For Taylor the history of human identity in the West has been a story of "interiorization." By that he means that modern humans show a turn inward for their moral sources, and that turn within has also been a turn away from moral sources that exist outside of themselves.

Pinzak: Sources such as religion.

Emile: Correct. For Taylor religion and the cosmic order are casualties of the turn within.

Pinzak: The source outside of ourselves that we moderns rely upon is not religion but science, and religion is incompatible with scientific empiricism.

Emile *(nods):* Therefore, Taylor claims, "Virtually nothing in the domain of mythology, metaphysics, or theology stands . . . as publicly available background today" (491).

Pinzak: That can't be. Today religion continues to be an important moral source for many people.

Emile: Taylor does not deny that. But as he sees it, religion is no longer a public background. It is only a personal background. So what he wants to see is the unification of the three domains—science, religion, and culture. Now Taylor does not tell us how to unite these domains, but he does provide a "hunch."[13] The source that Taylor thinks is strong enough to support our modern standards, and thus strong enough presumably to unite the three moral domains, is Judeo-Christian theism. Our greatest challenge, he supposes, is to retrieve a form of this theism divorced from its history of mutilation, savagery, and barbarism. Only in this way can we overcome the atrophy of spirit; overcome our preoccupation with the personal (and internal); and put into action, into life, "the promise of a divine affirmation of the human, more total than humans can ever attain unaided" (521).

Pinzak: The reason that Taylor's mission need not detain us, as you said, is that we are focusing on mysticism and thus do not have a problem with scientific empiricism.

Emile: Our position is not quite that straightforward, Pinzak. As we have already established, science can show us that there are physical or physiological correlates to what meditators report. But meditators are reporting their subjective experiences. As we said, scientists cannot tell us through their empirical studies what meditators are experiencing. Yet, we are not after the retrieval and reaffirmation of a belief system, as Taylor is. Instead, we are after a system of inducing experiences, mystical experiences, which can be replicated and validated in much the same way that any scientific experiment can be.

Pinzak (*scrolling through his computer files):* This reminds me of something Wilber wrote. Ah, here it is: Higher states of consciousness, mystical states, spiritual domains, are not hypotheses but conclusions "based on hundreds of years of experimental introspection and communal verification" *(Sex, Ecology,* 273). Is that what you're getting at?

Emile: It is. We no more want to unite Taylor's three domains of knowledge than we want to unite the four quadrants in the AQAL model. Each of the three domains—science, culture, and religion—corresponds to one aspect of our being, one aspect of our selves. Each domain is discrete, is real on its own terms, and pertains to an aspect of our human nature: body, mind, and soul or spirit. Each domain has associated with it a particular kind of knowledge, so that we can know these domains to be real and know what we find in them to be real. And while the methodologies for knowing each realm are different, the epistemological principles for all three domains are exactly the same.

Pinzak: Just to be clear, Emile, we're actually talking about mysticism and not religion, correct?

Emile: That is correct. We are not talking about the belief systems called religions, those with an emphasis on scriptural interpretation and a focus on institutions. We are talking about the experiential aspect of religion called mysticism. We shall also find, I believe, in this discussion about ways of knowing a reinforcement of the importance of dialogue for ascertaining moral and political "truths." This dialogue, democratic dialogue, is, as we have said, essential to cosmopolitan identity and Integral Politics.

Pinzak: Okay, so by focusing on the mystical or contemplative aspect of religion, we avoid the problem that Taylor identified.

Emile: . . . which is?

Pinzak: Taylor thinks that as we moderns moved inside, we eliminated moral sources that are outside. But Taylor's position, from the perspective of mysticism, confuses moving within for moving exclusively toward and within the personal. Instead, as Wilber shows in the upper-left quadrant, moving within can mean moving to the "interior," rather than the "internal." So what seems external is discovered, if not brought, within. In the cosmopolitan context, moving inside is not simply to discover what is peculiar to us, what is personal about us. It is also to discover that the interior we explore is the interior of everyone—not just what is personal about us but what is also common to and shared by all of us.

Emile: That is right.

Pinzak: Okay, but how do we know what is interior versus what is internal or personal?

Emile: "Inward goes the way full of mystery," as Novalis said. An answer to your question is the very topic of today's conversation, Pinzak. Patience, good sir.

Pinzak: Fair enough. So, I think that you and I agree with Taylor that all three realms are real and significant sources for our lives. If they are also, as you suggest, all sources of valid knowledge, then they are reflective of and therefore essential to understanding human nature and identity, especially cosmopolitan identity.

Emile: Correct. Each domain is discrete, but they are interrelated, even integrated, as we shall see. So let us begin with the domain of physical reality or "science." From there we shall move to the domain of morality or mind, which Taylor calls "culture," and, finally, we shall discuss the domain of soul or spirit. It is this last domain, understood as the realm of mysticism, that is really our target, since we need to see whether it is as a domain no less an experienced world of knowledge—that is, gnosis—than is science or morality. If it is, and this will be an answer to your question about interior versus internal, then mysticism, or its active component, meditation, can indeed be part of the foundation for the process of shifting identity toward cosmopolitanism.

The Three Domains of Knowledge

The Scientific-Empirical World
Pinzak: All right. To begin: Your contention is that the epistemological principles operating in each domain are identical, and, therefore, knowledge through mysticism of the spiritual world is no less real than knowledge of the physical world.

Emile: The principles are the same, but each domain or realm has its own particular methodological approach.[14] Each domain, that is, has its own particular way of being seen and examined. To see these realms persons must use different "eyes." So our physical eyes examine the material or empirical world and with it factual truth. Our second "eyes" examine rational truth.

Pinzak: These are what Hannah Arendt called "eyes of the body and eyes of the mind."[15]

Emile: And to those two "sets" of eyes we add a third, which Augustine called the "eyes of the Heart" or the soul.[16] With this third set we explore the world of spirit, the mystical world.

When any set of eyes wanders into the domain of another and declares exclusivity in that other domain, we have more than a category error; we have what Taylor calls a consequence that is "catastrophically wrong."[17] This collapses one domain into another. Then idealists claim that only ideas are real; logical positivists argue that statements not grounded empirically are meaningless; and some Christian fundamentalists, as we discussed earlier, declare that Earth is six thousand years old.

Pinzak: So, to follow along, you're saying that each set of eyes has its own domain to examine, but what we see with those eyes is validated identically in all three realms.

Emile: Exactly. Before discussing the domains individually, and while risking the label *terrible simplificateur,* which Taylor ascribes to Foucault,[18] let us first enumerate the steps for establishing epistemological validity in all domains. These steps are presented in this form by Wilber:

1) an instrumental or injunctive step: "a set of instructions, simple or complex, internal or external" that one must undertake to see anything in any realm. "All have the form: 'If you want to know this, do this.'"[19]

2) an illuminative or apprehensive step: Having followed the injunction(s), one then looks. When one looks, one sees—or does not see—something. What, precisely, has one seen; what has one experienced? Determining that leads to the third step.

3) a communal-validation step: This is the sharing of what one has seen, of one's experience in this realm, with others who are using the same eyes. When the sharing leads to agreement as to what has been seen, then we can conclude that we have "a communal proof of true or real seeing."[20]

Pinzak: This has to be more complicated than that. When the eyes of reason, our mind's eye, look into the domain of science or spirit, what results? It certainly isn't always agreement. That is, after all, how we generate various and differing hypotheses and theories, even theologies, in those realms.

Emile: Of course, there is not always agreement. When there is agreement, however, the knowledge generated, whatever the nature of that knowledge, rests on following these three enumerated steps.[21] The Yeats scholar T. R. Henn, for example, when helping Cambridge University science students with their writing, observed: "what the biologist does is comparable to what the poet does . . . close looking in the lab is like close reading of a complex poem."[22]

Pinzak: So in all three realms one first looks and then reports what he sees. Okay, I'll give you some leeway, Emile, you and Henn, on the first two steps, which seem straightforward, especially for the scientific domain. Yet the third step on its face requires far more explanation. Conferring "communally" or intersubjectively may result in agreement, possibly consensus, but how can this be construed as *proof* of *true* or *real* seeing? That would seem to attach proof to applause: What is true is what we agree on; our agreeing makes it true.

Emile: You raise a crucial point, but there is a straightforward response to it. Communal verification or validation rests on *why* we agree, not simply on *that* we agree. To clarify this point, and other issues, I shall begin with the most accessible realm, that of physicality and science.

If you come into the room where I am sitting and declare, "The sun is shining," and I counter you, "No, it is not," your response should be, "See for yourself." If I get up and head to the window, then I have taken the injunctive, the first, step. Looking out the window is the illuminative step: The day is sunny or not. When I return, I say, "You are right; the sun is shining." We now have intersubjective validation. This process is available to anyone who wants to know whether the sun is shining.

Notice, of course, in this prosaic example that very little is required: The instruction is simple to follow, the illumination is easily available and non-controversial, and confirmation is without problems, in large part because we bring to this "experiment" so much in common. In particular we share the same language. We do not have to quibble over what we mean by "shining"; it is part of the background that we share. So what we find already in this form of epistemological validation is a hidden assumption: We must share the same language. This is what Taylor calls being members of a "language community," and it is among such members that confirmation takes place.

Pinzak: But this would seem to make epistemology relative to the members of the community, because packed into the phrase "language community" are important background assumptions, among them qualitative distinctions—what is higher, lower, and so on—what Taylor calls our "strong evaluations."[23]

Emile: I shall take up that issue directly in a moment, but now I want to focus on another side of it: People in the communal-confirmation step must "speak the same language." If they do not, they cannot participate in the confirmation (or refutation). But speaking the same language does not simply mean, say, speaking English. It means that one has been adequately trained not only to articulate what one has seen, but also to be able to see in the first place. Thus, for example, "if you want to see a cell nucleus [and comment on its condition], then learn how to take histological sections. Learn how to use a microscope, learn how to stain tissues, learn how to differentiate cell components one from the other, and then look."[24] In other words, in whatever realm one is looking, the eyes must be trained until adequate to the illumination. In the physical world, where illumination is seen through our natural eyes, there is little training involved. But science is the realm of empirical illumination, empirical data, and that stretches beyond our "natural eyes"—our five senses—to their extensions: telescopes, microscopes, sonar, and the like.

Pinzak: So, communal confirmation is only among those who have adequately completed the injunctive and illuminative steps, and that may involve training.[25] But "trained adequately" can be subjective and biased. In fact, it might mean being trained until one adopts the prejudices of the group or community providing the training.

Emile: This is why in science experiments must be replicated to see whether others using controlled settings are getting the same results. It is also why there must be intersubjective validation. Critics are always on the lookout, and should be, for the kinds of biases that you are suggesting. Such biases must be exposed.

Pinzak: Anthony Appiah, in his book *Cosmopolitanism: Ethics in a World of Strangers,* makes a similar point about adequate training. *(Pinzak clicks open a computer file. "Give me a second to find that quotation . . . okay, here it is")* "When scientists looked at the tracks of charged particles in photographs of cloud chambers, they said things like, 'Look, there's the path of an electron.' That's what was reasonable for them to believe. Yet for the rest of us, who don't know the relevant physics or understand how the cloud chamber works, it all looks just like a fuzzy line in a photograph."[26]

Appiah's example shows both steps—the injunctive step and the illumina-tive step. One who refuses to look has not completed the injunctive step; one who has not been trained or refuses to be trained cannot complete the illumina-tive step. So if someone refuses to learn geometry, she cannot be allowed to judge the truth of the Pythagorean theorem; if Cardinal Bellarmine refused to look through Galileo's telescope, he was not eligible to judge the truth of Gali-leo's observations.[27]

Emile: That is correct, and the data we apprehend or experience with our five sense or their extensions seem to be objects that are separate from us. Even so, to avoid particularistic biases, science demands the testing and replication of findings. Replication is the way scientists try to minimize, if not eliminate, any prejudice resulting from the presence of norms, ideals, or biases inculcated dur-ing training.

Pinzak: We have excellent examples of the importance of replication in the cases of cold fusion and bubble fusion. In 1989 two researchers at the University of Utah claimed that they had generated energy through a form of fusion at room temperature, hence "cold" fusion. In 2002 Rusi Taleyarkhan claimed that he had created a small-scale kind of fusion by collapsing bubbles of acetone, hence "bubble" fusion. Unfortunately, no other scientists around the world have been able to replicate the successes originally claimed.

But the data scientists gather, the facts, observations, and experiments cen-tral to science, are not like rocks that scientists just happen to stumble over. They are selected according to a theory or hypothesis that motivates the scientist and that is itself not sensory data. So although truths about the physical world rest on sensory data, there can certainly be disagreements about and controver-sies over the nature of the data or what they "mean." Meanings are not given by nature; they are the product of interpretation.

Emile: Yes, and meaning or interpretation is part of communal confirma-tion.

Pinzak: But the realm that generates interpretations, meanings, and theories is not the sensory world, the world of empiricism, but is the world of the mind. In that realm the appropriate eyes are not the eyes of the body, but those of the mind. So you're already mixing up "eyes" and realms, which is, to borrow Tay-lor's phrase, "catastrophically wrong."

Emile: Not at all, Pinzak. The mind's eye can, and indeed must, look into all three realms. Scientists, just as philosophers and mystics, need to explain what they have seen. They need to fit their seeing and their explanations into a context of what has come before them, of how what they have experienced is different from or similar to what others have seen. All of that requires interpreta-tion. In all three realms someone can rightly ask, "What is the meaning of this?" Meaning, or interpretation, depends on the mind's eye.

Remember, the domains and the eyes appropriate to each are interrelated, even integrated. Thus, we want science to investigate mystical phenomena, where it is appropriate. Indeed, all confirmation, in whatever realm, proceeds through conversation, intersubjective communication, which requires the "mind's eye." The use of language central to mental work, as Taylor points out, "enables us to put things in public space." "Public space" means "that it [whatever is put there] no longer is just a matter for me, or for you, or for both of us severally, but is now something for us, that is, for us together."[28] The speech of conversation is not a series of monologues, but a series of responses to what the speakers say. Thus, public space is created in any conversation, because to converse speakers must join their perspectives. In this way every conversation creates a "space" that is neither yours nor mine but ours, and we see our views as one perspective among others. This is a public realm of intersubjectivity. As a public realm, this is also a political realm.

Language enables us to create a public space or a common vantage point from which we determine jointly and intersubjectively the truths in the world, whatever world we are surveying. This includes science. Anyone adequately trained, and who follows the epistemological steps—which must involve intersubjective communication to confirm or refute the illumination—is privy to that public space. The community is not public in that *anyone* is eligible, but it is public in that *anyone following the epistemological steps* is eligible. No one can be excluded simply because of political ideology; because, for example, as with the Nazis, he or she is Jewish. *That* is at best a category error, but more to the point, it is a position whose basis would be refuted either in the sensory realm or in the mental realm. What both realms, what all realms, provide is public knowledge—evidence that must be available to anyone capable of looking properly.

In the scientific realm data do not interpret themselves. The mind's eye must be used in that realm as part of intersubjective validation.

Pinzak: Hence the emphasis in the academic world on peer reviews for communal validation of one's work. These are scholars whose eyes are trained adequately to confirm or refute what another scholar has written.

Here also is what you alluded to about the importance of dialogue. Well, since we've moved to the topic, let's examine the world of the "mind's eye."

The Mental-Moral World
So we have stipulated that whether something is true, in any domain, is a matter of the communal confirmation of the evidence, but sometimes that evidence is "inconclusive." This would seem especially true for moral claims, which may be "testable," but not in an empirical way.

Emile: That is correct. Validation of moral claims differs from validation of scientific claims in that confirmation of "moral data" calls into question the very nature of what is seen. In the moral realm the question is not so much "Is it there, or isn't it?" or "Do you see it, or don't you?" The questions are, rather, evaluative: "Is this practice right and good? What does it mean?"

Pinzak: Yet the three epistemological steps do not seem to support this view. If we follow them, we simply learn to look at certain moral behaviors or statements and to confirm intersubjectively that we, indeed, saw them.

Emile: You are forgetting what the communal step demands. The confirmation in the mental-moral world involves validating the meaning of what is seen. It is not enough simply to see that a certain culture has an incest taboo and adheres to it. Required in knowing a moral practice is to understand its meaning—why, when, and how it is held and followed. Furthermore, to know the moral practice requires confirming whether it is true; in the moral world that means not only whether it is supported by the reasons offered for it, but also whether it is right and good, whether it should be held and practiced.

The criteria we use to judge meaning are not so readily agreed upon as they are in the empirical world. In the sensory world we confirm theories and hypotheses—the mind's eye looking at the physical world—in terms of empirical data. In other words, a proposition about the physical world is true if it matches or conforms to empirical data, gathered many times over through replication of observations (experiments). In the mental-moral world, both the propositions made and the data on which they rest are symbolic. Both involve meaning. A scientific theory, to be true and scientific, must rest on or refer to sense data—something we can "check and see." A philosophical moral theory, to be true, must rest on or refer to arguments or reasons—also things we can look at, that we can "check and see."

Pinzak: But reasons are not things "out there"; they are themselves symbolic or mental constructs. So how do we validate them? And who is in *this* "community of inquirers"?

Emile: In brief, we validate reasons by seeing whether those offered are *good* reasons according to some intersubjective structure of meaning. Those properly trained to look at and to see those reasons and who "speak the same language"—those, for instance, at a minimum, able to give reasons and follow reasoning—can be in that community. They may not accept the reasons, but they must understand them.

Pinzak: This makes the members of the community rather messy, even amorphous. There really isn't any special training necessary, as there is in some scientific community of inquirers. There is only the ability to reflect and to use and to identify reasons. But aren't you presupposing that those who are in the community already accept the reasoning being used in the confirmation? What do you mean, for example, by "good" reasons? How does someone know that his reasons are "good ones"?

Emile: Excellent question, Pinzak. How does anyone know what a good reason is? She is convinced by it. But how does she know that it is good? How does anyone know? Likewise, how does anyone know that she has the "right" values? Reasons and values must be presented, articulated, interrogated, defended, and one must do so publicly before a community of inquirers.

So how do we know that reasons are good or that moral values are right? We deliberate about and validate them intersubjectively.

Pinzak: But isn't it possible that in one culture what counts as a reason is radically different from what another culture accepts? Indeed, isn't it possible that those within a given community will have differing views on what counts as a reason?

Emile: In both instances, we want to know what counts as *their* reasons. Reasons themselves will be subject to scrutiny and dialogue. We want, and need, to understand how those in the culture view the world, how they construct their worldview. To do so we need to step inside—we need to see—their world. Then we need to join the community of inquirers to deliberate about their world, including what counts for them as reasons.

Pinzak: Okay, so those in this community of inquirers are those who can reason, who have what Taylor calls "linguistic articulacy" (1989, 92). That "articulacy" includes understanding and being able to use language to interpret and explain meanings, symbols, and concepts. To exist and to be known, these must be articulated; that is, these must be presented to the linguistic community, the community of inquirers. When we talk about the moral "good" of a person or culture, to see that good, we must "see" what it is that he sees or they see and how this moves him or them. Those not in the culture may not see the good in the same light, but they must see it in the same way. That is, they must publicly articulate what they see. Right? *(Emile nods.)*

Can one from outside the culture be a member of the community of inquirers who confirm the good that is seen? Must they not share the same structure of meaning, the same backdrop of strong evaluations, and thus does that sharing not place the outsider inside the culture? If so, no one can critique a culture from the outside.

Emile: One from outside the culture need not share the structure of meaning, but she must be able to understand the structure. That requires being able to speak the language of those whose good is to be validated. The nature of this community of inquirers is therefore similar to what Taylor describes as the "speech community."[29]

The training in this community for taking the illuminative step is, as you have pointed out, referring to Taylor, linguistic articulacy. That means, as you have also pointed out, that one must be able to express the ideas, ideals, purposes, norms, and customs important to and that constitute a background for a certain way of life. One can use, and therefore one understands, "a language of social life."[30] Behind this notion of articulation is the presumption that one understands the role and rules of the good in that life. Being able to articulate them implies an understanding of them sufficient to express what constitutes the good properly. More than simple language-use, articulation also presupposes some level of "experiential meaning." That is, inquirers have sufficient life experience—they have lived long enough and interacted enough—to understand the purposes of and feelings associated with these social practices and behaviors. In short, members of the linguistic community understand in general the motivations of others and the "meaning of a situation for an agent."[31] They can put themselves in the place of the others. To understand those experiential mean-

ings, to know how to respond appropriately—whether to laugh or to listen seriously—is already a sign of being within the linguistic community.

Pinzak: All of this underscores what we talked about with moves into dialectical thinking, being able to put ourselves in the shoes of others, especially
those who hold views divergent from our own.

Emile: Yes, all of that is central both to understanding cultural practices
and to validating them intersubjectively . .

Pinzak: . . . through dialogue or conversation.

Emile: Yes, but right now I want to emphasize a different point: Notice,
again, that the requirement for communally confirming the meaning and the
truth or goodness of a moral practice is to understand the nature of, reasons for,
and importance of that practice. It is not necessarily to *accept* that practice or to
accept the reasons for it. One must be able to share the common public language, to use it properly, and that includes understanding what Wittgenstein
called the "inherited tradition" necessary to make sense of talk of truth or falsity.
Part of arriving intersubjectively at the truth may well include scrutinizing that
inherited tradition. As a result, communal validation cannot simply be an adap-
tation of or conformity to traditional rules or practices.

Pinzak: So people in a culture, from this perspective, continue to define
themselves and their moral goods in conversations with others, presumably inside and outside that culture, but the community by which and through which
they define themselves is not necessarily the given historical community. They
define themselves by the linguistic community.

Emile: The linguistic community is open to all who can and will share the
public language. This community is therefore more inclusive than what might be
described as an "identificatory community." That is a community in which the
inherited tradition in part defines who one is. In that kind of community identity
is secured by social solidarity and conformity to social norms. Because dissension can lead to doubt and thus to insecurity and instability in such communities,
members might have to be brought into line with what the society or group ex-
pects one to believe.[32]

Pinzak: You're describing the membership self that we touched on in a
previous conversation.

Emile: Yes, and what is true of that kind of identity is not true of what constitutes a linguistic community. The linguistic community, being inclusive of all
public-language users, wishes to adjust to norms and standards confirmed in intersubjective communication. We can "stop simply living . . . within our traditions and habits and by making them objects for us, subject them to radical scrutiny and remaking."[33]

Pinzak: And we cannot do this kind of radical scrutinizing alone.

Emile: As Taylor points out, "The nature of our language and the fundamental dependence of our thought on language makes interlocution [conversa-
tion] . . . inescapable."[34]

Pinzak: What you, and Taylor, are describing here is really constructivism—that is, the idea that our knowledge, and in this case our moral knowledge, is socially constructed and historically contingent.

Emile: Yes. From this perspective knowledge is not discovered. It is not lying "out there" waiting to be found.

Pinzak: But, Emile, because the linguistic community includes all those who "see" these concepts, patterns, and linguistic constructs, and yet is not limited to those who accept these as good and true, it would seem that a clash is inevitable between those who speak the same language but are from different communities, whose knowledge constructions are different. Indeed, those from another community may well attack my standards because they are from a different community. When two different cultures have two different ways of describing and understanding the same phenomenon—say, the meaning of "honorable action"—then what we see is not simply "a difference of vocabulary, but also one of social reality."[35]

Emile: What you are describing is certainly going to be true for two "identificatory communities," as we were just saying. Sunnis and Shiites, for example, are surely divided on who should be or should have been the caliph to succeed Muhammad. This division, centuries old, will keep many of them from using their linguistic community for dialogue on multiple issues.

While that may well be true, we want to look deeper, underneath the particular issues that divide such groups. Look below the surface, though not to say "superficial," conflict. What both communities share is how that reality is negotiated. That is the level at which we approach two conflicting groups. What we must bear in mind is that social reality is not just what is constituted, but also how it is constituted. Social realities are "practices" and not independent of the vocabularies that describe them. "Language is constitutive of the reality."[36]

Pinzak: So what do we do when two communities disagree?

Emile: You are surely playing with me, Pinzak. *(Both men smile.)* When important issues are at stake for communities, when social worlds are at stake, then we examine together the parts of those social worlds that reflect disagreement. Perhaps the disagreement rests on a delusion or a partial misunderstanding or, as Taylor points out, "a projection of some quite ordinary desire" upon which we have conferred some exalted status as a moral good. How do we know?

Pinzak: If I may, Emile: We take up and face the particular positions or critiques involved in the disagreement.

Emile: But how do we know what we are talking about?

Pinzak: We know only by expressing thoughts and reasons to others; for example, by gauging their reactions to what I say and by listening and reacting to their own thoughts and reasons. This is a conversation, a display of intersubjective exchange. The two groups converse, share language and meaning, and interpret how they see or understand the moral constructs of the other.

Emile: What they hope to do, if we can introduce dialectical thinking here, is reconcile the opposing views. And "articulacy is the crucial condition of reconciliation" (Taylor 1989, 107).

Pinzak: How do they reconcile? We can't assume dialectical thinking here. That goes too far. In fact, if morality is tied to language, and language rests on and expresses an "inherited tradition," then can there be anything but a relative reply: What works for us is good for us; what works for you is good for you.

Emile: Well, what can we already assume? We can assume that the two groups are not incommensurable. We can accept that one group can call into question the nature or truth of the other's moral practices. We can assume that both groups are open to conversation, and thus an avenue is available for figuring out together how they differ. To come to reconciliation each group would have to demonstrate to the other that each had "seen"—that is, understood the meaning and importance of—the other's practices. As Thomas Kuhn said of two groups of scientists who differ over what they see, "Each will have to learn to translate the other's theory and its consequences into his own language."[37]

Pinzak: Yes, and both the scientists and our clashing cultures are looking for the same thing: evidence that supports the theory or the practice. The evidence for scientists is empirical facts and whether one of the theories better fits those facts. For the cultures the evidence is arguments or reasons for believing in and following the practice.[38]

Emile: Correct, and the first step toward reconciliation is to get to the third step in our epistemological sequence—the communal validation step. That step is to talk.

Pinzak: The first step is the injunctive step, which is to look at, in the case of clashing cultures, the practice in question.

Emile: So, whether one looks at a moral practice of her own culture or looks through translation at a practice of another culture, she tests communicatively first whether she understands it. This is, of course, especially important for translation, because it is not simply a matter of putting herself in the position of the other. That could mean interpreting the world of that other in one's own terms. Rather, the translation, her interpretation, must restate to the satisfaction of the other the nature of the other's practice. This is to understand the practice as if from the inside.

Once understanding is established, she conducts "ideational" tests, tests of arguments and interpretation. She asks the group to articulate, and thus to make public to the community of inquirers, an account of their practice. These are the reasons for their practice. Sometimes those reasons are in the form of general principles that provide the best justification. At other times, and more frequently, these reasons will rely on the group's moral and cultural background, so that their reasons will be a combination of principles, social history, and experience. This combination provides the best account of the practice and social life.

Pinzak: Let's take as a testing example the moral practice of witchcraft of the Azande, made famous by anthropologist E. E. Evans-Pritchard. Are their beliefs in and practices of witchcraft irrational? Are they therefore "bad" practices, practices to be condemned?

Emile: To know the answers to those questions, what must we do? We must get inside the Azande's system of rationality. We must see the practice as they do. In other words, we must fulfill the first two epistemological steps and follow the third—enter the community of inquirers. Once inside we can apply rules of reasoning to see whether the Azande made any mistakes in logical consistency and logical reasoning.

There are two implications here. The first is that the Azande do reason about witchcraft; that they think about why they do it, what it is, how to do it, when it is proper to do it, or when it has been done improperly. This they must do to give any kind of account of their lives in which witchcraft plays an important part. To know that it is a moral good requires articulating the good and thus subjecting it to public—communal—scrutiny. The second implication is that the Azande reason as we modern Westerners reason. While what counts as reason is relative, *that* the Azande reason and *how* they reason are not. Logic is about the propriety of relational statements in moving from premises to conclusions. Rationality requires at least self-consistency: propositions should be consistent with related ideas simultaneously held. For an act to be considered rational it must at a minimum conform to the norms of the community and fit in without contradicting those norms.[39]

Pinzak: So we examine the reasoning of the Azande and find no logical mistakes, and thus we can conclude that their beliefs are rational on that account. We may also find, however, that their premises are false and that we can argue epistemologically by offering counter-evidence, or even facts. Are these reasons that the Azande would accept?

Emile: Perhaps not, for they might well reject our premises. Perhaps they practice witchcraft because they believe it makes their crops grow and heals the sick by appeasing the spirits. This we reject, but they reject the basis of our scientific evidence. Perhaps they practice witchcraft because it is symbolic, a series of social ceremonies and beliefs essential to community cohesion. This we could accept. Depending on the reasons that both sides offered, we might not come close to any reconciliation; we might not change any minds. But if we are going to do either, this is how we must proceed.

Pinzak: So "experiments" in the mental-moral domain are designed to reveal reasons. Two opposing practices could rest on reasons that make both true. If witchcraft relies on empirical statements or facts, then we look at that evidence to conclude whether it is true.[40] But if it is a practice for social cohesion and one that works, we would have to conclude that it is true and for that purpose is perhaps even good.

Emile: This should not surprise us. We would not be surprised that two interpretations of James Joyce's *Ulysses* could both be solid, substantive, and brilliant, and yet could be opposite. This is not to be lamented but applauded, especially in the moral realm, for such possibilities manifest the fecundity of what constitutes the moral good.

We often seem ready to accept that the physical world is a domain of public and common objects. But concepts, too, are objects that when articulated become public and common. They are open to anyone who will follow the first two epistemological steps: learn the language and "see" what we are talking about. These concepts, moral concepts in this case, only become real when made public and common. Moral goods only exist for us through some articulation; they take place in the "space," the public space, between us. What is made manifest there is a world not only seen but also constituted through language. Morality in the narrow sense of the term—how humans find or determine what conduct among themselves is good or bad, right or wrong—is the product of language of meaning and interpretation. Actions take on moral attributes depending on what we take in our language to be suitable or unsuitable behavior: good or bad for what; in regard to what? Our cultural conversation provides such questions, and our actions and these questions are "directly available for all to see"— that is, are made public—through our language.

Pinzak: Emile, there's a problem with this approach, or I have a problem with it. You've made it sound as if participants in the epistemological inquiry must reason according to formal logic—you know, that any moral conclusion can only follow from a major premise about values and a minor premise about facts. For example, philosophers are evil; Socrates is a philosopher; therefore, Socrates is evil. So someone with a hidden or implied premise would have to lay that out and explain why that had to be done. Now maybe that's the way these epistemological conversations must go, that there will be pauses as philosophers point out that one participant has just uttered a non sequitur or committed the fallacy of the excluded middle or . . . .

Emile: I take your point, Pinzak, but I do not think that you have properly characterized the nature of the intercommunicative or intersubjective exchange. The pursuit in the exchange involves the meaning of propositions more than the relationships among them. So while there must be reasoning within the conversation, most of the dialogue is reason-giving. Participants are not trying to speak from an impartial perspective. They are not searching for reasons that all participants will find compelling. They are sharing their perspectives and experiences.[41] Bear in mind that sharing perspectives and experiences is not just about giving reasons. It is also about telling stories. People provide testimony as to why they see the issue in a certain way and how it affects them.[42] A person might say, "Here is what I have seen in our neighborhood. Here is how your proposal hurts my family and my neighbors."

Pinzak: Yet the basis or foundation of deliberation for generating epistemological validity must remain reason-giving. The community of inquirers is open to anyone adequately trained to the required illuminative level and who can give reasons. Participants are asked to give an account not only of what they see and what they do, but also of why they do it. They are asked to give reasons, and those who hear those reasons are then going to reason about them. So *reasoning* and *reason-giving* are other terms for *critical thinking* or *deliberation*.[43]

Emile: That is correct. *Deliberation* means being able to weigh evidence; to give reasons for and against various positions, including one's own; to form and advance arguments; to separate reasons from opinions and assumptions from conclusions; and to follow arguments of others and, when needed, mirror those arguments back to those others to their satisfaction. At bottom, the kind of reasoning that dialectical, or democratic, dialogue demands is what Aristotle called *sumbouleuesthai*. This is reasoning through consultation or talking things through with others. More simply, it is sharing, comparing, and contrasting reasons with others when ethical choices have to be made.[44]

Additionally, I think, the mental-moral realm also requires Aristotelian *synesis*. We speak of *synesis,* or understanding, "when it implies the use of one's faculty of opinion in judging statements made by another person about matters which belong to the realm of practical wisdom."[45] Carried within this understanding is a need for perspectivism that is essential to translation.

Pinzak: By "translation" here you mean the ability to step into the perspectives of others and to be able to reproduce their frames of reference accurately. This is similar to the kind of perspectivism found in dialectical thinking.

Emile: No, it is not just similar to but exactly like that kind of perspectivism. Whereas "tolerance" might be a value to a worldcentric perspective characterized by formal-operational thinking, "appreciation" or "embrace" might be the value central to the worldcentric perspective of dialectical thinking. Whereas one at formal-operational thinking sees the value of tolerating other perspectives, one at dialectical thinking sees the value in sharing disparate perspectives. She sees that these can enrich and enliven her own perspective through the acknowledgment of differences. Dialectical thinking requires, therefore, placing ourselves in the perspectives of others. What is universal about dialectical thinking is the desire, even the need, to do so and to honor our differences. In dialectical thinking the reasoning is not done in isolation, within the inner rational cathedral of one's own mind, and then brought into conversation. Instead, dialectical thinking is reasoning together. There is reason-giving, to be sure, but central also is the back-and-forth, the dialectic, of the conversation as minds are changed as well as made up.

What perspectivism does, as Taylor points out, is help us determine that one position or interpretation is better than another. It does so by bringing out in that position or interpretation an underlying coherence or sense.[46]

Pinzak: We talked about something related to this a couple of conversations ago, when talking about levels of human development. One level is higher than or superior to another if one of them is more comprehensive. Following that line, an interpretation would be more comprehensive if it were able to deal with more data in a more stable and consistent way. As a result, this interpretation could address, and even resolve, conflicts not addressed by other interpretations. Because it is applicable to a wider or greater range of situations and can handle more information more systematically, we can say that this interpretation is more comprehensive. But to be better than other interpretations this interpretation would have to be able to handle, and handle well, all the data and situations covered by those other interpretations. So, one interpretation is better if it includes but also transcends other interpretations. To know whether that is so, we must understand the other interpretations, and that understanding involves practical wisdom and perspectivism.

Emile: Very well said, Pinzak. Determining whether one interpretation is better than another requires, of course, following the three epistemological steps. We would have to ask people to look at these interpretations and to talk about what they see and whether and why one is better than another. Through discussion, critical reflection, empathy, perspectivism, imagination, interrogations, argument, and reasoning, some moral concepts or principles or positions will be the ones that we will accept and even enshrine.

Pinzak: Virtues or values such as "courage" or "honor" can then become the focal point for a culture or a group. In that sense, after dialogue, such ideas become real features of that social world.

Emile: Yes, but that reality is not a factual matter relating to the physical world; we cannot cut open a soldier and see his courage or honor. It is a hermeneutical matter: What do you mean by "courage"? Is it a virtue we ought to encourage?

Moral truth in this sense is not mere opinion, for then it would depend on who agreed or how many agreed. Those who agreed might decide by caprice that tomorrow they believe something else, making that true. If moral truth, or moral reality, rests on agreement alone, then no challenges, whatever the basis, brought against the agreement could themselves be true. But truth rests on reasons and evidence. Those are what we look at with the mind's eye; those are what we seek communally to confirm or refute.[47]

Pinzak: All moral truths in this sense must be affirmed through communal validation. That is how we establish their truth. But such truths must also be open to new deliberations, to renegotiation. They are not fixed, but rest on reasons and evidence in a context in which new reasons and evidence can come to light.

Emile: As Rawls wrote, "The search for reasonable grounds for reaching agreement rooted in our conceptions of ourselves and in our relation to society replaces the search for moral truth."[48] Rather than a stand-in for moral truth, agreement becomes (is) moral truth provided that the agreement is arrived at through open, and open-ended, dialogue. Truth lies not in *that* we agree, but in *why* we agree. Any such agreement rests on evidence seen and validated communally in a context of rationality. And what counts as truth, reality, and knowledge or gnosis in the spiritual realm depends no less upon this idea of insight, evidence, and communal validation—to wit, the three steps to knowing.

Pinzak: And so we turn our attention now to that realm.

Emile says, "Yes, but before we begin, what about some more coffee, and a glass of water for me?" Pinzak nods, stands, clears away the empty cups, and heads inside the café. He emerges moments later, quickly followed by Bobby, the waiter, who is carrying a small tray with the coffee and water. As Pinzak sits down, Emile says, "Thank you, Pinzak, and thank you, Bobby," as the waiter places the cups and the glass on the table.

The Spiritual World

Pinzak *(after a sip of coffee and as Emile takes a long drink of water):* When people report that, in a rapturous state, they have been spoken to by angels, or have felt one with the universe, or have taken all others as their self—a cosmopolitan sensibility, at the least—how do we know whether these experiences reveal something higher or whether they are simply reduced to a subjective phenomenon—a delusion, an emotional effusion, or the product of one's creative imagination?

Emile: Well, as we have suggested, and holding aside the laboratory experiments on meditation and brain states, those on the esoteric side of the world's sacred traditions argue that there is a way to know. That knowledge, they claim, is as real and true as any scientific discovery or philosophical theorem. Yet what makes such claims difficult to fathom is that what we experience, what we apprehend directly, is beyond logic, beyond reason, beyond the empirical world. The method used for seeing in this realm is meditation or what we can call more generally "contemplation."[49]

Pinzak: And contemplation, the eyes of the heart or the soul, to follow Arendt, cannot be reduced to or derived from reason or the five senses.

Emile: This is why, in part, philosophers and scientists dismiss it. Philosopher A. J. Ayer concluded that "the fact that [the contemplative] cannot reveal what he 'knows' or even himself devise an empirical test to validate his 'knowledge,' shows that his state of mystical intuition is not a genuinely cognitive state."[50]

Pinzak: But as you and I have already discussed, mystics and contemplatives do not claim that their intuition—their insight—is empirical. They claim that their insights are "transempirical" and "translogical."

Emile: They do claim, however, that their insights are public; they are available to anyone who undertakes the proper training, follows the proper instructions, and discusses what he or she sees with the community of inquirers.[51] In short, *gnosis* or knowledge of the spiritual realm follows from exactly the same broad epistemological principles as knowledge of the physical or mental realms. Philosopher W. T. Stace argued this point in *Mysticism and Philosophy:*

> We should believe in the existence of a newly discovered mountain in the Antarctic even though only one competent [trained] and reliable explorer had seen it. This is because we think there is good reason to believe that all normal men could observe it if they took the proper steps. Not all men perceive the mountains at the South Pole . . . but all men could perceive them if they would carry

out certain instructions which might in most cases and for most of us be so un-
enduringly rigorous and time-consuming as to be practically impossible. In like
manner it may be held that any normal man could verify the experience of the
mystic if he would . . . subject himself to a long and rigorous course of physical
and mental discipline. . . . And this means that mystical experience is just as
"public" as sense experience, since to say that an experience is public only
means that a large number of private experiences are similar, or would be similar if appropriate steps were taken.[52]

Pinzak: Give me an example to solidify the point.

Emile: All right. Zen Buddhist meditation takes the form of an injunction:
"If you wish to know whether there is Buddha nature, you must sit." "Sitting,"
or *zazen,* is the term for Zen meditation, and it often requires years of training
and discipline to see or experience the transcendental sphere. That sight is a
form of "intuitive apprehension" known in Zen as *kensho* or *satori,* both meaning a "direct seeing into the spiritual way." This looking, comments Wilber, is
"as perfectly direct as looking into a microscope." But, he adds, "Only a trained
eye need look" (1983, 60). This perception is called intuition to differentiate it
from sensory experience and from thought. It is beyond both.

Pinzak: And how does a Zen practitioner know that what she has experienced, what she has seen, is a direct apprehension of spirit, by spirit, as spirit?

Emile: That must be confirmed by both a Zen master and the community of
inquirers—fellow meditators. "This is a vigorous test. . . . Both in private, intense interaction with the Zen Master *(dokusan)* and in exacting public participation in tests of authenticity *(shosan) all* apprehensions are struck against the
community of those whose cognitive eyes are adequate to the transcendent, and
such apprehensions are soundly nonverified if they do not match the facts of
transcendence as disclosed by the community" (61).

In these contemplative or mystical paths no one is asked to accept any belief
or anything on faith. Pascal Kaplan studied as a representative sample of esotericism six spiritual teachers offering contemplative injunctions to contemporary
Westerners.[53] He concluded that all of these spiritual teachers separated mysticism or contemplation from any belief or belief system. Inayat Khan, for example, representing the Sufi tradition of Islam, declares that the true Sufi teacher
"never asks his disciples to accept any doctrine on mere faith. 'My work is only
to tell you in what way the faculty of revelation can be awakened. Do this practice, and this faculty will be awakened; you will then see for yourself.'"[54]

Pinzak: Well, that's still engaging the practice on faith. If Inayat Khan had
said, "Do this practice and see what happens," that would be one thing. But he
says, "This faculty will be awakened." So you undertake the practice on faith
that the faculty will be awakened, that Inayat Khan knows what he's talking
about.

Emile: There is a level of faith involved, I grant that. It is found in all three
realms. We have faith that when someone of greater experience, and wisdom,
tells us to do something to train us adequately to see and thus also to participate

in the validating community, we have faith that in following that program, whatever it is, we shall be adequately trained. The initial faith exists to get us to the requisite experience, not to substitute for experience. The faith is not "mere" or "only" faith.

Pinzak: I don't mean to quibble here, Emile, because the importance of the position on contemplation or mysticism that Inayat Khan is trying to make cannot be overstated. But let me understand: To avoid subjectivism—even a quasi-solipsism—we have to think that moral and spiritual "truths" do not lie captive within the limits of our creative imaginations. It is not a personal vision alone that defines the world. When the mystic tells us to turn within to find God, Spirit, Being, or Reality, he is not thinking that that discovery is the result of an intellectual deduction—"My thoughts are imperfect impulses from the perfect Creator; therefore, God exists." Instead, the discovery is preceded by an injunction—"If you want to know God, look within in this way"—and, after the looking, the validity of what is discovered depends on the intersubjective exchanges by the community of inquirers.

Emile: Well said, Pinzak. Through the epistemological steps the looking is beyond one's personal thoughts or sentiments or phantasms. Remember our earlier distinction: We are turning inward to explore the interior, not the internal. As Plotinus tells us, to see the soul "we must turn the perceptive faculty inward and hold it to attention there." But to what do we attend? "[W]e must let the hearings of sense go by." The soul is not found in the sensory, external world; "admiring pursuit of the external is a confession of inferiority." Nor is it found in the merely internal: "[W]e indulged [our] own motion; thus we were hurried down the wrong path. . . ." It is found beyond thought and beyond the senses and "needs no bodily organ for its thinking." Do not "seek any point in space in which to seat it; it must be set outside of all space. . . ."[55]

If contemplatives did no more than tell us to look within and gave us nothing but descriptions of transcendental states, then perhaps we could conclude with A. J. Ayer that "the mystic . . . is unable to produce any intelligible propositions at all" (1952, 118). But contemplatives provide injunctions, or meditative practices, for looking into the spiritual realm, for seeing the transcendental. And they insist that what is seen is public. What is seen can be and must be communally verified. Thus contemplation renews our spiritual aspects and does so not through belief but through experience. Such experience is not locked within, to be verified by how good or special it makes one feel. It is experience available to anyone willing to follow the procedures and to look.

Pinzak: This is at some remove from conventional religion.

Emile: What do you have in mind, Pinzak?

Pinzak: From the beginning religion has been associated with atrocities.[56]

Emile: Not all religions and not all sides of religion.

Pinzak: Of course not; we've established that all major religions have at least a mystical or contemplative side. So sacrifice, mutilation, a willingness and a felt need to immolate someone or something to please the gods or God are associated, it seems to me, with the exoteric, or theistic, side of religion and not with the esoteric side. Theism seems unable to survive without institutionalized bureaucracies set on saving souls through the one true way. Theism as it comes to us historically *is* its history. Judaism, Christianity, and Islam are religions established on the historical existence of sacred persons and/or covenants with God. How could theism therefore be divorced from history? The center of any theism is its clergy, sacred texts, and sacred practices sanctioned by, if not derived from, the historicity of the founding and of the teaching. That history justifies or legitimizes the ecclesiastical hierarchy while condemning other such hierarchies. These ecclesiastical hierarchies are used to instill and reinforce the faith, and the basis of that faith is theological. This means that theology in this sense is epistemologically mental-moral, and only epistemologically mental-moral, because it presents for interpretation theories and histories of the acts or the nature of God and the kingdom. But can theism be epistemologically spiritual?

Emile: You mean by that question, I take it, what we have been saying here about the three epistemological steps for validating contemplative experience. Can theistic religions rely on and demand spiritual experience, and not rely simply on belief or faith?

Pinzak: Can they rely upon experience, direct apprehension of the transcendental or divine, and not rely upon ecclesiastical hierarchies for the correct or accepted interpretations?

Emile: Here we must be careful, for theists hold that God is forever separate from the world. Could we then come to know God directly, and if we could, would this any longer be theism?[57] Can orthodox theistic traditions do anything but emphasize moral passion not just before experiential evidence but, indeed, in place of it?

Pinzak: Practitioners either avoid gathering hard evidence or rely on the clergy, or don't believe such gathering is necessary, or don't believe they can have such evidence—that it exists or that it is accessible. Spiritual knowledge gleaned from the public confirmation of direct experience, which is nothing but the experiential core present even in the theistic traditions, *is* hard evidence. And such evidence is available through esotericism or mysticism, which is downplayed. Have we not learned through science that the spirit is not empirical and that religion is not literal? Have we not learned through modern philosophers like Kant that God cannot be known or approached through reason?

Emile: God, to paraphrase W. T. Stace, is not to be found at the end of a telescope or at the end of a syllogism. This is not to say that conventional theism has no part to play in the lives of modern selves. It continues to offer solace to millions; it continues to lead our society in non-governmental organizations that do good works. Yet such actions are social, emotional, and psychological expressions and outlets. They miss what is unique to religion: spiritual knowledge or gnosis.

Pinzak: Nietzsche hyperbolized that God is dead. It is not God who is dead, but the form of institutionalized spirit erected in God's name.

Emile: Would Nietzsche agree?

Pinzak: I'm not interested in that, Emile; I'm interested in whether you agree.

Emile: I am inclined to. We moderns are in an advantageous position. Having come to know through science the nature and the limits of the empirical world, having come to know through reflective introspection the nature and limits of reason and creative imagination, we are poised, as the twelfth-century Christian mystic Meister Eckhart said, "to leave God for God," to escape the constraints of institutionalized religion and to look within, past the internal to the eternal. W. T. Jones, in *The Medieval Mind,* defined *gnosticism* as "the view that knowledge *(gnosis)* . . . is the means to salvation," and that this knowledge is "a special, transrational knowledge limited to a select few. . . ."[58]

Pinzak: Not limited any longer; not if what we've been talking about today, and the last couple of meetings, is so. We modern selves are different from the ancients, because we have experience, unavailable to them, as Taylor has shown, with reflective introspection. Thanks to Augustine and Descartes, we have learned to look within. With that experience, and with the availability of teachers of contemplation from our own traditions as well as those of the East,[59] we can say that one difference between the modern mind and the medieval mind is that gnosis is accessible not to the few but to the many. The modern age is the age of experience, of democratized gnosis.

Emile: I certainly agree with that. We are different from the ancients. For Plato it would have made no sense to imagine a rational person—a person whose desires were ruled by reason in conjunction with spirit—having false ideas about moral conduct or about the order of nature—say, about the movements of bodies in the heavens. These insights followed from being rational, from having the proper vision of the order of all things, from cosmos to nature to polis to the soul. Rationality was here defined substantially in terms of the order of being. Knowing the cosmic order provided knowledge of all the realms below it.

Political Implications: Generating Public Knowledge

Pinzak: But this turn within is both a blessing and a curse. Turning within can curse us, as Taylor also shows, by leaving the subject trapped within and trapped by her own personal visions, demons, fantasies; trapped within the endless stream of mental contents—thoughts, sensations, sentiments. So the desire of, if not the need for, science is to collapse or eradicate the inner world, leaving outside only a disenchanted world, a world that can be measured empirically. Yet the turn within is also a blessing—through it we can and do construct order in science and in life.

Emile: Again, we are different from the ancients because of the turn within. Because the ancients collapsed the world of reason into the world of the soul, they missed, or dismissed, a realm of intellect. They missed the intellectual domain in which procedures of thought compel us to justify our decisions and actions in intersubjective terms to which all, if properly trained, can have access.

Pinzak: We do not justify them, as the ancients did, according to a realm of Spirit or Being that we identify as the order of harmony, truth, and light. We no longer appeal to the Platonic Forms to justify our actions, and most of us look for reasons for our decisions beyond saying, "This is God's will." Because of the nature of proof that we accept today, and because of the multiplicity of moral sources available to us, many of us are no longer willing to subordinate what we think and experience to belief systems based on faith.

Emile: The turn within needs the three epistemological steps. Otherwise, as you have said, following Taylor, we can turn within and become trapped in our *personal* visions. Then my experiences remain only *my* experiences. They lack the intersubjective validation that comes through the public dialogue among the community of inquirers. Through intersubjective exchange, a publicly accessible cosmic order of meanings is possible, as Taylor further pointed out (1989, 512).

Pinzak *(typing):* So, we modern selves cannot, or should not, simply rely upon a set of meanings—moral, cosmological, spiritual—handed down by our theistic religious or even our philosophical traditions . . .

Emile: . . . which Taylor describes as our "canonical guardians."[60]

Pinzak: Right. Instead, our moral meanings and our moral sources must be steeped in our experience and validated by the community of inquirers.

Emile: But this is a predicament, is it not, Pinzak?

Pinzak: In what way?

Emile: We live in a modern world of pluralism. We live in a world of debates among moral philosophers as to the nature and substance of moral arguments, justifications, and theories. We live in a world of irreconcilable differences among conceptions of the good life. Differences over the necessities of life and over theories of human identity lead to questions that began in the eighteenth century about our own natures. Nature itself is no longer informed by an ontic logos.

Pinzak *(smiling):* Oh, I see what you're doing. This is one of your little tests, isn't it, to see whether I've been following, to see whether I'm adequately trained to participate in this conversation. *(Emile here chuckles heartily.)* Well, how's this: The modern world is in a predicament because we are faced with a multiplicity of possible moral sources with no apodictic way to sort through them. There is no realm of Platonic Forms or Ideas that orders self, nature, politics, and the divine, top to bottom. For moderns, then, the physical world and the mental world are their own domains, and while they are part of a cosmic order, they are both also independent of the world of spirit. These realms are interdependent, as shown by our own natures: We are constituted by and live in all three worlds, as Wilber's AQAL model shows. But meaning is not determined by an objective, cosmic order; our minds, our mental worlds, are not composed of *Ideas* but of *ideas*. Meanings are linguistic creations, constructed, interpreted, and validated according to a rational ordering of purposes by persons. Not all credible moral sources and meanings involve God, but they all involve intersubjective confirmation. Access to meaning, therefore, requires that we turn inward, that we reflect on ideas, sensations, sentiments. But that is not the only turn. Then we must turn "outward" to deliberate with others, to engage in intersubjective communication to verify meaning and knowledge. The world within can and must therefore go beyond "just me."

Emile: If this *were* a test, Pinzak, then I would say that you have done quite well. Do you recall the reason that we undertook this lengthy excursus?

Pinzak: I do. It was to ease my concerns about leaving a cosmopolitan identity even partly connected to . . .

Emile: . . . what I think you described as "mystical mumbo-jumbo."

Pinzak: I did.

Emile: And have your concerns been eased?

Pinzak: Largely they have, though the effects of these conversations about mysticism and meditation are still sinking in. But let me ask a question about the politics of this: If meditation is an important way to cosmopolitan awareness and cosmopolitan identity, then how are you going to implement meditation politically? You can't very well require people to meditate in order to have the kinds of experiences that can lead to the sense of unity that might eventuate in a cosmopolitan identity. I can't imagine a nationwide governmental recommendation, let alone an edict, that people should or must meditate, especially given the separation of church and state in this country and the spiritual tenets of meditation.

Emile: That is right, Pinzak. But recall that we talked earlier about a totally secular form of meditation that seemed to achieve similar results, at least physical and emotional results.

Pinzak: Benson's "relaxation response."[61]

Emile: Yes. Because Benson bases his relaxation technique on meditative practices—in fact, in most ways it is exactly like those practices—we can anticipate that some practitioners will have the same or similar metaphysical experiences. But introducing the relaxation technique comes without the spiritual trappings. So any group—a business or a school or a non-profit organization, say—could introduce the relaxation technique as a way to reduce tension and stress, just as Benson does.

Pinzak: That's a sneaky way into contemplation.

Emile: Is it? Is it not just what Benson says it is: a relaxation technique to induce a relaxation response? You are asking people simply to sit quietly, close their eyes, and silently repeat a world like "one." The technique reduces stress, the body relaxes, tension flows out. The person feels better, clearer, quieter, relaxed, and tension-free. Could not a school day begin with students sitting quietly for ten minutes practicing the relaxation technique? Could a business not have "relaxation breaks" instead of "coffee breaks"? Is it not so that schoolteachers and principals want their students to reduce or eliminate tension? Is it not also true that business executives and managers want to reduce the stress of their workers?

Pinzak: I can see by introducing a secularized version of meditation that one could make the practice more palatable politically and that people would then be more open to practicing it. *(Emile nods.)* Because people practicing it turn within and sit in silence, they are imitating the contemplatives that we have been talking about, and they could have similar kinds of experiences. Through the turn within, or so the contemplatives say, people can come to see and know the cosmic realm and, as we've been discussing in all of our conversations, would come to feel one with the cosmos, which, in a cosmopolitan turn, is feeling one with all persons.

Emile: Let us be true, here, to the logic of what we have been saying. If our experiences are verified intersubjectively in communal dialogue, then what is verified is what is.

Pinzak: Your point now, Emile?

Emile: We do not know whether there is a cosmic order that through meditation we tap into. That presupposes a cosmic order "out there" or "in here" that already exists in some form. Instead, we are saying something putatively more radical. We create or construct the cosmic order through what we intersubjectively verify. That is, no cosmic order exists apart from our intersubjective construction of it, for we cannot know of its existence unless we have both experienced and verified it communally.

Pinzak *(furiously typing and not looking up):* So what we verify communally is what exists. What we verify become real features of our world, part of the structure of our intersubjective worldview. Until something is experienced and verified, we cannot know that it exists at all.

Emile: That seems right. You might have an experience that is real to you, but it is not verified. You have a dream. It is real to you, but it is not real to me. We do not share what you dreamt.

Pinzak: Yet we do share dreaming. So we know that we dream, because the experience of dreaming is verified communally. The content of the dream is not, so it remains personal. So if we want to know what a dream means, we go to a dream therapist or a dream expert or we share it with our friends. We ask, "What do you think of that?" By doing so we seek shared interpretation; that is, we seek meaning together, and that requires dialogue.

Emile: And the same could be said for differentiating a mystical insight from a psychotic episode.

Pinzak *(still typing):* Thus the results of knowledge—what can be publicly and intersubjectively confirmed—may transform how we view the world and how we live our lives. The meaning of that knowledge, and the nature of what we know and have seen, must be explained and justified according to the epistemological method appropriate to the world of language and thought, the mental world. Therefore, *moral* commandments that putatively come from God, to be valid and true, must satisfy the criteria of sound knowledge in the mental-moral realm.

Emile: So if Swami Nananda tells us that his meditation reveals that all cancers are caused by viruses, we must ask for a look at his evidence. We should no more accept his pronouncements on medicine than we should expect him, now that he has seen into the world of spirit, to run a four-minute mile or to write elegant analytical philosophy.

Pinzak: *Elegant* analytical philosophy? That's oxymoronic, isn't it, Emile?

Emile *(laughing):* I take your point. My point is that realms are distinct; knowledge of one does not automatically translate into knowledge of and skill in another.

Pinzak: This is why we should not be quick to make contemplatives into kings. We need to hear about, to see, their evidence for what they propose to do in the political realm.[62]

Emile: Spiritual insight, seeing in that one domain, does not translate into political acumen. Seeing in one domain does not necessarily offer insight in another.

So we began our conversation trying to establish that mystical experience does, indeed, generate valid knowledge. That knowledge is as valid, and as real, as what we know through science about the physical world and through argument—reasons and evidence—about the moral and mental world. But now we are making the point that this real mystical or spiritual knowledge should not be used to subsume the other two domains.

Pinzak: Don't collapse the other two into the spiritual realm or domain.

Emile: Precisely.

Pinzak: And as you suggested this conversation has reinforced the importance of dialogue, which is at the heart of dialectical thinking and thus of cosmopolitan identity. In the world of politics, which is part of the mental-moral world . . .

Emile: . . . which should not be surprising since historically moral philosophy has had two parts: ethics and politics . . .

Pinzak: . . . we need to *see* what someone is talking about. Sometimes we cannot see the point of someone's position or belief; we ask for clarification and for reasons, or for more reasons, or for different reasons. We are asking the person to lay out and explain what he sees—how and why he thinks as he does. This is political dialogue, and it is through such dialogue that we generate public knowledge.

Emile: What do you mean by "public knowledge"?

Pinzak: Public knowledge is what citizens in dialogue and deliberation come to realize about the nature of social or political problems and policies and come to realize about the effects of problems and policies on themselves, their fellow citizens, and their fellow human beings. When a participant hears a diversity of views, he begins to understand the extent of the problem and the possible consequences of different solutions.

Public knowledge is something else, too. It is this public's view on what needs to be done or ought to be done, or what needs to be considered or ought to be considered before any policy is taken up. Public knowledge in this sense is a perspective or many perspectives generated by this group, this public, that could occur only by the participants' working together and not separately.

Emile: Political dialogue also helps generate among the participants a sense of community, a sense that they are themselves a public working together. This community of inquirers consists of participants interested in, concerned about, and affected by the politics of an issue. These participants bring to the dialogical deliberations their concerns, interests, ideas, dreams, passions, confusions, phobias. They bring all of those, for they are people just like us but often with particularities not like ours. Here, then, are the two sides of cosmopolitan identity: We recognize the connection to all others, the "beingness" of all others, as we equally acknowledge and seek to embrace the particularities of these others. Out of this cluster of discrete human beings comes a public. This public generates political knowledge through conversation.

Pinzak: This conversation or dialogue is truly integrative or integral, for from these partial perspectives that the participants bring together, this public tries to create a more encompassing, a more comprehensive, a more complete view of the issue or problem and of solutions.

Thus, we should treat moralities not as dictates from prophets or clergy or mystics, nor as facts derived from the empirical study of humans and nature. They are, instead, mental constructions created together through language and dialogue; made, that is, through thought and feeling and then confirmed, rejected, modified, or reinforced in our cultural conversation.

Emile: What is politics, especially democratic politics, but the attempt to work out some settlement among persons holding conflicting moral positions? What integral democratic politics should be, therefore, is a participatory forum of public deliberation that leads to political decisions, and possibly even agreement, on the basis of moral judgments. "Judgment" is here understood to mean a position taken after the exercise of practical reason and of empathy in the establishing of knowledge.

Pinzak: That participatory forum in our context is of cosmopolitan deliberation. In other words, some forums must be global. The dialogue, and the divergence of views, can be, must be, or will be on occasion as wide as the world.

Emile: Yes, but "cosmopolitan deliberation," as you phrase it, does not necessarily mean that the topic must be global or that the participants must come from around the world. Instead, it means that the deliberations must be dialectic or use dialectical thinking. In addition, the best dialogical setting would also involve a period at the outset for quiet reflection.

Pinzak: A period of meditation or the relaxation technique.

Emile: Something like that, to reduce the stress built up through the day and to quiet participants' minds. Yet the key element, it seems to me, is engaging in dialogue with people who are not like you, where the divergence of views is wide.

Pinzak: Not a "we" of people just like "me." What is a democracy, an active or deliberative democracy, but a community of strangers?

Emile: Precisely. With divergent views, one can think about, test out, probe and defend different values and insights. One can then hear about what other people "see," and one can "see" how other people construct worldviews and live within them.

You and I need to discuss the possible structures and kinds of such deliberative forums and institutions . . .

Pinzak: . . . always promised, never fulfilled . . .

Emile: Promised but not *yet* fulfilled. Our discussions are not over.

Pinzak: There is always tomorrow to think about cosmopolitan institutions. *(Emile nods.)*

Of course, not everyone will agree that a participatory forum of public deliberation, cosmopolitan or otherwise, should be the form of democratic politics. Some liberal democrats, for one group, won't agree. From their perspective liberalism shifts conflicting moral issues from public deliberation to private concern. Separating public from private enables liberals to accommodate disparate views by shunting off divergent views and practices into the private realm and invoking the virtues of tolerance and respect for others to do so.[63]

Emile: Yet moral issues are often political and thus public issues. Look at gay marriage, abortion, gun control, and cloning as examples, to say nothing of competing virtues and competing political ideals—liberty, equality, security. Divergent ideas and practices are competing claims of truth. As such, they require public debate and defense, not simply a guarantee that they can be privately held.

The ideal of politics, it seems to me, Pinzak, and here I am intruding on your territory, is to make our moral standards common. That is certainly the goal of any integral model. To do so requires a forum where standards can be fully articulated. For me this means a place where our moral conceptions can be discussed, analyzed, and clarified. To proceed to make those conceptions common, or to try to make them common, supposes, because our views are divergent, that some conceptions will be rejected, some accepted, and most repeatedly debated.

Pinzak: If by "repeatedly debated" you mean "renegotiated" or "never closed to discussion and deliberation," then I agree. This means that even "objective" knowledge, that which comes from the scientific method, is not certain and fixed. Scientific truths are themselves always open to scrutiny and renegotiation, in this sense. That is how science operates; indeed, that is how science gains its strength.

Emile: We have now made all of this common between us. *(Both laugh.)*

Pinzak: But not so fast, Emile. Are you suggesting that the aim of politics is to resolve deep moral and philosophical disagreements? That seems to ask too much, for opposing viewpoints, as we've said, can be equally "true" or right or good. Divergent perspectives and practices can have strong evidence and good reasons supporting them. There may be no clear way to choose among them.

There is every reason to believe that some, even many, moral disagreements cannot be resolved.

Emile: Yet we should approach such disagreement *as if* we can resolve them. In that way we demand of those holding divergent positions that they present the best account of—give the best reasons and evidence for—their positions. As a moral issue, for example, abortion cannot be resolved by politics. Yet in laying out the best arguments for the conflicting sides, we can come to see that both sides may be valid. Must we then decide which side is right? No, for what we may have established is that given what we know now, both sides are right (though for different reasons). That is why abortion will remain an issue. But because the issue makes a difference to us morally, we demand some *political* decision. The standards by which we make our arguments and render our judgments have now been established by intersubjective agreement. We now know which moral arguments for and against abortion are best and therefore which to use with care in making our public policy.

The decision-making procedures themselves are predicated on a presupposition of universality. That means that every participant is considered a self-reflective agent able to take up the perspectives of others as well as to criticize those perspectives, those of society, as well as one's own. At the same time, the content of the procedures rests on another presupposition: that participants are all different individuals, with unique perspectives, histories, biases, desires, even needs. These must be shared, understood, and taken into account.

Pinzak: So we approach moral issues as if we can resolve them, but what we cannot do is impose "consensus" on others. We try, in other words, not to impose our own structures on others, but to climb inside their perspectives and structures and procedures as much as is feasible.

Emile: This reinforces the value of respect, of mutual respect, especially if we demonstrate that we remain open to the perspectives of others.

Pinzak: It also shows that we value autonomy, living life from the inside. Persons must learn their own lessons rather than having such lessons imposed on them. If imposed, whose life are these persons living? Who is guiding that life?

Emile: We try to reach a consensus that combines or transcends the particular views of each side. By doing so through dialogue, we acknowledge the personhood of every participant.

Pinzak: If the notion of dialogue is to include plural perspectives in trying to reach consensus on values, especially moral values, then should not the value of dialogue itself be open to discussion?

Emile: Without question it should. Dialogue reposes on a bed of values that are necessary if the dialectic is to proceed. Those values include persuasion over coercion; not just tolerance of other viewpoints, but honoring and appreciating other viewpoints by taking them seriously; mutual respect; and the importance of autonomy: self-reflective, deliberative choices made among competing conceptions, even of the good life. These values must themselves be open to deliberation. Otherwise participants in the dialogue are arguing blindly on behalf of a bed of values that are simply their own parochial batting.

Pinzak: But how do we do that, Emile? How do we scrutinize the procedures without using the very procedures outlined in the deliberative dialogue? Won't any critique have to be phrased, explained, and argued for or against in the same way that the dialogue has been outlined?

Emile: Yes, it will be and should be in the same way. How else might we honor the divergence of the views at issue? The procedures themselves are universal. This should not surprise us or deter us, since the epistemological steps are themselves universal. We are simply following what any group must do to test, establish, or refute the epistemological claims before them. But this procedure is not imposed on anyone. Participants and prospective participants must come to see the value in the procedures themselves; in short, it is not just what morality we hold but why we hold it. We are looking for a convergence of people's understandings of morality and moral claims, not just because they share practices, but also because the convergence is the result of the discursive method.

Pinzak: Let me try to understand this, Emile. We are not looking for independent verification or justification of any claim; we are looking for comparative verification or justification. We judge on the basis of experience with, on the basis of reason and evidence within, multiple perspectives or contexts.

Emile: So far, so good.

Pinzak: If we found agreement or consensus across multiple perspectives or contexts, we might be tempted to say that we had absolute agreement. But to be true, that agreement would have to be with all contexts or perspectives, and we can't know that.

Emile: That is so. We cannot know that. Perception and interpretation determine what we think is true. But perception itself is a construction based on the social context, the familial and societal traditions, in which one is raised. This is why scientific claims need intersubjective verification. Scientific truths, in other words, are themselves constructed.

So, truth is a social construction, built up of and by interpretations and experience. We have to look at phenomena, examine them or experience them, and then share with others what we have seen or experienced. Thus we reason together with others about our interpretations and perceptions. We combine our subjective experiences and interpretations with those of others, and through this intersubjectivity we proceed toward "objectivity," depending on the domain and on the sharing and the agreement on reasons and evidence. According to the AQAL model, in the language of the quadrants, this is when subjects meet other subjects (Upper-Left Quadrant) and through intersubjectivity (Lower-Left Quadrant) move toward objectivity (Upper-Right and Lower-Right Quadrants). Thus agreement arrived at through intersubjective dialogue may even result in what is objectively true for us; that is, the agreement is a form of interobjectivity.

Pinzak: This is so whether we are talking about science or morals or mystical experience.

Emile: Correct.

Pinzak: Okay, so morals are constructed. They are constructed out of the collective experiences of people living together or living in proximity or simply sharing the same planet. Moral practices vary dramatically from epoch to epoch and even from culture to culture because the experiences are different. But all cultures construct some sense of morality. Are there similarities that connect if not unite how those moralities are constructed?

Emile: It would seem so. It would seem that any culture would construct moralities in much the same way. Something moves the culture, the people, or even the leaders of that culture, to change. All cultures have rules and norms and laws that represent how the cultures organize themselves. They refer to how persons within the culture are to behave and what rules they are to follow. This does not undercut the fact that persons within the culture may have diverse, even divergent, views and may disagree with some of the culture's rules, norms, and values. This does not negate the fact that different cultures have and have had different groups constructing those rules, norms, and values.

Pinzak: So then we ask how cultures come to agreement or find agreement that permits them to establish rules and laws and norms. How is diversity of views transcended?

Emile: The simplest answer is that much of the time that diversity is not transcended. Diversity can often be suppressed by an elite or by a tyrant. But our context is different. We are asking how self-reflective moral agents, persons with formal-operational capabilities, can come to live harmoniously in societies and across societies where some of these agents find some of the practices, norms, or laws deficient and even unacceptable. So how can these agents overcome not simply diversity of views but even this unacceptability?

Pinzak: They can if the values underlying these practices, norms, and laws are arrived at through dialogue among persons constituting that culture. They can if we treat participants with mutual recognition of moral seriousness.

Emile: What do you mean by "moral seriousness"?

Pinzak: I mean that we do not simply condemn a practice or a moral standard on the basis that we think it is wrong. We accept that the people performing that practice or holding that standard have reasons, good reasons, for doing so. Therefore, we engage in discussion of that practice or standard and don't dismiss it out of hand. When we condemn rather than challenge a practice, it is because we include in that condemnation the arguments that we think make it wrong. We assume those arguments in our condemnation, and to do that, to make that assumption, is to fail to treat those other persons with respect. We need to interrogate cultural practices, not roundly condemn them. We honor persuasion more than force; we exercise *that* as a moral value. We no more want to impose our moral views on others than we want them to impose theirs on us.

Emile: In such a dialogue participants must be given what they consider a fair airing and hearing of their views. When that occurs, then participants can accept the outcome of the dialectical or deliberative dialogue even when it goes against their own views.

Pinzak: Dialogue is the way to bring forth discussion of what underlies moral values. Deliberate about what people think and do and why they think and do it. There are, of course, groups that do not want to dialogue, because they consider dialogue a waste of time. Religious fundamentalists, irrespective of which religion we are talking about, might be such a group. They base their values on a reading of a holy work, and that work is considered infallible.

Emile: Yet even fundamentalists can disagree on where precisely that infallibility lies. Persons are interpreting that holy work, and different persons even within fundamentalisms can disagree. Thus they will discuss and deliberate, but many only among themselves. Still, it is a beginning.

If we recognize other humans as moral agents like ourselves, though their moral codes are diametrically opposite our own, do we not recognize that they are thereby agents with reasoning ability? What does that then convey to us? Under that circumstance is a dialogue not at least a possibility? And if there can be dialogue, can there not also be the possibility of convergence of moral views?

Pinzak: Now if we are talking about dialogue in politics, then the participants, the deliberators, in any democratic community of inquirers ought to include all citizens.

Emile: That would be a broad composition, broader than the kinds of community of inquirers that we have been discussing.

Pinzak: Yes it would, and that is intentional. Membership in any epistemological community depends on competence in seeing, in being trained in the requisite methodology. In the political community, *phronesis* is what is required. *Phronesis,* or what Aristotle calls "prudence" or "practical wisdom," comprises both "experiential learning"—learning that comes from experience through living—and judgment that guides deliberation—that reasons must be given and discussed with others.[64] No one is tested for *phronesis;* it is assumed that by a certain age one has it. This is so because we are not dealing with levels of expertise, but rather with threshold concepts of reasoning and experience, both of which are age-related, not mastery-related. So we assume the thresholds; we don't demand them. All persons of age, unless they demonstrate otherwise, are presumed to have the requisite capacities to deliberate.

Emile: So we need both Aristotelian *synesis* and *phronesis.* That is, we need the "phronetic" ability to deliberate or weigh evidence and give reasons, as well as the ability to put ourselves in the perspective of another so as to understand that other perspective.[65] This is what Richard Bernstein calls a "dialogical model of rationality" (1983, 172). It is the capacity to make practical judgments—judgments that lead to or explain actions—in the face of multiple factors. The capacities required of this kind of political dialogue do not necessarily require active participation. By simply attending to the proceedings one can gain epistemological insight.

Pinzak: That's right. Citizens, at the end of a deliberation, need not present an argument for their votes. And, short of unanimity, voting is the means by which a political decision is made. But because moral issues are not resolved by votes, the issue can be opened again at a later time. *Phronesis* is a way of knowing that according to Aristotle, the contingent positions or resolutions we arrive at are always open to additional interrogation. Politics is thus a rational enterprise, but the form proposed here would be and would need to be far more participatory than current democracies.

Emile: Such participation is warranted because public knowledge, as we have been saying, is formed and brought forth through political dialogue. If we want to generate such knowledge, then we need to bring people into dialogue with one another.

Pinzak: At the same time, if we want to encourage cosmopolitan identity, then we need to structure dialectical thinking into that dialogue as well. We want to encourage dialectical thinking because it requires the presentation of divergent perspectives, thereby leading to optimal public knowledge, or the integration of the most perspectives.

Emile: It is a "two-for-one." One process or procedure encompasses two aims or goals. The generation of public knowledge requires dialogue, and the best public knowledge requires dialogue of divergent views. Dialogue of divergent views stimulates dialectical thinking, which in turn stimulates cosmopolitan identity.

Pinzak *(typing):* This is splendid work that we've done today. We should celebrate with a drink.

Emile: We did . . . with coffee.

Pinzak: I was thinking of something stronger and more "consciousness altering."

Emile: If I imbibed such, and if it were not so late, then I would join you.

Pinzak *(somewhat sarcastically):* How about a larger cup of coffee then . . . at our next meeting. A DOUBLE espresso?

Emile *(laughing):* That I shall accept.

Pinzak *(closing his laptop):* You know, Emile, we can no longer avoid discussing the institutional framework for integral democracy.

Emile: We have done pretty well so far in that regard. But, yes, next time we must take that up. (*Pinzak packs away his computer, notebook, and pen, and stands. Emile rises simultaneously, and both extend their hands. Pinzak says, "Until then."*)

Notes

1. The conversation that Emile transcribed between the two senior monks will serve as the centerpiece of a future novel about the spiritual journey of Pinzak.

2. For a summary of some of this work, see Jensine Andresen, "Meditation Meets Behavioral Medicine," *Journal of Consciousness Studies* 7, nos. 11-12 (2000): 17-73. The most extensive studies of the effects of meditation have been conducted on Transcendental Meditation (TM). The first paper on TM's physiological effects appeared in *Science* in 1970, and researchers have continued studies up to the present. The five volumes of scientific research on TM contain over 500 studies. See *Scientific Research on Maharishi's Transcendental Meditation and TM-Sidhi Program,* volumes 1-5. This research focuses on beneficial changes in metabolic rate, plasma, cortisol levels, galvanic skin response, arterial blood lactate, cardiovascular and neural activity, motor ability, perceptual ability, learning, athletic performance, biochemical reactions, oxygen consumption, and the like.

Throughout this section of the Fifth Encounter I am not distinguishing between various kinds of meditation techniques. There is empirical evidence that different techniques produce different physiological results. For example, Dr. Herbert Benson and his colleagues found that some techniques decreased the metabolic rate of meditators, while other techniques raised the metabolic rate. (Cited in Andresen 2000, 28.) This is true between meditative practices—say, yogic mantra techniques and Buddhist mindfulness techniques—as well as within the same spiritual tradition, say the various techniques—*sutrayana* and *vajrayana*—within Tibetan Buddhism.

3. See Andrew Newberg and Mark Robert Waldman, *How God Changes Your Brain* (New York: Ballantine Books, 2009), and Richard Monastersky, "Religion on the Brain," *The Chronicle of Higher Education* 52, no. 38 (May 27, 2006): A15. See also Patrick McNamara's *Where God and Science Meet: How Brain and Evolutionary Studies Alter Our Understanding of Religion* (forthcoming).

4. Monastersky, "Religion," A16.

5. Quoted in Newberg and Waldman, *How God Changes,* 48. Newberg studied a group of nuns who had been practicing the Christian "Centering Prayer" for at least fifteen years. He found that the neurological changes in their brains were significant and matched closely the neurological changes seen in studies of Buddhist monks. Although the brain changes were similar, these two groups "obviously nurtured very different beliefs" (48). In brief, breathing, attention, and relaxation techniques used in various meditative practices produce physiological effects, even when stripped of religious or spiritual overtones. As Newberg said, "Our patients were taught a traditional Eastern meditation, using sounds and movements that had deep religious meaning, but we did not emphasize the spiritual dimensions of the ritual. No one reported having a spiritual experience, and no one mentioned God" (45). See also Newberg's books *Why God Won't Go Away* (2001) and *Born to Believe* (2007).

6. Decreased activity in the parietal lobe, the part of the cortex used to construct our sense of self, indicates a dissolution of a sense of self and an increased sense of unity.

7. Sam Harris, *The End of Faith* (New York: W. W. Norton & Company, 2004), 232, fn. 18. Harris notes that there appears to be credible scientific evidence even for reincarnation. Some might think that mystical experience itself is a paranormal phenomenon. But even reincarnation, an exemplar of the paranormal, can claim some scientific basis. See the work of Ian Stevenson, *Twenty Cases Suggestive of Reincarnation* (Charlottesville: University Press of Virginia, 1974); *Unlearned Language: New Studies in Xenoglossy* (Charlottesville: University Press of Virginia, 1984); *Where Reincarnation and Biology Intersect* (Westport, Conn.: Praeger, 1997). See also a book on Ian Stevenson's work, not mentioned by Harris: Tom Shroder, *Old Souls* (New York: Simon & Schuster, 1999).

Decades ago the scientific research on meditation focused almost exclusively on physiological changes in meditators. Other than measurements involving EEG, very little of that research looked at what interests many scientists today: psychological changes, alterations in brain structure, and changes in brain functioning.

8. Mario Beauregard and Denyse O'Leary, *The Spiritual Brain* (New York: Harper Collins, 2007), 263.

9. Antoine Lutz, Lawrence L. Greischar, Nancy B. Rawlings, Matthieu Ricard, and Richard J. Davidson, eds. "Long-Term Meditators Self-Induce High-Amplitude Gamma Synchrony During Mental Practice," *Proceedings of the National Academy of Sciences* 101, no. 46 (2004): 16372.

10. See Note 5 in this chapter.

11. See Sara W. Lazar et al., "Meditation Experience Is Associated with Increased Cortical Thickness," *NeuroReport* 16, no. 17 (2005): 1893-97. In a study testing sustained attention of meditators and a control group, Elizabeth Valentine, et al. found that meditators—those who practiced concentration techniques and those who practiced mindfulness techniques—outperformed the control group. Long-term meditators outperformed short-term meditators. See Elizabeth Valentine et al., "Meditation and Attention: A Comparison of the Effects of Concentrative and Mindfulness Meditation on Sustained Attention." This paper is available from Dr. E. R. Valentine, Department of Psychology, Royal Holloway, Egham, Surrey, England. Also, Newberg and Waldman tested some subjects who were new to meditation and meditated only twelve minutes per day for eight weeks. In these nascent meditators they found activation in the prefrontal cortex and in the anterior cingulate, which indicates improved memory and cognition, counters the effects of depression, and slows down or reduces cognitive decline (Newberg and Waldman 2009, 27-28).

12. In 2005 Newberg conducted an online survey of people's spiritual experiences, collecting data on their religious orientations and belief systems. By 2007 he had data from almost one thousand people (Newberg and Waldman 2009, 69-70). Nearly "three-quarters of our respondents indicated that they felt a sense of oneness with the universe or a unity with all of life." This was true for people, Newberg observes, "not just in a metaphoric sense, but in the way we conduct our lives" (2009, 81). Newberg and Waldman added that social interaction strengthens one's ability to respond to others. "We encourage you to interact with as many different people as you can" (2009, 127), which is certainly what I have emphasized throughout this book. See also Newberg and Waldman, 2009, Chapter 10: "Compassionate Communication."

13. Charles Taylor, *Sources of the Self* (Cambridge, Mass.: Harvard University Press, 1989), section 25.5, and also 518.

14. I shall use the terms "domain," "realm," and "world" interchangeably without, I hope, confusing the reader.

15. Hannah Arendt, "Truth and Politics," *Between Past and Future* (New York: Viking Press, 1968), 237.

16. The clearest discussion of these three eyes of knowing is in Ken Wilber's *Eye to Eye* (New York: Anchor Press/Doubleday, 1983). See especially within that volume the essays "Eye to Eye" and "The Problem of Proof." Anyone reading these essays will see the tremendous debt I owe to Wilber's discussion.

17. Charles Taylor, *Philosophical Papers 1: Human Agency and Language* (Cambridge: Cambridge University Press, 1985), 259.

18. See "Foucault on Freedom," *Political Theory* 12, no. 2, 1984.

19. Wilber, *Eye to Eye,* 31.

20. Wilber, *Eye to Eye,* 32.

21. In Jurgen Habermas, *Knowledge and Human Interests* (Boston, Mass.: Beacon Press, 1971). Habermas describes three different modes of knowing: a technical mode, a practical mode, and an emancipatory mode. The empirical-analytical sciences operate according to the scientific method to produce technical knowledge. Historical-hermeneutical approaches produce practical knowledge, and theory produces emancipatory knowledge—that is, emancipation from hypostatized powers (313). None of these three epistemological modes can be reduced to the others. Each explores, as it were, its own realm. Each is only one type of knowledge. And all three, argues Habermas, require open intersubjective communication about what is found and what is concluded.

Habermas later modified these epistemological modes into three dimensions of rationality: the cognitive-instrumental, the moral-practical, and the aesthetic-expressive. The reason for the switch seems to center around Habermas's difficulty in grounding emancipatory claims epistemologically and in delineating adequately his conception of self-reflection. Whatever the problems with his design, I wish only to point out the similarity between Habermas's first two modes and the first two eyes of knowing I have described. Note, moreover, that Habermas wants to distinguish three separate, non-reducible realms: empirical facts, social norms, and inner experience or self-reflection. While his emancipatory mode and my spiritual realm are quite different, we agree on the need in all three realms for intersubjective validation.

22. From T. R. Henn's *The Apple and the Spectroscope;* quoted in Ann E. Berthoff, *The Making of Meaning* (Montclair, N.J.: 1981), 116.

23. See "Responsibility for Self," in *The Identities of Persons,* ed. Amelie Oksenberg Rorty (Berkeley and Los Angeles: University of California Press: 1976), and Charles Taylor, "What Is Human Agency?" *Philosophical Papers 1,* especially 34-35.

24. Wilber, 1983, 32.

25. Wilber, 1983, 44.

26. Kwame Anthony Appiah, *Cosmopolitanism: Ethics in a World of Strangers* (New York: W. W. Norton & Co., 2006), 41.

27. Thomas Kuhn makes this point in *The Structure of Scientific Revolutions* (Chicago: The University of Chicago Press, 1962). One of his examples is of "seeing water droplets or a needle against a numerical scale." These are "primitive perceptual experience(s) for the man unacquainted with cloud chambers and ammeters." The man "who has learned about these instruments"—who has been trained—"sees not droplets but the tracks of electrons, alpha particles, and so on." When a student looks at a contour map, she sees only lines on paper. But the cartographer sees a picture of terrain. Only after training, when the student becomes an inhabitant of the cartographer's world, will she see what the cartographer sees (197).

Sam Harris gets at the same point when he comments that "[p]eople who believe that the earth is flat are not dissenting *geographers;* people who deny that the Holocaust ever occurred are not dissenting *historians;* people who think that God created the universe in 4004 BC are not dissenting *cosmologists*" (2004, 184; emphases in the original). When people have looked at the evidence, especially but not exclusively when they have been trained in such evidence, they do not dissent from these data before them. People who know geography, and they do not have to be geographers, do not argue that the earth is flat; similarly for people who can and have looked at the evidence for the Holocaust and at the science of cosmology.

28. Charles Taylor, *Philosophical Papers 1,* 259.

29. Charles Taylor, *Philosophical Papers 2: Philosophy and the Human Sciences* (Cambridge: Cambridge University Press, 1985) 234, 237. This is the same as the "linguistic community."

30. *Philosophical Papers 2*, 32.

31. *Philosophical Papers 2*, 23.

32. For a discussion of this topic, and related issues, see Jack Crittenden, "Veneration of Community," *Communal Societies* 9 (1989): 105-22.

33. Charles Taylor, *Sources of the Self,* 310.

34. Charles Taylor, *Sources of the Self,* 38.

35. Charles Taylor, *Philosophical Papers 2,* 33.

36. Charles Taylor, *Philosophical Papers 2,* 34.

37. Thomas Kuhn, *Structure,* 202.

38. Scientists rely on empirical facts, which are literally "something made through trial" *(facere,* "to make"; *en,* "through"; *peira,* "trial"). *Facere* is also translated as "to do" (thus a fact is a "thing done"). But in the sixteenth century "fact" came to mean not only the doing but also "the making" of an act. In addition, *factum* or *factus* refers to that which is made. See *The Compact Edition of the Oxford English Dictionary* (New York: Oxford University Press), 947. We, of course, are free to restrict the meaning of words as long as we make that meaning clear. So "empirical" has come to mean that which can be experienced through the five senses or their extensions. This has given science a great deal of precision. But it is curious that the literal definition makes no mention of this kind of "sensory" trial. Moreover, a fact is something that is "made," not found. So could there be other kinds of trials, other kinds of experiments that could yield facts? Are there other ways facts could be "made"? Could the three epistemological steps not only make or establish empirical facts but normative facts as well?

39. The anthropologist Ashley Montague concluded that "essentially the mind of the savage [sic] functions in exactly the same way as our own [modern mind] does, the differences perceptible in the effects of that functioning are due only to the differences in the premises upon which that functioning is based." So while the experiences and histories of cultures vary, the internal processes for reasoning about them are the same. And according to Steven Lukes, researchers Cole and Scribner have concluded "that thus far there is no evidence for different kinds of reasoning processes such as the old classic theories alleged—we have no evidence for a 'primitive logic.'" Note the open-endedness of their claim: There is no evidence "thus far." *(Culture and Thought,* 170; quoted in Steven Lukes, "Relativism in Its Place," *Rationality and Relativism* (Cambridge, Mass.: The MIT Press, 1982), 270. The truth of the matter is open to continued communal confirmation or refutation.

40. For the Azande to refute or confirm our evidence, they would, of course, have to train themselves adequately for the illumination, just as we would have to translate or see their practices properly.

41. Contrast this view with Joshua Cohen's notion of "reason-giving" in "Procedure and Substance in Deliberative Democracy," from *Deliberative Democracy,* eds. James Bohman and William Rehg (Cambridge, Mass.: MIT Press, 1997): "In an idealized deliberative setting, it will not do simply to advance reasons that one takes to be true or compelling: such considerations may be rejected by others who are themselves reasonable. One must instead find reasons that are compelling to others" (414). In other words, in Cohen's version, even if it is acknowledged to be an "idealized" setting, partiality of perspective is to be overcome, and it is overcome not by stepping into the particular

viewpoint of another, but by seeking out the universalistic perspective of the generalized other—that is, unanimity, if not an objective point of view, on what is normatively right.

42. See the Sixth and Seventh Encounters for the importance of storytelling and testimony in democratic deliberations.

43. For a detailed discussion of deliberation and critical thinking, see Crittenden 2002, especially Chapter Five.

44. In Aristotle, *On Rhetoric,* tr. George A. Kennedy (New York: Oxford University Press, 1991), 171. Aristotle also highlights through *sumbouleuesthai* the significance of combining *logos* or *reasoning* with *pathos* or *feelings.* This combination, of course, is one of the features of identity ("felt identity") in general and of cosmopolitan identity in particular.

45. Aristotle, *The Nicomachean Ethics,* trans., David Ross; revised by J. L. Ackrill and J. O. Urmson (New York: Oxford University Press, 1998), Book VI, chapter 10, 1143a12-15. *Synesis* comes from the Greek verb *suniemi* or "to set together" in the sense of coming to an understanding of someone else's position by working to put oneself fully into the other's situation. This attempt at understanding sets or binds the two together.

46. Charles Taylor, *Philosophical Papers 2,* 16-17.

47. Public validation—presenting to others through articulation what you know and how you know it—is the way Plato distinguished between opinion *(doxa)* and truth or true knowledge *(episteme).* See *The Republic,* Book VI, especially the "divided line." Aristotle used the term *endoxa* to refer to those beliefs and ideas that had been tested through argument among the citizens of the polis.

48. John Rawls, "Kantian Constructivism in Moral Theory," *Journal of Philosophy* 77, September 1980, 519.

49. As I use the term, "contemplation," I am not referring to Aristotelian contemplation, which involves more intellection than I intended here. But contemplation encompasses, to my mind, more spiritual techniques than does the term "meditation"—for example, the Christian Centering Prayer, which is a kind of mediation but also a kind of prayer.

50. A. J. Ayer, *Language, Truth and Logic* (New York: Dover, 1952), 118.

51. For a detailed discussion of these points, see Pascal Kaplan, "Toward a Theology of Consciousness," Ph. D. diss., Harvard University, 1976.

52. W. T. Stace, *Mysticism and Philosophy* (London: MacMillan, 1973).

53. Ken Wilber claims that these three epistemological steps are found in all of the esoteric traditions East and West; W. T. Stace concluded in *Mysticism and Philosophy* that the "introvertive experience" is in essence "the same all over the world in all cultures, religions, places, and ages." See also Fritjof Schuon, *The Transcendent Unity of Religions* (New York: Harper & Row, 1975).

54. *The Sufi Message of Hazrat Inayat Khan,* Volume 12 (London: Barrie and Rockliff,) 104; quoted in Kaplan, "Toward a Theology," 245.

55. All quotations are from Plotinus, *The Enneads,* "The Fifth Ennead," tr. Stephen MacKenna (London: Faber and Faber, 1969), 378-9.

56. Of course, certain atheistic visions also have this association—Hitler or Stalin or Pol Pot, for example.

57. See "Theism," *The Encyclopedia of Philosophy* 8 (New York: MacMillan Publishing Co. and The Free Press, 1967), 97-8.

58. W. T. Jones, *A History of Western Philosophy: The Medieval Mind,* Volume 2 (New York: Harcourt, Brace and World, 1969), 61f.

59. To understand the full extent of the spiritual realm and the experiences related to it, we cannot rely solely on William James's *Varieties of Religious Experience* (Cambridge, Mass.: Harvard University Press, 1985) on the stories of Christianity's and Judaism's great mystics, or on philosophers such as Stace. The full complexity and meaning of this realm can be revealed only through these sources in combination with non-Western sources—for example, the traditions of Hinduism, Buddhism Sufism, the Kabbalah, and Taoism. Here enter, also, the Native American traditions, as well as those of the Mystery religions, the Oriental cults, and the traditions of the Great Goddess.

60. See Charles Taylor, *Sources of the Self,* "The Moral Typography of the Self," 302.

61. See also the technique of "Compassionate Communication" developed by Newberg and Waldman, *How God,* 2009, 214-40.

62. On Plato's account philosopher-rulers could see the whole pattern, all segments of the "divided line." Perhaps, however, it was not their knowledge of specifics *(episteme)* that led Plato to wish them to rule, but their approach to knowledge, how they knew *(nous* or *noesis).*

63. For a sophisticated version of this, see John Rawls, "Justice as Fairness: Political not Metaphysical," *Philosophy and Public Affairs* 14, no. 3 (1985) and *Political Liberalism;* for liberal counters to this position, see Gutmann and Thompson, "Moral Conflict and Political Consensus," *Ethics* 101, no. 1 (1990) and Crittenden, 1992.

64. See Aristotle, *The Nichomachean Ethics,* Book VI, chapters 8 and 11. Practical wisdom as related to "prudence" and to *phronesis* is not to be confused with Aristotle's notion of wisdom as philosophical excellence. That "wisdom"—*sophia*—is a combination of intelligence as "intuitive reason" *(nous)* and "scientific knowledge" *(episteme).*

65. *Synesis,* then, corresponds to what Aristotle describes as "understanding"—that is, judging "soundly or well," which means accurately, what someone else says in matters under deliberation. See *The Nichomachean Ethics,* Book VI, chapter 10 and also chapter 11, especially on "sympathetic judgment."

Sixth Encounter:

Democratic Dialogue and Cosmopolitan Practices

In Lak'ech Ala K'in
—Mayan greeting meaning "I am another you."

In the several days since Pinzak had been to the Café Pamplona, fall had come to Cambridge. Pinzak could sense it more than see it. Before green had turned to red and orange and yellow fire, he felt the pulse of the city already slowing down; the pace, more relaxed. Sounds of the city—a shout across Brattle Street, the slap of the oars from the sculls and shells, the shrill of horns and the chime of laughter and bells—fell to whispers. Shadows elongated and lingered; birds flocked to their second homes. The city, the state, all of New England was contracting, compressing, pulling in. In winter it would crouch and huddle. Pinzak, mercifully, would be gone by then.

Tonight Pinzak was headed to the Cape for the weekend. His friend Bart (Barton Olney, III) had invited him for a weekend of lobsters and sailing. Pinzak looked forward especially to the midnight sailing that Bart loved to do in the light of a fall full moon. Bart had also invited another friend, a colleague from Brigham and Women's Hospital, who was also a pediatric oncologist and newly divorced. This weekend was not a "set-up" as such. It was simply a chance for Carly to unwind after a ferocious divorce. Was there any other kind? Pinzak had not heard of any. It was fall. It was time to constrict, not unwind. Pinzak had been through these kinds of "events" before . . . indeed, often. He was always running into friends or colleagues or acquaintances who just happened to have a cousin, sister, niece, neighbor, or who just happened to have met a lawyer, sous chef, bank teller, or personal trainer who would be perfect for him. "You're so much alike" or "She's just like you." Apparently Pinzak was not looking for someone just like him or even much like him. He was still single. He would play along, once again, however, because these friends and colleagues and acquaintances, just like Bart, had the best intentions. Besides, it was going to be Cape beaches, moonlight sailing, and steamed lobsters with Pinot Blanc, the wine as cold and crisp as the night air.

195

Pinzak arrived at the café to find Emile already sitting at their usual table, with a large cappuccino holding Pinzak's place. Emile himself had before him what looked like a double espresso. "Good afternoon, Pinzak," Emile said as Pinzak approached. "Good afternoon," Pinzak replied, looking up at the sky and squinting into the sun. Pinzak arranged his chair so that he and his computer would be in the shade, but he could easily shift into the sun from his seat if he wanted to. As he pulled his laptop from his bag, Emile asked, "Any plans for the weekend?" As Pinzak responded with news of his upcoming trip to the Cape, Emile was startled by the flat whisper in Pinzak's voice, words sounding like those from a man about to fall asleep. Emile opened his eyes and gazed at Pinzak, who was looking out onto the sidewalk at a man leisurely strolling by. The man was slim and wore a three-piece suit, European cut, that hugged his body. He had a closely trimmed beard and mustache and was smoking a cigar.

"Anything the matter?" asked Emile.

"That man is smoking a Punch Monarcas. I'd recognize the aroma anywhere."

"Punch Monarcas?" Emile inquired as he looked again at the man.

"It was my father's favorite cigar, a Cuban cigar. 'The best cigar in a tube,' he always claimed." Pinzak's eyes followed the man as he passed by. "Any time he went to a medical conference in Canada he'd buy some Punch Monarcas. He was so worried about being caught with them at customs that he'd stuff them in his suit and overcoat pockets to avoid packing them in his bags." Pinzak leaned forward to catch a final glimpse as the man disappeared from sight. "He never got caught." Pinzak finished unpacking his laptop, a notebook, and a pen.

"Those cigars carry a deep memory for me," he continued. "One year when I was teaching at Western, early in my career, I was visiting my parents in Albuquerque for the Christmas holidays. I had come into the house late one night and was turning off the hall lights, thinking them both asleep, when I heard my name called from my father's study. The study was dark, and so the voice surprised me. I went in. My father was sitting in the dark. I could see only the glow from the end of his cigar and smell the aroma of the Punch Monarcas. I said, 'Dad, what are you doing?'

He replied, 'Smoking in the dark.' I turned on a light. 'No, don't,' he said, 'I'm experimenting.' I quickly turned off the light and I said, 'Experimenting with what?'

'I don't think people smoke in the dark.'

'But you're smoking in the dark,' I responded.

'Yes, but only as an experiment. You can't see the smoke when you're in the dark. That is part of the enjoyment, and I think a big part, an integral part, of the experience. If you can't see the smoke, then you're not going to do it.' He paused. I had no response, not being a smoker at all. Then he said, 'I wonder whether you could get people to quit if you made them smoke in the dark every time they wanted to smoke?'

I don't know whether he would have done anything with this experiment. I doubt it. It was just something to think about and play with for a while. He died three weeks later from a massive coronary. That was totally unexpected, since he kept himself in good physical shape. Apparently he had a heart defect that went undetected his whole life. Ironic, no, his being a doctor?" Pinzak paused and rearranged his coffee cup on the table. "It was the last conversation I had with him. He was working at the hospital when I left for the university, and I never talked with him again."

The two were silent for several seconds. Then Emile observed, "So your father passed along his curiosity to you."

"If he did," Pinzak said, "it was about all he passed along." More seconds passed in silence.

"You two did not get along?" asked Emile.

"We had a casual relationship, almost more like acquaintances rather than father and son. He was totally caught up in his work, and, growing up, I was caught up in myself. We didn't really share many interests. For him, work was everything, even more than family. I kept my own life and interests secret from him and my mother. Neither of them probed, so that was pretty easy. Eventually, when I turned seriously to political theory, my father dismissed it as 'ethereal mental groping' and 'a waste of a good intellect.'"

"He wanted you to be a doctor?"

"I think he did, but he never said it. He wouldn't have. That would have been too intrusive and directing."

Both men drank from their cups. Then Pinzak said, with a small smile, "But I've never forgotten the smell of Punch Monarcas. That will always remind me of him."

"And of smoking in the dark?" asked Emile.

"That, too." Both men sat in silence for a while. Emile closed his eyes and soaked in the sun; Pinzak scrolled through a file on his computer. Their conversation began.

Pinzak: You know, Emile, I think I understand why we kept postponing any talk about cosmopolitan institutions.

Emile *(with eyes still closed):* Oh?

Pinzak: Because from the perspective on cosmopolitan identity that we've been developing, it doesn't matter as much what institutions we have, as much as it matters how the institutions are structured internally. That is, it doesn't matter what kinds of specific institutions of global governance we have, though we must have some; what matters is how decisions at whatever level are made. They must be made democratically, deliberatively, and integrally or through dialectical dialogue.

Emile: We might even go so far as to say that the institutions themselves are secondary to those procedures, or the essence of those procedures, because they are an organized or ordered reflection of those procedures. The focus is, therefore, on institutionalizing the process or procedures. Any institutions might do, provided they are built on the combination of dialectical thinking and deliberation . . . what we can call "democratic dialogue."

Pinzak: "Any institutions might do?" Isn't that position too extreme, Emile? We need to have some discussion of the political impact of democratic dialogue in institutional settings to see where dialogue ought to be established. Otherwise, the political and moral force of the presentation is weakened.

At the same time, thinking about institutions helps us imagine how to move toward global democracy and a cosmopolitan worldview. There will surely be people who argue, plan, and act on behalf of both global democracy and a cosmopolitan worldview who are not dialectical thinkers or who lack, or don't care about, cosmopolitan sensibilities. Their motivations are philosophical, or philosophically moral; they are moved by possible consequences of failure to act on global issues like nuclear proliferation, global warming, or the spread of pandemics. They are motivated to create images of a global world order, including the institutions for addressing global problems, because it makes sense philosophically.

Emile: What we wish to ensure is that those institutions, whatever forms they take, will be built upon democratic dialogue. *(Pinzak nods and types.)* We do not want our thinking about dialogue dismissed because we failed to imagine effective political institutions for an Integral Democracy.[1] At the same time, our thinking will not be so comprehensive that we can predict the many different ways that people might "transcend but include" the various perspectives on the topical political issues of today and tomorrow. Instead, we may offer an outline—a "recipe" if you like—of the ingredients essential to a democratic dialogue that permit and even require participants to hear and engage pluralistic perspectives. The ingredients are essential, but how they are ordered or emphasized or used must be left up to the participants themselves.

Pinzak: So our emphasis, then, is on what might be called "micro-level processes" rather than on institutions themselves.

Emile: Well, not entirely, because that seems to suggest that we shall not talk about politics at a mass level. We need to address that level, as you said. There is another reason why we should do so, and it fits with the overarching perspective that we have been taking in our conversations. We can see that if we recur to Wilber's AQAL model. In the model the institutions are the "hardware" or the Lower-Right Quadrant essential to running the "software" of dialectical thinking, or the Lower-Left and Upper-Left Quadrants.

Keep in mind that the processes or procedures themselves are visible structures and thus also part of the hardware, so it is not as if we are avoiding the Lower-Right Quadrant by talking more about the procedures themselves and not so much about the institutions. But we need to introduce and develop the democratic dialogical structure, more than we already have, and then link that structure to possible institutional changes or innovations.

Pinzak: One of my chief concerns at this point is the imposition from above, by elites, of both a democratic dialogical structure and those concomitant institutions that the people subject to them have not helped create, have not endorsed, and don't necessarily want.

Emile: The issue does not have to be seen as one of imposition versus choice by the people. We are offering suggestions that people can choose to implement, to alter as they see fit, or to use to generate their own thinking about how to proceed. Our position is that if you want to induce movement toward cosmopolitan identity, then you ought to use something very much like democratic dialogue, replete with dialectical thinking and deliberation. To that end, and as I said earlier, we are providing a foundation, not a blueprint, for structuring democratic dialogue, including recommendations for institutional changes. A foundation sets some parameters as to what may be built on top of it. Yet you cannot determine by looking only at the foundation what will be or must be built above it. The problem arises when there is no reciprocity or insufficient reciprocity so that the people actually affected by the procedures cannot make changes to them. Instituting democratic dialogue and institutions that rely upon such dialogue is not an imposition, so long as the people have some power to influence the structures themselves. Of course, the more people you have involved in planning and implementing the structures and institutions, the better.

Pinzak: The budgeting system in Porto Alegre, Brazil, I think, illustrates your point. The system was put into place in 1989 by the Workers' Party (the *Partido dos Trabalhadores* or PT) that won the mayoral election on a platform of social justice. Once in power, the PT replaced the system of deciding the municipal budget by the city council with a participatory system using both representatives and direct participation by the people. Now, every January "people's assemblies" are held in the city's sixteen districts to discuss the forthcoming budget, usually around two hundred million dollars per year, regarding such issues as waste disposal, education, housing, health care, and public transportation. The assemblies also elect representatives to participate in later stages of the budgeting.[2]

In 2002 *(reading from his computer)* fifty thousand residents in a city of one-and-a-half million took part in the budgeting process. No one who wanted to was prevented from participating or had to pass a test.

In 1989 seventy-five percent of the households in Porto Alegre had running water. David Lewit writes that by the end of 2002, when he reported on Porto Alegre,

> 99 percent have treated water and 85 percent have piped sewage. In seven years, housing assistance jumped from 1,700 families to 29,000. In 12 years, the number of public schools increased from 29 to 86, and literacy has reached 98 percent. Each year the bulk of new street-paving projects has gone to the poorer, outlying districts. In addition to these achievements, corruption, which before was the rule, has virtually disappeared.[3]

According to Lewit, "poor people, less well-educated people, and black people are not inhibited in attending and speaking up, even though racial discrimination is strong in Brazil" (Lewit, "Porto Allegre," 2002).

The participatory system in Porto Alegre might not fit exactly how we envision democratic dialogue, but it is surely an example of the people, working in concert with city officials and elected representatives, designing a democratic decision-making mechanism and institutionalizing it.

Emile: It is, but as you describe it, the mechanism may lack the essential ingredient of dialectical thinking. The residents of Porto Alegre have gained some political power over the city's budget and have democratized the budgeting process, but do they deal with disparate perspectives? If not, then we would not expect that mechanism to generate cosmopolitan sensibilities, let alone cosmopolitan identity. It might, but that would seem to be inadvertent.

Pinzak: I see your point. Listen, Emile, I don't have a problem with presenting an outline of or a foundation for democratic dialogue, but I do have a problem with presenting an outline for institutions built on that dialogue, because even an outline of these can potentially foreclose imagining different possible forms for those institutions.

Emile: I do not agree. We may present the institutions as suggestions only, as tentative suggestions. We may also reiterate that plans for institutions always come both from the bottom up, from the grassroots, as well as from the top down. That, too, is democratic reciprocity.

"The Great Mediocrity"

Pinzak: There's another concern I'd like to address right off. How do we handle what Ken Wilber calls "the great mediocrity"? He uses the term to describe those persons who seek to level all hierarchies and who inflate their own sense of importance, which takes the form of high narcissism, such that every decision must be in agreement with "me."[4] The presence of many "me's" with varying and opposing views makes this proposition dicey, to say the least. They may entertain, even tolerate, disparate perspectives, but they dig in their heels and refuse to budge from their own positions.

This was the fear of the "democratic elitists" like Mosca, Pareto, and Lippmann, that the featherheaded masses in a democracy would rule thoughtlessly. If anyone paid attention, for example, to the presidential elections in the United States in 2000, 2004, and 2008, one would see campaigns focused on playing to this great mediocrity; campaigns, that is, centered not around issues facing the nation, but around the personalities and character of those running. This was passed off as a significant strategy, because the personality and character of the candidates were thought to be reflections on how they would govern the nation and, maybe more important, how they would represent "me." Pundits reduced these elections to the central question, which seemed to resonate with the electorate: "Which candidate would you rather have a beer with?" John Kerry, for example, in 2004, was portrayed as an effete elitist who ordered Swiss cheese on his Philly cheese steak, liked to wind surf, and spoke French. George Bush, on the other hand, was presented as a brush-clearing cowboy who would stand up to terrorists and make us safe. He was portrayed as a regular guy, just like us, who didn't read newspapers and liked his politics in black-and-white.

Apparently, these are the kinds of campaigns American voters want. "Sarah Palin is one of us" was the cry of many women across America in 2008 who thought that this criterion alone was sufficient for being one massive coronary away from the Oval Office.

From the perspective of democratic elitists, if you give the masses political power, they will simply vote their desires and interests and think little about, because they do not care about, the common good. They are narrow-minded, entertainment- and shopping-obsessed, egocentric, law-and-order individuals dipped only in conventional thinking. Not only won't they think about the common good, but they also *can't* think about the common good unless it fits with their own conventional and personal views.

Emile: I see. What we have here, then, is the unattractive combination of an uninformed and largely apathetic public subjected to self-serving nominees, campaign officials, and powerful—that is, money-laden corporate or union—special interests. This amounts to little more than a system in which the benighted masses are outmaneuvered by the moneyed special interests. In other words, politics is all about self-interest. Yet the masses lack the political voice to have their self-interests satisfied, whereas lobbyists buy access and maybe influence to have their self-interests addressed, if not fulfilled.

Pinzak: For Wilber the situation is not simply about moneyed interests controlling politics. Ordinary citizens are not necessarily even in favor of demonstrable common interests unless those interests conform to one's own perceived interests. In another conversation Wilber said *(Pinzak reads from his computer screen),* "One of the reasons that an actual democracy [rule by the people] will never work is that if we took this country [the United States] as an example, somewhere between 60 and 70 percent of the population is ethnocentric or lower. So the moment we put into play an electronic democracy where everyone over the age of twenty-one has an automatic vote, you'll have Kansas outlawing the teaching of evolution and Wyoming will make it legal to discriminate against homosexuals."[5]

On the other hand, there is for Wilber an opposite of this mediocrity: those who recognize that excellence and growth are good, good for individuals and for society. According to Wilber, the only way to handle the "great mediocrity" is to enable, or inspire, ten percent of the population to attain the dialectical or vision-logic level. Only then will we have leaders with "the broadest, widest, deepest, most inclusive values" as part of our governance system (Wilber and Ury 2004).

Emile: Of course, Wilber is right if by "actual democracy" we mean, as he suggests, a plebiscitary democracy, apparently freed of the "fetter" of the Bill of Rights, in which every eligible voter has one vote to use electronically regardless of what she knows about the issues or the candidates. But that is not what we are talking about. A plebiscitary democracy makes no demands on the voters or the participants other than to push a button. They certainly do not have to deliberate with others or pay attention to opposing perspectives or to *any* perspectives, for that matter. Nor is there any demand for them to change their behavior.

We are obviously pressing for a democratic system quite different. Let me use an example to highlight one difference straight off. In the preface to his book *Deliberating in the Real World,* John Parkinson differentiates between two instances that informed his view of democratic deliberation.[6] In 1985 New Zealand tried to decriminalize homosexual behavior, but the measure was defeated, much to Parkinson's consternation. To Parkinson the defeat said something about the insights of the electorate. Later, political elites had to push the decriminalization changes onto the voters. Only in that top-down manner could the changes be made. Yet, when Parkinson was asked to consult with businesses on their internal communications projects, he found that it was the managers and not the rank-and-file workers who resisted change. To the contrary: the workers were the ones who came up with creative solutions to the problems.

Pinzak: So what accounts for the difference?

Emile: The difference lies in what people are asked to do when making decisions. Parkinson observed that people of all sorts deliberated well when placed in "well-designed procedures to help them make decisions," and when they had "the power to design and implement the changes themselves" (2006, viii). Parkinson's study of deliberation in the real world led him to conclude that ordinary people have "remarkable capacities" (viii). This view is echoed by David Mathews's experiences with National Issues Forums. In 1991 these Forums dealt with the issue of energy sources and policy:

> Deliberation on this issue was particularly interesting because the subject was full of scientific and technical considerations, which are supposed to overwhelm average citizens who have little scientific or technical expertise. However, on this and other issues of similar complexity, forum participants were not the least overwhelmed. Although complaining about the lack of information on some options and conflicting information on others, they had little difficulty assessing the pros and cons of renewable sources of energy—including nuclear power.[7]

Pinzak: How do we square this view with the seeming apathy of most of the American electorate who can't be bothered to turn out to vote when they have the opportunity? Consider the attendance at municipal meetings, school-board meetings, any public meetings: It's paltry, across-the-board and across the country. All of that argues, doesn't it, against any rush to install participatory mechanisms in the face of such indifference?

Emile: One aspect is left out of your perspective: dialogue. People are underwhelmed by what is demanded and expected of them politically. Their most significant political act amounts to voting every couple of years for the same faces, or even different faces, to represent them. But what does that amount to?

How much influence, to say nothing of control, over their own public lives do they have? Matt Leighninger points out that virtually all public meetings are structured so as to rule out small-group deliberation, to discourage people from talking about their own experiences, and to prevent citizens from "a meaningful chance to be heard."[8] This is deleterious, because, as Leighninger says, most people come to meetings to have an impact on an issue they care about (39). "If you want to succeed," he comments, "you can't just involve citizens in ways that supplement the political process—you have to construct new arenas where citizens are at the center of the system" (47). Indeed, in Leighninger's experience, when officials introduced dialogue and deliberation, "citizens didn't just complain, they actually learned about the issue and the various policy options. Activists were part of the discussions, but they weren't able to dominate them. Participants were able to think through the recommendations carefully" (15). Self-interest, which often seems like selfish interest, takes a turn toward the collective when expressed in certain kinds of settings, deliberative settings.[9]

Pinzak: Tocqueville observed this when he reported to the French on America's fledgling democracy. Citizens move out of the closed societies of their friends and family, out of what Tocqueville called "individualism," and into the public-at-large when they operate out of "self-interest rightly understood." That is, citizens come to see that they need the help of others to realize projects that interest or suit them, because those projects also interest and suit others.[10]

Men quickly learned that even one's own private ambitions and personal business require the aid of others.[11] It is the recognition that we are in this together that brings citizens to the realization that they must work with others both toward defining interests and toward achieving them. Over time, Tocqueville noticed that repeated public participation led citizens to work not only for mutual interests but also for interests when they themselves had nothing personal at stake. Citizens working together in this way is in itself an expression of the common good. This is what Tocqueville meant by "self-interest rightly understood."

So, it's getting out of our "holes" and into our "wholes," even into our new "holons." What starts off as the pursuit of an individual self-interest, which is seen to require for its success participation with other citizens, soon becomes a habit of citizens' working together in pursuit of common or collective interests.

Emile: Of course, nineteenth-century America, as Tocqueville observed, offered citizens ample opportunities to participate locally in political associations, associations in which they made actual political decisions. We are suggesting returning to such widespread participation in actual political decision-making.

Pinzak: But we still haven't addressed Wilber's concern about "the great mediocrity." You're simply suggesting that we make available political participation in associations or institutions that are built on dialectical thinking and deliberation. Wilber's point about the 60 or 70 percent of the population who are ethnocentric is that they won't want to hear, or be able to hear, the contradictory and antagonistic positions held by others.

Emile: There is always the possibility that as you make the participatory procedures more demanding, many people will self-select out of participation. If it is too demanding, many will not do it. But that is a defeatist attitude and, I think, misperceives how people will respond when the political issues on which they can make decisions are *real* issues, issues important to their lives.

Pinzak: Do you really think that most people can handle the required deliberative aspects?

Emile: Yes, I think they can. For example, a study done by Gerald Holton and Marcel LaFollette found that a statistically representative sample of the general public, a group of seventy participants divided into six groups and asked to deliberate on research projects involving complex technical issues and data, came to judgments that coincided with the judgments of scientists knowledgeable about the science and technology of the projects.[12]

The structures of governance are crucial both for bringing about persons of cosmopolitan consciousness and for bringing about good deliberative democratic decisions. There is no reason that those in charge of workplaces, schools, prisons, clubs, and the like cannot introduce dialogical deliberative procedures. That can be, and is, the responsibility of those in charge, at the top, in the elite corps. Wilber's concern about imposition from the top is legitimate; his concern about the "great mediocrity," less so. His position is not much different from those who think that guidance should always be directed from the top down to the masses, to what Lord Lytton, the British politician and writer whose reputation for bad writing overshadowed his talent for aphorism, called "the great unwashed." This position, while it rests on the very important democratic quality of accountability of representatives and officials, undercuts and ignores the literature on the collective wisdom of the masses beginning as far back as and championed by the likes of Aristotle.

Wilber has stated that the Founding Fathers who wrote the United States Constitution were men of the Enlightenment who established a government on the basis of high principles.[13] The people who would live under this constitution were clearly not all persons of high principles. The genius of the system, according to Wilber (2000a, 59), is that they did not have to be. They did not have to be enlightened rationalists who could argue their way to and from universal moral principles and thus be guided by them. They simply had to behave in public as if they were. So, a Pennsylvania farmer might not care for what his neighbor has to say and might like to prevent him from broadcasting those views. The farmer might object to his neighbor's strange dress and peculiar religious views and might want to see such expressions curtailed. But that Pennsylvania farmer had to honor the right of that neighbor to say whatever he wanted whenever he wanted and to dress and to worship however he wanted. Therefore, the high-minded principles structured into the Constitution required the people to follow those principles, even if people did not or could not accept those principles as their own. They had to behave, however, as if they did. That is the key: *behav-*

ing as if they did. The social and political situation, the context created by the Constitution, demanded that they do so.

Pinzak: So the argument is that democratic dialogue, based on dialectical thinking, doesn't require persons to understand dialectical principles or even to think dialectically. But they must behave in the democratic procedures as if they do follow those principles. *(Emile nods and sips his coffee.)* To participate people must adapt their behavior to the rules based on dialectical thinking and to do so to the best of their ability. Thus, higher forms of thinking, without all participants necessarily grasping them, influence the very procedures that they are working with and in. As David Mathews comments *(Pinzak reads from his computer screen),* "How people behave politically may be . . . a function of what the political norms expect of them" (1994, 64). Just as higher principles structure the U.S. Constitution but require only higher-order behavior, so, too, democratic dialogue is built upon dialectical principles but requires participants to behave only as if they were dialectical thinkers. Thus, for example, while they all can't process, balance, or handle ambiguity, all can listen attentively to positions divergent from their own.

Emile: I think so. It is impossible to identify the dialectical thinkers and to reserve political decision-making to them. How do you find these thinkers? Do you give every eligible voter a dialectical test? Who makes up such a test? Who evaluates such a test? It would be a self-selecting and self-congratulatory group, would it not?

Pinzak: More to the point, Emile, this violates the very tenets that we established earlier when talking about the kind of knowledge and insight needed to participate in political decision-making, and it violates the participatory tenet we discussed earlier still: *Quod omnes tangit:* "what touches all must be decided by all." Most important is how people behave once they are in the democratic dialogue and participating in the decision-making process.

Emile: This is just what we have been arguing. Behavior in the process is determined largely by the structure and strictures of the process itself. It is not that to participate people *must* be dialectical thinkers; rather, they must behave in the process *as if* they are. Behaving as if they are might well spark the first step toward their becoming dialectical thinkers.

There is abundant evidence now in social psychology that shows that people's behavior is to a large extent heavily influenced by the characteristics of the situation and by variations within those characteristics. What a person brings to the situation is relevant, but the circumstances of the situation usually overwhelm the "disposition" of the person. The circumstances themselves can be transformational. Depending on what they are, they can transform behavior in benign and beneficent directions or in malignant and evil directions.

Pinzak: So good people can do evil acts, but situations can also create and reinforce good behavior. That's what we're aiming for in our dialogical settings: to reinforce a behavior—dialogical interaction—among all the participants. But, what, now you're arguing that character and personal qualities are unimportant, that the external circumstances are what matter?

Emile: I am arguing that the context, the social and political situation, highly influences how we behave. Personality and situation interact. It is not always one or the other. Here is another reminder of, and lesson from, the AQAL model: We need to take into account both an individual's interior psychological states and the exterior social and political circumstances in which she finds herself. Humans are not dispositional selves who act only according to rationally or socially established principles or to genetically determined programs. Acts always occur within a behavioral context that creates its own directions and pressures. Yet we are not slaves to social situations either. Our behavior is not dictated by the circumstances in which we find ourselves. Persons are active participants in these situations, and they can redirect or alter the circumstances, challenge the settings or those responsible for them, and resist the demands made within the settings.[14]

Pinzak: The argument, then, is that context or situations exert pressure on behavior. That's all that you're claiming here and not that situations determine how we behave or everything about our behavior. *(Emile nods as he reaches for his coffee, cold by now. He thinks better of drinking any and removes his hand from the cup.)* Behavior is the result of a complex interaction between organism and environment.

Emile: That is correct and should not be surprising, given all that we have said in our various conversations about developmental psychology and about the AQAL model of integration of the individual, the collective, the institutional, the cultural, and the psychological. We can look to the work of Philip Zimbardo, the Stanford professor of social psychology who ran the Stanford Prison Experiment, for some insight. Zimbardo points out, when analyzing why someone commits a heinous act, that situational factors are too often minimized in our Western culture that prizes individuality. As a result, we are often biased in expecting people to behave according to ethical principles independent of any situation. People of good character and robust moral dispositions, we believe, will not succumb to temptations to do evil. Strong moral character is a bulwark against bad behavior. Social psychology, however, shows us something quite different, to which we must be sensitive when discussing behavior. "The situationist approach," Zimbardo comments, "preaches the lesson that any deed, for good or evil, that any human being has ever done, you and I could do—given the same situational forces" (2007, 320, 211). Asking rhetorically how important situationism is as a force in shaping behavior, Zimbardo refers to a statistical meta-analysis of twenty-five thousand social-psychological studies over one hundred years involving eight million people. "Across 322 separate meta-analyses, the overall result was that this large body of social psychological research generated substantial effect sizes—that the power of social situations is a reliable and robust effect" (323).

The social psychology experiments show us also that context can be structured so that positive aspects of behavior can be reinforced. Instead of a rapid descent into evil, we can have a slow climb to the good. That is our goal for structuring democratic dialogue. For example, Zimbardo (2007, 448-51) tells us that pro-social behavior can be encouraged when there is "reciprocal altruism" present—that is, when someone thinks that others will respond to her as she wants them to, and thus this is how she responds to them. Mutual respect then, is hereby reinforced, which is one quality that we want in our democratic dialogue. Participants should also be engaging in critical thinking (453), which is, of course, another aspect of democratic dialogue.

Perhaps the most significant factor that Zimbardo introduces for promoting pro-social behavior is one that he calls giving someone "an identity label." One ascribes to a person the very characteristic one wants her to evince. "[I]f we tell someone that he or she is a helpful person, he or she will take on the manners and actions consistent with that identity label" (451).

Pinzak: Where do you see all of this leading?

Emile: It leads to a social-psychological reason for structuring democratic dialogue as we do. We require participants in the dialogue to behave like dialectical thinkers in concert with other dialectical thinkers. Underlying those behaviors is the expectation that participants can and should act this way. Moreover, the context affixes to the participants an identity label that they are dialecticians. Within this view of social psychology meeting political science, we might also conclude tentatively that we could have more cosmopolites if we had sufficient contexts or situations for developing them. In other words, people are not often enough immersed in or part of situations that require them to think and act "cosmopolitically."

Pinzak: Remember when we were discussing dialectical thinking and the work of such researchers as Susanne Cook-Greuter.

Emile: Of course.

Pinzak: The research found that there are very few dialectical thinkers. One reason for that might be that our culture doesn't offer enough opportunities for dialectical thought. We leave adults to their own devices, and so dialectical thinkers are rare because people have to come to that kind of thinking on their own. Our institutions and social contexts don't provide sufficient stimuli to get people thinking dialectically.

Emile: That seems right. Without such contexts or situations we cannot develop the habits that may elicit or instill cosmopolitan sensibilities or weave those sensibilities into a cosmopolitan identity. The institutional framework itself must generate or demand certain behaviors and attitudes. Give participants sufficient opportunities to take part in democratic dialogue, and the identity label might well stick beyond the institutional adhesive.

Pinzak: Okay, so participants engage in a variety of psychological processes that appeal, as Lincoln said, to "the better angels of our nature." This in turn creates expectations for or of the participants. Expectations then modify behaviors as people become what they are expected to be.[15]

Emile: That is correct. How do we temper Wilber's "great mediocrity"? How do we deal with persons who refuse to listen or present their views and instead wait only to vote their preconceived positions? Place them in a context where it is difficult to do so. Place people in a dialectical context, where integrative thinking is encouraged even if the people cannot quite think that way yet—cannot quite hold ambiguous or divergent views in mind. This will fundamentally change the context in which they are thinking. This will spur them to grow into more comprehensive, open, and integrative—that is, dialectical—thinkers.

Plus, we want to look also at another extreme: How to prevent a minority from corrupting or hijacking the process. Zimbardo argues that "the power of the many may be undercut by the persuasion of the dedicated few" (2007, 266). How does that happen? According to Zimbardo, a dedicated minority can do this only if the majority has *not* engaged "the systematic thought and critical thinking skills of the individuals in the group" when making a decision (266). In other words, our democratic dialogue should establish the very conditions that militate against a dedicated minority undercutting the majority and, at the same time, against a majority mindlessly holding to a position contraindicated by the evidence. Engaging in systematic and critical thinking, thereby eliciting dialectical thinking, is the heart of democratic dialogue. It also helps assure the health and beneficial function of the group.[16]

Pinzak: Constructing democratic dialogue in a specific way, then, is crucial to its success in enlisting participants to be dialectical thinkers. Doing that, we think, might induce movement into cosmopolitan sensibilities and toward cosmopolitan identity. In a way, that's a given, because dialectical thinking itself really is the expression of cosmopolitan sensibilities.

We pull people out of "the great mediocrity" by pushing them toward dialectical thinking. We'll still have leaders; we're always going to need leaders, and we hope that they will be those with "the broadest, widest, deepest, most inclusive values . . ."

Emile: Yes, if we can find them and figure out how to get them to run and how to elect them.

Pinzak: But the issue is no longer trying only to identify and elect those individuals. The issue is not to elect only a certain type of thinker or certain kind of character into elected offices. It is, instead, to ask how we might encourage all participants to think in a way or at a level that is integral or dialectic. How do we encourage all participants to express their dialectical thinking or, more important, to stretch themselves to reach into dialectical thinking if they are not yet there?

So trying to have us ruled by genuine philosopher-kings, as we discussed previously, is not our goal. Even if it could be done, it is not a system that permits people to participate in deciding those issues that affect their lives deeply, immediately, and fundamentally. And, if we limited their participation because they were judged, somehow, "unworthy," then we'd be denying them an avenue of possible development toward or into dialectical thinking.

Emile: There is nothing more destructive to democratic dialogue than a view that those with dialectical experience and expertise should devise for all of us the policy or action outcomes that affect us all. Of course, dialectical thinkers need to share their expertise and their dialectical thinking with us, but one aspect of their dialectical thought is appreciation for the thinking of all the levels below the dialectical. That appreciation in itself is a mandate for the dialectically proficient to bring along the less adept.

Pinzak: Another of their responsibilities is to translate dialectical thinking and alternatives into terms that those less capable of such thinking can understand. Give me one example of an issue or perspective that persons below the dialectical level cannot understand; if a dialectical thinker cannot explain that issue or perspective to someone of, say, concrete operational thought, then that dialectical thinker himself does not understand the perspective well.

Of course, some can think more dialectically than others. The purview of the dialectical thinker ought to be, then, to work through democratic dialogue to bring into context the different kinds of thought on a subject and to show how dialectical thinking integrates the perspectives expressive of those kinds of thought. *(Pinzak takes his first sip of coffee.)*

Democratic Legitimacy

Emile: So let us examine the nature and structure of democratic dialogue. It seems to me that we should begin, in a sense, where we left off. *(Pinzak looks quizzically at Emile.)* Here is what I mean: In our last conversation we established that democratic decision-making procedures themselves are predicated on a presupposition of universality. That means that every participant is considered a self-reflective agent able to take up the perspectives of others as well as to criticize those perspectives, those of society, as well as his or her own. The content of the procedures rests on another presupposition—that participants are all different individuals, with unique perspectives, histories, biases, desires, even needs. These must be shared, understood, and taken into account.

Pinzak: I'm with you so far.

Emile: Good. We also said that democratic procedures, if we are interested in possible ways to generate cosmopolitan sensibilities and cosmopolitan identity, must have at the core dialectical thinking. Dialectical thinking provides a "worldcentric" perspective of a particular sort. Whereas "tolerance" might be a value central to a worldcentric perspective characterized by formal-operational thinking, "appreciation" or "embrace" might be the value central to the worldcentric perspective of dialectical thinking. Whereas one at the level of formal-operational thinking sees the value of tolerating other perspectives, one at the level of dialectical thinking sees the value in sharing disparate perspectives. She acknowledges differences and contradictory perspectives. Yet she does more than simply leave them alone, let them be. She appreciates what they have to offer and may even embrace them as a way of enlivening and enriching her own perspectives.

Pinzak: Dialectical thinking requires, therefore, placing ourselves in the perspectives of others. You referred at this point, as I recall, to Aristotle's *syn-*

esis, the idea that we come to understand someone else's position by working to put ourselves fully in the other's situation. By the way, the psychological situationism that we were just talking about reinforces the importance of understanding someone else's context.

Emile: What is universal about dialectical thinking is the desire, even the need, to exercise *synesis* or perspectivism and thereby honor and appreciate our differences. In dialectical thinking the reasoning is not done in isolation, within the inner rational cathedral of one's own mind, and then brought into conversation. Instead, dialectical thinking is reasoning together. There is reason-giving, to be sure, but central also is the back-and-forth, the dialectic, of the conversation as minds are changed as well as made up. We called this reasoning process, in large measure, "deliberation."

Pinzak: We also said that dialogue does not just involve reason-giving; in addition participants can and must tell stories. People provide testimony as to why they see the issue in a certain way and how it affects them. Someone might say, "Here's what I've seen in our neighborhood. Here's how your proposal hurts my family and my neighbors." *(Emile, sipping his cold coffee, nods.)*

All of these—reason-giving, storytelling, perspectivism, and embrace of differences—help to create relationships among the participants. The sharing and the relationships foster mutual trust, which is crucial if participants are to work together to come to some agreement on issues where they seem fundamentally to disagree.

Emile: Ideally that agreement would be a consensus on an issue that transcended all perspectives but also included all perspectives.

Pinzak: Yes, but heavily emphasizing "ideally."

Emile: Agreed.

Pinzak *(after a long gulp of coffee):* Also, as we added today, all participants would behave in the dialogue as if they were already dialectical thinkers. They conform to meet the expectations of the political context to the best of their abilities, and one expectation is that they are already capable of dialectical thinking. By steeping them in democratic dialogue, time after time and setting after setting, the hope is not simply to come up with good outcomes, but also to develop or educe cosmopolitan sensibilities and move the participants toward cosmopolitan identity.

Emile: Last, we said that democratic dialogue and its constituent parts must themselves be open to deliberation. That is so because democratic dialogue reposes on a bed of values that is necessary if the dialectic is to proceed. Those values include what we have just been talking about: persuasion over coercion; not just tolerance of other viewpoints, but honoring other viewpoints by taking them seriously; mutual respect; and the importance of autonomy: self-reflective, deliberative choices made among competing conceptions, even of the good life. These values themselves must be open to deliberation. They are settled, true, but not settled forever. Otherwise participants in the dialogue are relying blindly on a bed of values that consists of their own parochial batting.

Pinzak: This is one way of skirting the charge that the procedures are imposed on participants. *(Emile nods.)* And yet, Emile, the procedures *are* imposed on participants, at least at the outset before they have had a chance to challenge them. How is that justified? On the grounds that this is one way to generate cosmopolitan identity?

Emile: That is one possible justification, but I do not think it is the strongest. The strongest, I would say, is political legitimacy. Deliberativists—as persons concerned about direct deliberative decision-making may be called—argue that democratic decisions gain legitimacy only insofar as they are reflections of open, deliberative procedures.[17] Even David Miller, whom we encountered in an earlier conversation as a proponent of national identity and hardly a champion of cosmopolitanism, lists "legitimacy" as one of the three conditions that characterize deliberative democracy: It is legitimate in that every participant "can understand how and why the outcome was reached even if he or she was [sic] not personally convinced by the arguments offered in its favor."[18] Of course, one might ask why participants whose favored position has not prevailed would or should consider the outcome legitimate. Granted, they have participated in the procedure and knew going in that their position might not prevail, but does participation, then, generate legitimacy in their eyes?

(There is a pause as both Emile and Pinzak look at their coffee cups. Pinzak waits for Emile to say something. "Another round?" Emile asks. Pinzak nods, picks up both cups, and heads inside. Emile merely sits, looking out onto the street. Pinzak soon returns with two cups of fresh coffee.)

Pinzak *(with mock irritation as he sits):* So those were rhetorical questions, Emile? You're not going to answer them? *(Emile shrugs.)* You're playing with me, aren't you? What, are you tired of talking and want a break?

Emile *(after a sip of coffee):* This is your bailiwick, Pinzak. You can summarize the argument and then we may move on.

Pinzak: Fair enough. Participation in deliberation is exactly why the participants should consider the outcome legitimate: They had a fair chance of winning the day themselves. Had they prevailed, would they then consider the outcome legitimate? Is it only winning that generates legitimacy? If an elected body passes a law that you oppose, is that law nevertheless legitimate? If it is not, then laws that you favor cannot be legitimate either. What generates legitimacy is the authority vested in the institution and the procedure. Legislation passed by a recognized authority is legitimate, though it might be a bad law. Bad laws can be overturned, even resisted, but they still have legitimacy. Martin Luther King, Jr., went to jail as a consequence of and in protest against bad, immoral laws, but he accepted that consequence, because he recognized the legitimacy of the laws that he opposed.

Emile: It seems a stretch to view rules and laws, for example, as impositions on us if we are ourselves involved in making those rules and laws. No doubt, persons and groups may be discriminated against, and, thus, although they may present their views, those views are never part of the outcome. Yet such a situation *is* discrimination and a violation of the very participatory and deliberative structures that we are creating.

Pinzak: This raises a different, but germane, point: Legitimacy rests not only on how a decision is made—that is, deliberatively—but also on who is making it.

Emile: Yes, we can imagine, can we not, that some persons are not interested in cosmopolitan identity or cosmopolitan sensibilities or cosmopolitan anything. What if some people think that global governance, indeed all governance, ought to be left to the experts? They do not want to participate, and, more to the point, they do not think that ordinary persons ought to participate in making such decisions. Some people may think that cosmopolitan identity is too arduous an undertaking or too diffuse or too ambitious. Some people may think that strengthening nation-states is a better way to protect people's rights.

Pinzak: Our argument isn't based solely on how attractive or unattractive one finds cosmopolitan identity. We've been arguing that to have effective global governance and Integral Democracy through participatory forums, we need to promote the kind of identity formation and global awareness that moves us into a felt identity with all of humanity.

Emile: What we called a planetary consciousness.

Pinzak: Precisely. But underneath that argument, or at least next to that argument, is a normative perspective, beyond the desire for cosmopolitan identity, that lies at the heart of deliberative democracy: People have the right, or should have, to participate in making those decisions that affect their lives. That is part of the argument for legitimacy, and that point takes us back to our moral and political tenet: what touches all should be decided by all. If we accept that perspective, then we see that some issues related to those lives do not necessarily stop at certain borders. They are global issues.

Emile: Look at the implications of what you are saying. Should workers at a Ford Motor Company plant in Missouri be involved in deciding whether Ford moves the manufacturing in that plant to China?

Pinzak: Shouldn't they? Let's imagine that Ford wants a deliberative democratic decision made about that move. *(Emile raises his eyebrows.)* We're speaking strictly hypothetically now. Anyway, Ford wants that kind of decision. But the ones affected are not simply workers in the plant, but stockholders of Ford, persons who sell Ford parts and products, executives at Ford, workers in other plants in the United States and overseas who work for Ford, merchants and civil servants and residents who live in the community, and the Chinese themselves. All of these perspectives, and perhaps more, need to be considered in the decision-making. After hearing all of these considerations, might the workers agree that it is best for Ford to move the plant's operations to China?

Emile: Speaking hypothetically also, we can imagine that they might. But there would have to be assurances of possible jobs elsewhere within Ford or job training provided by the company or severance packages or buyouts.

Pinzak: Yes, and those issues must be addressed if the workers who participate in the deliberations are to agree in general with the move. Otherwise, Ford executives and management might pay lip service to the concerns of the workers, but not honor the damage, and ways to mitigate the damage, that moving the plant's operations will cause to the workers and to their community.

At issue here is not really whether the plant in Missouri closes and the operations move to China. It is doubtful, given the economic justification for the move, that Ford is going to be dissuaded. At issue is the chance for the workers to express their concerns and to have Ford and others listen to them. There are factors to be introduced that all involved in this decision need to hear. This is one way that the workers and residents of the community can gain some reciprocity with Ford. It is a way to move out of a sense of being dominated by forces beyond one's influence, because reciprocity is a form of power. Failure to acknowledge the fundamental reciprocity working in the deliberations—failure, that is, to consider seriously the positions of others seemingly tangential to the company's concerns—is to betray Integral Democracy at its base. Workers might not influence the actual move to China, but democratic dialogue, bringing these different perspectives into the conversation, can express concern, bring insight into options and outcomes, and gain concessions. Ford is therefore accountable to more than just the stockholders.

Emile: Of course, Ford is not going to agree to any of this. Why should it? They do not have to invite workers or community residents into the decision-making process. The power differential is completely uneven. So what if the workers in this one plant and one community are not happy about having their jobs "outsourced"?

Pinzak: Ford probably won't agree now. Their stockholders won't agree now. If China offers the lowest costs and that translates into new or renewed profits for Ford, then there seems to be little at stake for them. But hearing the issues and concerns of the workers and residents could have an impact, as you point out, on the future lives and livelihoods of those left behind. Imagine there is a context of more and more deliberative democracy—democratic schools, national initiatives, citizen juries, democratic conversations springing up throughout the country and around the world. Could there then be mounting political and social pressure to bring democratic dialogue to the workplace and humble Ford into introducing a dialogical forum?

Solidarity, the labor movement in Poland that led to the overthrow of communist rule there, began with fewer than a dozen workers talking among themselves about the sacking of one of their colleagues, Anna Walentinowicz, at the Lenin Shipyards in Gdansk. By the end of the month they had over nine-and-a-half million members nationwide. That's almost ten million members within thirty days! From small movements, from intimate conversations, can come significant, even transformative, change or the beginnings of change. Pressure from below can have monumental effects.

Emile: There is an old, and familiar, Catholic maxim: "Better to light a single candle than sit and curse the dark." That is what we are talking about here.

Each of us, metaphorically, is a single candle, and when we bring our light, our energy, our attention to an issue, then we chase away some of the dark. One single candle can light a room that is pitch-black. That act changes the atmosphere from darkness to light. The more "candles" you add to that room, the brighter it becomes. You cannot bring a cloud of darkness into a well-lit room and alter the illumination really in any way. Each of us brings her candle to add to the illumination. Each of us contributes her insights and interests, ideas and concerns, to the issue to generate illumination. But that illumination is not simply external, related to the group insight, but is also internal.

Pinzak: The ineluctable interconnections found in the AQAL model . . .

Emile: Precisely. Internal change is always accompanied by external correlates and vice versa. Over time, through the introduction of more and more insight into our own "darkness" or limits, we modify our own internal structures. We transform our sensibilities and identity.

Pinzak: We bring light into the world of shadows, into Plato's cave.

Emile: Speaking, as we were, of the external and of small contributions leading to significant changes reminds me of a wonderful story told by the Aztecs. At one time the earth was covered with forests. A huge fire started and quickly spread. All the animals tried to flee. As he fled, Tecolotl, the owl, saw a small bird flying back-and-forth from a nearby river and the fire. Tecolotl flew closer and saw that it was the Quetzal bird, Quetzaltototl, who was filling his tiny beak with water and dropping it onto the flames. Tecolotl scoffed at him. "You can't achieve anything by doing this. Are you stupid? Flee and save your life." Quetzaltototl replied, "I'm doing the best I can with what I have." The Aztecs tell this story as the time the forests were saved from the great fire when a small bird, an owl, other animals, and people joined together to put out the flames.[19]

Each bird, each person, does his share. At some juncture their work creates a critical mass, or a tipping point, that helps save the forest or saves the day or catalyzes action into a transformation, internally or externally. We saw the results of such "mass action" in Poland, in Czechoslovakia, in South Africa. Those who gathered and demonstrated lacked the political power to overthrow their governments. What they had was political will, which translated into mass movements that brought immense and impressive political pressure.

Pinzak: It's a different kind or different expression of political power. Democratic dialogue can provide persons with processes and structures of deliberation and decision-making that can compensate for an absence of officially recognized or sanctioned political power. If the legitimacy of government derives from the will and consent of the people, and that will and consent are expressed through a dialogical outcome, then it seems difficult for government at any level, or the officials of any organization, to ignore that outcome. This is how political pressure can be built and then brought to bear. Through dialogue persons can generate political will and the relationships to coordinate and perpetuate that will.

One of the problems with the normative claim, that what affects all should be decided by all, is determining who, exactly, is affected. Even if we use the example of Ford moving a plant to China, we have to decide, as you suggested, where the notion of "being affected" ends. There are secondary buyers and sellers involved in the transactions involving the Ford plant in Missouri: providers of electricity and water and sewage, people who provide or prepare food eaten by workers and management, companies that supply the parts used in the plant, consumers who buy the vehicles whose parts were manufactured in the plant, states on whose highways or along whose rails the new vehicles or transported parts move. Who's in this last group? Representatives from the states' governments? Members of the Federal Interstate Commerce Commission? People from railway or highway commissions? Aren't all three levels—state and local and federal—affected by Ford's decision?

Emile: The issue is complex, no doubt. Strategies must be devised to deal with the complexity but also to handle decision-making efficaciously.

Pinzak: One way might be to consider the scope or boundary of the public addressed by the formation of an institution. By that I mean that every governmental institution or commercial institution or financial institution creates a "public" of some dimensions. That public is created to address the interests or needs of some constituency. The constituency is the "public," even where, as with Ford, the "public" might be consumers worldwide and the "private publics" of stockholders who invest in the company and workers who labor there. These are constituents affected by Ford's decisions.

Emile: So are you suggesting, then, that decisions should not be made by all those affected? Instead, decisions should be made by those most *directly* affected?

Pinzak: We need to think of something like that, though what "most directly affected" means is itself problematic. Perhaps any constituency that wants to be included needs to make a case for why. Some constituencies are automatically included given their relationship to the institution involved. But others would have to argue how their fundamental needs, obviously connected to rights, would be directly and strongly affected. So, a weak or weaker connection would be someone whose consumer options would be limited or threatened—for example, a company is thinking of closing its blue-jeans manufacturing plant. The community where the plant is sited would suffer as a consequence of the closing. Livelihoods would be jeopardized and thus the ability to provide basic necessities for families—food, clothing, shelter—would be at risk. Life expectancies and life chances would be at issue, and so community members would face a strong and immediate connection to any decision made by the company. So, in comparison, a consumer who favors this company's blue jeans and buys only this brand of blue jeans would suffer only a minor or insignificant loss, given that there are other kinds of blue jeans available and certainly other kinds of pants.

Emile: So it is, then, a case of serious injury or harm versus disappointment or frustration. I do not mean to make light of restrictions that people find have been imposed on them. Yet surely we can see a difference between deprivation and need, as opposed, say, to a narrowing of preferences when other good preferences or alternatives remain.[20]

Still, persons should be allowed to plead their case to have its merits discussed, as you seem to suggest. But make a case to whom or to what? Some kind of court? And at what level? Who decides that? Federal court? State court? Local municipality? Does it go through all those levels?

Pinzak: I don't know that there's an easy way to create a generally applicable principle, regulation, or law here. I'm thinking that there must be some kind of common-sense solution: We know the ambit of authority when decisions must be made. A school deciding on how to structure democracy within its walls does not need to include the trucking company that brings in the foodstuffs prepared and served in the cafeteria. That company is not affected much, if at all, by what kinds of democratic structures exist within the school.

But such a decision does need to include the students, parents, teachers, and staff of that school. A decision on whether to permit a school in the first place to create democracy within its walls would require participation of those constituents plus members of the school board or school committee, representatives from the central administration of that district's schools, and possibly the superintendent of schools as well. This decision probably doesn't involve the state's superintendent of schools, but if it does, the decision does not include the state's governor. Those who want to be involved must make a case for why they should be included, and that case must be made to the immediate "public" or constituencies involved—in this case, people involved daily and directly in the schools or their business.

Emile: So you are suggesting, first, a principle of subsidiarity. That is, political decisions are made at the appropriate level and by the appropriate parties. Where there is dissension about and disagreement over which level and which parties are appropriate, then there needs to be some kind of judge or court of appeals. Yet I do not think that those judging who can participate should be persons or groups already involved in deciding the issue. Such persons might well have biases against the persons or groups bringing the case. The judge or court should be independent. The judge or court would then decide who has standing. "Legal standing" is not far from what we are discussing here. Can the interested party show injury or harm? Is there some relationship, causal relationship, between the interested party and those involved in the case? In our particular example, who has standing within a particular school or school district? The interested parties and those people on the periphery with standing, given the circumstances and scope of the decision to be made, should also be involved.

Pinzak: Decisions in these cases shouldn't be made by individual judges, which would eliminate democratic dialogue in decision-making. But the venue could be a court of some kind. There seem to be two ways that we could go here. One way would be to have a judicial or permanent court; the other would be to have "ad hoc" courts. At all levels of political decision-making, from local to global, these would be "democratic courts," not with judges, however impartial, hearing the cases, but with citizen juries hearing them.

Contrary to your perspective, Emile, I think that the "democratic courts" themselves should be made up of precisely those constituents who have a clear right to be involved in the decision-making on this particular issue—in our case, that school. Their participation underscores the legitimacy of democratic dialogue: The participatory context takes into account the very biases that you fear might doom a fair outcome.

Emile: Participants deal with those biases through deliberations and seek to transcend them.

Pinzak: Yes. *(He sips his coffee.)* Those constituents then hold a hearing to determine whether others wishing to participate have a good case for doing so. This would be a deliberative democratic process involving all pertinent perspectives in the deliberations and decision-making, even in this situation about who should be included in the decision-making. The point of the deliberation is to determine who really has an authentic interest in the outcome. Persons who are excluded can always try to have their case reconsidered by bringing pressure on the constituents, on the "court," through publicity and public opinion.

Emile: Of course, people may always weigh in by communicating with constituents through op-ed pieces, blogs, e-mails, "tweets," phone calls, text messages. They may do all of this before, during, and after the deliberations. Thus they might well have a say in what is done. But what these people lack is knowing that their "say" translates into definite influence. They lack the power to participate directly in the deliberations and outcome.

Pinzak: In that situation, then, the "democratic court" would have ruled that these people don't have standing in these particular deliberations and in the decision-making process. But your point makes it seem as if people outside the democratic dialogue have only symbolic influence and not real influence, a "say" but no real power. I don't think that this is true. People can organize, protest, boycott, and draw media and public attention to the issue. They do have power, as we noted in the Aztec story about Tecolotl and the story about Solidarity in Poland, but that power does not always translate into effective political influence and action.

There are institutions that have mandated authority and thus institutional power. The political officials of any state—governor, attorney general, judges, elected representatives, and the like—have the power to implement certain kinds of changes. But citizens may organize and use their collective political power, as we said, through communication, persuasion, protest, and publicity to bring attention to a particular issue and to bring pressure on those with institutional authority to consider or reconsider their positions. In this way, any group may take part in any public issue, even though they are not formally recognized participants. It is also how they might eventually gain admission as participants.

Emile: So one kind of political power is mandated authority, which is official. Another kind is fluid and ad hoc and depends on the coming together of persons for some common purpose. This kind of power is unofficial and can be permanent, like a consumer watchdog group, or evanescent, arising when necessary and fading when its purpose is served.

Pinzak: An example might be seen at the meetings of the World Trade Organization, which is run by elites and is exclusive. Protesters bring attention to the nature of the closed-door WTO meetings and through public and quieter means seek to open those doors to wider participation.

Another approach for attracting attention, rather than relying on protests that can be tenuous, unpredictable, and capricious, might be to set up temporary "public juries" within governmental agencies and departments, within private companies and firms, and within NGOs and organizations within civil society to offer critiques, suggestions, and innovations about how to open up decision-making within these institutions. Public juries would be composed of ordinary persons and citizens, not experts or elites, who would be given the authority to deliberate about systems and operations and decisions made within those institutions. This would be one way to introduce broader input and insights into how the institutions are structured and how they operate. It would also introduce another venue for democratic dialogue.

Emile: Institutions might welcome this as another way of gaining insight through differing perspectives into the institution's functions and procedures and outcomes. Citizens and concerned persons would welcome this as another avenue of empowerment, however temporary, and of democratic dialogue. So we have here a combination of dialectical forums given a top-down mandate by officially recognized and empowered institutions—the public juries—and those arising spontaneously or through organization from the bottom-up—deliberative social justice forums growing out of the WTO protests. But we need to be honest here, Pinzak. These forums do not really empower the citizens or jury participants. Instead, such forums offer "pretend" power. Unless the institution stipulates that it will deliberate about the results of the jury's work, then the participants themselves lack power. They are like advisers. The institution or company may take their advice; they may also reject or ignore it.

Pinzak: Participants lack reciprocity and thus power to influence the institutions.

Emile: That is correct.

Pinzak: So the juries need to know that their work will be taken seriously, and that means that their work will serve as the focus for democratic dialogue within the institution itself, presumably with some or all members of the jury participating in this new democratic dialogue. So reciprocity here isn't necessarily that the institution now gives back to the jurors something that speaks to their specific needs or interests as individuals. Instead, the institution gives back by involving the jurors in sharing power, however temporarily, in helping shape, for example, the procedures or outcomes of the institution. This will be good not simply for those involved but also for those whom the institution serves.

Emile: And questioning why those who are affected by the institution's outcomes are not more fully or more often represented in decision-making might be one good outcome, even if a side-benefit, of public juries.

You know, some people like to think of government as a business, with citizens as customers or clients and elected officials as officers who run the business. Often businesses, such as banks, want customer feedback, but they do not involve the customer in making decisions about, for example, how the bank operates. Banks, and other enterprises and institutions, should not be required to stop working as they do. They might, however, improve their image and treat their own operations more like a democratic government in which they seek involvement from customers and others to help shape the systems and direction of the company.

Pinzak: We need to keep in mind that participants in democratic dialogue are not involved only to grow personally, to develop cosmopolitan sensibilities or even to transform into a cosmopolitan identity. If that were so, then democratic dialogue could rest on the notion that it exists simply to give people a chance to speak and to be heard. But democratic dialogue demands more. It's more than advising; it's more than having a say. Participants want to see whether and to what extent their contributions may be worked into a solution or resolution or dialogical outcome. Moreover, they want to see their work reflected in policy positions and political action. It's not, then, just about the talk; it's also about the walk—how the outcomes of deliberations are used.

Emile: Participants also come to learn from others. They come to try to understand the positions, interests, needs, and concerns of others. There is no race to get to a solution or agreement. Initially, there might be resistance to the discordant views. One may surely understand why. Over time, however, one may see how defenses might well begin to break down and allow for reconsideration of one's own positions, including one's sense of self. This seems especially so in informal groups where participation is voluntary and the group is often self-selecting; that is, those who join see similarities or likenesses to themselves.

Pinzak: So let's talk more specifically about how to structure democratic dialogue . . .

Emile: . . . which is, again, the combination of deliberation, conversation, and dialectical thinking.

Pinzak: Last meeting we established that moral systems are put together intersubjectively. We follow the same epistemological steps to arrive at moral codes and truths as we do to arrive at scientific truths and even spiritual truths. Because we put together moral truths in this way, we should not be surprised to find the logic in creating cosmopolitanism or cosmopolitan identity in the same way. Cosmopolitanism arises through dialectical dialogue and communicative exchange.

Emile: The dialogue is an actual dialogue among real participants, not an abstract and hypothetical exercise conducted in the solitude of one's own library. While that dialogue is built of real, concrete contributions and perspectives, there is always the goal of transcending the participants' own limitations.

The Dialogical Process

Pinzak: So, what are the elements that you see essential to democratic dialogue?

Emile: To my mind such dialogue must have four phases:

1) an introductory phase of storytelling and trust building;

2) a phase of laying out of perspectives, ideals, and options;

3) a phase predominantly of deliberating or reason-giving when the perspectives, ideas, and options are critically explored and examined; and

4) the attempt to find a common policy, solution, or resolution based on or arising out of the perspectives and positions that remain after the third phase.

Pinzak *(while typing):* Just a quick note of clarification on the last point: the final stage is an integral stage where, after pooling their perspectives and examining them, participants then try to embrace as many as possible in cobbling together a solution. They attempt to transcend the parts by finding or creating a new whole.

Emile: That is correct. As we have been saying from the beginning dialectical thinking—the foundation of democratic dialogue—involves not simply tolerating perspectives. Such thinking involves appreciating those perspectives. One participant in a National Issues Forum, which we shall discuss later, commented that "people find their views not just tolerated; they are welcomed."[21] Also, since there are no absolute perspectives, no Archimedean point, the outcome is contingent. That is, the issue may not finally be settled. Further dialogue may well be necessary.

Pinzak: How about our taking each of your four phases or stages one at a time? *(Emile nods as he reaches for his glass of water.)* So, why a stage of storytelling?

Emile: Before we get into that . . .

Pinzak *(with real exasperation):* . . . Oh, come on, Emile!

Emile *(puts up his hand):* I just want to use an example that will illustrate many of the elements of democratic dialogue that we shall be talking about. Okay? *(With a deep sigh, Pinzak nods a couple of times.)*

Emile: Three weeks after the attacks of September 11, 2001, on the Pentagon and the World Trade Center, Ms. Gearhy's tenth-grade World History class postponed their lesson on ancient China and instead held a discussion on possible U.S. responses to terrorism. The discussion was based on the curriculum project Workable Peace, designed by the Consensus Building Institute.

First, students were presented with four different perspectives on how the U.S. should respond to terrorism and asked to choose the perspective that most closely resembled their own positions. Then, based on their individual choices, the students were placed in one of four groups. Each group, representing one of the four perspectives, was to map out what it thought were the most important elements that made up their perspective. After these group discussions, the class reconvened to discuss together and to compare and contrast the perspectives from each group. Stacie Nicole Smith and David Fairman (2005), representatives from the Consensus Building Institute, summarized the discussion in the following way:

> [S]tudents not only defended their own deeply felt views but were also asked to listen to, restate, and acknowledge the needs and concerns underlying their classmates' perspectives. Rather than scoring points . . . the goal of this discussion was to develop a better understanding of how and why Americans might legitimately disagree on what the United States should do in response to September 11th. Among the skills that the students practiced were explaining their views clearly, listening actively, acknowledging others' legitimate concerns, brainstorming options that reflected the needs of all points of view, and examining how the key issues might be resolved in ways that would meet the primary needs and concerns of others.[22]

All of these skills are important, if not central, to democratic dialogue. They help students address different perspectives and process new knowledge. They help break down stereotypical thinking and categories and, instead, highlight common interests, values, and ideas. Missing from this example are two of our four phases. First, the students did not have a storytelling phase, for the simple reason, I think, that they did not need one. Such a phase is first and foremost for participants to get to know one another and to build trust and mutual respect. Knowing one another already, the students did not need that phase. But also, and more important, given the level of personal development of most tenth-graders, the point is not to push their identities toward cosmopolitanism. Storytelling is a vehicle for revealing assumptions and aspects of oneself. This kind of self-reflection and self-revelation may not be appropriate for many students at the secondary-school level. Causing identity confusion of this kind at that level could well be harmful.

The second missing phase is the final phase. Here participants try to come to some kind of agreement on a solution or resolution. They try to find some way to accommodate the "primary needs and concerns of others" by combining or transcending perspectives—by "brainstorming options that reflected the needs of all points of view," as Smith and Fairman express it—in order to find or build a common solution. When you add in those two missing phases, you have what I think is democratic dialogue.

Pinzak: Your example also displays something else you mentioned earlier today. We are offering a foundation for democratic dialogue, not a blueprint that must be followed precisely. The tenth-graders were presented with four perspectives from which to choose, and they divided their group into four smaller groups. These seem to me to be modifications and not necessarily essential ingredients.

Emile: I think that that is right. Different groups, associations, or agencies will wish to shape the dialogues in accordance with the interests, needs, and wishes of the participants or the problems/issues they address.

Pinzak: So *now* let's return to phase one, storytelling . . . please.

Phase One: Storytelling

Emile *(laughing):* All right. *(Emile takes a sip of coffee and then a drink of water.)* In her influential article "Against Deliberation," Lynn Sanders comments that deliberation is most often a demand for a certain kind of rational and controlled talk. That demand leaves out impassioned and even extreme talk.[23] Such a demand also minimizes, if not eliminates, the participation of people who prefer or are accustomed to the second kind of talk. Sanders, therefore, proposes an alternative model of deliberation, which she calls "giving testimony" or "telling one's particular story to a broader group" (370). Because the emphasis in the first phase is on this kind of talk, I call it "storytelling."[24]

Pinzak: I recall that Sanders further suggests that giving testimony or telling stories encourages participants to present different perspectives instead of trying to conform to making arguments or giving reasons. They have the liberty to say whatever they want in the way that they want.

Emile: This phase is important for giving people that liberty: To say what they want without fear of censure or critique. Not only does storytelling permit the presentation of different perspectives, but it also introduces the speaker to the group. Storytelling is about who one is; testimony is personal experiences of or reflections about the issue at hand. When people talk, comments John Forester,[25] those listening learn about the speaker's perspectives and ideas, but they "learn still more from the way [one speaks]. . . . [F]rom the way they talk and act, from their style, we learn about who they are, 'what they are like,' what sort of 'character' someone has . . . whether they are arrogant or not, trustworthy or not, reliable or not. . . . We learn not only from the points people make but from the details they present—and often the unintended details" (310-11).

Pinzak: There is another important aspect of storytelling that needs emphasis. Storytelling elicits a different kind of listening. Often when someone speaks, we immediately judge whether we agree or disagree. That judgment can color our hearing of what the speaker is saying. Storytelling, on the other hand, bypasses or undercuts such judgments. It is someone else's personal experience, whether the speaker's or another actor's, and so we can relax and simply listen. We don't feel the urgent need to filter what is said.[26]

Emile: That is so because storytelling engages us emotionally, not just intellectually. We connect with the speaker in a more open and more complete way. We listen to the stories with openness and at times with sympathy and empathy.[27] This connection makes it far more difficult to keep people at a distance, at arm's length. As Chickering and Turner point out, "with engagement comes *trust.*"[28]

Pinzak: That is the reason you described this phase as one that helps generate trust and respect.

Emile: And when we respect someone, comments William Isaacs, then "we accept that they have things to teach us"[29] This acceptance in turn builds a sense of connection and community among participants.[30] "Sharing personal stories inspires trust by helping us understand each other from the inside out. . . . When we open . . . our lives to each other, we create a safer environment for forming new relationships."[31] Daniel Yankelovich comments that this approach is especially important and highly effective when the issue under consideration is deeply felt, such as health care, abortion, or capital punishment.[32]

Pinzak: Learning from people's stories is important for more than building trust and respect, as significant as those elements are in any dialogue. Stories also reveal ideas and information that at first blush might seem inconsequential or irrelevant.

Emile: That is an extremely important point, Pinzak. We need also to keep in mind, as we shall discuss again in the deliberative or Third Phase, that storytelling and swapping stories is also a way that people deliberate. As a result, telling stories will not be, and should not be, consigned solely to the introductory session. Stories will appear throughout the dialogue.[33]

Pinzak: So the literature on dialogue shows that people are generally more comfortable entering into a dialogue if they begin by talking about their own experiences or begin with stories tied intimately to their lives.

Emile: Yet people also want to start slowly, even discreetly, because they do not wish to open up too quickly among strangers. So there is a fine line of balance here that perhaps a facilitator must take into account.

Pinzak: Not pushing people—encourage them but do not rush them. *(Emile nods.)*

Emile: This seems like a crucial step, because if scholars like Katherine Cramer Walsh[34] are correct, then this phase of democratic dialogue is that part of the process where participants really delve into mutual understanding. This, then, is the most fundamental aspect of dialogue and one that is often missing from deliberations. Participants, in telling their stories and giving their testimony, are not offering positions that must be defended. They are simply saying, "This is how I see it. This is how the issue affects me." Those listening do not feel a need, and certainly not an urgency, to interrogate the speaker.

Pinzak: It's a kind of "easy listening." *(Emile groans, and Pinzak shrugs his shoulders.)* It's a way for participants to learn about the perspectives of others and try to gain insight into why others hold the positions they do. Storytelling permits the listeners to hear the assumptions that people hold. That requires empathy and careful listening, which are really the same thing. What we have, then, in this first phase is a way for persons to open up and, equally important, for listeners to hear perspectives, especially divergent perspectives, in ways that are non-threatening. With a story or testimony a listener can more easily slip into the position of the other.

Emile: Organizers of dialogues and facilitators within them must emphasize that this kind of listening and learning leads to greater trust and openness among participants. The evidence from such dialogues shows that trust and openness further lead to outcomes that participants holding diverse and conflicting views can find acceptable. This is so even if those outcomes do not include all the interests, perspectives, or desires.[35]

Phase Two: Laying out Perspectives

The participants then move from a focus on giving testimony to one on hearing testimony. Phase Two is the period for gathering information, for hearing expert testimony, if there is any, on the issue and for the presentation of as many perspectives as possible. This, too, is a phase of careful listening and questioning. Phase Two is the phase of discussion where information is presented and elucidated so that participants can absorb it. But in addition to information and testimony, participants at this stage must be encouraged to explore other options, ideas, positions, and possibilities. It is important at this stage to allow participants the freedom to explore and create options not yet presented and to examine from as many angles as possible options and ideas that have been presented. Creativity of this sort relies on participants' suspending judgment about what other participants are saying. This is the time for gathering ideas. This phase is sometimes referred to as "mapping" the issue.[36] Criticizing or reacting to the participants' contributions comes at the next stage.

Pinzak: As I see it, the difficulty here will be that as positions on the issues are laid out by participants, people will want to defend those positions. Some defense is, of course, necessary, especially when positions are scrutinized. But the more one person defends his position, the more others wish to defend theirs. Soon defending positions becomes the only mode of interaction, and dialogue is lost. Instead of exploring—hearing—the perspectives of others, taking in what others are saying, one is interested only in and even consumed by trying to bolster his own. Then inquiry stops and defensiveness rules the discourse. Reflection becomes difficult, and movement from established positions becomes almost impossible.

Emile: Let us consider an example to illustrate the need for and the difficulty of truly hearing the perspectives of others. The example comes from Daniel Yankelovich. Organized labor and management were at loggerheads over the need to maintain competitiveness in the steel industry by downsizing the workforce in a steel mill. There was not enough goodwill to establish any kind of dialogue between the two groups. "In the early sessions, the mistrust was so intense that participants from both the union and the management sides called each other insulting names, stormed out of meetings, and even threw chairs at each other" (1999, 111). Eventually, both sides, mediated by William Isaacs, then of the MIT Dialogue Project, agreed to some ground rules. Participants would meet every two weeks, sitting together in a circle, without any agenda or specific task or detailed timetable. But why? Why would they agree to these steps? What did dialogue offer them that they could see might help?

Apparently, though Yankelovich does not say so, there was no alternative. Both the union and management knew that the future of the steel mill and thus their own futures were at stake. It was the intercession of the facilitator, William Isaacs, which kept the two sides meeting together. Isaacs had to reinforce each side listening to the other through weeks of preliminary meetings, without either side becoming immediately defensive in light of comments that they found challenging, mistaken, or offensive.

The format of listening to the perspectives of others without judgment was unfamiliar to the two sides. Yankelovich says that the format was disorienting. Yet such disorientation is what can induce cognitive dissonance of sorts. The dissonance or internal turmoil produced through the need to listen attentively to the other side, to empathize with those who spoke and with what they said, shifted the tone of the meetings. Attentive listening heralded a shift of approach and attitude—a shift in sensibility—inside the participants themselves. As one union member commented: "You know, I can't tell who is on what side anymore" (1999, 112).

Pinzak: It is apparent to me that the key to the first two phases is careful listening.

Emile: Yankelovich, for one, agrees with you. He calls it "empathic listening." Such listening is enhanced when participants are asked to paraphrase what another has said (1999, 136).

Pinzak: I've heard this referred to as "mirroring." When participants hear someone mirror back to them what they have just said, then they are assured, or reassured, that they have been heard. The speaker can then repeat a point that has not been heard, or can modify or clarify a point that was correctly heard but is not what was intended. Mirroring is especially important, because without it, putting oneself in the position of another, even when the intentions are noble, could mean interpreting the world using one's own terms and not using the terms of that other person. Restating to the satisfaction of the other the nature of the other's position reinforces that the other person has been heard. This process generates trust, as participants come to trust that they are being heard and to trust those who are listening.[37]

Emile: So participants must be reminded repeatedly that the purpose of dialogue, the early stages of dialogue, is understanding. The onus is to listen to and to learn from the perspectives of others.

Pinzak: The emphasis on listening in dialogue reminds me of Susan Bickford's argument that listening requires the person to slip for that moment into the background and to concentrate on the speaker as the foreground.[38] Of course, as she also points out, we cannot hear anything unless there is a person there to receive what another says. Her point is that we cannot concentrate on our own inner voice as we listen; we cannot hear simultaneously the other and our self "at the same volume."[39]

Listening, then, seems to imply a kind of openness on the listener's part so as not to "mishear" what is being said, so as not to prejudge or prejudice what we are hearing.[40]

Emile: Obviously, there is a difference between being true to how someone is conveying the world as he or she sees and experiences it and you, as the listener, coming to know and live the world as the speaker does. The second seems an impossibility. The listener must, instead, have some appreciation for an accurate account of that speaker's world, not living in or pretending to experience that world.

Pinzak *(opening files on his computer):* Bickford captures this sentiment well. *(There is a long pause as he looks for the passage.)* Here: "I try to experience the world as you construct it for me, but this is not the same as experiencing it as you do" (1996, 147). The construction of your world and experience takes place in my head as my experience of your world. It is the joint effort—the speaker's expositive construction, the listener's reconstruction in his own head, the listener's questions back to the speaker, the speaker's next story used to illustrate or clarify an aspect of his construction, and so on—that constitutes communication.

By this joint effort, Bickford continues, "speaking and listening together may engender a change in consciousness" (1996, 149). Unfortunately, Bickford says little beyond this about what she means by consciousness and what role it plays in identity. But, for us, it is at the heart of the matter. The necessity within democratic dialogue to take up seriously the different, sometimes discrepant, positions of others can lead to the opening of one's own worldview and thus of one's own identity.

Emile: Presumably, given our use in democratic dialogue of dialectical thinking, that opening up of worldview and identity could be toward cosmopolitan identity.

Pinzak: I think so.

Emile: Interestingly, the physicist David Bohm applied his background and insights from science to the study of dialogue. He found that if structured properly, dialogue could result in a change of consciousness among the participants. Dialogue, argues Bohm, enables us to focus our collective thoughts, which are usually, like ordinary light, scattered and conflicting and canceling out one another. The focus through dialogue creates coherence. That coherence generates power in our communication and, presumably, in the outcome of the dialogue. [41]

The basis of dialogue, for Bohm, is to arrive at the different assumptions that motivate participants. When assumptions come up, especially your own, then you and others are to hear but not judge those assumptions (2004, 23). This, of course, is difficult to do. If your assumption about yourself is that you are not well educated enough to speak, then you will remain silent during the dialogue. You will do so not out of choice, but because your assumption about yourself dictates how you should behave. Likewise, someone whose assumption is that he ought to speak often because he is well educated, experienced, and smart, will dominate. These are strongly held and deeply felt assumptions. They are parts of our identity and will not be suspended easily. Introspection and self-reflection are crucial, but it is both the group and the procedures themselves, the situation or context, that can help us here as well. [42]

Pinzak: This isn't surprising. Bohm's language fits in with dialectical thinking and with this phase of laying out perspectives—hearing others' viewpoints without judging them: Simply acknowledge that those viewpoints exist, that they are important to others, and that they have a place in the dialogue. Even if the group polarizes, then that polarization must be recognized and acknowledged. What Bohm is arguing for is the nurturance of non-judgmental attention to what others are saying.

Emile: Nor will we be surprised when Bohm observes that in this way, then, the whole group "becomes a mirror for each person" (2004, 22). Bohm's dialogical process is designed to have a "group think" together, through what he calls "the free flowing of meaning among all participants" (1985, 175). Instead of having individual participants express an idea, then having others defend that idea as still other participants attack it, instead of such back-and-forth, Bohm believes that participants acting as mirrors for one another will come to "think together" (2004, 30). If a participant can suspend judgment of others' views and assumptions, then she can take on those views and assumptions as if they were her own. The practice of that activity can lead to coherence, to a flow of thought and not the jumble of assertions, defenses, attacks, and reassertions that characterize negotiations.

Pinzak: This is what we have been saying about the first two phases of democratic dialogue. All of this for Bohm must rest on trust, just as it does for us.

Emile: He acknowledges just that (2004, 30). Trust leads to the "thinking together" that is the focus of his dialogue. When we can suspend our assumptions, when we can share a common content, then our thinking is flowing and we are thinking together. Here is the connection to the change in consciousness that Bickford was talking about. The content of our consciousness, comments Bohm, "is essentially the same. Accordingly, a different kind of consciousness is possible among us, a *participatory consciousness,"* in which each group member is participating in and partaking of the entire meaning of the group (30-31, emphasis in the original). In short, the group now has a group or common consciousness (38) built of or by participating in the pool of common meaning that constantly develops and changes in the dialogue. This participatory or common consciousness reflects the new meaning generated by the group's being together and thinking together. So, Bohm comments, we have "a harmony of the individual and the collective, in which the whole constantly moves toward coherence (32).

Here is the integration of the individual and the collective, the interplay between and harmony of the upper quadrants of the AQAL model. That interplay and harmony, that integration, leads to the integration of the lower quadrants, as thinking together individually and collectively can generate common values, interests, and worldview (LL) expressed through common institutions, laws, and procedures (LR).

Pinzak: Do you think that Bohm's "participatory consciousness" is somehow our cosmopolitan consciousness?

Emile: The two seem very close. Bohm's kind of dialogue moves participants "out of ego-consciousness" and into "dialogical consciousness." This is a new kind of mind, Bohm says,[43] that arises out of the "new dynamic" of dialogue in which "no speaker is excluded and in which no particular content is excluded" (1985, 175). Because participants must hear the comments of others whose own views are diametrically opposed to the listeners', they must remove themselves temporarily from their own egocentric positions to listen with open minds and even open hearts. The possibilities of dialogue, Bohm suggests, could lead to the transformation not only of relationships among participants but also, and even more significant, "the very nature of consciousness in which these relationships arise" (175).

Pinzak: We might hypothesize, therefore, that over time repeatedly exercising such listening can open the participants' identities to transformation, fundamental transformation. By encountering the other, by opening to the other, we move toward embracing the other and appreciating otherness itself. The very nature of our consciousness changes to cosmopolitan consciousness and to a cosmopolitan identity. If we are opening repeatedly to others, then why must that stop at the boundaries of our group or community or nation, especially if we establish dialogical contexts with those from outside our borders?

For many participants this requirement to listen, although sounding innocuous in itself, can be profound . . . profoundly disturbing. It requires participants to "open themselves" so as to take the perspectives of others seriously, to hold those perspectives as if they were their own. Doing so makes the participants vulnerable, certainly vulnerable to change, because unfolding before them is another way to view the world, or at least one issue within it. This can lead to participants' challenging their own worldview and thereby to challenging their own identity and sense of self.

Emile: This is precisely what we have, in part, been talking about and striving for: the unfolding of cosmopolitan identity through dialogue. Bohm himself says that through dialogue "we have this very high energy of coherence," which "could make a new change in the individual and a change in the relation to the cosmic" (Bohm 2004, 175). Kay Pranis and her colleagues, who are experts at running dialogues as Wisdom Circles, have found that participants often come away from dialogues sensing that they "are connected to all other beings, and so what happens to them affects us too."[44] Here is an expression of cosmopolitan sensibility that is not theoretical. It comes from those who have participated in, conducted, and observed dialogues.

Pinzak: Bohm's ideas on transformation of consciousness through dialogue are not far from our prior conversations about meditation, which is also a mechanism for transforming consciousness. The structure of dialogue permits us to explore our minds and our boundaries together.

Emile: Whereas in meditation, we attend to our breathing or a mantra, in dialogue we attend to meaning—the meaning that we all share and that we also create together. In the Foreword to *Dialogue*,[45] Peter Senge comments that dialogue is close to meditation. Senge calls dialogue a "collective meditation" (xxxviii), which is reminiscent of Bohm's view of dialogue as transformative.

To Senge, meditation, regardless of the kind or style, is about cessation, where we cease paying attention to our own mental chatter as we listen. Meditation is about silence, levels of deeper and deeper silence. Listening, claims Senge, is like that, where listening begins in silence. Our backgrounds—our histories and prejudices, our impulses and proclivities—are silent, so that we may tune into what others are saying and not to our own mind's programs.[46]

Pinzak: Another approach to silence might help us understand its role in dialogue: There is a gap, which we might call a moment of silence, between the time when one participant finishes speaking and another begins. There may also be a gap or moment of silence between the time when someone stops talking and we aren't yet thinking, because we've just been actively listening, and then we have a thought. These gaps or silences are the in-between that allows thoughts or statements to be distinct. They are the ineluctable and essential backdrop. Silence is ever-present; it is never absent; it is the ineluctable and essential backdrop for all communication.

Emile: Silence, I think, also conveys a sense of emptiness. In silence we are empty of thoughts and judgments. We are listening and waiting. In that silence we are open to letting in the contributions of others. We are waiting and simultaneously "inquiring" of another; we are literally "asking or seeking into" another. There is room in that waiting, in that silence, to allow or to *admit,* in both senses of the word, something new. When the listener is silent, the speaker can be heard.

Pinzak: How much silence is there in a Quaker meeting, with Friends waiting for the "light" of the "God within"? Do you think anyone has ever quantified how much of those meetings consists of silence versus how much of talk?

You know, Emile, as we suggested earlier, we could introduce at the very outset of any democratic dialogue a period of silence, a time for all participants to experience meditation or Benson's secular relaxation response. That would enable us to combine the two aspects of identity change that we've been talking about—meditation and dialectical thinking—thus making dialogue all the more powerful. Plus, the period of silence could be presented as nothing more than reduction of stress, release of tension, and a way of quieting the mind for better listening and reflection, all of which we mentioned before and all of which would be true. *(Pinzak and Emile both sit for a time in silence. A member of the staff comes by and clears away their empty cups. Pinzak looks at his watch.)*

Pinzak: You know, when we are in a dialogue, we must also listen to ourselves, to our own responses as they arise in reaction to what someone else has said. All of the demands of listening and sharing that we've been talking about, all of this makes transformative dialogue risky or at least challenging.

Emile: Yes, it is risky, because you risk a deep connection to others. In that you risk opening to the possibilities of new worlds or perspectives that can transform you. Perhaps this is nowhere stated better than in Plato's comment in his "Seventh Letter" about the power of dialectic, or what we call dialogue: "[A]fter long-continued intercourse between teacher and pupil, in joint pursuit of the subject [the first and highest principles of nature], suddenly, like light flashing forth when a fire is kindled, [insight] is born in the soul and straight-away nourishes itself' (1997b, 341c6-d1).[47]

Dialogue is also challenging, but not impossible. People listen with whatever skill and focus they can muster. They do not have to attain a certain meditative state, even though such states, as Senge points out, are possible in dialogue. Dialogue challenges every participant, because every participant tries to listen without projecting onto others her own prejudices, proclivities, or point of view. Yet, at the same time, the person must be aware of, must listen to, her own reactions, as you say. The task is not to let those internal reactions dominate or be projected onto others.

Pinzak: So each participant must hear what another is saying and, at the same time, must hear his own reactions to what the other person is saying. Whenever a participant speaks, each participant listens to and reacts to that reaction. Over the course of the dialogue, in reaction to what is said, each participant brings to the foreground in his comments on the issues his own basic assumptions about life and about how the world works. He needs to be aware of those assumptions, even critically aware of them, but not let them dictate or get in the way of listening. And inner silence can permit one to acknowledge the internal reactions but not attend to them. One lessens the inner chatter and, by doing so, one might then "hear" the feelings and meanings that come from deep within what we might miss if we are too "noisy."[48]

Emile: Yes, this is all part of the challenge. That challenge may enrich one's worldview by questioning those assumptions and leading to changes in them or by reinforcing those assumptions through the addition of factors not seen or considered before. What unfolds is an identity that, as we have argued, is more encompassing and more compassionate than previous levels of identity. Observe how participants in democratic dialogue open to the views, lives, and meanings of others. Observe the connections or interrelationships that develop out of that openness and the shared meanings that ensue. Finally, observe the sensibilities—cosmopolitan sensibilities—that can manifest and develop into cosmopolitan identity.

Pinzak: Society is based on shared meanings. If we don't have them, then society falls apart, if it ever begins. The issue over headscarves in France is an example that calls out for creating shared meanings.[49] As Benhabib points out, the girls who wore headscarves to school, in defiance of France's ban on displays of religious application but in accordance with their own Muslim beliefs, were themselves never consulted. They were not asked to give testimony as to why they wore the headscarves or what doing so meant to them. Nor were they consulted about what should follow from the national and international attention that this issue garnered. Instead, state and school authorities "dictated to these girls" what the wearing of headscarves meant. A forum of democratic dialogue would at least have given the girls a chance to lay out their own interpretations. The state *(reading from his computer)* constrained "these women's own capacity to write the meaning of their own actions, and, ironically, reimprison[ed] them within the walls of patriarchal meaning from which they are trying to escape" (2006, 57).

Emile: If we do have "meaning coherence" (a phrase we might invent following Bohm's logic), then society might well be stronger or, as we would phrase that, integrated. If we have this shared meaning across borders, then we are talking about a coherent social order, an integrated social order, that we might call cosmopolitan. Shared meaning should precede the institutions, laws, and procedures that concretize it, and those "concretions" can reinforce the shared meaning that engenders the coherence and integration. Shared meaning leads to a "new kind of culture," as Bohm says (2004, 32). A new culture founded on shared meanings through dialectical thinking and democratic dialogue is the basis for a cosmopolitan culture, as multiple groups, using democratic dialogue, engender changes in consciousness toward planetary or world consciousness.

This cosmopolitan culture and consciousness are not identified as persons holding to the same content. Differences of perspectives and interests, ideas and values will still exist. What will change is how persons view those perspectives and interests, ideas and values. Cosmopolites will not agree on everything, thank goodness. They will agree on how they look at and think about the world and their connections to others. They will have what Bohm calls "an attitude of dialogue" (41). Cosmopolites are marked by their dialectical thinking and by the desire, if not the need, to do that thinking in a democratically dialogical setting.

Let us set this important insight into the context of democratic dialogue. This kind of dialogue has a twofold purpose. One purpose is, as we were just discussing, to engender a cosmopolitan identity and planetary consciousness by opening up to different and divergent perspectives and then by seeking to reconcile or to find the unity underneath them or to transcend them. That seeking underscores the other purpose, the political purpose. We seek to generate through democratic dialogue a "compound common good," which is a good political outcome. We do not want to lose sight of either one of these purposes.

Pinzak: You think that we went too far afield with the topic of empathic listening?

Emile: On the contrary, I think that we emphasized the importance of listening while participants present their own positions and then work with others to create new positions. This topic also serves as a segue into the other two phases of democratic dialogue, which are the more "political" phases. Let us move on, now, to Phase Three.

Phase Three: Deliberating on Plural Perspectives
Creating respect and trust begins with our Phase One, introductory storytelling, as a way for participants to introduce themselves through personal experiences, insights, or testimony related to a particular issue. Once some level of trust and respect has been established, it is easier to move to the stage of scrutinizing people's positions, our Phase Three. Katherine Cramer Walsh points out, interestingly enough, that scrutiny is actually seen by many of the participants she

observed in dialogues as a form of respect.[50] That is, one respects the other person enough to offer some criticism of her position. For dialogue "to constitute a joint project, a credible joint attempt by people . . . it has to involve the scrutiny of all participants" (198). Such scrutiny shows that others are taking all positions or perspectives seriously. Such respect leads to greater trust. How do participants gain one another's trust? They do so, observes Walsh of the participants in the groups she studied, "by being respectful to you, by listening to you, by acknowledging you're different" (251). Respect and trust make it easier for participants to be open-minded.

Pinzak: Building trust, then, needs to occur before any deliberations on participants' contributions or on expert evidence takes place.

Emile: Trust does not make deliberation possible. It simply makes deliberation easier if one is to hear and openly respond to oppositional points of view. Deliberation is the heart of the third phase. Of course, difference of viewpoints, ideas, interests, and values characterizes both Phases Two and Three. It is deliberation that distinguishes between those two phases. Whereas Phase Two is about simply listening to different perspectives that have been laid out, Phase Three is about examining and exploring the merits and consequences of those perspectives, or their lapses and deficiencies.

Pinzak: And to elicit dialectical thinking, to engage in it, requires different, even opposite and divergent, views and positions.

Emile: This has been one of our most consistent points about dialectical thinking. Cass Sunstein argues that deliberative democracy itself, irrespective of any use of dialectical thinking, requires diverse perspectives.[51] Sunstein posits that groups polarize if they do not hear and deal with diverse perspectives. The evidence shows that persons who talk, and deliberate, only with those of like-minds tend to hold strongly to their pre-formed positions. Moreover, they are also far more likely to adopt more extreme positions, being confident in the correctness of their shared views. According to Sunstein, understanding group polarization helps us explain how discussions and activities of in-groups establish far stronger ethnic identifications among members (2001, 34).

Furthermore, Sunstein points out that there is evidence showing "that cohesive groups of like-minded people . . . often suppress dissent and reach inferior decisions—whereas heterogeneous groups . . . tend to produce the best outcomes" (2001, 44). Sunstein cites as one example the case of the creation of the South African constitution, which he calls "the most admirable constitution in the history of the world" (261): "The astonishing success of constitutional design in South Africa was possible largely because people of one view were constantly in discussion with people of opposing views" (50). This, then, highlights the need in deliberative democracies for persons to deliberate with those who do not share their viewpoints. It highlights as well the need for an expansive pool of perspectives from which to draw possible solutions.[52]

Pinzak *(typing):* The easy path is for people to interact only with like-minded folks, because if they deliberate only within their own homogeneous groups and share only similar, if not the same, perspectives, then they can protect themselves from challenging and competing views.[53] The result will be narrow views that are not only reinforced but also pushed to more extreme positions. So, how can we guarantee interaction with diverse and divergent views?

Emile: Sunstein is not particularly helpful in laying out procedures or plans as to how persons "are not isolated from conversation with people having quite different views" (2001, 41). He does not tell us how this can or will be done in a deliberative democracy. But I think that our procedures might have some advantages here.

Pinzak: You mean, first, try to assure some diversity by composing groups that are a mix of races, ethnicities, socioeconomic statuses, ages, religions, occupations, locales, those sorts of things? Or by composing a group through random selection?

Emile: Such selection might work for something like a national deliberative opinion poll,[54] or if you were gathering a small group from around the world to discuss global issues. But if the issue is local, if the group meeting is in a school or factory or office, then there is a strong likelihood that you will not be able to tailor the group sufficiently to achieve diversity.

Our procedures have built into them the idea of participants' hearing public or expert testimony on an issue. We can assure that that testimony is diverse, but guaranteeing that the entire array of perspectives and options is represented in the evidence and arguments made available to participants is difficult. One model that we ought to consider seriously for our own dialogical groups is the National Issues Forums, about which I shall have more to say when we talk about institutions.

Pinzak: I, for one, don't want to leave Sunstein's position unchallenged. Simply because persons agree, even when pushed to more extreme positions, is not necessarily negative. Deliberations among the like-minded, especially the marginalized, can promote coherent presentations of ideas and positions that might otherwise go unheard and unheeded.[55] Nevertheless, I take his major point, especially considering our emphasis on dialectical thinking, that considering divergent views can help to solidify one's position or jettison those aspects of it that are weak, including, one can hypothesize, most of that position. *(Pinzak takes a sip of his coffee, now stone-cold. He seems not to notice or mind. He finishes the coffee and glances at his watch.)*

Listening to someone who disagrees with you is difficult. Listening to someone whose views are antithetical to your own, whose positions strike you as fatuous, even dangerous, without any evidence or support, seems almost impossible. We react strongly and immediately. Perhaps we don't say anything to that person; we are, after all, respecting the idea of toleration, civility, and restraint. But we may very well stop listening.

Emile: We have talked about the importance of listening, and listening to stories at the outset is one way to listen to someone's views and experiences without feeling a need to judge them. When someone is saying, "This is my experience; this happened to me," we are less likely to feel threatened or annoyed or angry. When the same person then offers some ideas about or reasons for a certain position, we might well refrain from judging, believing that we know, as the saying goes, "where he or she is coming from."

But, yes, you are correct. Remaining open and attentive when listening to positions that are opposite one's own is difficult.[56] Bohm tells us to try to create some critical distance from those opposite positions by suspending judgment.

Pinzak: Easier said than done.

Emile: True. (*Emile takes a sip of his water.*) This topic brings up for me Senge's view on the meditative aspect of dialogue. Certain Buddhist traditions have a practice called "mindfulness" or witnessing. The meditator simply attends to her thoughts and feelings, whatever they are. She observes them. She does not try to control or alter them, and she does not try to have them; she simply lets them be. She also watches her reactions—a pain in her leg, a change in her breathing. If they linger, observe that. If they grow and lead to agitation, observe that. When she is aware that she has been lost in a thought, she simply releases it, lets it go. She remains a witness to them rather than the person who has these thoughts and feelings.

This observational or witnessing perspective permits the meditator, or anyone, to gain some distance between the thinking and the thought. That distance can create a certain detachment from the thoughts and feelings and permit the meditator to remain neutral in the face of thoughts and feelings.

Pinzak: Of course, that neutrality, that witnessing, could be useful in dialogue, as the participant remains open and attentive when hearing the perspectives of others.[57] But can someone merely witness when the thoughts are expressed by someone whose view is totally opposite one's own?

Emile: Listening well is a skill. How do we develop the skill, especially with views that are radically different from our own? We try to create some critical distance, not between the others' views and our own, a distance that already exists and one that must be bridged. Instead, we need critical distance from our own views and our reactions to others' views. We need to develop a curiosity about how others see the world, instead of being overwhelmed by a knee-jerk reaction to what we perceive as the obtuseness, limitations, or perniciousness of those other views. We need to involve ourselves in the worldviews of others: "How did you come to see things this way? Help me understand how you view this issue. What is your thinking process?"[58]

Pinzak: In other words, we need to exercise our moral imaginations, to put ourselves in the others' shoes. We need to be curious about the perspective that someone is offering and invite him to amplify that perspective.

Emile: Remember, the procedures themselves call for participants to hear the perspectives of others sufficiently that the participants can mirror them back to those who offer them. Of course, participants may and will disagree. This is the heart of Phase Three: deliberating on the array of perspectives, options, and information now before the participants. During this phase participants probe and challenge the perspectives and positions of those with whom they disagree.

The group has to understand the scope and nature of the option or viewpoint or idea that someone has brought forward, because any of these could be the cornerstone of a decision that comes in Phase Four.

Pinzak *(after trying to gather a few drops of coffee from his cup, already drained):* I recognize, Emile, that this is a perfect time to transition to Phase Four, but I've got an issue to discuss that I think is significant, an issue I'd like your insight into.

Emile: I shall be a candle against your darkness.

Pinzak *(smiling as he concentrates on scrolling through a computer file):* So . . . in her analysis of civic intergroup dialogue, Katherine Cramer Walsh claims that dialogue aims at understanding, whereas deliberation aims at decision-making (2007, 34). This strikes me as a strong claim, Emile—too strong, I think—and in her book she offers no argument for it. I want to know what you think. *(Emile nods as he sips his water.)* I see no reason why deliberation necessarily aims at decision-making. Surely, we can deliberate on or about an issue and use those deliberations to gain greater understanding of the issue itself. Equally, we can use deliberation to see where the group stands on an issue. Weighing arguments and evidence and considering them well, which is the literal definition, and essence, of deliberation, in no way implies needing to make a decision. It can have an educative purpose instead, like Ms. Gearhy's tenth-grade World History class.

Emile: Good example, Pinzak. I agree with Walsh that the term *dialogue* connotes far more than *deliberation,* though I agree with you that deliberations are surely "speaking across" or "speaking through" two or more people, which is the literal definition of *dialogue.* More fruitful might be to contrast *dialogue* with *discussion.* A *discussion,* which comes to us from the Latin combination of *dis* or "apart" and *quatere* or "to shake," is really a focused examination of some topic. It is the same as or at least similar to an *analysis,* which means in ancient Greek "a breaking up." A discussion, then, dissects or analyzes a topic, shakes it up or breaks it apart into smaller or finer pieces. That is its purpose. A dialogue, on the other hand, is more open-ended and involves more than a focus on a topic. It involves revealing aspects of the participants as well.[59]

Pinzak: And I agree with both you and Walsh that dialogue involves generating greater understanding of one's own position and the positions of others. But in my view of democratic dialogue, deliberation has to involve not simply coming to a decision, but also generating greater understanding of the issues. Otherwise, we can never build an integrative outcome.

Deliberation, then, combines the educative function and the decision-making function, though I maintain that there is no necessity that deliberation must be about or lead to decision-making. A Citizens' Jury impaneled in October, 1993, to deliberate about President Clinton's health care reform package illustrates this dual role for deliberation. Button and Mattson report that on the first day of the deliberations *(Pinzak reads from his computer),* "Twenty-nine percent of the participants believed that President Clinton's proposed health care plan would be 'bad for the country'. . . . At the end of the five-day process, those numbers changed to 46 percent of the Citizen Jurors believing that the President's plan would be bad for the country. Before the Citizens' [sic] Jury panel, 54 percent reported that they did not understand most of the major points of the health care reform plan. By the end of the session, only 4 percent of the participants reported being confused about the issue."[60] Their deliberations appear to have educated them about Clinton's reform package even if the group was not making a collective decision about health care reform.

Button and Mattson comment that this educative role may turn participants into pupils; that is, they become more passive as they soak up information and learn from the "experts." So within this framework of testimony, our Phase Two, the process must be structured to assure that participants have ample time to interact with, even interrogate, the experts to make certain that they understand what is presented to them. There is little reason that expertise cannot be translated from technical language. That happens in courtrooms all the time.

Emile: Having time to question the experts lessens the passive-pupil status of the participants and moves the expert testimony from a lecture to a discussion, as in a seminar. Here the participants are, indeed, trying to "shake apart" or "break up" the testimony into digestible or understandable bits.

Pinzak: There is a time, of course, for accumulating information, for hearing and processing the testimony or evidence, and, as with all good pupils, there is also a time for putting that information to use. This is the second purpose of deliberating—using the information in dialogue about the issues among the participants as they move toward decision-making—and this is our Phase Three. So, I'm suggesting that democratic dialogue is not either discussion or dialogue or deliberation. It is all three. Part of the process requires discussion and analysis and evaluations; another part involves opening to the perspectives of others, embracing differences, connecting to others, making meaning with others. Plus, deliberations involve analysis and scrutiny of positions, which is Phase Three. But they also involve finding common ground and constructing an integrative outcome. The issue, then, is not whether to use dialogue or discussion or deliberation, but *when* to use one or the others.

Emile: Daniel Yankelovich, another student of dialogical processes, both agrees and disagrees with you. Somewhat like Walsh, he distinguishes between dialogue and decision-making, because the two processes require quite different approaches. Yet he agrees that there can be deliberation within dialogue, as long as the two processes are kept separate. This is possible by having a dialogical aspect during which participants tell stories; share personal accounts, experiences, assumptions; and express their values, convictions, and ideas. All of this is included in our Phases One and Two. We also have deliberation, with discussion built in. This is our Phase Three, where the participants scrutinize the different perspectives presented regarding the topic at hand. That is part of the decision-making process and is far more discussion-oriented. Yankelovich writes, "[T]he act of seeking mutual understanding through dialogue should come before all of the practical constraints and clash of interests involved in practical decision-making are brought to bear" (1999, 57).

Pinzak: That is precisely what we're suggesting we do before Phase Four, the decision-making phase.

Emile: I agree. Yankelovich introduces as well another aspect of dialogue worth paying attention to. He argues that dialogue, unlike discussion and certainly unlike debate, implies treating all participants as equals (1999, Chapter 2). We can see that in a discussion, say in a seminar, there are unequal roles. The professor has a level of authority that the students lack. It may not be warranted within the discussion of a particular topic, but it exists as a difference in status between the teacher and the students. No one might object that the discussion took place within this framework; it happens all the time. Yet if that discussion were to turn into a dialogue, then the status of the professor would have to change to that of one participant equal to any other.

Pinzak: Our term "democratic dialogue" does convey a sense of participants as equals meeting to address, resolve, and/or make a decision about a political issue important to the participants' lives. In this sense democratic dialogue aligns with McCoy and Scully's term "deliberative dialogue" (2002), a term that lacks, however, a definite political aspect. The kind of equality that is important within democratic dialogue is what I call "equality of reciprocity." That is, there is unequal status if I want you to change your mind, or assume that you ought to and will, but I'm not willing to change mine. There must be a sense felt by all parties that you can change your mind and I can change mine.

Emile: That reciprocity reflects not just equality but also openness, open-mindedness.

Pinzak: And that open-mindedness is essential to dialogue, because the process of changing one's mind swings on the hinge of empathy. We listen to understand the perspectives, experiences, and assumptions of others. We listen, first, to learn about those perspectives, experiences, and assumptions, to try to understand them, and to respond to them from a position of trying to put ourselves in their shoes.

Emile: As Yankelovich points out, there can be discussion without the requirement of empathy, but there cannot be dialogue (1999, 43). As we have said, the focus is different.

So from a perspective on reciprocity we see the importance of empathy. From a perspective on empathy, which we talked about in some detail at our last meeting, we see the importance of respect.

Pinzak *(speaking excitedly):* That's right! One can't listen empathetically without having respect for the person and what he is going to say. You might disagree with his comment, but your respect for him, and your open-mindedness, leads you to suspend judgment and to listen attentively to try to understand what he is saying.

Emile: In contemporary parlance, to understand "where he is coming from."

Pinzak *(smiling):* I'm not sure how contemporary that is anymore, Emile.

Emile *(with a slight salute with his right hand):* I defer to you regarding what is colloquially *au courant.*

Pinzak: After Phase One—testimony and storytelling—and Phase Two—laying out of all perspectives—we welcome critique in Phase Three primarily as reason-giving. I say "primarily," Emile, because we don't rule out storytelling after the initial section, after Phase One. To argue their positions persons might well use a story to make their points. So there are dialogical moments possible within any section of the process. That's one reason for calling our process "democratic dialogue."[61]

Emile: Those moments are moments when participants connect to one another and create a group sense of meaning, especially when dealing with differences of perspectives and values. When conflicts appear, then emphasizing differences rather than commonalities may be one way to deal with them. Storytelling, however, undercuts that approach by bringing us into contact with the internal world of another person who is sharing that world and not offering up a position for discussion.

Pinzak: He or she is sharing experiences, not making arguments. And in an argument or a conflict, that sharing helps defuse the tension and overcome differences by bringing us closer through our hearing those stories.

Emile: Stories, as we have been saying, ease the tension between self and other and enable the group to work together more readily. Stories are an easier invitation than argument to help us understand both ourselves and others, because it is easier for us to open ourselves to the other person's experience, rather than her argument. The *argument,* which I use here as a stand-in for "reason-giving," might call into question our own position and thereby raise our defenses. A story, on the other hand, asks us to hear the other person's experience or situation. We do not have to defend or impose ourselves or overturn any long-held or deeply felt attitudes or positions to accept what she is saying . . . at least not at the outset.

Pinzak: The storyteller is really revealing something about her, more than about her position, though her position might be the cause and focus of the story. She's revealing something about her identity or how she identifies herself. At the same time, her story allows us easier access to her perspective, for the reasons you cite. Thus, we can take up her perspective; we can walk in her shoes. So not only can these "dialogical moments," as you call them, happen any time during the proceedings, but they also *ought* to happen to permit more, or easier, perspective-taking.

Pinzak looks at his watch again.

"I think that is the third time in the past few minutes that you have looked at your watch," Emile says.

"I'm sorry, Emile, I know it's rude, but I've got to go to meet with my mentor from my undergraduate days before I head to the Cape. It's the only chance I'll have to see him while I'm in Cambridge."

"Your mentor cannot spare more time than that to meet with one of his star pupils?" Emile asks with a small smile.

"I'm hardly that. Actually, he's spending most of the year in Washington, D.C., consulting for the State Department with two of his truly star pupils. He only comes back to Harvard to meet occasionally with his graduate students."

"Who is this mentor of yours?"

"It's Herman Kleinschmidt."

"Of course, Kleinschmidt."

"You know him?"

"No, not personally. But anyone who has been around Cambridge for any time has heard of Kleinschmidt." Emile watches as Pinzak begins packing up his computer. Then he asks, "What is a historian of political thought doing consulting with the State Department?"

Without looking up as he continues packing up his computer, Pinzak responds, "As you probably know, Kleinschmidt is a historical contextualist. To understand the political thinking of any philosopher, the contextualists think that you need to recover the philosopher's intentions, and to do that they must reconstruct the historical period in which the philosopher wrote. Only then can you truly understand and appreciate what the philosopher thought and why he thought it. Reconstructing that context requires prodigious work and results in encyclopedic knowledge, at least in Kleinschmidt's case. So two of his former students now in the State Department somehow convinced someone high up in the pecking order that to understand better Europe's relation to the Middle East, they should consult with someone who knows the historical periods and philosophical underpinnings of Europe's era of colonization." Pinzak finishes zipping his bag closed. As he stands up, he adds, "In terms of encyclopedic knowledge, Kleinschmidt is like you."

Emile, too, stands. "No empty flattery, Pinzak, please. It is unseemly." Emile smiles.

"I'm really sorry to race off like this, Emile. We haven't even finished talking about all of the phases of democratic dialogue, let alone cosmopolitan institutions."

Emile extends his hand and says, "That is quite all right, Pinzak. We are at the end of Phase Three, and it is a good place to stop. We have next week for Phase Four." Pinzak extends his hand as well, and both shake hands. "Besides, as we said earlier, we keep postponing that discussion because the heart of the matter is institutionalizing the dialogue, whatever the level. It is the process of the dialogue itself that is most important, and that is what we are now talking about . . . or were."

Emile smiles again, as he begins to walk out of the café. Pinzak smiles as he says, "Until Monday, Emile. And thank you for everything."

Notes

1. As I see it, and I shall have more to say about it in this encounter and the next, Integral Democracy is both individual and collective (in keeping with the AQAL model). As such, it has both a horizontal dimension and a vertical dimension, which need to be integrated. Essentially, Integral Democracy is the integration of democracy in the multiple areas of a person's life; it is the recognition of and action on the idea that democracy is integral to one's life going well. If the heart of democracy is the idea of self-governance, personal and collective (Crittenden 2002), then we ought to see democracy present and active throughout a person's life. So Integral Democrats seek to establish democratic dialogue on the vertical axis from global settings, down through regional and national settings, to local and personal settings. Similarly, Integral Democrats want to see democratic dialogue along the horizontal axis—that is, in the important venues of a person's life: work, education, recreation, and the like. Nowhere is democracy—deliberative and dialectical democracy—more necessary than in the workplace. Not only should workers be able to participate in creating the structures and nature of their work and the places in which they work, but such participation should also lead them to see connections between their own working lives and conditions and larger social and political issues—a living wage, health care, education, public transportation, day care, neighborhood security, quality of food, child care for parents who want to attend evening deliberative dialogues, and so on.

2. See Gianpaolo Biaocchi, "Participation, Activism, and Politics: the Porto Alegre Experiment and Deliberative Democratic Theory," *Politics and Society* 29 (2001): 43-72, for a discussion of the method of electing representatives from the assemblies.

3. David Lewit's article, "Porto Alegre's Budget Of, By, and For the People," can be found at www.yesmagazine.org. Posted December 31, 2002, (accessed June, 2009).

4. See Ken Wilber's conversation with James Turner, former "Nader's Raider" and lawyer: "The Integral-Political Imperative, Part 3: A Trans-Partisan Vision for America," broadcast April 18, 2008, at http://in.integralinstitute.org/contributor.aspx?id=180 (accessed June, 2009).

5. See Ken Wilber's conversation with Bill Ury, Director of Harvard's Global Negotiation Project: "Towards an Integral Theory of World Governance: The Importance of Stages of Development," http://in.integralinstitute.org/talk broadcast December 6, 2004 (accessed June, 2009).

6. John Parkinson, *Deliberating in the Real World* (New York: Oxford University Press, 2006), viii.

7. David Mathews, *Politics for People* (Urbana, Ill.: University of Illinois Press, 1994), 187.

8. Matt Leighninger, *The Next Form of Democracy* (Nashville, Tenn.: Vanderbilt University Press, 2006), 14.

9. Pete Hamill, writing for the *New York Daily News*, describes a scene illustrative of this position on deliberation, even when it involves New Yorkers: "New York, July 20, 2002: 'We came to the vast hangar at the Javits Center expecting the worst. Put 5,000 New Yorkers in a room, charge them with planning a hunk of the New York future, and the result would be a lunatic asylum. We would erupt in waves of mega-kvetch. Shouts, curses, tantrums, hurled objects, nets hurled to make mass arrests. All laced together with self-righteous sound and obsessive fury. . . . None of that happened. . . . We [were] broken down into groups of 10, seated at tables equipped with a computer. . . . We came . . . expecting the worst. Instead . . . [we] debated in a sober, thoughtful, civil way. . . . All

around the vast room, you heard citizens saying politely to others, 'What do you think?' And then listening—actually listening—to the replies. In this room, 'I' had given way to 'we.' Yes, the assembly was boring to look at, too serious, too grave, too well-mannered for the standard TV presentation. And it was absolutely thrilling.'" Pete Hamill, *New York Daily News,* July, 20, 2002, http://www.deliberative-democracy.net/resources/, accessed July, 2009.

10. Through participation, Tocqueville wrote, "Each man notices that he is not as independent of his fellows as he used to suppose and that to get their help he must often offer his aid to them." Alexis de Tocqueville, *Democracy in America,* ed. J. P. Mayer, trans. George Lawrence (Garden City, N. Y.: Doubleday, 1969), 510.

11. "It is difficult to force a man out of himself and get him to take an interest in the affairs of the whole state, for he has little understanding of the way in which the fate of the state can influence his own lot. But if it is a question of taking a road past his property, he sees at once that this small public matter has a bearing on his greatest private interests, and there is no need to point out to him the close connection between his private profit and the general interest" (Toqueville, *Democracy,* 511).

12. Cited by David Mathews, 1994, 187-88. See John Doble and Jean Johnson, *Science and the Public: A Report in Three Volumes,* (New York: Public Agenda Foundation, 1990), and Jean Johnson, *Science Policy Priorities and the Public,* (New York: Public Agenda Foundation, 1989).

13. Wilber refers to the U.S. Constitution as "a moral-stage-5 document," which is a reference to Kohlberg's stages of moral reasoning. On Kohlberg's scale, stage 5 is one of two levels of postconventional principled moral reasoning. See "Introduction," *The Complete Works of Ken Wilber,* Volume 8 (Boston, Mass.: Shambhala Publications, 2000a), 17n, 59.

14. Philip Zimbardo, for example, suggests that persons who resist orders to commit evil, or resist temptations to do so, are often those who have had some prior experience with or knowledge of, however unwittingly, techniques of resistance. Philip Zimbardo, *The Lucifer Effect* (New York: Random House, 2007).

15. See Zimbardo's section on "The Social Construction of Reality," (2007): 221-24.

16. Research also shows that the decisions of a group are more thoughtful and creative when there are dissenting views present. See C. J. Nemeth, "Differential Contributions to Majority and Minority Influence," *Psychological Review* 93 (1986): 23-32, cited in Zimbardo, *The Lucifer Effect,* footnote 15, 507.

17. Viewing deliberation as the basis of democratic legitimacy is hardly a startling insight, as anyone familiar with the vast literature on deliberative democracy can attest. Interested readers in pursuit of the topic might begin with Bernard Manin's article "On Legitimacy and Political Deliberation," *Political Theory* 15, no. 3 (1987): 338-68; Jon Elster's "Introduction" in *Deliberative Democracy,* ed. Jon Elster (Cambridge: Cambridge University Press, 1998); and Joshua Cohen's article "Deliberation and Democratic Legitimacy" in *The Good Polity,* ed. Alan Hamlin and Philip Petit (Oxford: Blackwell, 1989). Readers might then move on to any number of excellent books on the subject. Among those are *Deliberative Democracy,* ed. James Bohman and William Rehg (Cambridge, Mass.: MIT Press, 1997); John Dryzek, *Deliberative Democracy and Beyond* (New York: Oxford University Press, 2002); and Amy Gutmann and Dennis Thompson, *Democracy and Disagreement* (Cambridge, Mass.: Harvard University Press, 1996).

18. David Miller, *Citizenship and National Identity* (Malden, Mass.: Polity Press/Blackwell, 2000), 142.

19. Margaret Wheatley, *Turning to One Another* (San Francisco: Berrett-Koehler Publishers, 2002), 158.

20. See David Held's discussion of strong, moderate, and weak impacts on peoples' lives in *Globalization Theory: Approaches and Controversies,* ed. David Held and Anthony McGrew (Malden, Mass.: Polity Press, 2007), 253. The phrase "life expectancies and life chances" is also his and found in this article.

21. Harold H. Saunders, *Politics Is About Relationship* (New York: Palgrave/Macmillan, 2005), 152.

22. See http://cbuilding.org/ and www.workablepeace.org, accessed July, 2009.

23. Lynn Sanders, "Against Deliberation," *Political Theory* 25, no. 3 (1997): 370.

24. I hesitated about including this footnote, because it seems self-evident to me what a "story" is and what "telling" it means. Then I thought that literary critics, rhetoricians, and highly inquisitive types might find my failure to define "story" as problematic, if not weak, especially in the absence of any distinction between "narrative" and "story." So, a story has a beginning, a middle, and an end in chronological order; is a "sequential, explanatory account of self-motivated human action" otherwise known as experience; often has a moral or makes a point, sometimes reaching beyond the account itself, that underscores the value of its telling; and is open to interpretation. These are not my ideas, though I accept them readily, but those of Francesca Polletta, *It Was Like a Fever* (Chicago, Ill.: The University of Chicago Press, 2006), 10, 192, footnote 9.

25. John Forester, "Beyond Dialogue to Transformative Learning," in *Political Dialogue: Theories and Practices,* ed. Stephen Esquith (Atlanta, Ga.: Rodopi, 1996), 310-11.

26. Polletta points out that telling stories in deliberative settings helps participants "hear different opinions and experiences as different but not incomprehensible or threatening." Polletta, *It Was Like a Fever,* 89.

27. To my mind, and perhaps no one else's, *sympathy* and *empathy* are not the same. They often seem to be used interchangeably. But *empathy* is the ability to "feel oneself" into the position of another; it is literally "feeling into" another's position (from the Greek *empatheia).* It is to consider someone's circumstance as if you were yourself in that position. *Sympathy,* on the other hand, is the ability to feel another's emotion. In 1992, when Bill Clinton said to a voter attending his town-hall debate with George H. W. Bush, "I feel your pain," he was sympathizing with her. He could feel in himself the anguish or fear or worry that she was expressing. When you see someone else crying and your own eyes fill with tears, you are sympathizing; your response arises regardless of why the other person is crying. You are not reacting to the person's situation but to his or her show of emotion. *Sympathy* is crying because someone else is crying; *empathy* is crying for the same reason that someone else is crying.

One reason *sympathy* and *empathy* are interchangeable terms is that both are at the core about reading and responding to the emotions of others. When someone tells us a moving story, we can place ourselves in that circumstance not so much because we understand cognitively what the person is saying, though we do, but because we feel ourselves into the story. We empathize; we see ourselves in the same position and thus have the same emotions. Sympathy is sharing their emotions; empathy is having their telling of the story elicit from us the same emotions. In one you cry because the person is miserable; in the other you cry because you know why she's miserable and you would be too if you were in her position.

28. A. Lawrence Chickering and James S. Turner, *Voice of the People: The Trans-partisan Imperative in American Life* (Goleta, Calif.: da Vinci Press, 2008), 77, emphasis in original.)

29. William Isaacs, *Dialogue and the Art of Thinking Together* (New York: Random House, 1999), 114-15.

30. For more on the role of narrative and storytelling in connecting participants into a sense of community, see David Ryfe, "Narrative and Deliberation in Small Group Forums," *Journal of Applied Communication Research* 34, no. 1 (2006).

31. Kay Pranis, Barry Stuart, and Mark Wedge, *Peacemaking Circles* (St. Paul, Minn.: Living Justice Press, 2003), 139.

32. Daniel Yankelovich, *The Magic of Dialogue* (New York: Simon & Schuster, 1999), 131.

33. John Parkinson, *Deliberating in the Real World* (New York: Oxford University Press, 2006), 42, argues that "reasoning together" is quite consistent with "a range of communicative styles" and that concerns by Lynn Sanders and others that deliberation leans on, if it does not require, reasoned arguments "may well be theoretical possibilities but empirical rarities in genuinely deliberative processes."

34. Katherine Cramer Walsh, *Talking About Politics* (Chicago: The University of Chicago Press, 2004), and *Talking About Race* (The University of Chicago Press, 2007).

35. See Isaacs (1999) and Yankelovich (1999) on this point.

36. See Saunders, *Politics,* 21-22; and 21-25 for an outline of what Saunders calls "Citizens' Political Process." One of the best methods for creating and exploring policy possibilities on important social and political issues is through the discussion process pioneered by the Interactivity Foundation. See www.interactivityfoundation.org.

37. For more details on mirroring, see Crittenden 1992, 103-04. I wrote about mirroring in the context of participants' hesitation in democratic forums to reveal their perspectives for fear of facing ridicule or losing emotional control. Participants must feel confident that fellow participants will seek first to understand their positions rather than seek only to demolish them. Phase One as discussed here helps in that regard.

38. Susan Bickford, *The Dissonance of Democracy* (Ithaca, N.Y.: Cornell University Press, 1996), 23.

39. Bickford, *The Dissonance,* 24, fn. 14. Bickford cites the experimental work of Don Ihde, who shows that we can no more hear another's voice and simultaneously our own voice than we can see different objects simultaneously. We cannot, for example, see simultaneously two faces and one vase in the same-silhouetted picture. Instead, we must draw back and concentrate on one view or the other.

40. According to Bickford, Simone Weil thought that such openness was possible only "supernaturally," in a meditative or mystical state, such as Weil's "waiting on God" (1996, 145). But openness of the kind discussed here does not require the vacating of any sense of self. Moving oneself to the background is not the same as making oneself disappear altogether. Yet, we can appreciate how the sense of oneness gleaned by meditators, about whom we have talked, might contribute to the ease of evincing this openness—of opening to others—and slipping into the background of silence.

41. David Bohm, *On Dialogue* (New York: Routledge, 2004), 15-16. Bohm sees dialogue as necessarily purposeless; that is, he does not think that transformative dialogue can arise if decisions must be made or if the topic is determined beforehand. The dialogical space must be "empty," as he puts it, so that any topic can come in (2004, 19). I am not persuaded that this is necessarily so; why, that is, the emptiness of the dialogue is crucial to transformation. It is true, in a sense, as he says, that this emptiness makes the dialogue free. From one perspective that is self-evident; the dialogue is free of content.

But this does not necessarily translate into participants being or feeling internally free, even if they have no set collective objectives or conclusions to reach and share. Bohm's dialogue is solely educative. His concern is with creating coherent communication, which flows from trust among participants and changes within participants. Shared meaning is important, but not apparently the translation of that meaning into policy or political outcomes. I see no reason why that kind of translation cannot occur within a dialogical structure, as in democratic dialogue, that has aspects built on a kind of emptiness but that also honor and strive for policy or political outcomes. I talk more about this later when addressing "silence" in dialogue.

But Bohm's dialogical groups are not without any purpose; they are without fixed purpose. The purpose, really, is educative: to sustain the dialogue so that changes can occur, transformations can occur, within the participants and therefore in their communications. Such change occurs, in Bohm's experience, when basic assumptions of group members are voiced, heard, and challenged. If you stick with the dialogical process, then "deep assumptions will comes the surface" (22).

42. Some of Francesca Polletta's research on online dialogues in *It Was Like a Fever* (2006, 98*)* supports Bohm's position. She observes from her own work with five hundred sixty-two active discussants participating in an online dialogue between July 31 and August 12, 2002, on the future of Lower Manhattan in the wake of the terrorist attacks on September 11 that their storytelling "the narrative character of people's accounts[,] . . . engaged people imaginatively in experiences quite different from their own. The interpretatively open character of stories demonstrated participants' willingness to scrutinize their own assumptions." Polletta also finds something else that we have thought significant about storytelling: "[I]n asking for and telling stories of people with views different from their own, storytellers communicated their respect for those views (98). Polletta concludes her chapter by observing that having participants telling stories at the beginning of a deliberative forum is effective for building solidarity and trust (207).

43. David Bohm, *Unfolding Meaning* (Mickleton, U.K.: Foundation House Publications, 1985), 175. See also David Bohm, 2004, 54: "I'm suggesting that there is the possibility for a transformation of the nature of consciousness."

44. See Pranis et al., *Peacemaking Circles,* 68. Participants also find that the variety of perspectives that participants hear leads them to investigate different aspects of themselves. That investigation encourages participants to find a balance within themselves and simultaneously to seek connections with others (63). I shall have more to say about Wisdom Circles in the Seventh Encounter.

45. Linda Ellinor and Glenna Gerard, *Dialogue: Rediscover the Transforming Power of Conversation* (New York: John Wiley & Sons, 1998).

46. See also, as already mentioned, Newberg and Waldman's discussion of "compassionate communication" that "integrates an awareness-based meditation directly into the dialogue process" (2009, 219).

47. Plato, "The Seventh Letter," in *Plato: The Complete Works,* trans. Stanley Lombardo and Karen Bell (Indianapolis: Hackett Publishing Co., 1997b), 341c6-d1.

48. See William Isaacs, 1999, Chapter 4, "Listening," for more on this.

49. Seyla Benhabib, *Another Cosmopolitanism* (New York: Oxford University Press, 2006), 57.

50. Katherine Cramer Walsh, *Race,* 2007, 236.

51. Cass R. Sunstein, *Designing Democracy* (New York: Oxford University Press, 2001), 34.

52. Katherine Cramer Walsh reinforces through her studies what might be painfully obvious: Persons join groups where they feel comfortable and where they see likenesses among themselves and fellow members. Such groups create a collective perspective that expresses the positions held by the group. When discordant views arise, they are easily dismissed or disparaged, because they do not fit the group perspective. Walsh observes of such groups: "This strong sense of who is one of us and how such a person should behave serves as a useful guideline for both preventing and dealing with dissent" (2004, 111).

On the other hand, if one is in a democratic dialogue where one's central purpose is to hear and deal with the views of others, then the crafted social identity brought to the group, the context in which an individual situates himself, might be questioned and disrupted, at least internally. Here, then, is an opening, a painful opening no doubt, for change of identity. Democratic dialogue will not, then, have the transformative result if held within like-minded groups.

53. Sunstein warns that "[w]ith greater specialization, people are increasingly able to avoid general interest newspapers and magazines and to make choices that reflect their own predispositions. The Internet is making it possible for people to design their own highly individuated communications packages, filtering out troublesome issues and disfavored voices" (2001, 35).

54. The deliberative opinion poll is the idea of James Fishkin. See *Democracy and Deliberation* (New Haven, Conn.: Yale University Press, 1993).

55. Sunstein himself acknowledges that like-minded sharing is not categorically negative. He points out that the abolitionist movement might well have been furthered by such "extremists" whose like-minded sharing fueled and intensified one another's views.

56. Here I advert, of course, to the earlier discussion of listening.

57. Linda Ellinor and Glenna Gerard, *Dialogue,* 72, recommend the following exercise for sharpening listening skills: The next time a judgment shows up and shuts down your listening skills, mentally "pick up the judgment between thumb and forefinger of your right hand and literally suspend it at a distance in front of you. Once you've suspended it, let it go. It will simply float there." That suspension creates the mental space to permit you to continue listening without the judgment. They comment: "If you practice this exercise with any regularity, it is guaranteed to result in a deepening of your listening skills" (73). To ascertain whether their view is so requires, of course, following their injunction and noting the results—following, that is, our epistemological steps.

58. William Isaacs offers two steps that a dialogue facilitator or a participant could try to defuse the defensive posture of those bolstering their own perspectives instead of inquiring into the perspectives of others. First, he writes, call attention to what is going on by naming it: "The way we are talking right now—each one advocating, no one inquiring, everyone defending a position—repeats the exchange we have [been having]. Do people see this? Can we make an effort to do something else" (1999, 368)? Notice that the facilitator or participant does not suggest what that "something else" is or might be. That is up to the group.

If this step does not elicit a shift toward inquiry and listening, then Isaacs suggests the step of "engagement." Directly engage the participants in challenging questions:

> Advocating this way is unlikely to move us to the point of reflecting on why we have these views. So let me ask: Why does each of us feel pressured to defend ourselves? What stops us from slowing down and inquiring? . . . What might we be learning that is new from each other? Can we begin to ask what we are missing that we do not want to hear? (1999, 368, emphasis in original).

59. According to Ellinor and Girard, *Dialogue,* Chapter Three, participants in dialogue also seek to see the whole among the parts and the connections among the parts, which is one way that I have characterized dialectical thinking.

60. Mark Button and Kevin Mattson, "Deliberative Democracy in Practice: Challenges and Prospects for Civic Deliberation," *Polity* 31, no. 4 (1999): 622.

61. David Ryfe, "Narrative and Deliberation in Small Group Forums," *Journal of Applied Communication Research* 34, no. 1 (2006): 73, concludes from his studies of five National Issues Forums that participants tell stories when they deliberate. They also discuss and argue, but Ryfe says that storytelling is for many the preferred method. As Ryfe also points out, however (88-89), groups that engage predominantly in storytelling "will gravitate toward a single narrative and spend much of their time congratulating themselves on its discovery." What is wrong with that? Is that not the point of deliberating? Not when it often results, as studies reveal, in consensus positions that show "biased judgments or decisions" made without fully considering differing viewpoints and contradictory information (89). This is one reason, and a strong one, why there ought to be dialogical or storytelling moments in the more deliberative section of our democratic dialogue, Phase Three, but not a focus on storytelling in that phase. There is a time for predominant storytelling and a time for reasons, evidence, and argument.

Seventh Encounter:

Institutionalizing Democratic Dialogue

For I dipt into the future, far as human eye could see
Saw a Vision of the world, and all the wonder that would be. . . .
Till the war-drum throbb'd no longer
And the battle-flags were furled
In the Parliament of man, the Federation of the world.
—Alfred Lord Tennyson, "Locksley Hall"

Pinzak left Widener Library through the rear exit and crossed Massachusetts Avenue. This was his usual route to the Café Pamplona, but instead of turning left as he normally did, Pinzak turned right and headed to John F. Kennedy Street. Once there, he turned left and walked to the Charles River. At the river Pinzak walked under the elms and maples on the swath of grass that separates the Charles from Memorial Drive. He headed west toward the Eliot Bridge. He had left the library early so that he could take this walk in the afternoon sun. It was a gorgeous fall day for so late in the season, and this walk reminded him of his undergraduate years. The scene did not seem to have changed at all. Pinzak stopped, unshouldered his computer bag, placed it on the ground, and lay down on his back, his head resting on the bag. He gazed up at the sky, a deep, dark cloudless blue, a perfect background for the reds and oranges and yellows on the trees.

What seemed like only a moment later, Pinzak, startled, opened his eyes. "What the . . ." he exclaimed as he looked at his watch. As unlikely as it was, and therefore as unexpected, Pinzak had fallen asleep. He was not a napper, by habit, and he never could fall asleep on his back. But yet here he was, scrambling to his feet after dozing off. And now he was late. He seized his computer bag in his right hand and began the trot to the Café Pamplona. He was not concerned that Emile would leave. He was concerned because it was rude to be late, and on Friday he had left in a hurry, which Pinzak thought was rude, despite Emile's good humor about it. Now Pinzak was compounding the rudeness. But a trot was at this point all that he could manage.

He arrived at the café slightly out of breath. Emile sat at their usual table, what had become their usual table, much as he had when Pinzak first met him weeks ago. His overcoat was buttoned to the top, and he was catching the fading rays of the setting sun on his face. Unlike the past few visits together, there were no drinks on the table. "Pay back," Pinzak wondered, "for my rudeness?"

"I am so sorry to be late, Emile."

"Oh?" exclaimed Emile softly. "Did we have a set time?"

"No," Pinzak answered, "but I don't usually come this late."

"Do not fret, Pinzak. The sun is shining. The air is fresh. It is a lovely day."

Pinzak unzipped his bag and extracted his computer. "I fell asleep on the grass by the Charles. That's not like me at all."

"What is not like you? Falling asleep, or falling asleep on the grass along the Charles?" queried Emile.

"Falling asleep during the day. Outside. On my back. With my clothes on." Pinzak spoke each word with great deliberation as he opened his computer and arranged it on the small table.

"Too much library work, Pinzak. Too much stale air and eye strain. You are fortunate that we can still meet outdoors." Emile paused, opened his eyes, and looked at Pinzak for the first time since he had arrived. "If I notice you dozing off, I shall give you a nudge."

"Very funny," Pinzak said as he sat down. "No coffee yet, Emile? Are you expecting me to pay as compensation for bolting on Friday?"

"That would be petty of me, Pinzak, would it not? Actually, I thought that you might want to try something different today. Perhaps as compensation for 'bolting' on Friday," replied Emile.

"See, I knew you were . . ."

"Stop. I am teasing you. Do you like chocolate, Pinzak?"

"I do, but only dark chocolate."

"Excellent. What you and most patrons do not know is that Angela Varney, the new owner of Pamplona, is a historian of chocolate. She has studied recipes from all over the world and from all epochs. Each fall she offers a menu of special chocolate coffee drinks that she does not publicize but does make available to the discerning. In addition to being a historian, Angela is also an artisanal chocolate maker, making fresh each week the small batches of chocolate wafers that she uses in the drinks. This week Angela is using the historical drinking chocolate of the French court at Versailles during the reign of the Sun King, Louis XIV, produced from a recipe published in 1692. The chocolate drink is highly scented, dark, semi-sweet, and includes cloves, Ceylon cinnamon, and oils of Ambergis and Musk. Blend into that some espresso, and you have a true elixir. Will you try some?" asked Emile.

"Given how much I owe you, Emile, how can I refuse? And only if you're joining me," replied Pinzak.

"But of course." Emile turned in his chair, raised his right arm, and waved his hand ever so slightly at the waiter standing by the door. The waiter nodded and walked inside the café. Emile turned his face back toward the sun and closed his eyes. "How was your weekend?"

"It was absolutely average. The weather and sailing and food were all superb, but the company was not. There was tension the whole time."

Emile asked, with his eyes still closed, "Oh, why was that?"

"Well, apparently my friends invited someone as a 'fix-up' for me. I suspected that, but I did not expect the blatant attempts to thrust the two of us together. From the outset, she and I knew that nothing much was going to come of the weekend. Neither of us was in the mood for romance or a relationship. Somehow our hosts felt obliged to try all weekend to make something happen between us. So our hosts were tense, because they were trying so hard, and we were tense because they were trying so hard. Finally, last night, right before we left, Carly—my 'friend'—and I cleared the air. We told the others that their plotting had almost ruined the weekend for the two of us. Fortunately, the sailing, food, wine, and stories were strong enough to make up for it."

"And how was the meeting with your mentor?"

"It went well, though we spent most of the time talking about you. Kleinschmidt certainly hadn't expected that. I think he thought that we'd be talking mostly about his consulting work in Washington." Emile did not react at all. He remained, eyes closed, sunning his face. "He wants to meet you."

"Oh?" Emile opened his eyes and turned toward Pinzak. "Well, here I am."

"He didn't mean today." Emile smiled at Pinzak and then turned back to the sun. Pinzak typed on his keyboard and moved his hand on the mouse pad. "He thinks that I should write my cosmopolitan book as a dialogue."

At this, Emile opened his eyes and turned his body toward the table and Pinzak. At that moment, the elixir arrived. Emile waited for both Pinzak and himself to be served; thanked Bobby, the waiter; and raised his cup. "To your book," he said as he held out his cup to Pinzak, who touched his to Emile's. They both sipped.

"Oh, my God!" Pinzak exclaimed. "This is fantastic. It's spicy, with a bite, but yet it's smooth, too."

"And as the flavors of coffee and chocolate mingle, it becomes smoother still," remarked Emile. "So, he thinks that you should write a dialogue. What a splendid idea."

"Really? You think so?"

"My goodness, Pinzak. You are writing a book on dialogue. What could be better for that than the dialogue form? It is a dialectic, a back-and-forth between two persons . . ."

"Between you and me."

"If you wish . . . a back-and-forth between two persons 'thinking together,' as Bohm said. The format worked for Plato."

"Emile, I'm not Plato."

"I am not saying that you are. But why did Plato write dialogues instead of treatises, as Aristotle did?"

"That question itself raises philosophical questions that I certainly cannot answer," answered Pinzak.

"Humor me, Pinzak. Try."

Pinzak: Well, one possibility might be that the dialogue is not, and is not meant to be, a definitive statement on any issue. When we enter into a Platonic dialogue, we are in the midst of a conversation in which characters try out positions. The dialogue opens up questions and leaves them open, once the dialogue proper has ended.

Emile: So, the point of a dialogue is to open up the reader to the questions and positions discussed within it. The dialogue stimulates the reader's thinking and imagination.

Pinzak *(warming to the topic):* Yes, and imagination is as important to Platonic dialogues as is philosophizing, for Plato has given us a dramatic structure for the presentation of philosophical ideas. Thus, the reader must seek to integrate both the dramatic and the philosophical aspects. For those interested in the philosophical ideas in Plato, the dramatic aspects are often overlooked, and they ought not to be. Thus, the callow perspectives of Socrates's interlocutors in *The Republic,* for example, provide the dramatic tension that propels the dialogue forward.

Emile: It sounds as if you are warming to the idea of writing your book as a dialogue.

Pinzak: Well, it would be easy and fun to write, I think, given that we've been having a dialogue on cosmopolitanism for weeks now. It might write itself. *(Both sip their elixirs.)*

Speaking of the topic of cosmopolitanism, on Friday we were talking about David Bohm's idea, in *On Dialogue,* of creating what he called "a new kind of culture."[1] In our case, that culture would be a cosmopolitan culture. Persons in such a culture won't agree on all values and interests and views of the good life. Instead, they will agree *(Pinzak scrolls through a file and continues)* on what Bohm calls "an attitude of dialogue" (41). That is, cosmopolitans will want to use dialectical thinking and democratic dialogue when they look at and think about the world and its problems.

Emile: Yes. When we concluded our conversation, we had just finished laying out the third of four phases in democratic dialogue.

Pinzak: I apologize again for abruptly ending our conversation.

Emile: It is not at all a concern. But let me say, by way of short review, that Phase Three is the time for scrutiny. During this phase, participants may challenge viewpoints and seek clarification and amplification of those viewpoints. Contrary to other modes of argumentation that are traditionally adversarial—in which predetermined positions are staked out and the purpose of argument is to expose the vulnerability of others' positions and the superiority of one's own—

the key concept in Phase Three is exploration. Participants must defend their positions through the presentation of reasons and evidence. Persons holding views that are challenged are expected to make the best case for them. Yet such scrutiny and deliberation are not conducted solely to uncover weaknesses or contradictions in those positions, thereby to dismiss them. Instead, they are also examined to ascertain whether anything in them is beneficial or "salvageable" and ought to be incorporated in the final result, the outcome of Phase Four. Positions and perspectives, ideas and options, are analyzed or broken down, and the constituent parts are examined for salutary, suitable, or substantial elements.

Phase Four: Finding the Compound Common Good
One way to move into Phase Four is to look at the outcomes of some groups that have used dialogue as the centerpiece of their proceedings. Some groups use the format of Wisdom Circles. Especially interesting about these Circles is that they not only aim for integrative outcomes, outcomes that transcend but include all the perspectives presented, but they also often result in transformation of the participants as well.

Pinzak: I know a little bit about Wisdom Circles, having grown up in New Mexico and having taught for years at Western. They come out of the Native American or First Nations People's tradition of the "Medicine Wheel" or "Peacemaking Circles," which themselves come out of the tradition of Talking Circles.[2] All are built on dialogue, and all take place in a circle, symbolizing the equality of all participants and the inclusion of and connection among all participants.

The Medicine Wheel, also known as the Sacred Hoop, is itself a pictographic depiction of the universe, a circle marked off in quadrants presenting and representing the four directions; four winds; four elements (air, earth, wind, fire); four seasons; and four types of creatures: those that fly, those that crawl (insects), those that walk on four legs, and those that walk on two legs. Given our discussions of the AQAL model and of labyrinths, we should not be surprised to find Native Americans using an encircled four-quadrants as a symbol for unity and diversity. In this case, each quadrant on the Medicine Wheel is an aspect of individual life: body, emotions (heart), mind, and soul or spirit. All aspects must be "encircled" or integrated; all persons must also be "encircled" or integrated with all others.

We can extrapolate, however, and envision the quadrants as also pertaining to communities or collectivities. The "body" of the community would be its physical layout and properties—farms, factories, mills, houses, roads, and so on. The "head" would be the "average mode of consciousness," as Wilber puts it, of where the community members are psychologically. The "spirit" of the community would be the ethos or attitudes and values that underlie and define the community's norms and way(s) of life. Finally, the "heart" of the community would be the center of the community, the house of worship or meetinghouse or other vital place that brings the community members together and that expresses in concrete form the rules, roles, and regulations that give structure and order to the community's life.

Emile: In terms of democratic dialogue the four quadrants are represented in any dialogical circle. Each person shows up physically and remains present—that is, does not leave. Each person also shows up emotionally by expressing feelings and sharing stories from the heart. Each also keeps her head during the proceedings by listening to, reflecting on, and sharing about what is being discussed. Finally, persons are present in spirit when they connect with others. Each person remains open emotionally (sympathy), intellectually (empathy and maintaining an open mind), physically (staying awake and being aware of body language), and spiritually (remaining open to connections—whether through values, ideas, interests, needs, physical contact, and for sharing emotions).

All of these "openings" are essential for reminding us that a circle dialogue, indeed any democratic dialogue, is more than simply a discussion or intellectual exercise. It is a deep sharing of ourselves with others, as well as a connection, if only temporarily, to those others. One circle participant summarized this idea of connection, of unity, well:

> I've never experienced that before and really haven't since, not that strong. But when we were all feeling her pain and her daughter's pain, we were in pain. It was the closest moment I've ever had to feeling like family to strangers. You could say everyone in that Circle began to be one with each other. Some people in there I didn't know before, but for a while there, I knew them—knew they all walked on the same trail and would continue on the same trail as me in a way.[3]

The sense of being one with others is what we have been describing as the cosmopolitan sensibility, "feeling like family to strangers." Participants in Peacemaking Circles, again those forums built of democratic dialogue, experience or are in the context for experiencing this kind of connection. As Pranis and her co-authors say, in these dialogues we meet one another as equals. We reveal and embrace through feeling another's pain and placing ourselves in her shoes "our shared human condition." We go "into our hearts . . . bring down walls, release burdens," and come closer together (2003, 66). Each Circle creates the potential for and experience of "deeper, more authentic level of connectedness" (74).

Pinzak: Over time, as we hope and suggest, repeated experiences of this kind might transform those cosmopolitan sensibilities of connectedness into cosmopolitan identities.

Emile: Pranis and her co-authors have themselves observed and experienced, through years of running Peacemaking and Wisdom Circles, "unexpected shifts" in temperament and identity as people "reconnect with themselves, their values, and each other" (74). "This can happen," they say, "to any participant, not just key players" (74). No longer theory, this becomes practice: "[W]e experience what it means to open our hearts, give voice to our souls, be present with others" (66-67).

Pinzak: So, what we see in or through these Circles is an integration of different aspects *within* each person, as well as the potential for integration through repeated experiences *among* persons.

Emile: Yes, and the participants use their sense of connection then, when they examine the perspectives of one another. Participants in the Circles, as "they feel more grounded and connected to wholeness," come to examine conflicts and problems "not as conquerors but as explorers" (76). The result, Pranis et al. report, is that participants experience a sense of expanded awareness that enables them to see more sides of an issue and more sides—especially the needs—of the people participating. Participants ask one another: "What potential is hidden in this conflict or problem that we need to see? How can we use this situation constructively, even creatively?" Problems and conflicts are not debated, where winning or losing are at stake. "Conflicts are openings, doorways to new ways of being together . . . conflicts invite us to explore how to change" circumstances and relationships to reinforce or create connections (77).

The experiences of Pranis and her co-authors show that the dialogue in the Circles uncovers deeper solutions to problems. "Solutions are often entirely different from what anyone originally thought. . . .[W]hen a Circle creates a place safe enough for people to search their lives and share their stories, the dialogue can explore how to cure deep wounds" (78-79).

Pinzak: Therefore, Circles have a dual benefit: They enable participants to delve deeply into the different sides of issues, and they call upon participants to explore their own and their fellow discussants' feelings, values, standards, ideas, and perspectives. Participants not only learn about issues, themselves, and others, but they also connect to or discover aspects of themselves and others not known to them before. These connections and discoveries can lead beyond learning to transformation (80).

Emile: The Circles do so through a process that is similar to our democratic dialogue. There is an initial or introductory phase where the Circle "keeper" or moderator (less a moderator than a "foreman," because the keeper participates just as any other Circle member does, but has additional duties as well) introduces the topic, clarifies the Circle's purpose, and reviews the Circle guidelines.[4]

This is also the phase of welcoming when participants engage in personal storytelling. Persons sponsoring Circles argue that this phase is essential for opening up, creating bonds, and building trust among the participants (137-40). Persons come to the circle, come to democratic conversation, as peers; that is, as equals. No one is coming to fulfill or fill certain roles. This recognition is a way to build trust, to have people tell their stories and listen to others' stories in an atmosphere of equality. This is important, because early on in the dialogue, there will be comments made that do not connect. But at this point, they do not have to or should not be expected to connect. This is the time for letting persons talk and for listening, for making certain that everyone's voice is heard. Simply listen; do not strive to make sense of or connections among comments.

The next phase is identifying and expressing the needs and interests of the participants, to which we would add identifying and expressing positions and perspectives, our Phase Two. Meg Wheatley is a long-time practitioner of learning through conversations and a facilitator of conversations. She writes that when hearing something with which she disagrees, even and especially when she thinks the position wrongheaded or foolish, "I silently remind myself that they have something to teach me."[5] This, she claims, keeps her open-minded and less judgmental.

The third phase, a combination of our Phases Three and Four, is the exploration of options, at which time the participants test out possible consensus options for action plans and search for solutions. Then, before the closing phase, the participants attempt to build consensus from the options offered during the third phase. Consensus in Circles, according to Kay Pranis, "does not require enthusiasm for the decision or plan, but it does require that each participant is willing to live with the decision and support its implementation."[6] Circles do not end without either an agreement to come back again to take up this problem or issue or an agreement about a course of action.

Finally, a few words of summary from Pranis and her co-authors, which seem to get right to the heart of our concerns about democratic dialogue:

> In a nutshell, Circles generate long-term personal, relational, community, system, and cultural transformation. Evidence for this transformation is found in a community's increased capacity to resolve differences and to forge outside-the-box solutions. But Circles generate less tangible fruits as well—understanding, trust, empathy, love, as well as a greater awareness of how connected we are. The more Circles yield these intangible results, the easier it is for people to achieve the more tangible outcomes—agreements, plans for implementation, or joint projects. Circles are not, therefore, about dispensing quick fixes but about crafting deep, sustainable changes (2003, 210).

Pinzak: Notice the interactive effect that takes place within and among participants. There is transformation within persons, as they come to integrate aspects of themselves. There is also transformation among participants, as they come to see their levels of connection and to nurture that sense of connectedness. From those transformations, or concomitant with those transformations, comes greater ease in creating "tangible outcomes" as agreements on and solutions to the problems or issues that brought participants together in the first place. All of these aspects, from the tangible to the intangible, are reinforced, even deepened, through repeated practice of Circles dialogues.

Emile: Perhaps nothing more needs to be added to elaborate on or to explain the quotation, or your comment, but I wish to highlight one particular aspect. The authors allude to the "evidence of transformation" found in their research on and running of Wisdom Circles. We are speaking about people who have actually witnessed the results of these kinds of dialogues. The results are not simply theoretical constructs . . .

Pinzak: . . . what might happen if . . .

Emile: Precisely. Moreover, the authors observe that Circle members come to see one another "as fellow human beings." Such a designation permits members the space and encouragement to transcend their roles, social statuses, and inbred prejudices and to "work through issues *with* others rather than *against* others" (2003, 215; emphases in original).

Pinzak: The structure of dialogue within the Circles and within our democratic forums encourages, if it does not demand, that participants see one another, or come to see one another, as human beings. We all have different perspectives that we are bringing together to or for a common purpose. This enables us to appreciate those differences and to acknowledge the complexity of the issues involved and the solutions pursued. Through open dialogue, participants try to see everyone's interests, needs, and points of view.

Emile: According to Pranis et al., "In this context, expressing differences doesn't lead to further opposition but to a better grasp of what's at stake. . . . [I]nterjecting . . . stories, needs, experiences, or feelings can trigger breakthroughs. . . . [T[hey may lend new perspectives that suggest unconventional solutions" (2003, 215).

The authors conclude that participation in Circles trains people to appreciate differences and to work with, and not against, those differences. Openness becomes contagious (215), as they say, and this is precisely the fertile ground necessary for developing cosmopolitan sensibilities.

Pinzak: Katherine Cramer Walsh finds that dialogue on sensitive issues such as race relations is not all "roses and chocolates," however. Deep-seated resentments and long-standing prejudices are not quickly or easily deflated. Still, there is movement as *(reading from his computer screen)* "Participants compel each other to face the reality of different realities,"[7] which we refer to as different worldviews and identities. The race-relations dialogues that Walsh studied show "a constant struggle with the desire to find common ground and yet respect difference. . . . The results suggest that the deliberative system can and does include listening to difference" (13). Indeed, one of her conclusions is that it is the struggle itself that unifies civic life today. The same is true, we think, for internal struggles, not just collective or group struggles, in a context of democratic dialogue—struggling with diversity and divergence can yield integration within and greater connections among persons.

Emile: Where do you see us now, exactly, in our conversation about Phase Four?

Pinzak: Well, we've established through looking at the structures of and evidence from Wisdom Circles and through other sources[8] that participants in dialogues can and do listen to divergent perspectives, can and do deal with them, and try to honor those differing views by integrating them into the dialogical outcome. Creating that integrative outcome is the purpose of Phase Four, no?

Emile: It is. Amassing different perspectives on an issue is important in the dialogical process, because from these perspectives any solution, any compound common good, may be built. Underneath the divergent and even discrepant perspectives may be the seeds for a common interest that may be the foundation for a commonly perceived good outcome.

Pinzak: Let's take as an example affirmative action. Participants discussing this social policy can be divided about it. Some see affirmative action as necessary for promoting justice, while others see it as unwarranted special treatment or pushing for racial quotas. Can these views be united by a common desire to pursue what is fair? Can fairness serve as a common interest to create an outcome that all agree enables participants to integrate or transcend their divergent views?

Emile: Good questions, Pinzak, and I suppose the answers depend on the composition of the dialogical group. All participants are encouraged to bring their differences—different perspectives, different beliefs, different practices, and the like—to the democratic dialogue. The procedures themselves acknowledge and honor these differences. Yet the procedures also call upon or uncover enough commonality to generate a compound common good. Daniel Yankelovich commented from his experience that, "Often, to their surprise, participants discover affinities with people with whom they strongly disagree. This experience transforms a battle . . . into a human encounter between people who feel a bond with one another even though their life experience has led them in different directions."[9]

Pinzak: Conflict can be seen as creative, not just adversarial, and as an opportunity to develop or grow. One can use conflict as a way of learning about one's own perspective as well as those of others. Dialectical thinking is in some ways predicated on the idea of a search for transcendence, although dialectical thinkers acknowledge that human beings are in many ways defined by their differences, differences that often collide. Yet, simultaneously, human beings share universal characteristics that unite all of us. So dialectical thinkers appreciate both difference and sameness. Transcendence is the term for this appreciation, and it points the way toward overcoming conflict and ambiguity in moral crisis.

Emile: Say more about this, Pinzak.

Pinzak: Okay. *(He pauses, reaches for his elixir, but changes his mind and puts the cup back down.)* What comes out of democratic dialogue, the attempt to create a common outcome? *(He holds up his hand.)* That's a rhetorical question, Emile. *(Both men laugh.)* At least two results, regardless of the final decision or outcome, should obtain. First, participants should feel that they have had adequate opportunity not simply to say what they want but also to be heard. This leads to the second result: Participants should have a better understanding of the perspectives of others. Such understanding means that those holding opposing views can nevertheless recapitulate the perspectives discussed in the dialogue. Participants should have listened to and heard, therefore, concerns about their own positions, just as they listened to and heard good reasons for holding positions opposite their own. All of this sharing is built upon and thus rests on a foundation of respect and trust. So, at the very least, what is created out of democratic dialogue is a new context for looking at, understanding, and respecting, if not accepting, differences. From that new context ought to come some idea of generating alternative outcomes. By acknowledging the concerns that others have expressed about his own positions, a participant might well see that his positions are incomplete. In this way he holds open the possibility of modifying those positions. He remains open to new possibilities and to finding common ground with opponents.

These moves are forms of transcendence. In the first instance participants strive to transcend old labels, patterns, and arguments by generating a context in which the opposition can hear contrasting opinions. In the second instance participants transcend typical interactions and outcomes by searching for common ground or a new fit or a better, more complete perspective. This is not to say that conflicts can easily be resolved or resolved at all. The point is to strive to do so, and the purpose is to undertake the process as if it can be done. But if the conflict is irresolvable, then at least participants have generated new contexts, have expressed honest concerns about the assumptions of and ramifications and reasons for various positions—that is, they have heard and understood the positions of others and have heard and understood the concerns about their own positions. What is exchanged intersubjectively among participants, however, is more than positions. What is exchanged is mutual respect for one another and mutual concern about participants' perspectives.

Emile: Transcend the context by finding a broader or wider context in which to view the specifics of the conflict. That is one of the goals. For example, in a debate pro-choice and pro-life advocates would shout their positions back-and-forth and be done with it. But in a democratic dialogue, participants build trust among themselves through stories and testimony. Then they lay out their positions and scrutinize those positions. The purpose of doing so is not to score points or simply to eviscerate one's opponents. It is, instead, to introduce a context for exploring how moral and political decisions of any kind may be made. That is, have the participants discuss first a broader context before narrowing the focus, say, to an issue such as abortion. That might help establish common ground before a dialogue focuses on the actual conflict.

Pinzak: What do you think is required to construct such a context where participants with divergent and even hostile views can discuss their positions and then together seek options for reconciling, resolving, or transcending conflicts?

Emile: Well, here is an example. It comes from Mary Parker Follett, the early twentieth-century American social worker, political activist, and democratic theorist:

A cooperative association had formed an agreement to have the members market their crops through the association. The Executive Committee of the association discovered that a third of the members were not doing so, despite their contracts. Some on the committee wanted to prosecute the offenders; others felt that in many cases the extenuating circumstances of the offending members militated against prosecution. Plus, it would have been costly and time-consuming to investigate every case. So the matter was resolved in the following way: No prosecution could proceed unless a local committee from the association had first investigated the circumstances. Thus, comments Follett, "Both sides were satisfied: One because the policy of prosecution was to be continued; the other because the responsibility for prosecutions was placed in the hands of a local group."[10] The local committee that handled any individual case consisted of members who lived within the locale of the offender. Additionally, the cooperative membership overall saw this as an opportunity to create an educational program for the association. Not only did both sides participate, but they also were satisfied with the outcome.

The outcome was an integrative solution, rather than a mere compromise. A compromise more often than not leaves both sides with less, even if slightly less, than they wanted, but with enough to comply. Comments Follett: "Compromising between the old ways, or even combining the old ways, keeps us always with—the old" (160).

Pinzak: In a compromise both sides give up something; with integration, they do not.

Emile: Follett expresses it this way: Integration is qualitative; compromise, quantitative. The former is inventive; the latter, a form of barter. Integration shows "qualitative change in our thinking. . . . Through an interpenetrating of understanding [among ourselves and others], the quality of one's own thinking is changed; we are sensitized to an appreciation of other values" (163).

Pinzak: If we simply bargain from our position, then both sides give in a little, but the thinking remains the same.

Emile: If we disagree with someone because there is a misunderstanding, then it is easily rectified, but no change has occurred in our thinking. On the other hand, if we disagree because of a real difference in outlook or value, then, as Follett says, "we can unite what was of value in each point of view, [and] it is a step in our growth" (174).

Pinzak: Beware what John Stuart Mill called "the deep slumber of decided opinion."

Emile: Precisely. Remain open and look for commonality. Walsh points out that the pursuit in dialogue is not for oneness, but for wholeness (2007, 75, 138ff, 251). Oneness is the attempt to reduce the group to unity, if not uniformity, to create a likeness among participants that elides difference. Wholeness, on the other hand, is not oneness. It is, in our terms, integration of different perspectives into a common outcome, a common good. Such notions retain the idea of differences brought into harmony. Different parts are still different, but they mesh to create a wholeness.

Pinzak: But Walsh's differentiation really misreads, I think, what unity means and even what oneness means. We can feel "one" with all human beings without necessarily feeling that there are no differences among us. That's not what oneness or unity connotes, as far as I'm concerned. Oneness is the absence of separation, not the end of difference. So, too, with unity. We can all be united behind a common cause, but there need not be any sense of sameness or uniformity. People do not have to do the same thing or look and think and act the same when they are united. When the thirteen colonies united to form the United States, they didn't cease having their own characteristics as individual states.

The pursuit in democratic dialogue, and particularly of dialectical thinking, is of integration within and among people. That is also an expression of unity. Cosmopolitan identity is not expressive of having the same tastes and preferences, choices and values, ideals, and practices as others also holding a planetary worldview. It is, instead, an expression of the connections one feels and commitments one has to other human beings simply as human beings. Differences still exist, but not necessarily as dividers.[11] It is a "being-to-being" connection. It is an expression of how one sees and handles difference and not an affirmation about how differences disappear in a global goo of sameness.

One final point on this topic, Emile: Our democratic dialogues need to be "radical" in the literal sense of "to the root." Participants must be willing to express and to hear the underlying values, assumptions, and experiences that inform their own worldviews but that also inform their fellow participants' worldviews. We need to get to the root of what people think and why they think it. By plunging to such depths we can get below the surface differences that separate us and find those hidden connections that we can use to resolve or transcend conflicts.

Emile: Do not forget Phase Three. Radical dialogues must also be critical dialogues. Getting to the basic assumptions upon which one has built beliefs and worldviews is to bring those assumptions to light. Once in the light they can be explored and examined, reinforced or modified. Persons with and persons opposed to certain assumptions should be able to reason together about those assumptions. The first goal of such a dialogue is to understand the position that someone holds before issuing any critique of that position. To borrow from those at the National Issues Forums, deliberations begin when a participant is able to make a good case for the option or choice that she least prefers.

Pinzak: And deliberations end when all participants can support an outcome even when it is their least preferred. They can do so because they have had a fair hearing of their own perspectives, have had a chance to interrogate the perspectives of others, and have seen that their own perspectives were taken seriously when the group came to its final decision. Through democratic dialogue participants may generate the kind of solidarity and connection that will permit those who do not vote for the substance of a decision to accept it as if it were their own. Though not initially held to in common, the decision was made in common.

Emile: Making the decision together facilitates acceptance of the decision. To summarize: In the final phase participants strive as best they can to embrace and nurture contradiction rather than yield to or expel it. Each participant's perspective is potentially enlarged and enriched by considering the various perspectives of others. This is so because each can incorporate the viewpoints of others, either as additions to one's own perspective or as emendations or rectifications of that perspective.

Pinzak: Considering multiple perspectives and contradictions in tension allows one to see one's own view as partial and limited and enables one to find what is valuable and true in the positions of others. And if one cannot reconcile or transcend the contradictions?

Emile: Then one chooses a viewpoint, or a composite viewpoint, from within the context of the broadest and soundest understanding possible; namely, one in which disparate views and arguments have been presented. Thus, even if an integrative view is not possible, the context of choice, the range of choice, has been expanded.

It is this integrative approach that points toward cosmopolitanism, because the dialectical thinker, in order to embrace viewpoints, ideas, or attitudes that conflict with her own, must have both an open mind and an open self-definition. He sees that every system or worldview, including and especially his own, is partial and leaves something out.

Pinzak: In needing to integrate viewpoints or perspectives, the dialectical thinker attempts to construct with others an inclusive solution. Being open to all perspectives leads him to see that no boundary separates him from anyone else. We are not only tied to all others; we are like all others, and they are like us. Carmichael describes this as "the awkward embrace": the preservation and holding of "all available contradictory views and perspectives" and the attempt to generate from them one inclusive perspective.[12]

But keep in mind that if an inclusive solution is not found, a decision must nevertheless still be made. Then what happens? I'd suggest taking a vote. Voting in such a case is not always a sign of defeat. It does signify that unanimity was not reached, but that is not our criterion. Wholeness is not necessarily betokened by unanimity. As we've been saying, not everyone will agree with the outcome, but everyone will agree that it is legitimate and made in good faith. There should be in the group sufficient trust and respect that the outcome of a vote is a sign of a good decision. The vote is taken only after everyone who wants to voice a viewpoint has had an opportunity to do so, after those who speak have been listened to and heard to their satisfaction, and after everyone's perspective has been treated seriously in the third and fourth phases. As a result, all participants can accept the outcome as fair and reasonable, especially when the outcome goes against their position or option. These points highlight what has gone into the deliberation, and they reinforce the idea that no outcome rests simply on the special status or standing of any individual, group, or nation.

Emile: These conditions that we have set in our democratic dialogue are crucial. Otherwise, having to vote may be seen by some as demeaning and as a sign of defeat.

Pinzak: What we're talking about, then, is consensus. The term is confusing, because many people often think that consensus means unanimity. But unanimity is, well, unanimity and not consensus. Consensus doesn't mean that everyone agrees; rather, it indicates that everyone can "live with" the outcome, can accept the decision and see the decision as the best result for everyone, given everyone's different perspectives and circumstances.

Emile: Indeed, *consensus* comes from the Latin *consentire,* which means "feel together." From that feeling we then agree.

Pinzak: Also, seeking to incorporate all perspectives coming out of Phase Three doesn't mean making a checklist of all perspectives and then cobbling them together into an amalgam. It means ensuring that each participant is able to speak and is heard. This is the expression of equal respect and concern. To build a consensus, the areas of disagreement are the very ones that ought to occupy the most time and attention. By making an effort to incorporate all views, participants will feel that their views have been given due attention and that the group has made a good-faith effort to include those views. If the final outcome does not include an aspect of someone's perspective or interest, then that person must feel that he had an equal opportunity to present his case or his arguments against someone else's case and that the group has heard him. He can live with the outcome, knowing that he was honored within the group but that his perspective, although taken into account, did not work into the solution.

Emile: "Did not work into the solution" this time. Differences in outlook or opinion do not usually melt away. But the dissenter must feel that she had adequate opportunity to articulate her view, that it was heard and considered, and that she can open the issue again at a later date.

Institutionalizing Democratic Dialogue

We have spent a lot of time and much of our daylight *(The wait staff is placing lit candles within glass hurricanes on each table, though it is not yet dark.)* talking about the dialogical process. We have yet to discuss how we might institutionalize it.

Pinzak: Let's do so now, finally. *(Both drink from their cups.)*

Emile: We have emphasized how important it is within democratic dialogue to permit participants to express their views and to have those views heard and addressed by others. This process allows a participant to feel a sense of trust in and respect for her fellow participants. For that reason, when others criticize her views, she should recognize that those criticisms may add perspectives that help clarify, enrich, or even modify her views. As a result, she may come to appreciate and embrace the views of others. In this kind of open environment, then, participants may work together to try to find some common solution to the problem. At the very least, participants within a dialogue may see in greater relief what they hold in common rather than what keeps them apart.

Pinzak: I'm with you on all of that, Emile. The purpose is not to change people's minds; it is to arrive at a just conclusion—a decision that all participants see as just. In the process some might change their minds, while others might adhere ever-more strongly to their own views. But because all participants have had an opportunity to affect the outcome, to speak, to be heard, and to hear other views, then all participants can accept the outcome as legitimate. Plus, participation of this kind, in this political context, requires persons to act like dialectical thinkers, to open their minds or to keep an open mind. That can lead to developing cosmopolitan sensibilities and may eventuate in a cosmopolitan identity.

Well and good. But here's my problem: We have not talked about the optimal size of the group. We can imagine a multitude of perspectives, maybe so many they could overwhelm the effort to address them all in Phase Four. How does the group keep all the perspectives straight? How does the group try to accommodate so many?

Emile: Your questions lead into one way of instituting democratic dialogue: "Legislative Juries."[13] I think that this model may accommodate a constituency of any size, from local politics to state, regional, national, and global politics. Such a format may also address the concerns that the price of gathering to share political perspectives on an important issue is simply too high. As Diana Mutz comments in *Hearing the Other Side,* participants may be unsettled by political conflict and by the embarrassment and awkwardness that may accompany taking a stand that friends and associates may oppose.

Legislative Juries

Let us imagine right now a democratic dialogical context in which members of a club directly create club rules. Or perhaps the management and employees of a business together make new workplace regulations. We may imagine residents and town or city officials, as in Porto Alegre, jointly passing local ordinances. We may imagine citizens working on and deliberating about provincial initiatives, national initiatives, and even global initiatives.

Only with the last three do we begin to worry that the size of the constituency might be too big to manage. The size of the constituency notwithstanding, initiatives are one way of institutionalizing direct, deliberative democracy, because through them constituents make laws and rules directly. The process of creating and presenting ballot initiatives is an excellent context for instituting democratic dialogue at any political level we wish—local, national, regional, or global.

Pinzak: But the size of those constituencies, Emile, must create problems.

Emile: Legislative Juries, modeled on Citizen Juries, may help us see our way toward institutionalizing our dialogical form of direct, deliberative democracy.

Citizen Juries bring together randomly selected groups of eighteen to twenty-four citizens, just like our judicial jury system, to deliberate on an important policy or on possible policy options. The jurors, over the course of a few days, will hear testimony on the topic from expert witnesses and others involved with the policy. Like a grand jury, the citizen jurors may cross-examine the witnesses. Having heard all of the testimony and having received all the requisite information, the jurors then deliberate to reach a decision or recommendation in the form of a citizens' report.

Pinzak: What happens to the report? Who gets it? How is it used?

Emile *(after finishing his elixir):* The agency or sponsor who called the jury together receives the report. This agent or sponsor might be a government official, a government department, or an elected representative. Anyone who wants to hear citizens' views on the subject—citizens, that is, who have deliberated using information and expert testimony—may call a jury together.[14]

Pinzak: I see the appeal of gathering six or twelve or twenty-four randomly selected citizens to deliberate on public issues if you want to institute democratic dialogues. But what about the quality of the outcomes?

Emile: In part we have already addressed that issue when we talked about what happens in dialogue and what we predict might happen when participants use dialectical thinking in a dialogue. The issue that you are raising, on the other hand, is directed, I take it, toward the value inherent in juries themselves.

Pinzak: That's right. How good is the idea of placing ordinary citizens, mere amateurs, on a jury that may deliberate on technical and sophisticated issues?

Emile: Worried still, Pinzak, about the "great mediocrity"? *(Pinzak does not reply and reaches for his cup.)* Kalvin and Zeisel, in the mid-1960s, did an extensive investigation of juries and compared their decisions with those that would have been made by judges.[15] Kalvin and Zeisel found that of 3,576 jury trials, judges would have agreed with the juries' decisions about 76 percent of the time. In addition, when the jury and judge agreed on issues of evidence, the disagreement percentage dropped from 24 percent to 12 percent.

Pinzak: Holding that finding aside and going strictly on the jury-judge agreement of 76 percent, we can see that judges—the professionals involved—agreed with the juries a little over three-quarters of the time. That tells me that juries do a pretty good job.

Emile: Kalven and Zeisel concluded that juries do a *very* good job.[16]

Pinzak: What about verdicts that are reversed by higher courts?

Emile: The statistics show that verdicts are usually reversed because the higher court determines that the law has been misapplied. Application of the law is the purview of the judge, not the jury (Campbell 2004, 137).

Pinzak: So, the jury system is a bona fide method for gathering citizens to deliberate, and the Legislative Jury has citizens, randomly selected, deliberating on ideas or policy that will become law?

Emile: That is the general format, but the process itself is more detailed than that. The process for Legislative Juries is built also on elements found in the format of the National Issues Forum (NIF).

National Issues Forums are organized and promoted around the country to enlist members of the public in deliberations on important public issues. Topics have included such issues as health care, immigration policy, U.S. foreign policy, racial tensions, physician-assisted suicide, Social Security, legalization of drugs, and nuclear proliferation. Over the past twenty years or so, the National Issues Forum Institute, which is the non-profit organization chartered to promote NIF, has sponsored forums involving, as their website states, "thousands of civic clubs, religious organizations, libraries, schools, and many other groups." Participants in forums, again according to their website, "range from teenagers to retirees, prison inmates to community leaders, and literacy students to university students."[17] The actual forums themselves range in size from small study circles, akin to Wisdom Circles of one to two dozen people, to auditorium-sized gatherings.

In partnership with the Kettering Foundation of Dayton, Ohio, the NIF Institute publishes booklets that describe the issues under deliberation, as well as provides information and costs and benefits of alternative policy options. These options are limited to three or four choices for participants to discuss.

Pinzak: So participants are limited to choosing one among three or four options? That seems really constraining.

Emile: At first view, I agree. Limiting options seems a constraint. But recall the context of this part of our conversation. You were worried that too many perspectives might overwhelm and even paralyze participants.

Pinzak: But now we seem to have gone too far in the opposite direction.

Emile: Again, at first blush, it may seem so. Yet the way the NIF comes to these three or four options, I think, will allay your concerns. Moreover, one of their missions is to help people of diverse views find common ground on public issues important in their lives.[18] So, it is not the case that anyone's perspective is closed down or shut out. Instead, participants funnel their diverse perspectives into these three or four possible outcomes or policy options.[19]

Pinzak: So it's not the NIF Institute or the Kettering Foundation that comes up with the options? It's the forum itself?

Emile: In part, yes. There are actually two forums for every issue. The first is a "framing" forum. The purpose of the "framers" is to decide on the three or four most salient options. Their mission, really, is to find those options that capture or encapsulate the most perspectives.

Pinzak: The "framers'" objective, then, is to create what we call the compound common good.

Emile: Not exactly. Their objective is to present to the second forum, the "naming" forum, three or four options that offer a spectrum of possible outcomes. The spectrum is, indeed, a compound of the perspectives presented during the forum. Instead of being a compound of only one outcome, the spectrum presents the "namers" with several disparate options in tension with one another. That tension demonstrates that there is no ready outcome on the issue under consideration.

Pinzak: Why are they called "namers"? What are they naming?

Emile: The very short answer is that they are naming, in our context, the option that will constitute the initiative that members of the public—whether local or regional or national or global—will decide. But let us return to the framing forum for more detail before we take up naming.

As David Mathews, the president of the Kettering Foundation, wrote: "There is a public dimension to every issue. . . . For the public to relate to an issue, it has to be framed in terms of what is valuable to people in their everyday lives, not just in terms of technical considerations."[20] Framing an issue, therefore, is about generating the most salient, though not necessarily the most conspicuous, frames of reference for understanding an issue and its consequences. The three or four issue options that participants deliberate on are those that capture the "values or deeper motivations that are at play" in the issue (Mathews 1994, 108).

Pinzak: So the forum booklets prepared by non-partisan research centers like the Kettering Foundation and the Public Agenda Foundation replace what a jury would hear as sworn expert testimony. That's what they are deliberating about. And as they do so, they not only share and hear different perspectives, but they also come to share meaning—or create shared meaning, to recur to our talk about David Bohm last week—and reflective judgments.

Emile: In Mathews's experience part of those shared and reflective judgments is the reconstruction of what participants understand as their identity. As one community organizer said, "You begin to see your interests as broadening in relationships with other people, particularly as you begin to have serious conversations and you begin to identify with other people's experiences" (1994, 180). The broadening of our interests and identifying with others' experiences need not stop at the borders of our nations.

Pinzak: Let me see whether I've got the concept of the NIF so far. A forum meets to deliberate on an important issue. Their objective is, as we said about dialogue, to share and hear the perspectives on the issue—let's take, as an example, legalization of drugs in the United States.

Emile: Forgive me for interrupting, Pinzak, but also keep in mind that the forums as we envision them would proceed through our four phases of democratic dialogue . . . if the forums are to be a proper model for our purposes.

Pinzak *(typing as he talks and thus not, for the time, looking at Emile):* Right. The first forum will be the framing forum. Framing an issue means finding options that accommodate the interests, values, and concerns of the participants in the forum. Those experienced with running the National Issues Forums find that three or four options are best, provided that the options taken together offer a spectrum of possible positions on the issue.

In our example of the legalization of drugs in the United States, participants want to find four options that encapsulate and also capture the disparate views held by those participants. These are options that the participants have deliberated about and are the most prominent ones, the ones that they think ought to be considered by those deciding about legalization. These might comprise a) full-scale legalization of all drugs; b) legalization of "soft" drugs such as marijuana and hashish, but not highly addictive drugs such as heroin, cocaine, crack, or methamphetamines; c) decriminalization of possession and even sale of "soft" drugs or maybe all drugs; and d) strict enforcement of current drug laws and opposition to legalization in any form.

Emile: Go to the head of the class, Stan. *(Pinzak looks up, startled, and then slightly aggrieved at the use of his first name. Emile laughs.)* I just wanted to see whether you were listening amidst all that typing.

After participants have decided on the three or four options, and after having generated a spectrum of prominent perspectives on the issue, the topic is set for a naming forum.

Pinzak: As you said, the framing forum will follow the four phases of democratic dialogue, as will the naming forum. So, there will be an introductory phase when participants tell their stories as they see fit, though sharing experiences related to the topic under discussion would be highly beneficial. This is followed by Phase Two, or laying out the perspectives. In the case of the naming forum, however, and unlike the framing forum, the "perspectives" are already laid out in the sense that they have been reduced to or compounded into three or four alternatives.

Emile: Yes, and the participants themselves may have perspectives on the alternatives, some of which, of course, might well have come out initially during Phase One.

Pinzak: Granted. Phase Two is also the stage when experts appear before the participants and give testimony, in which they provide evidence and arguments for and against the options. Then, after the evidence has been presented and all participants are satisfied that they have been able to share their views and that others have heard those views, then the forum, or dialogue, proceeds to Phase Three. This is the stage of active deliberation, where participants challenge, modify, reiterate, and even transcend their positions. This is the phase of critique, when participants distinguish and identify strengths and weaknesses.

That "identification" helps, then, with Phase Four, when the forum decides on which option it favors.

But what if the naming forum decides against all the available options? What if it presents a new option not thought of by the framing forum?

Emile: I do not know, but it strikes me that in such a case, the issue must go back to a new framing forum. It might be that a naming forum could arrive through deliberation and dialogue at an option that transcended but also included the options resulting from the framing forum. The naming forum might do so through the consideration of perspectives that the framers did not include. We, then, could introduce another step. The first naming forum would deliberate simply to ratify the framing of the issue. If that framing is not accepted, then it goes to a new framing forum, now armed with the critiques of the original framing, to determine how to reframe the issue. If the framing is ratified, then we move on to another naming forum that deliberates to decide the issue.

Pinzak: Regardless, each forum, whether framing or naming, is composed of new participants each time.

Emile: That is correct, and the same would be true for Legislative Juries. We should have a framing jury different from the naming jury.

Pinzak: I understand the purpose of the naming forum; it states what the participants think is the best option on the issue. Yet we're considering these forums as models for Legislative Juries. Decisions made by juries are binding. When we add the term "legislative" to "jury" we create a repetition, if not a redundancy: Legislation is binding on some set of people. But if the legislation proposed and authorized by a jury were on a global issue, then who exactly would be bound by it? No Legislative Jury, indeed no democracy, can pass binding legislation on the entire world. Thus, a cosmopolitan legislative jury, for example, is only a regulative ideal. That is, it serves as a key to what a sample of "persons of the world" thinks on some issue. This may then be broadcast throughout the globe and carried out wherever appropriate, in whatever form—publicity, articles and books and reports, e-Parliament,[21] initiatives by village or regional councils, by states or provinces or nations, and so on. The democratic results from cosmopolitan legislative juries are not binding, then, on any territorial constituency. They are, instead, insights from and the policy decisions of a collection of deliberative cosmopolitans—"mundus-populus" or people of the world—who point the way to a possible cosmopolitan solution or resolution.

Emile: Yes and no, Pinzak. Yes, the policy decisions of a collection of deliberative cosmopolites do indicate a possible cosmopolitan solution to or resolution of a global problem. But, no, that is not what Legislative Juries do. Recall what I said early in our conversation about the NIF as a model for Legislative Juries. If we substitute the word *jury* for *forum*, then we have established the process for the juries. That process, as we said, uses our four phases but sets them in the context of framing and naming. Legislative Juries, however, have the purpose of setting the language and the parameters for ballot initiatives. The outcome of a naming jury is to provide the phrasing of the issue that will appear on a citizen- or member-originating initiative or referendum, which might be state- or province-wide, national, regional, or global.

An initiative is a proposed resolution that is to be acted or voted on by the electorate or some membership as a whole. It is proposed in writing and printed, or otherwise copied, and distributed, not for initial approval or consideration, but to secure the signatures of some number of fellow citizens or members who support the bringing of this resolution before the appropriate "public."[22] I use the term "public" here, because I am thinking broadly of initiatives as proposals generated by Legislative Juries involved in naming that could even be used on issues that pertain only to members of a private club or by employees in a workplace, as well as by residents of the planet. So I envision initiatives as proposed resolutions that can be used at any level of group or political organization, from private concerns to global governance. Thus, I use "public" as a term of art to refer to the appropriate audience eligible to participate in democratic dialogue on the issue.

Pinzak: Thus your point that initiatives are one way to institutionalize democratic dialogue broadly.

Emile: Yes, and they provide a good way to do so. Initiatives by their nature carry an expectation that the public will participate directly in making laws, rules, ordinances, and the like. By using initiatives shaped by democratic dialogue, we assure that the "public" is not involved in a plebiscitary kind of democracy. Instead, the public is deliberating on the issues and thereby arriving at shared reflective judgments.[23]

Pinzak: Using jury-derived initiatives involve the people in two ways: the people decide how the issue itself is phrased on the ballot and they then vote on the initiative. As you've introduced the term, "initiatives" also bring in the principle of subsidiarity that we talked about last Friday—political decisions are made at the appropriate level and by the appropriate parties. A national initiative on gun control in the United States is not open to regional or global participants just because their region or other parts of the globe supply numerous tourists each year who are thereby susceptible to being shot. The initiative is decided by all eligible members in the United States and only the United States.

Emile: You see, then, that Legislative Juries may be used throughout the legislative levels of subsidiarity.

Pinzak: Sure. Just as a committee of elected officials draws up a bill to be presented to and considered by the full representative body, so, too, could Legislative Juries draw up bills, ordinances, regulations, referenda, and initiatives for consideration by an appropriate body—whether public or private, whether in a hospital or school, in a workplace or house of worship. Initiative topics could include interstate or intrastate trade policy, workers' compensation or insurance, a national policy on physician-assisted suicide, or how to address the global AIDS epidemic. Juries are a reliable and feasible way to gather persons together, present expert testimony, elicit comments and perspectives from participants, deliberate on that information, and come to agreement on the best course of action or phrasing of the prospective legislation.

Emile: H. G. Wells proposed a form of government by jury. In his model, these citizen juries—and Wells envisaged a cosmopolitan or "Grand Jury" at the apex of a series of juries taking on national, regional, and local cases—were regulative and not really legislative. That is, Wells wanted the juries to consider only those cases that were referred to it by other governmental agencies or bodies. The matters for these juries to consider were suits brought by "the individual or some state organization . . . *on behalf of the common good* either against some state official or state regulation. . . ."[24] Wells's Grand Jury also convened in an ad hoc series of summit meetings whenever an issue of global significance arose.

Pinzak: How did Wells propose to select the jurors for his "Grand Jury" or world jury?

Emile: His idea was to use a draft or some kind of lottery. Wells thought that persons who conducted a nation's draft or lotteries had the kind of experience that would be ideal for devising a method of selecting or finding jurors for the global jury. It could be done, he thought, "by any actuarial expert" (Partington 2003, 143). Wells thought that first you could divide the world into two-and-a-half million areas of about equal population. Then from these areas you could randomly select twenty thousand areas and by lot select one person from each of those twenty thousand.[25] Wells also proposed using "sub-juries" to select jurors for the juries above its authority, in a nod to our principle of subsidiarity. He also argued that the Grand Jury should sit permanently, though the composition of the jury would change every year or three years or seven years; he had not quite made up his mind on the issue of jurors' tenure.

Pinzak: According to Wells's scheme, then, the Grand Jury would consist of twenty thousand jurors. *(Emile nods.)* He thought that was manageable?

Emile: He did. He thought that organizing twenty thousand jurors was no more difficult than managing a really large conference.

Pinzak: Yes, a *really* large conference. Even the ancient Athenians in the Assembly didn't have twenty thousand citizens in attendance.

Emile: Wells wanted his method of global governing-by-jury to end electoral politics. He despised the system of political parties with their partisan bickering and narrow self-interests. He thought that his method could be used from the global level down to and through the subsidiary levels of government below it. Then, according to Wells, all electoral politics could be abolished.

Pinzak: That's not quite the method I envision.

Emile *(Watching Pinzak drain his elixir, Emile asks, "Another round, Pinzak?" "Only if you let me pay for both rounds, Emile." Emile shrugs his shoulders in assent. He then turns toward the café door and motions to Bobby, the* *waiter, just as he had done earlier.)*: All right, Pinzak, what kind of method or setting do you have in mind?

Pinzak: I have two ideas. The first idea is to divide every town, city, village, and rural area into Jeffersonian wards of one hundred residents each. Every ward would then have a democratic dialogue on the initiatives. The wards would decide.

Emile: Wards were one of Jefferson's "two hooks of the republic." The other was education. Wards were Jefferson's way of assuring that every citizen—all of whom were white, property-owning males in his day—would have an equal voice on political concerns.

Pinzak: That's right. Jefferson proposed his ward system in the spirit of Pennsylvania's "little republics." A ward was the division of . . . wait *(Pinzak scrolls through a file),* I've got his description right here:

> Every county into hundreds [100 adult citizens or males], with a central school for all children, with a justice of the peace, a constable and a captain of militia. These officers, or some others within the hundred, should be a corporation to manage all its concerns, to take care of its roads, its poor, and its police by patrols. . . . Every hundred should elect one or two jurors to serve where requisite, and all other elections should be made in the hundreds separately, and the votes of all the hundreds be brought together. . . . These little republics would be the main strength of the great one.[26]

When Jefferson mentions "all other elections," he has in mind those political decisions that the one hundred citizens would reach together. *(Pinzak continues reading further):*

> We of the United States, you know, are constitutionally and conscientiously democrats. We consider society as one of the natural wants with which man has been created; that he has been endowed with faculties and qualities to effect its satisfaction by concurrence of others having the same want; that when, by the exercise of these faculties, he has procured a state of society, it is one of his acquisitions which he has a right to regulate and control, jointly indeed with all those who have concurred in the procurement, whom he cannot exclude from its use or direction more than they him. . . .[27]

To Jefferson the people were competent to judge and decide political issues, assuming that we follow the principle of subsidiarity. He imagined tiers of government, with the wards having an essential place *(Pinzak begins reading again):*

> [T]he way to have good and safe government, is not to trust it all to one, but to divide it among the many, distributing to every one exactly the functions he is competent to. Let the national government be entrusted with the defence of the nation, and its foreign and federal relations; the State governments with the civil rights, laws, police, and administration of what concerns the State generally; the counties with the local concerns of the counties, and each ward direct the

interests within itself. It is by dividing and subdividing these republics from the great national on down through all its subordinations, until it ends in the administration of every man's farm by himself; by placing under every one what his own eye may superintend, that all will be done for the best.[28]

The elementary republics of the wards, the county republics, the State republics, and the republic of the Union would form a gradation of authorities. *(Pinzak begins reading once more):*

> . . . standing each on the basis of law, holding every one its delegated share of powers, and constituting truly a system of fundamental balances and checks for the government. Where every man is a sharer in the direction of his ward-republic, or of some of the higher ones, and feels that he is a participator in the government of affairs, not merely at an election one day in the year, but every day; when there shall not be a man in the State who will not be a member of some one of its councils, great or small, he will let the heart be torn out of his body sooner than his power be wrested from him by a Caesar or a Bonaparte. As Cato, then, concluded every speech with the words, *'Carthago delenda est,'* so do I every opinion, with the injunction, 'divide the counties into wards.'[29]

Wards are for local administration and the resolution of local political problems. "Divide the counties into wards of such size as that every citizen can attend, when called on, and act in person. Ascribe to them the government of their wards in all things related to themselves exclusively." Such division thus makes "every citizen an acting member of the government. . . ."[30]

Emile: We can further imagine a tier of global governance to take up and deal with global issues. *(Pinzak nods. Bobby brings over the two cups of elixir and clears away the empty cups. "A glass of water, with lemon, for me, please, and, when he is ready [gesturing toward Pinzak], the bill for my friend.")*

Pinzak: Yes, we can. Missing from Jefferson's wards, unfortunately, are deliberations among the members, though it is only the organization of wards that interests me. I can imagine dividing the nation—and maybe the globe itself, but let's deal for now with the United States—into wards of one hundred members.

Emile: You are not suggesting, I take it, that you would abolish all representative bodies and replace them with deliberative wards.

Pinzak: I'm not suggesting that. I see a mix, an imbrication, of representative and participatory institutions. Whatever the mix—and we might follow, for example, the schemes and arguments of two political theorists: Jane Mansbridge (1980) or Benjamin Barber (1984) on that—deliberation and dialogue must hold a prominent place in the life of the polity. A society would have to sort out through democratic dialogue which tiers would be participatory, and when.

Emile: And for the global level of governance? Perhaps a world constitution? Perhaps we should take up that topic? *(Emile waits as Pinzak sips his elix-*

ir. "This really is incredible, Emile." Emile smiles and sips from his cup. Bobby brings Emile's water.)

Pinzak *(putting down his cup):* We should, but in a moment. The wards would all be linked electronically to a central computer that would receive the decisions on an issue in the form of reports or ballots or polls over every, say, five thousand wards. These reports or ballots or polls would be relatively detailed, carrying minority positions, caveats, serious points of contention—divergent positions that could not be reconciled—and other noteworthy results, if any, coming from the wards. These central links of five thousand wards would themselves be hooked into another central computer, this time covering one thousand central links or centers rather than five thousand wards. The computers at this "grand center" would use software programs to read the details coming in to check for overlaps. The votes would then be tallied and the reports consolidated and sent from the "grand center" to headquarters for final tabulation and creation of minority and dissenting reports. The results of the initiative would be published online and by the mainstream and alternative media. The issue can, of course, be raised again if the people think that there is sufficient dissent to warrant it and they can gather the necessary signatures.

Emile: Have you completed your thoughts on wards? *(Pinzak nods as he sips again.)* Then what is your second method? You said that you had two, no?

Pinzak *(busily scrolls through files on his laptop):* I did. The second is the model favored by John Parkinson: the Electronic Town Hall *(Pinzak reads from his computer):* "in which thousands of people are split into groups of ten, each with a moderator and a minute-taker, and each linked electronically to all the others in order to share issues, take quick polls and reactions, and vote on proposals once they had been discussed."[31] Parkinson sees no reason why such electronic town halls could not be run simultaneously out of multiple locations, thus involving hundreds of thousands, if not millions, of people (2006, 170). This is not far off from Jeffersonian wards, although if millions of people are involved in, say, national or global initiatives, then finding enough moderators and minute takers, a problem itself for wards of one hundred persons, would seem even more daunting for thousands and thousands of groups of ten.

Emile: Given your comments, I, too, prefer the ward model. Let me share with you my view on how it might work, and you tell me what you think. First, once the Legislative Jury has named the initiative and before the wards meet, there must be publication or dissemination of information, in booklet form and on the Internet, about the reasons behind the three or four options named. At the same time, there might well be televised and printed and streaming video of testimony for and against the options.

Next there would come the meeting of citizens and persons throughout the state, county, city, nation, region, or globe in wards or village councils to discuss those options. Ideally limited to one hundred persons, as Jefferson imagined them, the wards and councils need not have any stringent time restrictions, provided there are opportunities for people to talk together in small groups (around ten or twelve participants) within the ward or council. Wards may set their own timetables. Persons unable to attend these meetings, for whatever reason, could have small-group meetings via the Internet, through blogs, or through a toll-free conference call. The small groups give persons a chance to express their positions, ideas, and concerns. Then after hours or days of such small-group work—the groups might meet, for example, two hours a day, one day per week, for three weeks—the entire ward reconvenes for a plenary dialogue and deliberation. The plenary meeting itself might be for three hours, one day per week, for two more weeks. Remember, Pinzak, democratic dialogue is used with issues of major salience, the ones most important to the people, and thus it is unlikely that there will be "quick fixes" to any of these problems.

Proceedings of the ward/council meetings are then reported to a central office, your central computer, where a newsletter/broadside is prepared for dissemination to everyone, just as you laid out. This could be posted, e-mailed, mailed, and placed on a website on the Internet. It could be a podcast or streaming video for those who do not choose to read or who cannot. The information is preparation for the next round of ward/council meetings.

The first meeting involves deliberating about the different options, and the newsletter/broadside would reflect the various perspectives, popular and unpopular, that arose from the offered options. The next meeting is to decide on the outcome. Participants are asked to argue on behalf of their preferred option. Once this is completed, then participants vote.

Pinzak: Must a voter have participated in the ward or council meetings?

Emile: Yes, though a voter does not have to attend both meetings (deliberating on the options and arguing preferences) to vote. Any voter, then, would have a dual registration: the overall voter registration appropriate to the level at which the decision is made, as well as the registration for voting on this specific policy, initiative, or bill, given after attending one of the two ward/council sessions.

Pinzak: I want to stress the importance of meeting face-to-face when involved in democratic dialogue. I understand, as you suggested, that sometimes people can't meet and have very good reasons for not doing so. Face-to-face meetings, however, introduce non-verbal communication: body language, inflections, intensity of feeling, and the like, that are often missed when someone relies on transcripts, instant messaging, posted discussions, and conference calls.

Emile: Teleconferencing helps with some of that.

Pinzak: It does, but it doesn't help with my second concern. In a dialogical group it is much more difficult to turn away from someone with whom you disagree, just as it is much more daunting to shut off someone's story or shut down their story when you are face-to-face with that person. Clicking "Escape" or "Delete" or hanging up on a conference call is an easy way to avoid disagreement and dissension. It's too easy to revert to knee-jerk reactions and biases when we hear divergent views. When we can simply and easily shut them off or tune them out, then easy exit might well be a participant's standard reaction, instead of yielding to the demands of democratic dialogue and asking the other person in a spirit of inquiry: "How did you come to see things this way? Help me understand how you view this issue. What is your thinking process here?"

Emile: I agree with you on that point. Of course, some persons, shut-ins, for example, are unable physically to get to wards and meetings and dialogues. Others have a host of reasons, at various times, for why they cannot make it. Perhaps information technologies will help in this regard. *(Emile sips his elixir. Some of the waiters begin firing up the outdoor gas heaters.)*

Global Governance I: Reforming the United Nations
I have another concern. Institutionalizing Legislative Juries in particular and democratic dialogue in general is going to take a great deal of orchestrating. This is especially the case with the introduction of subsidiarity and thus multiple levels of possible participation. Whatever the level or locale or venue, the appropriate authorities must ensure that there is an extensive outreach effort to enlist participant involvement in the wards/councils, especially from populations that do not usually participate. Such recruitment efforts will necessitate outreach through trusted persons and organizations within the community, however the community is defined.

Also, keep in mind that we have talked about the dual pressure of institutionalizing democratic dialogue from the top-down and bottom-up. Alongside any formalized institutions, or set forms of democratic dialogue, is an inchoate, ad hoc, free-flowing, evanescent kind of democratic dialogue lying low but bubbling up from the grassroots level. One hopes that these various bottom-up democratic encounters and engagements are insolent, clever, humorous, and bold. One hopes that they appear in all walks of life and all sorts of settings. One hopes that they get the attention of scholars, writers, politicians, and the media. From these renegade or contrary forms of democratic dialogue, the authorized or sanctioned forms may learn new methods or at least use the renegade, the epitome of divergence and the non-institutional, to interrogate their own methods.[32]

Pinzak *(typing rapidly):* I like how you said that, Emile. I have a strong sense that these "renegade forms," as you call them, reinforce the importance of reciprocity. People can bring new ideas to the structures of dialogue; it isn't the case that people must only fit in with the system as prescribed and as it functions. This is another form, an important form, of integration: trying to integrate the grassroots and the elite and all in between.

One place where we might look for immediate leadership on orchestrating democratic dialogue at the global level and integrating these forms of democratic dialogue is the United Nations.

Emile: The economist Jeffrey Sachs has commented, "No major problem can be solved by government, or the business world, or one community alone. Complex social problems have multiple stakeholders who are all party to the problem and who generally must be part of the solution."[33] Who is able to undertake sufficient outreach to all of these stakeholders? Who is able to organize to get all who are party to the problem involved in seeking solutions to that problem? How do we move governments to cooperate? How do we lead nations to set global goals and timetables? How do we convince them to share finances and to mobilize populations? The United Nations offers one prospect for doing all of this.

Pinzak: It does, and another one that we should consider is a global federation of some sort. At the moment, however, let's focus on the United Nations. As it currently operates and is structured, the UN seems too dysfunctional to be relied upon, and it is certainly under-funded for the tasks that you've outlined. The total annual spending of the UN, including administration, peacekeeping missions, and all its programs, is ten billion dollars. The total spending of world governments on their militaries alone is over one trillion dollars.

Emile: It sometimes seems that the United Nations only garners headlines when there is a scandal or problem. So we need to be reminded that, among the kinds of work that the UN does, it has monitored dozens of elections and election results. It has sent peacekeepers on over sixty missions to hot spots around the globe (and not just to Srebrenica where, in 1995, UN peacekeepers did nothing as Serbians selected for murder nearly eight thousand men and boys). It has negotiated more than one hundred seventy peace agreements that ended regional conflicts. It funnels aid to millions of refugees each year, bringing attention to such issues as world poverty, human rights, child mortality, AIDS prevention, and the plight of indigenous peoples who are disadvantaged and victimized.

So, the UN does good works, but it can do more. One essential step is to make the internal operations of the UN dialectically and dialogically based. Another is to have the UN serve as a coordinator of democratic dialogue among its member states, whether those dialogues are within the UN organization itself or whether they are held as bilateral or multilateral dialogues among and between the member states on their own.

Pinzak: In addition, Emile, the UN can serve to coordinate the democratic dialogues of those actors beneath or aside from the state level, who interact among themselves as well as interact with states. I'm thinking here of transnational civil-society networks. These networks comprise citizen- and civil-society organizations throughout the world whose interactions and policy positions challenge global power. These cross-border organizations, coalitions, and campaigns are having an increasing impact on economic and political power structures in both industrialized and developing nations and thus have become an increasingly recognized, significant political phenomenon of non-state action. Some examples of such groups, include Amnesty International, the WTO protesters in Seattle and Genoa, Doctors Without Borders, and the Slum/Shack Dwellers International, a transnational movement of those marginalized within cities.

Finally, there are the grassroots movements and events that we've alluded to a few times. These movements are ongoing and often independent, though not chaotic, local or locally produced and targeted political action aimed at or across borders. One of the best examples of this level of political action is happening at the border between the United States and Mexico. There is an extensive network of persons aiding persons trying to cross from Mexico into the United States, without regard for their status as citizens, subjects, subaltern actors, marginalized persons, or heroic saviors. They are simply people aiding people in need. Such groups and individuals already are or seem to be cosmopolitans, but democratic dialogue of the type pioneered by Paulo Freire can help immeasurably with raising the consciousness of those who continue to be victims of oppressive social and political conditions.

Emile: These transnational groups, movements, and organizations are of central importance. They are outside of formal state and governmental institutions, and yet they work on behalf of and express the needs of people throughout the globe who have little or no voice. These organizations and other civil-society groups, these NGOs, can function alongside any global governmental institutions. They, too, are sites for democratic dialogue and can serve as governors on global governmental institutions. Is your view that the United Nations might serve as a bridge for connecting, if not integrating, all of these different networks and groups and movements?

Pinzak: Yes, the UN could if it is reconstituted.

Emile: Reconstituted how?

Pinzak: Well, picking up on your point, I'd recommend that the civil society, which is constituted by the sorts of NGOs that we've both mentioned, have its own formally recognized Assembly or Congress within the UN.

Emile: How do you see such an assembly functioning, given that there are thousands of non-governmental organizations and other such civil-society groups now operating around the world?

Pinzak: Frankly, I'm not sure. I don't want the inadequacy of my imagination to be a hindrance when thinking of ways to empower civil society at the global level. Certainly, I haven't studied issues such as reconstituting the UN or organizing global institutions for global governance.[34] I'll need your assistance here, Emile.

Emile: Do not look at me, Pinzak. I know even less about this than you do.

Pinzak: Nevertheless, it is important that we put forward ideas to get people thinking seriously about these issues. We want to ensure that participation is not "empty," that it offers participants real power to influence political decisions. To do so there must exist institutions that connect decision-making with real outcomes. This isn't to say that the mere practice of dialectical thinking and deliberation is without consequence; sensibilities, as we've argued, can develop and identities can change. But that restricts change to the personal and not the political. Institutions are needed for political change. But in recognition of the poverty and paucity of our background information, we put our ideas forward tentatively and guardedly.

Emile *(after sipping his drink):* Maybe someone will organize a democratic dialogue using your ideas as the centerpiece for deliberation.

Pinzak *(also after sipping):* That's amusing, Emile, especially before you hear what I have to propose.

Emile: Then let us proceed.

Pinzak: Perhaps the Civil Society Assembly or "chamber" should be nothing but a bank of computers to tally decisions or votes that come from transnational organizations and NGOs from across the globe, decisions made through and after democratic dialogue. Supermajority votes, here as elsewhere, would determine the position favored by the Civil Society Chamber (CSC). Representatives for reconciling CSC decisions with the UN General Assembly—again, through democratic dialogue—would be selected every two years from a random list of NGOs and similar organizations or movements, perhaps even multinational corporations, all of which would have to be registered with the UN. Once those NGOs and other groups were chosen, the groups themselves would determine how to select their actual representatives to the Chamber for those two years.

Emile: Instead of a bank of computers, perhaps the representatives should simply serve their terms the same way that elected and appointed representatives to the General Assembly do.

Pinzak: Regardless of the method, surely transnational, multinational, and civil-society organizations need a voice. There are now, for example, approximately forty-four thousand non-governmental organizations and sixty-six thousand multinational corporations (MNCs) spread around the world.[35] Of the one hundred most powerful economic entities in the world today, over half (fifty-one) are corporations. The remaining forty-nine are states.[36] Don't their perspectives and interests deserve their own separate voice-chamber?

Emile: Furthermore, putting NGOs and MNCs and other transnational groups together in the same chamber will enable them to discuss and criticize positions taken, strategies used, and responsibilities shared throughout the globe. Then there is the additional benefit of creating joint committees made up of delegates from the General Assembly and from the CSC, where, again, disparate views may be shared and deliberated.

May I assume, beyond establishing the Civil Society Chamber, that there is more reform to come? Habermas, for example, summarizes the minimum required reforms of the UN as the need for "a functioning Security Council, the binding jurisdiction of an international criminal court and the complementing of the General Assembly of government representatives by a 'second chamber' made up of representatives of world citizens."[37] You have mentioned such a second chamber, but not one made up of world citizens.

Pinzak: Such a chamber is definitely necessary; it's what we might call, as some do, a "Peoples' Assembly."

Emile: You would add that chamber to your newly structured UN, made up of the General Assembly and the Civil Society Chamber, to form a "tricameral" structure?

Pinzak: I would. The UN would consist, then, of three legislative chambers: the General Assembly of appointed or elected officials who represent nation-states, the Civil Society Chamber, and a Peoples' Assembly that is nonterritorial and inclusive. There should also be joint committees made up of members from these three assemblies. Each assembly has perspectives that the others need to hear. All of this is in the context of cross-border and trans-border cooperation, especially related to human rights. Each assembly, to say nothing of those within the Civil Society Chamber, has much to learn from the others; talk about diversity of views!

Emile: In your view, then, the General Assembly represents states, the Civil Society Chamber represents transnational and multinational organizations and groups, and the Peoples' Assembly is constituted by the people, *simpliciter.*

Pinzak *(finishing off his elixir):* That's right.

Emile: So how do you propose choosing the representatives?

Pinzak: Through direct global elections.

Emile: But such elections would penalize poor persons and the illiterate or undereducated who might not have access to polling places or who might lack functional knowledge of, to say nothing of access to, the Internet or other devices involved in a global election. We can imagine that establishing fair methods for directly and globally electing members of the Peoples' Assembly from around the globe would be difficult indeed.

Pinzak: Okay, how about this: To ensure that there would be fair global elections, each member nation of the UN, even tyrannies, would have to guarantee polling places and would allow, where necessary, UN representatives to oversee the elections. A member nation failing to offer fair global elections for the Peoples' Assembly—failing, for instance, to provide an adequate number of polling places for its population—would forfeit its membership in the UN for some pre-established period of time.

Emile: Who would appear on the ballot in each country?

Pinzak: Well, the election would be regional, not national. Candidates would represent entire continents or blocks of nations. So persons voting in Kenya would vote for a slate of candidates drawn from regions of Africa or perhaps from the entire continent. In this way the election would be transnational. Similarly, there could be regions made up of Southeast Asia or South Asia, Southern Europe, North America . . . regions that would transcend the idea of national candidates. You could divide the regions so that the populations were relatively equal, or you could make the number of representatives from each region proportional to its population.

Emile: This system might offset the problem of any one country having too many representatives. Voting in this way guarantees, based on the size of the population of a region or continent, that no one region or continent or country is over-represented. Even if the slate of candidates from the United States dominated the elections, those candidates would be offset by the elections in other regions.

What, however, if only 5 percent of the world's population votes for candidates? How representative, then, would the Peoples' Assembly be?

Pinzak: It would be more representative than the General Assembly's composition of appointed ambassadors. People would be given an opportunity. If they choose not to avail themselves of it, then that is their choice. On the other hand, they have to be *able* to make that choice. Hence the need, as we said earlier, for supervision of the elections.

Emile: Would not most of the candidates be drawn from the same ranks as those who stand for parliament or congress in their countries? Would the slate of candidates in every region not consist of the most prominent players from within the countries of that region? What if an elector does not like any of the candidates on her ballot?

Pinzak: You're going beyond my imagination here, Emile. Perhaps we could deal with the stipulations on who can run. We could exempt people who have held national offices in the countries within the region; encourage to stand for election those who work in local politics, activist movements, trade unions, religious organizations, or retirees; try to put forward teachers, farmers, wage-earners, and small-business owners and their employees. We could try for a different slate of candidates.

Another method of election initially could simply have representatives elected from the national legislatures of the countries. This approach might make establishing the Assembly more feasible. Amendments to the UN Charter require approval by two-thirds of the United Nations General Assembly. Members might be more likely to vote for an amendment establishing a Peoples' Assembly if they knew that representatives to that Assembly would come initially from national legislatures. Such representatives have already established legitimacy and credibility by winning elections in their countries, though, of course, the nature of the regimes in which the elections were held may call legitimacy and credibility into question. At the very least, these representatives already have experience in the legislative processes.[38]

Emile: Electing representatives directly from national legislatures could be a transitional method that would permit the UN to work out the logistical issues for moving to direct global elections. But it would be risky. The Peoples' Assembly might find itself favoring policies and positions that the national legislatures also favor. Despite the use of democratic dialogue and General Assembly oversight, the Peoples' Assembly might often resemble an Assembly of International Parliamentarians, merely an offshoot and mouthpiece of powerful national assemblies looking to advance domestic policies on an international scale or at an international level.

Regardless, Pinzak, none of this is going to happen until there are changes, as Habermas observed, to the Security Council. The Security Council's permanent members still hold veto power over any amendment to the United Nations Charter. Would all of those members agree on the idea of a Peoples' Assembly? Would the United States like to see a second UN body that might thwart or challenge its influence?

Pinzak: You and Habermas are, of course, right. The obvious problem with the Security Council, and the first area to reform, is that it isn't democratic. It has five permanent members—the United States, the United Kingdom, Russia, China, and France—each of which holds veto power over any decision made within the Council. This structure exists for good reason: to prevent the main nuclear powers from fighting one another. Although each of these countries holds nuclear weapons, and perhaps the most nuclear weapons, they are hardly the only nuclear powers today. Additionally, especially if we hold China aside, they represent very little of the world's population and thus do not themselves represent a sizable portion of that population. The end result of this is that the Security Council does not have democratic legitimacy, given its distinction between "great powers"—those permanent members with veto rights—and the rest of the UN member nations. The veto power of its permanent members renders the Council unwieldy, if not dysfunctional.

As we established last week, democratic legitimacy may only come with the democratization of the Council itself. Thus, although the Security Council functions, contra-Habermas, it does not function democratically and thus does not function well. How might the Council be reformed to make it functional and democratic?

Pinzak: It's difficult to imagine that any of the permanent members would voluntarily surrender their permanent seat or their veto power. Perhaps it might be possible to tackle, first, the idea of democratic representation on the Council. The Council was expanded in 1965 from eleven members to fifteen members, with all but the permanent five seats rotating every two years among UN member nations. Such expansion could be done again, say, to twenty-four members, as suggested in the reform proposals of the Razami Ismael group in 1997. This would at least provide more diversity of views on the Council. More significant than this, though, would be to bring the Council under the guidance of the General Assembly, itself a more diverse and open body of largely, but not only, democratic states.

Emile: Well, the General Assembly is democratic in that the members all have "sovereign equality." Each country is treated equally; no country has more than one vote. But certainly the Ambassadors to the UN are not democratically determined within their home countries, nor, as you suggest, do they necessarily represent democratic states or represent their people. They are representatives of states, regardless of the kind of regime, more than of persons. Nevertheless, if power could be shifted from the Security Council to the Assembly, then there would be an incremental move toward democratic oversight of decisions made by the UN.

Pinzak: But how is that really a democratic move when tiny Luxembourg would have the same voting power as Brazil, or Belize would have the same voting power as China?

Emile: How about offering "proportional voting"? The larger a country's population, the more votes it may cast. An additional factor in deciding the number of votes a particular country receives might be the amount a country contributes to the UN's budget.

Pinzak: But wouldn't small, rich countries have more votes than middle-sized poor countries? Dictatorships with large populations would have more votes—ironically, would have "more" democratic influence—than countries with democratically elected governments? This is getting complicated.

Emile: There is nothing wrong with complexity or complication.

Pinzak: Unless it's unnecessary or impossible to overcome. How and why would the United States and Germany, say, agree to a plan in which China and India, with massive populations, would wield the most power? Anyway, I think that these proposals are beside the main point: The General Assembly represents states, not people. We should leave the General Assembly as it is, though have it oversee or somehow override the Security Council, or abolish that Council altogether, and introduce the Peoples' Assembly as the main deliberative and even legislative body.[39]

I have another idea for institutionalizing democratic dialogue among the world's population . . . this time at the UN itself.

Emile: Yes, I know. We have already talked about the Peoples' Assembly.

Pinzak: I mean besides that. I'd like to see institutionalized immediately at the UN a legislative jury pool of six hundred persons that changes every six months. Remember H. G. Wells's idea of dividing the world into two-and-a-half million areas of about equal population, then randomly selecting twenty thousand of those areas and by lot selecting one person from each of these twenty thousand? Well, the six hundred could be drawn each year from those twenty thousand. Then the following year the UN General Assembly would randomly select twenty thousand areas again. So every year there would be a new pool of areas and thus a new pool of twenty thousand persons from whom to select the six hundred.[40] The remaining randomly selected twenty thousand persons could constitute cosmopolitan sub-juries in different geographical regions of the globe to serve as "naming" juries to name the initiatives framed at the UN by the six hundred.

Emile: Selecting jurors in this way would certainly accomplish the goal of providing multiple perspectives and could do so without interference and engineering by political elites. Why six hundred?

Pinzak: I borrowed the number from the number of members of the European Parliament—626—and rounded it off for symmetry.

Emile: Where and how would these juries convene? Given all that we have said about the value of face-to-face meetings, I assume that they would travel somewhere to meet?

Pinzak: Remember John Bolton, the highly controversial ex-ambassador to the UN from the United States? *(Emile nods.)* In 1994, before his days at the UN, he told a gathering of the World Federalists, who believe in world government as Bolton does not, that so little goes on at the UN that if you lopped off the top ten floors of the UN building nothing would really change.[41] Well, maybe the UN does have ten floors of underutilized, if not wasted, space. I'd like to see them renovated and turned into small but well-appointed apartments and small conference rooms to be used by the six hundred.

Emile: You envision that they would do what Legislative Juries do?

Pinzak: Yes. They would follow the system that we outlined for the Legislative Juries. They would frame and maybe name—different juries for each—the way that a global referendum or initiative will be phrased. Multiple juries would meet on the same issue to see how and whether the framing and naming changed from jury to jury. When there were discrepancies, the juries would work toward consensus.

Any finalized referendum or initiative would then be deliberated on globally, with the UN providing testimony, even sworn testimony, to be broadcast worldwide via radio, television, telephone, the Internet, and through print media as well, including broadsheets to be posted in villages and peripatetic criers to read aloud much of that testimony. Decisions would not be taken solely by a small group, but must be open to deliberation among the people and finally decided by the people.

Additionally, the six hundred would also raise, dialectically think about, and come to a consensus on any issues that they find germane to their groups. Once they have arrived at consensus, then they would deliver their consensus statements to the UN General Assembly, or the Peoples' Assembly, if it exists, for broadcast and dissemination to the world. The point is to publicize the positions and policy recommendations that a deliberative group of world residents finds significant.

Emile: Does it seem odd in this scenario that an undocumented worker from Costa Rica, living in the United States, could be selected to participate in the approximately six hundred or so in the cosmopolitan Peoples' Assembly and thereby take the place of a citizen of the United States?

Pinzak: No, it does not seem odd to me. The goal is to have people represent themselves and the interests, values, ideas, or beliefs that motivate them. The goal is not to represent a country. It is irrelevant where someone lives or where someone is from. For purposes of convenience mostly, we have said that anyone may apply to participate from anywhere; all any applicant needs is contact information. The selection of participants will be completely random. Whether any particular country is represented—that is, whether persons residing in a certain country are selected—is irrelevant to the process. If a country can take a census, then it can offer to place in contention any person who wishes to be included; if a country can advertise state lotteries, can launch "get-out-the-vote" campaigns, and can broadcast or publicize public-service messages, then it can find ways to announce the pool of prospective participants in the Peoples' Assembly.

Emile: Practicality suggests that there will be people who will never be able to participate. There will also be many who will not want to engage in the democratic dialogical format.[42]

Pinzak: Lots of people, I should think, will not want to give up their time or give up whatever they are doing to participate. Others cannot or will not suspend their own ideologically driven commitment to their cause, whether that cause is religious, political, economic, or whatever, and thus won't want to participate. Fundamentalists of all stripes hold tenaciously to their worldviews. Loosening their hold on those views is tantamount to surrendering themselves.

Emile: That from our perspective is a central purpose of the dialogical format itself.

Pinzak: That's true, and so it is going to be very difficult for many of them to participate . . . perhaps over time. . . . Anyway, to answer your first question, and holding ideology aside, why would people not be able to participate? All participants in the six hundred, and in the sub-juries, should be paid a "living wage" for their time. If the living wage is below their yearly earnings, then within reason the UN should pay their current yearly salary. For everyone the UN will pay for their travel expenses and apartment.

Emile: Can you see any country or group of countries or the UN itself actually acting on such ideas? (*Pinzak shrugs his shoulders.*) So we are back where we started, with the need to reform the Security Council, but no way to do it. The permanent members will always resist any proposal that erodes their power or jeopardizes their veto. Power is really held not by the whole council, and certainly not by the rotating ten members elected by region every two years, but by the five permanent members, each having veto power.[43]

Pinzak: This is why we need to consider other ways of institutionalizing democratic dialogue within other forms of global governance. Considering Habermas's third required reform, the International Criminal Court, will lead us to another form of global governance: a world federation.

Global Governance II: Integral Democracy
The centerpiece of the International Criminal Court ought to be cosmopolitan law. That law, which is nothing other than the institutionalizing of human rights, is on the horizon but is still some distance from us. As Habermas says, when countries intervene to stop human-rights abuses, "the force they exercise does not yet possess the character of a legal coercion legitimated by a democratic cosmopolitan order" (2006a, 29). Reforming the International Criminal Court

with cosmopolitan law as its base and with the articulation of that law through democratic dialogue is a step toward that legitimacy. At the very least, using democratic dialogue reemphasizes the legitimacy of the decisions made and the actions taken.

Emile: Thus the Court would be the only legally sanctioned institution in which groups and individuals could sue states for violations and abuses of human rights. States found guilty would face sanctions against them and would possibly face military action.

Pinzak: Whose military?

Emile: Now you have caught me in your "imaginary" . . . perhaps there could be armed forces under the direction of the UN General Assembly or under the auspices of a federation of liberal democratic states. But here I seem merely to be reverting to Kant's idea of a federation of republics, or in our case a federation of liberal democracies.[44]

Pinzak: Well, the multiplicities of transnational organizations and agencies, the presence of transnational rights, treaties, and agreements, and the existence of a supranational entity like the European Union all mean that cosmopolitan norms are increasingly evident. So we might think of the current global situation therefore, as a transition stage, as we move more and more toward a mode of following cosmopolitan norms and adjusting to cosmopolitan law, all of which is Kantian.

Emile: Moreover, as Benhabib concludes, "[T]he spread of cosmopolitan norms from interdictions of war crimes, crimes against humanity and genocide to the increasing regulations of cross-border movements through the Geneva Conventions and other accords, has yielded a new political condition: the local, the national and the global are all imbricated in one another."[45] Dialogical democratic forums can help speed us through the transition.

Pinzak: Yes, it can and will, but I want to focus for the moment on the imbrication of levels of influence and decision-making. One argument against those who oppose a federation because it could lead to tyranny—as Kant, for example, opposed a world federation—is to point out that a federation of liberal democracies, following the principle of subsidiarity, would have jurisdiction only over global issues. Nations, states/provinces, and localities would continue to have jurisdiction over their own issues. Where there is overlap, where there is imbrication or hints of it, then perhaps a World Court, limited to hearing and settling only disputes of this sort (disputes on jurisdiction and on suits related to global issues) could decide where jurisdiction lies. By the way, this court or another one like it could serve as a Federated Supreme Court to assure that no outcomes violate the human rights that are the very foundation of the federation itself.

Emile: Why do you envision a federation?

Pinzak: The concepts of "federation" and "federalism" capture the idea of "subsidiarity." Federalism does not establish a "national" government. That is, states continue to be self-governing in all matters pertaining to them. So, as in subsidiarity, leave local governance to localities, provincial governance to provinces, national governance to nations, and governance related to global issues and only to global issues to the Federation of Liberal Democracies. That would be why the Federation exists: To address global concerns.

In short, there are, or can be, multiple levels of federations. The term is derived from Latin, *foederare,* or "to league together." That means that any group of persons that leagues together regularly, however "regularly" is defined, is a federation. So there can be all sorts of federations, from neighbors to communities to clubs and associations to counties or regions or states or inter-states. Why can't one be an active member of these diverse federations? One can be. It's not as if a federation of liberal democracies would suddenly supersede participation in all other federations. The purview of each level of "federalism" must be clearly delineated and the form and formation of institutions and activities at each level must be influenced both top-down and bottom-up. This is, again, part of the integrating nature of Integral Democracy.

Emile: We have a wholes/parts issue here, as we discussed with Nussbaum's concentric circles of identity and with Wilber's AQAL model. Persons may be members at different levels of federalism, just as they have varying commitments to different groups or associations. At each level democratic dialogue is the "whole" of that level, meaning that all public issues pertaining to that level may be addressed through those forums. But those forums are themselves only parts of the level of federalism "above." Just as states in the United States have their own individual constitutions that overarch local ordinances, rules, and statutes, and just as nations have constitutions that overarch the constitutions of the states, so, too, the Federation would have its constitution that only in certain areas would overarch the national constitutions.

Of course, as you say, there may be conflicts at a certain level of federalism and between levels. It might happen, for example, that a member of the Federation decides that a certain level of particulates may be released annually into the atmosphere. The Federation decides that the acceptable level is much more stringent than the levels to which the people in that country agreed. Both parties will need democratic dialogue to sort this out, since both will want their "day in court" to present their cases. Perhaps these conflicts would be better handled through democratic dialogue in the Democratic Courts that we talked about last week. Such courts would be preferable in that the people, then, would have another venue for political decision-making.

Pinzak: I like that idea, Emile, because it is in concert with our desire to create multiple, even ubiquitous, democratic forums for dialectical thinking and deliberative decision-making. Indeed, we've talked about the need for a cluster of democratic forums or centers—local, countrywide, statewide, regional, national, continental, global—where persons can interact in democratic dialogue with those having similar concerns but different perspectives.

Speaking of clusters, keep in mind that direct democracy through democratic dialogue does not supplant, but rather supplements, representative government. The United States Congress won't disappear, nor will the governance system of the European Union, which is itself a regional federation. We cannot discount, nor should we, the need for representation at different levels of political activity. For example, some decisions taken at the trans-regional or transnational level may require a decision made by representatives. This means that political participatory membership must include not just local and regional and national organizations, but also international and transnational organizations.

Wherever there are to be representatives, there must be reciprocity and accountability. That is, when a local group sends a representative to a regional or national association, that representative will be held accountable to his constituents. Those constituents can demand transparency in transactions and decisions and must be able to recall, interrogate, and replace that representative if they are not satisfied. Constituents must have equal and immediate and sustained access to their representatives, regardless of the level of the association.

Emile: Even if representation remains, are not democratic dialogue and direct, deliberative democracy asking too much of people? I am reminded of Oscar Wilde's quip that the problem with socialism is that it took too many evenings.

Pinzak: It takes as many evenings as one wishes to devote to it. "Integral Democracy," which is the term for the overall scheme of federated levels of democratic dialogue, makes available opportunities to participate, or not, at multiple levels of political decision-making. My position is that whatever you're involved in, whenever decisions must be made that affect the collectivity, however bounded and defined, you decide whether and when to participate. It's the availability that's significant . . . that and the way that the dialogue is structured.

Emile: So you imagine each person having available to her a network of democratic forums or clusters of interactions with others for making decisions that affect her life. Everyone, then, in Integral Democracy is self-governing. Everyone is fully autonomous in that she brings herself and her interests, values, ideas, and concerns to the forums. She participates in democratically deciding how the company or agency or country or globe will live with this particular issue. Participation is determined by how the "self" in "self-governing" is defined and understood—what are the boundaries, if any, to the collectivity deciding? Do you belong to or are you within that boundary? That is the initial question that any person would ask.

Pinzak: Of course, Integral Democracy does not mean the end of boundaries. Boundaries can and must exist, if only for feasibility of decision-making. Not everyone needs to be or ought to be involved in every democratic decision. Whether the city of Pittsburgh, Pennsylvania, shuts off Liberty Avenue to all motorized vehicles except delivery vans, emergency vehicles, and public transportation is not a decision that the residents of Boston, Massachusetts, or Calcutta, India, ought to be making or need to be making . . .

Emile: . . . or surely want to be making.

Pinzak: Because persons define themselves not only by what they do, value, think, believe, and the rest, but also by those with whom they do many of these things, then we can see that identity itself is relational. That doesn't mean that I must have an "out-group" against whom to define myself, for I can also define myself by those with whom I share my essentials. To form and express myself, my identity, I interact with lots of persons in lots of settings. When I and other persons in those settings need to decide something important for the group, we do so through democratic dialogue. Now imagine that those dialogues take place not just at Joe's Diner, when the Night Watchmen's Club wants to revise its founding document, or in the neighborhood when the Crime Watch group wants to expand its responsibilities, but also in Human Rights Watch, a global NGO, when it is deciding whether to partner with Amnesty International in a new global campaign. Every member of these groups has a right to participate in democratic dialogue to shape the policies and decisions. Non-members are excluded, because of eligibility, though that can be contested in the Democratic Courts and the World Court.

Emile: What is the basis of this right? How is it formed and expressed and protected?

Pinzak: Well, perhaps through an integral constitution. As I see it, an integral constitution is not the same as a cosmopolitan constitution. The latter is concerned with the establishment and enactments of cosmopolitan law. A cosmopolitan constitution would govern a supranational sphere of politics, however conceived, that would be concerned with enforcing and protecting human rights. Our example, of course, is the Federation of Liberal Democracies. An integral constitution, on the other hand, is a document that tries to coordinate the several federated levels or layers of democratic governance available to individuals, groups, and states. The constitution of the Federation speaks to or for only those member nations, and it speaks to or for its members only on global issues. But the integral constitution would seek to integrate all levels so that persons wishing and eligible to participate would know where to go to effect changes and to share policies related to different needs, interests, values, and even aspirations. An integral constitution is the framework for governance within Integral Democracy and would be the foundational document for any Federation of Liberal Democracies under which would be subsumed the Federation's cosmopolitan constitution. The integral constitution would be, in other words, the coordinating and integrating document for all levels of federalism.

Emile: Let us look at both of these: a cosmopolitan constitution, and with it cosmopolitan law, and an integral constitution. At this point, it seems unlikely that nation-states would join together to write and ratify even a cosmopolitan constitution, let alone an integral one. Of course, from our perspective, any such constitution would have to be written and ratified through a dialectical democratic process. If legitimacy in a democracy emanates from the consent of the governed, and given that a cosmopolitan constitution must institutionalize global or transnational democracy as we have described it, then the people must be involved in creating the constitution if it is to be democratically legitimate. This normative position—that the people must be involved in decision-making—may be assumed for the purposes of discussing cosmopolitan institutions. Yet getting national and international authorities to agree to such input could be messy, time-consuming, and nearly impossible. Would sanctioned power holders want, and do we really want, to institutionalize, or constitutionalize, a set of institutions and democratic procedures that have not really been tried, especially when those institutions could siphon off some of their political power? At the very least, any such constitution would involve some loss of sovereignty, as nations would have to surrender exclusive decision-making power on issues within and across their borders.

Pinzak: All excellent points, Emile. We're speculating here, of course, about institutions of global governance, and right now these speculations gesture only toward regulative ideals. They point in the direction of what we'd like to see or might like to try. Would member nations of the Federation really be losing sovereignty, or would they be gaining sovereignty? *(Pinzak looks at Emile quizzically.)* Here's what I mean: Sovereignty rests on the consent of the governed, the people. The people must consent through democratic dialogue on what human rights are and mean. We talked about this at our last meeting. When the people consent, then the Federation's cosmopolitan constitution is formalized. Member nations and their citizens are held to upholding those rights, both within their nations and across those nations. Sovereignty, then, has expanded beyond the borders of any member nation and now rests among the people of all the member states. I might even go so far as to suggest that the people of the Federation could even claim sovereignty on behalf of human rights over those nations that violate or fail to honor those rights. In a real sense, here, we are making the Hegelian point that honoring and protecting such rights is the only way to be rational and ethical. If a state cannot or will not honor and protect those rights, then perhaps it is not worthy of sovereignty and forfeits that sovereignty to the people of the Federation.

Emile: In this case the Federation would become the final and absolute political authority within the state that is violating human rights. That is, the Federation literally becomes sovereign. This is not unlike Hobbes's position: When the sovereign no longer protects the subjects, then subjects are no longer obliged to obey the sovereign. In fact, one can say that that sovereign ceases to be sovereign.[45] States in general and communities at large are not in themselves valuable. They are, instead, instrumentally valuable for the development of individuals and for the development of their concomitant and ineluctable relationships and fellowships. When states inside or outside the Federation violate or fail to protect the rights of citizens, then those states have little ground for arguing that their sovereignty ought not to be violated or, as you say, forfeited. But whose justice is this? The Taliban will want to institutionalize, if not constitutionalize, *Sharia* or Islamic law. By doing so, and in the interest of saving souls and ensuring righteous living, the Taliban will violate what we have determined are fundamental, universal human rights. So, then, the Federation would impose its will on the Taliban?

Pinzak: That statement might be too strong, Emile. The Taliban would be in danger of having sanctions placed on them. The nature of those sanctions and measures beyond sanctions would be determined through democratic dialogue at the appropriate levels. But, always, intervention of any sort in the internal affairs of a nation is a serious matter. Any form of intervention must not result in worse consequences for the very people who are in jeopardy and who need help.[46]

This part of our conversation is within the context of human rights, which are individual rights, and this gets right to the heart of cosmopolitan law. Cosmopolitan law has one significant difference that separates it from mere international law: For us, as for Kant, cosmopolitan law was not of states, as is the case today with international law, but of individuals. Legal status shifts from whether and how one is a member of a state to legal protection of rights on the basis of simply being human. A cosmopolitan law would transcend all national boundaries and as such would require all nations, regardless of their political systems, practices, or beliefs, to abide by it. If a nation did not, then other nations—in our case, the Federation of Liberal Democracies—would take action to bring the recalcitrant nation into compliance. This would mean, of course, that cosmopolitan law is binding and thus must be enforced.

Emile: How could it be enforced? Could it be enforced? Does it mean, for example, that the Federation would declare to the world that it will enforce cosmopolitan law irrespective of what other countries follow and believe? If cosmopolitan law is based on the view that human rights trump national sovereignty, as you have implied, then the Federation would have to take action against any country that violates its own citizens' human rights or violates the rights of citizens in other countries.

Pinzak: I didn't mean to imply this; rather, I meant to *state* it. This is exactly what it means, and we talked about this at one of our earlier meetings when we discussed the doctrine adopted at the UN World Summit in 2005: A state that treats its citizens criminally, that commits "gross human rights violations" against its citizens or fails to protect those human rights, has forfeited its moral right to sovereignty. That doctrine and our cosmopolitan law go one step further and declare that such a country has also forfeited its legal right to sovereignty when failing to protect its citizens' human rights.

Emile: All right, but what if the violation is in a "gray" area? The delegates who signed that Summit Document in 2005 agreed that states have the responsibility to protect their citizens against "atrocious crimes." For the delegates those crimes include, and may be limited to, "genocide, war crimes, ethnic cleansing, and crimes against humanity." Failure to protect citizens from those crimes will result in action, from diplomatic to military action.[47] But what if the violation were of some political rights? We and the Federation might see such a failure as a violation, but the people within that country support that "violation." For example, suppose the issue is about a country eliminating any right to vote in a monarchy, and the people fully support that. Would such a violation warrant intervention, irrespective of what the people themselves want and value?

Pinzak: Cosmopolitan law would transcend the Summit Document precisely because, as I said, it insists on the protection of *all* human rights, however those are eventually and democratically defined. But certainly the definition will include virtually all of the Universal Declaration of Human Rights. Also, your case shows why the Federation itself would operate internally according to the guidelines and procedures of democratic dialogue. Deliberations among member nations might well lead to the conclusion that no intervention is warranted under these circumstances.

Emile: So, then, how binding is the cosmopolitan law?

Pinzak: It's like any kind of law, Emile. There will be extenuating circumstances that alter how persons view the situation. Murder is both morally and legally wrong, and laws are passed within and among nations to prohibit it and to punish those who commit murder. But not every case is handled the same way. Not every charge of murder eventuates in a conviction, nor does every murderer receive the same sentence. There are always mitigating factors to consider, and those are presented during trials and considered during deliberations. The same conditions exist when applying cosmopolitan law. The Federation announces to the world, and not simply to its members, how it may enforce cosmopolitan law. But that does not mean that it will enforce the law in the same way in all cases.

Emile: This line of inquiry, I think, is taking us in a direction that skirts a more significant issue: If we already have the doctrine from the UN Summit in 2005—"the responsibility to protect," also known as "R2P"—then why do we need a cosmopolitan law?

Pinzak: One reason is that the cosmopolitan law, as opposed to a mere doctrine, is presented as a law binding on all humans and all states and is the central law binding the member nations to one another in the Federation. It is a statement of a commitment and an obligation to act on that commitment.

Emile: So in your estimation having cosmopolitan law would make intervention easier. R2P currently exists, but is not exercised enough, even though people say they support it?

Pinzak: Support dissolves into mere lip service when countries don't have to intervene. Unless there is popular support, governments don't mount efforts to take action. Popular support, of course, is crucial in democracies, and the cosmopolitan law is a clear statement by the Federation that action will be taken in cases of clear violations of the law.

Emile: Will people want to uphold cosmopolitan law when it involves personal sacrifice?

Pinzak: We're back to our earliest discussions. When people feel a connection to what is happening, when they feel the need, then they will respond and will support action. How do we engender that feeling, that cosmopolitan sensibility, so that people feel that, in Kant's words, a violation of rights anywhere is felt everywhere? That's why you and I, are on this excursion. *(Emile smiles.)*

We can't hide the implications of what we're saying here about cosmopolitan law. If the Federation is to uphold it, then it will intervene in whatever ways it deems necessary to effect a remedy.[48] But ultimately, this must mean that unless a government is prepared to change its policies toward its people, then that government might well have to be changed.

Emile: Regime change? *(Pinzak nods, and Emile sighs.)* That seems inevitable. If a country has violated cosmopolitan law to such an extent that the Federation decides to intervene, how could the people of that country ever feel safe that their rights will not be violated again? After all, it was their government that failed in the first place to protect their rights. That government might even have participated in violating those rights. When the cyclone struck Myanmar . . .

Pinzak: . . . Burma . . .

Emile *(with a slight head nod toward Pinzak):* . . . Burma. . . . When the cyclone struck in 2008, and the government refused to permit foreign aid or aid workers into the country, surely our Federation would have taken some action. But what action? Would it have interceded militarily to get the aid into the country? And would it have stopped there? I doubt it. The source of the problem in the first place, the reason aid could not come in, was the government itself.

Pinzak: It seems to me, Emile, that at that point there would have to be some significant protest or resistance movement among the people of Burma themselves to warrant overthrowing the government. We might expect such movements, because the citizens and residents might no longer trust their government to protect them. With Federation forces inside the country the people might also feel more confident that changes could actually happen, that those forces could help bring about positive changes for their country. If the government were overthrown, then whatever form was to replace it must be the outcome of democratic dialogue among the people of Burma themselves.

Emile: You refer to the Federation as a Federation of Liberal Democracies. Do you include the adjective "liberal" to encode, if not enshrine, individual rights?

Pinzak: I do so in part. Individual rights are particularized within nations, but they are also reflections of universal human rights that inform any particularistic expressions of them. For this reason, liberal rights, as I use the term, serve to limit or restrain democracies from creating policies and passing legislation that violates these rights.

Emile: So any nation that fails to protect the freedom of speech or association or religion of its citizens would be ruled out as a member of the Federation? What if there were only one state religion?

Pinzak: To be a member of the Federation, a state cannot prevent its citizens from worshipping as they wish, provided that their worship does not violate the tenets of human rights. A nation may have a state religion, but citizens of that nation cannot be required to adopt it as their personal religion.

Emile: We are talking about the institutionalization of the rights described in the Universal Declaration of Human Rights in its broad outlines. So, in accordance with that declaration, you would not include, for example, specified paid vacations or the length of workweeks? How are you going to require nations to honor rights that you do not specify?

Pinzak: The human rights that underlie the Federation's cosmopolitan constitution must be rights upon which the member states agree. For example, rights such as specified paid vacations and the length of workweeks would have to be approved through democratic dialogue and through framing and naming Legislative Juries. Then those proposed rights would have to be presented as initiatives to the citizens of the member states.

Emile: What if a country does not want to govern democratically? What if a country wants instead an aristocracy or a monarchy?

Pinzak: That country can have whatever form of government it wishes, but it cannot be a member of the Federation of Liberal Democracies. A country that believes in the divine right of kings, and that its own king has been chosen by God and sanctioned by priests, without input from the people themselves, has a right to live as it chooses without interference from those outside that country.

Emile: Without interference, provided, of course, that that country and its king do not harm the subjects. What if a country is a liberal democracy, but is only in a limited way a dialogical democracy? What then?

Pinzak: We're assuming, of course—after all, it's our context—that member states of the Federation will be dialogical democracies. But questions such as how many procedures in each country will involve direct citizen decision-making, how many of its institutions will be representative, and how true to dialectical deliberation the procedures will be must be answered by each country itself. Members of the Federation will decide whether each applicant country has the requisite liberal democratic conditions to be admitted. Not all countries will look exactly alike as democracies.

Emile: No federation of this sort is going to succeed without the willing surrender of some national sovereignty, because on some issues the Federation will have to override the desires of the officials and/or of the people in that nation.

Pinzak: You're right, and this is an essential requirement of membership in the Federation. In *Another Cosmopolitanism,* Seyla Benhabib (2006) points out that since the passage of the Universal Declaration of Human Rights in 1948, the world has witnessed the growth of interrelated and overlapping global and regional human rights regimes. By such a "regime" she means the rise in the number of human rights treaties such as the International Covenant on Civil and Political Rights; the International Covenant on Economic, Social, and Cultural Rights; the European Union Charter of Fundamental Rights; the Convention on the Rights of the Child; and the Convention Against Torture and Other Cruel, Inhuman, or Degrading Treatment or Punishment. These treaties can be enforced and have been enforced, as in cases of humanitarian intervention and through prosecutions in international courts. In these cases human rights violations trump state sovereignty but, as we mentioned earlier, such interventions are difficult to orchestrate for the very reason that they violate a state's sovereignty and thus are seen by many as creating a parlous precedent.

If intervention is necessary, then the use of armed intervention must be a possibility.[49] Without armed forces of its own, the Federation would be toothless in the face of a defiant member nation or against threats from outside that might divide members within the Federation. Let's say that a block of Federation states has a trade agreement with a country outside the Federation. That outside country refuses to curb piracy coming from ships along their coastline or from their shores. The trading block within the Federation does not want to confront the country; so they oppose the use of the military, even after all diplomatic entreaties and democratic dialogue have failed. But, in actuality, the matter would be out of their hands, since the Federation's armed forces would be under the control of the Peoples' Assembly of the Federation . . .

Emile: . . . yes, I can see that we would have to have such an assembly . . .

Pinzak: . . . and not only of the individual member states. The Federation should have its own armed services. Part of the Federation's budget would be spent on military personnel and materiel.[50] The armed forces could be entirely voluntary, and its officers and enlisted personnel could all be retired and/or experienced veterans.

Emile: If there were Federation forces, then why would there be a need for armed forces within the member nations? Why would those nations retain their military forces at all?

Pinzak: They would do so, presumably, for the same reason that states within the United States, for example, have their militias called "National Guard" units. Their duties are often different from those of the regular armed forces, though their call-up to service in Iraq and Afghanistan demonstrates that this is not necessarily so. But I would imagine that the duties of each of these armed-service branches would be reevaluated and integrated, which is another aspect, though a smaller aspect, of Integral Democracy.

Bear in mind, also, that the armed forces of the Federation would be voluntary only. Some nations within the Federation might want to continue with their own policies of mandatory-armed service, and those nations might want to expand that service to include volunteering to serve in the Federation forces. Having Federation forces available for peacekeeping might also allow mandatory national service to replace mandatory military service, thereby opening up greater service options for their populations.

Emile: For example, service as teachers or nurses or geriatric assistants could replace military duty.

Pinzak: Right.

Emile: The Federation of Liberal Democracies would be a prime example of integrating individuals and communities. That is, the cosmopolitan constitution underlying and supporting the Federation is a framework for uniting countries or nation-states. Yet the cosmopolitan law that is the heart, or spine, of that constitution protects all individuals within the Federation, regardless of where they reside or of their citizenship or lack of citizenship. The commitment of all nations within the Federation is to human rights. No state or community within a state, or any groups or individuals within or between states, will violate those human rights. Moreover, individuals within the Federation are free to conduct business and travel across boundaries. Individuals are free to move to and reside in whatever states they want.

Pinzak: For Kant cosmopolitan law *(Weltbuergerrecht)* meant the extension of and conditions for "universal hospitality"—"the right of a stranger not to be treated with hostility when he arrives on someone else's territory."[51] When the stranger arrives on your shore or at your door, you have an obligation to treat him or her with concern and respect. That duty mitigates, if not eliminates, any urge or intention to shun or turn against the stranger as one who does not belong. This hospitality was Kant's proposal for enhancing mutual relations among diverse countries and persons. In today's parlance such hospitality may be construed as honoring human rights, which transcend state boundaries and do not depend on citizenship or even legal residence. Enhancing such relations might lead, in our terms, to cosmopolitan sensibility. By requiring hospitality one engenders a cosmopolitan sensibility, an opening to and embracing of others, much as we are requiring certain structures or formats in democratic dialogue to express a cosmopolitan sensibility and to engender a cosmopolitan identity through listening to, even embracing, divergent voices and views.

Emile: Cosmopolitan law would be the law for and of all persons living within the Federation. Yet all of our speculations simply reinforce how far we are from living according to cosmopolitan law. This moral ideal of unconditional hospitality is in reality bounded, limited, and all too often ignored. We see this in states that refuse entry to immigrants and refugees. There are countless manifestations across the globe of hostility to rival ethnic groups, different religions, or foreign cultural practices and traditions.

Pinzak: Still, cosmopolitan law provides an ideal that we can and want to approach, and we can use it as a regulative idea until such time, however distant, when it can be transformed into an actuality. That transformation will be a product of the full integration of the cosmopolitan worldview that we seek. That our global situation and ethos might be transformed into a reflection of unconditional hospitality turns this from a Kantian regulative ideal, and as such unrealizable, into what I'd term a "regulative idea." We speculate about ways both to describe and to enact a cosmopolitan constitution and its "parent" document, an integral constitution. The integral constitution is the framework for establishing the structures of worldwide democratic dialogue, with obvious implications for how democratic dialogue functions at and below the global level. But the constitution must not be seen as a fixed document somehow reflecting natural law. This constitution is an ongoing, living process of and conversation about establishment, interrogation, modification, and reenactment. People will engage in democratic conversations at all levels of politics, as they seek to integrate the different levels by arranging, creating, and rearranging institutions and procedures to come into harmony throughout the entire cosmopolitan system. Thus, the conversations themselves will be ongoing, constant processes, with input from the grassroots as well as from the elites and all those in between. As we said earlier, what starts off as small local instances of democratic dialogue can help foster instantiating democratic dialogue in ever-rising and widening circles.

From one perspective it is irrelevant whether we could all live out the moral ethos of unconditional hospitality found in cosmopolitanism. It is a goal worth striving for, an ideal worth pursuing to modify our behaviors. Therefore, we must work our way politically—that is, democratically—through the tensions that arise between our nation's particular laws and moral codes and our impetus toward a cosmopolitan identity and concomitant worldview.

I feel as if we've suddenly reversed roles, Emile; changed seats, as it were. I'm usually the faultfinder and the skeptic in our conversations, and you've remained remarkably, and refreshingly, consistent. Now we seem to have swapped perspectives.

Emile: Perhaps that is so and even inevitable, given how we have opened to each other and to each other's perspectives over these several weeks. So, I am curious: What, if anything, leads you to think that transformations, personal or collective, toward cosmopolitanism might actually be possible?

Pinzak: I have a couple of thoughts on this. First, I can imagine that people will find attractive the notion of making those decisions that directly and deeply affect their lives, or their conceptions of the good life, and that they might well find that the best way to make these decisions is through democratic dialogue. Finding such dialogue attractive, they will also be drawn to having multiple democratic-dialogical forums, outlets, and institutions for exercising their political power in making these decisions. It might be easiest to establish these outlets and forums at local levels, as the National Issues Forums, as one example, demonstrate. The empowerment found at the local level, in clubs and schools and workplaces and associations, can then motivate people to seek to create additional and more inclusive kinds of dialogical democratic forums and institutions.

Emile: The ever-rising and widening circles.

Pinzak: Exactly. These can be joined with or forged in the context of movements toward integration and universal rights and justice that are palpably visible around the world today.

Emile: Along with your outlook, Pinzak, is the presence of many transnational groups, movements, and even institutions functioning and springing up all the time. These groups could be amenable to adopting democratic dialogue. So it is not as if we need to invent new organizations, so much as we need to support and perhaps expand current ones.

Pinzak: It's almost as if we are at a historical juncture. We are between the old Westphalian system of international governance through nation-states and a glimmer of a new kind of global federalism. This isn't to suggest that we are trending headlong toward the new and away from the old. Rather, it's only to point out that the rise of multinationals and NGOs and transnational organizations signals movement, or potential movement, of some kind. After all, as Jeremy Waldron points out, the international recognition and system of human rights started off in just such a slow and inchoate way *(Pinzak reads from his computer):* "It consisted largely at the time of what we now call 'soft law'—diplomatic declarations and assurances, a patchwork of treaties and conventions subscribed to by some states and not others, the sentiments and expressions of concern recorded at public meetings, the proceedings of conferences, miscellaneous protocols, the deliverances of tribunals whose status was unclear, and so on."[51]

So there will be activism on all political levels, from local associations and groups of all sorts utilizing dialogical democracy and pushing for it at other venues and other levels. There will also be calls for and movement toward a cosmopolitan federation of like-minded democracies and the increasing recognition of a need for such global venues as the United Nations's Peoples' Assembly.

Emile: We want to take advantage of this time to cultivate cosmopolitan sensibilities. We would like to see all of these institutions be or become forums for democratic dialogue.

Pinzak: Yes, and I'm encouraged by more than simply the presence and growth of multinational and transnational organizations. *(Pinzak here clicks on his keyboard and then scrolls through a file.)* Results from the University of Michigan's *World Values Survey* indicate that people around the globe, with the exception of Africa, are moving into a "postmaterialistic" era of "a rational ideal of a secular community," replete with an emphasis on greater individual self-expression and greater freedom to make significant life choices. This development *(reading from his computer)* "makes people mentally free, motivating them to develop, unfold, and actualize their inner human potentials."[52]

Emile: That is pretty vague. What are our inner human potentials?

Pinzak: They include, Emile, the very kinds of values—cosmopolitan sensibilities and dialectical thinking—that we've been talking about.

Emile: And the development of these values goes along with democratic reform?

Pinzak: Yes, just as the University of Michigan researchers conclude *(Pinzak reads),* "A central component of rising self-expression values, postmaterialistic liberty aspirations, generates a democratic reform potential by driving people to place more emphasis on democracy while making them more critical of the actual democratic performance."[53]

Emile: So people want more democracy, but they will be critical of how it functions and is structured. There is a good chance, given the developments that we have been talking about, that people will want "real" democracy, the kind of direct, deliberative democracy that we have been discussing, if they want to make significant life choices.

Pinzak: When you factor in as well the global issues that face and potentially threaten us all, then the idea of the United Nations as an institution for democratic global governance, perhaps even in the ways we have conceived, becomes more likely.

Emile: In *The Magic of Dialogue,* Daniel Yankelovich asked the question, how do we get millions of persons within single countries and across the globe to participate in democratic dialogues about crucial public issues? He asked this in the context of spurring national (U.S.) debate on Social Security, as one example. Should we have small groups of citizens meeting throughout the country? Should we use the Internet and offer to conduct dialogues through that medium? Should we have experts on the subject use radio and television to explain different aspects of the issue? Should we hold a series of town hall meetings and invite elected and appointed officials to discuss with the public their views on Social Security? (1999, 163).

Pinzak: We should do all of these. Each suggestion offers a different approach that is important to any national, regional, or global dialogue. Small groups provide ample airtime for participants and serve as ways to build trust. The Internet is vital for people who are shut in or cannot make small group meetings. Experts are necessary for providing insights into and reasons for and against public issues—the basis of evidence for deliberations—and there is no reason why their expert testimony can't be delivered via television and Internet, provided there are participants available to cross-examine those experts. Finally, town hall meetings are ways for constituents to hold their representatives and officials accountable. All of these are parts or reflections of our democratic dialogue, and an Integral Democracy will find ways to integrate all dialogical approaches to make sure that they are each and all appropriate, manageable, and thus useful.

Emile: Sheldon Wolin wrote, "Political identity is shaped by the ways a society chooses to generate power and to exercise it."[54] Generating power through democratic dialogue will shape a new political identity, a cosmopolitan identity, depending on how the people exercise that dialogue. That exercise is determined in part by the dialectical procedures used and by the institutions in which they are used. Reaching those institutions will involve a bubbling up from the grassroots of groups and associations and organizations of all sizes and kinds that use dialogical democracy. It will also involve top-down decisions by elites already holding some or much of society's power.

Pinzak: Why would the elites make such a concession?

Emile: Playing devil's advocate, Pinzak? *(Both men smile.)* In part they might do so, because it would be prudent and efficient. In part they might do it because of political results and political pressure arising from the prevalence and outcomes of democratic dialogue at those lower levels.

Pinzak: How it's done is not as significant as that it's done, though we must acknowledge that moving to generate political power through democratic dialogue will most likely involve movement both from the bottom and from the top.

Emile: I am reminded of something that Harold Saunders said about his experiences organizing and running dialogues: "As citizens grapple with their questions and possible approaches together, they begin to change the quality of their relationships. They emerge with a sense of what is tolerable and intolerable for each actor—and why."[55] Dialogues build relationships of power—the capacity to influence the course of events (2005, 86). During South Africa's National Peace Accord, the dialogue between Afrikaners and the African National Congress "created its own public impact" (119-20). Dialogue among all levels of government and by persons outside of government, among themselves and with government officials, is one reason, maybe the principal reason, that South Africa avoided a post-Apartheid bloodbath. Zimbabwe, which lacked such dialogical processes, did not (119-20).

Pinzak: Saunders's observation has a dual significance. The context of the dialogues that Saunders set up and even moderated involved such warring groups as Palestinians and Israelis discussing the political issues separating them. Granted, the mere fact that persons from these groups were willing participants indicates some level of interest, if not cooperation, prior to the dialogue. Nevertheless, the fact that participants on both sides could hear and see the causes and consequences of the opposing side's behaviors evinced a change in attitude, at least temporarily, toward the other side. This changed the relationships of the participants, which could herald or at least make easier through repeated experiences of this kind a more established shift in attitude or sensibility. The direction of that shift is, of course, toward greater openness, which is also the direction toward cosmopolitanism.

So the first significance of Saunders's observation is the change in possibility of an internal shift toward greater openness. The second significance is the possibility through changed relationships of producing a satisfactory outcome, given that participants understood the limits of options and approaches for those on the opposing side and were willing to take these seriously and into account. Thus, there is a greater likelihood of coming to agreement on an outcome, in the sense that the outcome is acceptable to all participants, though no one will necessarily be satisfied with all aspects. At the least the outcome has been developed through dialogue and deliberation.

Emile: So, we return, as always, to where we began: to ways of engendering greater openness toward cosmopolitan sensibilities. But we return not as if we have completed a circle. Rather, we have "circled" back in a spiral, which is emblematic of a return but from a higher level. What we have discovered in our conversation today and last week is that institutionalizing democratic dialogue, the heart and soul of our attempt at generating cosmopolitan sensibilities and identity, will require subsidiarity and an imbrication of different settings. Just as nations have towns and cities, counties and provinces, states and regions, so, too, will the global order be composed of multiple layers of democratic dialogue, political power, and functional sovereignty. Just as nations and the world reflect a diversity of customs, practices, values, standards, and beliefs, so, too, will the global order reflect the diversity of political institutions, from representative to participatory. Just as a foundation of values and practices undergirds each nation, so, too, will such a foundation—of cosmopolitan values and democratic practices—undergird the global order. At every level and in all corners we shall see the operations and effects of democratic dialogue.

Pinzak: Creating identities for modern nation-states was a long, even a prolonged, process. As Habermas pointed out, forming national identities in Europe required specific historical conditions and lasted the entire nineteenth century (2006a, 100). We can foresee, then, that the process of generating cosmopolitan identity will not be short or easy. But national identities are constructs, and thus cosmopolitan identities can be constructed as well. There are steps in that construction. The first step is to understand the nature and scope of democratic dialogue. The second is to institutionalize democratic dialogue within multinational, transnational, and supranational organizations; within nation-states from the top down and bottom up; and through all the levels of civil society, as well as local organizations, grassroots social justice movements, and the spontaneously arising and disappearing pockets of everyday resistance.

In our efforts to construct and educe cosmopolitan identity, we ought not to be stymied by our inability to imagine the most effective political institutions for a democracy, global and otherwise, built on dialectical thinking and dialogue. At the same time, we ought not to be stymied by our inability to predict the different ways that people might "transcend but include" the various perspectives on the hot-button and pressing political issues of today and tomorrow: abortion, gun control, AIDS, global warming, and the rest. We simply start with the premise where you and I, Emile, began: Within the community of humankind how a violation of someone's rights anywhere can be felt everywhere.

At this point, Emile stretches and says, "It is very late, Pinzak. Has our conversation caused you to miss dinner?"

"No, Emile," Pinzak replies as he begins to pack up his computer. "I wasn't planning on eating until later anyway. I have a pick-up basketball game in an hour. I'll eat after that. How about you?"

"Oh, I am not one for dinner. I eat my largest meal at midday."

Pinzak places his computer in his bag and zips it closed. He signals to Bobby for the bill. "Emile, I definitely have enough right now for a book. You've been so generous with your time."

"Well, I trust that it has been edifying for you, as it has been edifying and enjoyable for me. And speaking of edification, I shall write out for you the quotations and references that I have used during the past couple of conversations."

Pinzak says, as Bobby arrives, "You can remember them all?"

"Please, Stan, do not insult me," replies Emile. Pinzak was reaching for his wallet to pay Bobby when Emile called him "Stan." He shoots Emile a look of annoyance. Emile smiles broadly and says, "You have business to conduct with Bobby. So I shall leave you now. Good bye, Pinzak."

Pinzak straightens up. They shake hands as Bobby waits for Pinzak to pay the bill. "And good night to you, Emile."

Notes

1. David Bohm, *On Dialogue* (New York: Routledge, 2004), 32.

2. Kay Pranis, Barry Stuart, and Mark Wedge, *Peacemaking Circles* (St. Paul, Minn.: Living Justice Press, 2003), 7.

3. Pranis et al., *Peacemaking,* 67.

4. Peacemaking Circles also utilize a "talking piece," an object, sometimes symbolic but not necessarily so, that any participant who wishes to speak must hold to do so. No participant physically holding the talking piece can be interrupted. This provides each speaker the time and space to pause and to search for words without needing to rush or fear that he or she will not be able to complete the thought. Participants may also hold the talking piece in silence without needing to speak aloud.

5. According to the experts who have studied Wisdom Circles, listening is perhaps the most important skill. Margaret Wheatley, *Turning to One Another* (San Francisco: Berrett-Koehler Publishers, 2002), says that during the Truth and Reconciliation Commission hearings in South Africa, "Many of those who testified to the atrocities they had endured under apartheid would speak of being healed by their own testimony" (89). Knowing that so many people were listening to them was enough to help them deal with and overcome what they had experienced. If people do not heal, they cannot be whole. One way to help them is not so much to lend a hand, to do something, but to lend an ear.

6. Kay Pranis, *The Little Book of Circle Processes* (Intercourse, Penn.: Good Books, 2005), 13.

7. Katherine Cramer Walsh, *Talking About Race* (Chicago: The University of Chicago Press, 2007), 8.

8. One would find, in looking at the recommendations from various organizations that promote civic or public dialogue (or as we have called it, "democratic dialogue,") steps similar (though not exact) to what I have outlined. For example, in "Tips for Study-Circle Participants" put out by the Study Circle Resource Center (SCRC), the proponents of study circles include the following guidance: "Make sure your remarks are relevant"; "Speak your mind freely, but don't monopolize the conversation"; "Really try to understand what others are saying and respond to their ideas, especially when their thinking is different from yours"; "Be open to changing your mind. This will help you listen to others' views"; "Don't personalize disagreement; try to identify the ideas that are in conflict"; "Search for the common concerns beneath the surface"; and "Help to develop another's ideas; listen carefully and ask clarifying questions." (Listed in Walsh 2007, 42-43.)

For an excellent overview of some of the groups promoting and propagating political or public dialogue, see Walsh 2007, Chapter Three. In footnote 58, 284-85, Walsh lists the ground rules used by a study circle on race relations in Kenosha, Wisconsin, and reiterates the invitation to participants to modify the rules as they see fit. She comments that of the six study circles she observed, five accepted the rules as presented, with the sixth creating their rules from scratch. These ground rules cover the list already presented, though the sponsors added these rules: one person speaks at a time (respect); speak up if a comment offends you (respect and trust); speak briefly (respect, which is a reminder that facilitators are not experts but are present to help the process along); and use "I" statements so that any participant speaks only for herself or himself and not as a representative of any group.

9. Daniel Yankelovich, *The Magic of Dialogue* (New York: Simon & Schuster, 1999), 105.

10. Mary Parker Follett, *Creative Experience* (New York: Peter Smith, 1951/1924), 158-59.

11. D. Carmichael, "Irony: A Developmental and Cognitive Study" (Ph.D. diss., University of California, Berkeley, 1966), 176.

12. Walsh herself acknowledges that it is through these differences, not in spite of them, that intimate connections are made (2007, 251).

13. The term "Legislative Juries" was coined by my former student and current friend Debi Campbell. For her treatment of this topic, see Debra Jane Campbell, "Taking Democracy Seriously: A Proposal for Citizen Lawmaking," (Ph.D. diss., Arizona State University, 2004).

14. For details on citizen juries and how they are used, go to www.jeffersoncenter.org. The Citizens' Jury Process, started in 1974, was developed by Ned Crosby, one of the founders of the Jefferson Center.

15. The results of Kalven and Zeisel's study are found in their book, *The American Jury*; discussed in Campbell 2004. For details of their study and of other studies of jury efficacy, see Campbell, 134-140.

16. Campbell 2004, 136. According to Campbell, "that conclusion remains either unchallenged or affirmed by the few empirical studies done since that time (137).

17. See www.nifi.org/about for these quotations and for more information. According to Harold H. Saunders, in *Politics Is About Relationship* (New York: Palgrave/Macmillan, 2005), 149, 150, there has been a veritable explosion of National Issues Forums held since the 1990s on a variety of topics; for example, causes and consequences of alcoholism and drug addiction, the future of Social Security, U.S. national debt, abortion, collapse of the family, domestic violence, affirmative action, race relations in the United States, the direction of U.S. foreign policy, U.S.-China relations, and democracy in post-communist Russia. The number of forums held is matched by the types of civic organizations holding them; for example, adult literacy programs, high schools and colleges, corrections facilities, academic extension services, 4-H clubs, environmental groups, high school dropouts, residents of housing projects.

18. See www.nifi.org/forums for more information.

19. The Interactivity Foundation, mentioned earlier, also produces printed discussion guides on important social and political topics. But in order to capture greater diversity these reports usually contain six to nine policy possibilities, not three or four possibilities. See www.interactivityfoundation.org.

20. David Mathews, *Politics for People* (Urbana, Ill.: University of Illinois Press, 1994), 44.

21. e-Parliament uses the Internet to link democratically elected Parliamentary and Congressional representatives. That link serves as a means of creating communication among democratic legislators who might otherwise lack a forum for discussing policy ideas on global issues. e-Parliament is, then, a possible precursor to a full-fledged world parliament.

22. North Dakota, for example, requires ten thousand signatures for an initiative and twenty thousand for a state constitutional amendment. Most states in the United States require signatures from roughly eight percent of those who voted in the previous gubernatorial election. For the kind of national or global initiatives that I am proposing, the figures would vary, of course, from state to state and around the globe, depending on the size of the electorate and their territorial distribution. A national initiative in the United States, for example, might require something like three million total signatures divided proportionately among the states, similar to a measure proposed in the 1970s by Senators James Abourzek (Democrat from South Dakota) and James Jones (Democrat from Oklahoma). To avoid undue influence, if not domination, by regional interests, there might be a requirement that a specific number of signatures must come from twenty to twenty-five states. If the number of required signatures is set too high—say, for ten percent of eligible voters—then the danger is that proposing initiatives could be taken out of the hands of "ordinary" citizens and monopolized by the well organized and well financed. See Laura Tallian, *Direct Democracy: A Historical Analysis of the Initiative, Referendum, and Recall Process* (Los Angeles, Calif.: People's Lobby, 1977), 80-82. Similar criteria, with different numbers and percentages, should be proposed for global initiatives as well. Irrespective of the political level of the initiative, the signature-gathering process would be a step after the framing but before the naming.

23. Democratic theorist John Parkinson, in *Deliberating in the Real World* (New York: Oxford University Press, 2006), 171, who himself confesses to being highly critical of citizen-initiated referendums, which we in the United States refer to as initiatives, agrees that the use of three or more options, generated through citizen deliberations, would offset the principal drawbacks that he sees in the process.

24. H. G. Wells quoted in John S. Partington, *Building Cosmopolitanism: The Political Thought of H. G. Wells* (Burlington, Vt.: Ashgate Publishing Co., 2003), 142; emphasis in original.

25. See Partington's quoting of Wells 2003, 143.

26. Thomas Jefferson, *The Writings of Thomas Jefferson,* ed. Albert Ellery Bergh (Washington, D.C.: Thomas Jefferson Memorial Association, 1905), Volume 12, Letter to Governor John Taylor, 26 May 1810, 525-26 and his letter to Joseph C. Cabell, 31 January 1814.

27. Thomas Jefferson, *Writings,* Letter to John Tyler, 26 May 1810, 391.

28. Thomas Jefferson, *Writings,* Volume 14, Letter to Monsieur Dupont de Nemours, 24 April 1816, 487-88.

29. Thomas Jefferson, *Writings,* Letter to Joseph C. Cabell, 2 February 1816, 421. See also Volume 15, Letter to Samuel Kercheval, 12 July 1816, 37.

30. Thomas Jefferson, *Writings,* Volume 14, Letter to Joseph C. Cabell, 2 February 1816, 422-23; Volume 15, Letter to Samuel Kercheval, 12 July 1816, 37-38.

31. 2006, 170. Parkinson refers readers to www.americaspeaks.org as the source of this model. If so, then it appears that the Electronic Town Hall has been superseded by Americaspeaks "21st Century Town Meetings." See their website.

32. For more on such renegade reforms, especially as forms of political resistance, see Shannon Wheatley, "Everyday Cosmopolitical Practices in Contested Spaces: Moving Beyond the State of Cosmopolitanism," Ph.D. Diss., Arizona State University, 2010.

33. Jeffrey Sachs, *Common Wealth* (New York: Penguin Press, 2008), 315.

34. It is beyond the scope of this book, and beyond my abilities and interests, to discuss the manifold organizations now involved in the area of global governance and global democracy. Here are a few sources to explore: 1) The CIVICUS Society, a clearinghouse of sorts for civil society organizations. One of their programs is to promote the "CIVICUS World Assembly." See www.civicus.org. 2) World Social Forum, an annual meeting of social-justice and civil-society activists. See www.wsf2008.net. 3) Human Rights Watch, which itself is a member of the International Freedom of Expression, a global network of NGOs that monitor censorship throughout the world. 4) Amnesty International, dedicated to the eradication of capital punishment, torture, forced disappearances, slavery, inhumane treatment, and political killing, with 1.8 million members worldwide. 5) *Pro Mujer* (pro women), started in Bolivia by two women, provides services for approximately 130,000 of the poorest women in Argentina, Bolivia, Mexico, Nicaragua, and Peru. 6) World Democracy Campaign through the World Citizen Organization (www.worldcitizen.org). 7) World Youth Movement for Democracy, an Internet community started in India by youth and their allies working to support and implement democracy throughout the globe.

35. Jeffrey Sachs claims that there are "millions of NGOs around the world" (2008, 324). Sachs here refers to NGOs working within nations and not those working internationally, a number closer to what I have offered.

36. Andrew Kuper, "Reconstructing Global Governance: Eight Innovations," in *Globalization Theory: Approaches and Controversies,* ed. David Held and Anthony McGrew (Malden, Mass.: Polity Press, 2007), 227.

37. Jurgen Habermas, *Time of Transitions* (Malden, Mass.: Polity Press, 2006a), 26.

38. Another idea is to use Article 22 of the United Nations Charter as a means of bypassing the perilous amendment process. Article 22 empowers the General Assembly to establish subsidiary organs to carry out its functions. The Peoples' Assembly could be one such organ, though how much oversight the General Assembly would necessarily exercise, given the "subsidiary organ" status of the Peoples' Assembly, I do not know. Unquestionably, however, the Peoples' Assembly would be answerable to the General Assembly. Perhaps after some passage of time, and under pressure from Peoples' Assembly representatives and citizens worldwide, the General Assembly could be convinced to vote through Article 108 to amend the Charter and thereby make the Peoples' Assembly an independent chamber. For more on such a gambit see Erskine Childers and Brian Urquhart, *Renewing the United Nations System* (Uppsala, Sweden: Dag Hammarskjold Foundation, 1994).

39. Speaking of representing states and not people, Daniele Archibugi points out that the Security Council, too, represents states. He suggests that the Council be opened up to "global public opinion" by creating a world parliament whose "executive organs" would have access to the Security Council. See Daniele Archibugi, *The Global Commonwealth of Citizens* (Princeton, N.J.: Princeton University Press, 2008), 163-65. Better yet might be to have representatives elected directly to the Security Council by the Peoples' Assembly or a world parliament.

40. My friend Alisa Kessel suggests choosing participants at random from a global census.

41. The actual statement is: "The secretariat building in New York has 38 stories. If you lost ten stories today, it wouldn't make a bit of difference." Bolton made the statement during a panel discussion at the World Federalist Movement office on February 3, 1994.

42. One issue of concern is whether participants speaking arcane dialects would be excluded for that reason. It does not seem unreasonable, on its face, to provide an interpreter for each of the six hundred and stipulate that each interpreter, and thus all interpreters, must speak English, which, as Daniele Archibugi, in *The Global Commonwealth of Citizens* (Princeton, N.J.: Princeton University Press, 2008), 265-66, is the *lingua franca* of the world.

43. The High-Level Panel on Threats, Challenges and Change of the UN proposed two models for reforming the Security Council. The first, Model A, proposed adding six new permanent members but without veto power, plus three new two-year rotating memberships. Each region of the world was guaranteed representation. The second, Model B, proposed having no new permanent seats, but would have eight four-year renewable seats and eleven two-year seats. As Douglas Roche, in *Global Conscience* (Toronto: Novalis Press, 2007), 142, points out, neither model altered the five permanent, veto-holding seats. In the end, neither model garnered enough support to be accepted.

44. I am not here trying to imply any kind of strong definitional significance by using the term "federation." I am certainly not following any of the juridical differences laid out by Hans Kelsen in *General Theory of Law and State* (Cambridge, Mass.: Harvard University Press, 1945) that distinguish *federation* from *confederation.* In the context of my ideas on a federation of liberal democracies, here and to follow, I am much more in the mode of Daniele Archibugi's model of *Cosmopolitan Democracy* (2008, 101-12).

45. Seyla Benhabib, *Another Cosmopolitanism* (New York: Oxford University Press, 2006), 74.

46. See Hobbes's *Leviathan,* ed. Michael Oakeshott (New York: MacMillan Publishing Co., 1962),especially Chapter XVIII.

47. Daniele Archibugi points out that in many cases of humanitarian intervention, "the victims one proposes to save suffer to a greater extent the fallout from the intervention than the perpetrators, as the means used are too clumsy to strike at the criminals without harming their potential victims (*Global Commonwealth,* 2008, 190).

48. The document is known as *The World Summit Outcome Document.* On page 27 of the document the signatories make clear that human rights will be protected, including "the rule of law and democracy," but they stop short of including all human rights. See www.un.org/summit2005/documents.html.

49. Mark Olssen, *Toward a Global Thin Community* (London: Paradigm Publishers, 2009), 199: "When states act against life, they must face the gaze and discipline of others, including scrutiny, humiliation, pressure, and if necessary, of action."

50. In 2000 the European Union agreed to establish a "Rapid Reaction Force" made up of military armament and personnel from member nations, based on each state's military budget and capabilities. Using this "Force" requires unanimous agreement among all member states in the EU.

51. Immanuel Kant, *Kant's Political Writings,* ed. Hans Reiss (Cambridge, U.K.: Cambridge University Press, 1970), 105.

52. Jeremy Waldron, "Cosmopolitan Norms," in *Another Cosmopolitanism,* Seyla Benhabib, 2006, 96.

53. University of Michigan, *World Values Survey,* available at www.worldvaluessurvey.org.

54. All quotations are taken from "A Human Development View on Value Change" by Christian Welzel; available at www.worldvaluessurvey.com.

55. Sheldon Wolin, "The People's Two Bodies," in *democracy* 1, (1981): 10.

56. Harold H. Saunders, *Politics Is About Relationship* (New York: Palgrave/Macmillan, 2005), 22.

Epilogue

God loves from Whole to Parts; but human soul
Must rise from Individual to the Whole . . .
Friend, parent, neighbor first it will embrace
His country next, and next all human race.
—Alexander Pope, "An Essay on Man"

Throughout New England fall had caught a cold. People left fall alone, wrapped in its gray blanket. They postponed pilgrimages to their favorite shrines of color in the face of the steady drip of rain and the coughs of thunder.

When fall dried out and smiled again, Pinzak resumed his ritual of afternoon coffee at Café Pamplona. He was eager to see Emile and to talk with him about cosmopolitan education. In 2003 the Pew Research Center for the People and the Press released the results of a survey on global attitudes. Six in ten people in the United States agreed with the statement that "Our people are not perfect, but our culture is superior to others."[1] Could there be a stronger indication of a need for the development of a cosmopolitan sensibility and the need for cosmopolitan education?

Simply put, what needs doing, it seemed to Pinzak, was to prepare people, especially young people, to participate actively in democratic dialogue(s). Such dialogues could and should be the basis of democracy locally, regionally, nationally, and globally. Preparing for one such forum is preparing for all such forums. Thus, educating people to participate in local or national democratic dialogues simultaneously prepares people for democratic participation on a global level . . . or should. Is it ever too early to begin educating children about the cultures, customs, values, ideas, and beliefs of people from around the world? Would that undercut a youth's callow and tender commitment and even devotion to family, neighborhood, region, and nation? These were the kinds of questions gnawing at Pinzak. He thought—no, he was sure—that Emile would provide some insight.

Right now, however, as he walked to Pamplona, Pinzak was preoccupied not with thinking about cosmopolitan education but with Jean-Henri Dunant. On June 21, 1859, the French Army of Napoleon III, allied with the Sardinian Army, fought against the Austrian Army near the village of Solferino in northern Italy. The purpose was to unify Italy, but there was a side outcome. Jean-Henri Dunant, on a business trip to Italy and witness to the battle, was so horrified by the brutalities that he saw, brutalities committed by both sides, that he decided to form an emergency aid service for wounded soldiers, regardless of for which side they were fighting. Dunant's book, *A Memory of Solferino,*[2] led to the formation of the International Red Cross and was an inspiration for the eventual creation of the Geneva Conventions. Here was an example of transcending boundaries, transcending categories of "friend" and "foe." Here was an example of "being-to-being" connection, which epitomizes and even defines "cosmopolitanism." Dunant exemplified cosmopolitan sensibilities, if not cosmopolitan identity. What ignited inside Dunant that led him to see and to act on this connection? Why Dunant and not others, countless others?

Pinzak was musing about all of this when he arrived at Pamplona. He stood on the sidewalk and surveyed the patio. Before him was their usual table, partly bathed in sunlight, but no Emile. This was the first time in a long time that Pinzak had arrived first. He moved to the table and began to unpack his computer. He set up his computer so that the screen faced the shade and so that his face would capture the sun. Until he had met Emile, Pinzak had not thought much about whether he took his afternoon coffee in the sun or the shade; now that orientation was his first thought. He sat at the table, turned on his computer, and shifted in his chair so that his face fully faced the sun. He closed his eyes and let the warmth wash over him. He was startled when he opened his eyes and saw that Bobby, the waiter was standing in front of his table.

Pinzak looked up at him. "Hello, Bobby."

"Good afternoon, sir. I have something for you, from the gentleman you have been sitting with regularly."

"Oh? He is not here yet?" Pinzak asked as he looked around.

"No, sir. He simple ordered a double cappuccino for you," Bobby said as he placed the drink on the table, "and left you this."

Pinzak barely looked at what Bobby handed him as he asked, "He came and left?"

"Yes, sir. He paid for the cappuccino and asked me to give this to you as well. Oh, yes, and he left a generous tip . . . though not quite as generous as yours from the last time that you . . . ."

But Pinzak was not listening. He was flummoxed. Perplexed. He looked down into his hands and noticed for the first time what Emile had asked Bobby to deliver. It was long and cylindrical, wrapped in powder-blue tissue paper, tied at both ends with dark blue ribbon. It looked like an oversized Christmas cracker. Pinzak glanced up, but Bobby was gone, and Pinzak had not even said "thank you."

Pinzak frowned slightly, looking at Emile's package. He was wondering whether Emile was coming back later, or tomorrow; or, was he ever coming back?

Pinzak unconsciously began unwrapping the tissue paper. Underneath was a cigar tube, a Punch Monarcas tube. "Where in the world," he thought, "did Emile find . . ." Pinzak smiled as he uncapped the tube. He looked at the open end as he placed the cap on the table. The tube was stuffed with cotton. Puzzled, Pinzak pulled the cotton out of the tube, tilted the tube with his left hand and held his right palm under the opening. Out came a clump of paper tightly wrapped as a cylinder and held in place with two rubber bands. Pinzak slid the rubber bands off the cylinder and placed them on the table. The papers—there were several folded sheets—contained the references that Emile had promised at their last meeting. Apparently, thought Pinzak, it had not simply been their last prior meeting, but possibly, their last meeting.

Then Pinzak smiled again and broke out into a laugh. The papers were wrapped not around a cigar, but around a black pen, an exquisite ebony pen with gold trim and finely etched red annular rings. It was Emile's Conklin Endura Long Cap; it certainly could not be anyone else's. Pinzak was stunned. "This pen is a rarity," he thought. "Now he's passing it on to me? From the Prince of Wales, to Emile Whyte, to Stan Pinzak. He hasn't allowed me even to accept the gesture and to refuse the gift. It's too much; this is all too much."

Wrapped tightly around the pen itself was more paper, a small piece, held in place by a tiny rubber band. Pinzak removed the band, placing the pen on the table while continuing to look at it as he unwrapped the paper. It was a short note, in Emile's script and written, no doubt, using the Conklin. The note read: "Alexander the Great once watched bemused as Diogenes sifted through a pile of human bones. 'How strange,' Diogenes finally announced, 'that I cannot make a distinction between those of your father and those of his slaves.'"[3]

Pinzak stared at the words and thought, "Emile brings us, brings me, back to the beginning, to Diogenes as the 'citizen of the world.' And he does it with a vignette that captures the heart of cosmopolitanism." That seemed fitting to Pinzak; indeed, it seemed almost perfect. Pinzak smiled as he recalled the story of when Alexander first met Diogenes. As legend has it—and the entire story might be apocryphal—Diogenes, needing little, lived in a large tub or barrel and spent his days sitting in the sun and spouting fulgent insights to anyone around him. Alexander came to see Diogenes and asked whether there was anything that he could do for him. Diogenes, sitting on the ground, looked up and said, "Yes, you can step aside a little so as not to keep the sunshine from me." So, Emile, like Diogenes, is a "heliotrope." This connection made Pinzak laugh again.

Pinzak stopped laughing as he began thinking of Emile. This man, this stranger, had become over the past several weeks a central figure in Pinzak's life. "What kind of figure?" he thought. "A mentor? A teacher? He was surely both. A father figure?" Pinzak paused and picked up the pen. The thought of Emile as a father figure wounded Pinzak, and he was unsure why. Was it thinking of his father that hurt, or the sense that Emile had abandoned him? Had Emile abandoned him? Pinzak knew some things about Emile, but he did not really know him. They had met quite a few times, but they had not been intimates about their personal lives. Or had they been? Pinzak felt a profound sense of loss. He liked and admired Emile; he trusted him. It was not only the conversation that Pinzak had appreciated; it was Emile's demeanor, his way of being in the world. Now Emile appeared to be gone, and Pinzak had no way of getting in touch with him, no way to thank him for the pen and notes and coffee and insights. He had no way of thanking Emile for the companionship over the past several weeks that more than anything else had made Pinzak's time in Cambridge indelible.

Then Pinzak realized that what he did have from Emile—aside from the notes, the pen, and the coffee—were those insights; Pinzak had their dialogue. That would simply be the backbone of his book—the dialogue between them would BE the book. And when Emile saw the book—as he surely would; he was, after all, a reader—then Emile would know firsthand how grateful Pinzak was for all that Emile had given him. Plus, Emile knew how to contact Pinzak; he knew where Pinzak taught. Pinzak felt immensely relieved. Emile could contact him, and Pinzak felt confident that Emile would do just that.

Pinzak also felt confident that Emile knew him well. He knew that Pinzak was at a point where he could write the dialogue without Emile's continued assistance. Emile had conveyed that message by bringing him full circle through the anecdote about Diogenes. But, Pinzak mused, what about cosmopolitan education? It was the last topic that Pinzak had wanted to discuss with Emile. Was Pinzak ready to take on that subject on his own? He put down the pen and turned to his computer. He hit the space bar and watched the screen come to life. Pinzak took a sip of his cappuccino, opened a new file, and began to type:

Me: Emile, if we're promoting cosmopolitan politics and democratic dialogue, do you think that there is a concurrent need for cosmopolitan education for the young? Must persons be educated to perform their roles in democratic dialogues? *(Pinzak stopped typing and read over what he had written. "These are two different questions," he thought. "Well, that's a comment that Emile would make.")*

Emile: You have raised two different questions, Pinzak, or so it seems to me. One is about preparing students for cosmopolitan politics, a politics yet to come. The other is about preparing them for democratic dialogues, some forms of which are already extant.[4] Thus, democratic dialogues do not necessarily comprise cosmopolitan politics. The two are right now, and can be for the foreseeable future, separate.

Let me begin to answer your questions by making obvious what has been evident but unstated in our conversations. Cosmopolites *(Pinzak here uses*

Emile's preferred term and not the more common "cosmopolitans") are made, not born. As such, education must be a good idea, since we want to use the best means possible in creating cosmopolites and not just hope that people simply stumble toward cosmopolitanism. The best means for creating cosmopolites is through the use of democratic dialogues and all the steps that constitute them. Those steps, given all that we said about opening one's identity to others and to others' perspectives, can certainly point the way, if not lead, toward cosmopolitanism.

Me: But do we leave it there, pointing the way and not assuring the way?

Emile: That is the issue, then, about instituting cosmopolitan education. *(Pinzak noticed as he wrote that he avoided the use of contractions in Emile's imagined responses. He had not thought about that before, but, after a brief recollection, he realized that he had never heard Emile contract verbs. So, in creating Emile's comments, Pinzak would follow that practice.)* So, first, we must consider what we mean by "cosmopolitanism."

Me: Haven't we already determined that? Hasn't cosmopolitanism been the ground and focus of all of our conversations?" *("Am I writing myself into a box," Pinzak wondered, "simply repeating here what I'll write about at the beginning of the dialogue?" He paused for a moment, and then began typing again.)*

Emile: It has, but not in the context of education. Historically, education for global citizenship has often passed as cosmopolitanism. That kind of cosmopolitan education is not a new idea. The Council for Education in World Citizenship in the United Kingdom, for example, has been using this kind of education, or trying to do so, since 1939.

One reason that world citizenship has been considered a brand of cosmopolitan education is that cosmopolitanism was considered to be a knowledge of, if not an appreciation for, the customs, standards, ideas, and cultures of people around the world. In that regard, look at the model of "cosmopolitan" education laid out by H. G. Wells in an address in 1937 to the Educational Science Section of the British Association for the Advancement of Science. *(Pinzak here opens the file with his notes on this topic and begins typing again.)* In that address, "The Informative Content of Education," Wells outlined an educational curriculum that was presented as the core of the studies for students during their school years, but was also intended to serve as a program for lifelong learning. Wells thought, as we do, that cosmopolites had to be created. Just as nationalism is not a natural outgrowth of human maturation, neither is a cosmopolitan outlook. Devotion to either, Wells believed, had to be inculcated. British education helped establish the nationalist outlook, but that education virtually ignored the cosmopolitan outlook. Without a cosmopolitan outlook, there would be no popular support for global governance and thus no peace. Without receiving an adequate cosmopolitan education, the population would be unable to operate a global system. *(Here Pinzak cuts and pastes the following from one of his files:)* "It is clear that if a world-league is to be living and enduring," wrote Wells, "the idea of it, and the need and righteousness of its service, must be taught by every educational system in the world."[5]

Me: So one form of cosmopolitan education is to teach the young about the practices and beliefs and ways of life of those living around the globe. *("This was, of course, a variation of the very question that I was thinking about on my way here earlier this afternoon," Pinzak thought as he typed.)*

Emile: Yes, and note that Wells emphasized in his address, as the title shows, the informational content of his educational plan. It was, for Wells, the content that made the education cosmopolitan. We certainly do not discount the content.

Yet, our emphasis on raising cosmopolites has been in pursuit of cosmopolitan identity and sensibilities and the dialogical structures that can engender them. In that context cosmopolitanism is about the connections felt between and among human beings and not simply learning about foreign customs and ways of life. These feelings exist independent of bonds of community or citizenship. They are feelings stripped of affiliations and particularities. They exist as one human being's feelings for another simply because of their shared humanity.[6]

Me: So a cosmopolitan education from our perspective would have two parts: one part would consist of the content and the other, the process of democratic dialogue. We need the practice that comes from participation in dialogic democratic procedures, but we also need knowledge that informs that participation. This is also the mandate of our schools. Students need to learn about the world, about different ways of life, different value systems and worldviews, different ways of structuring social, political, economic, moral, and cultural life.

Emile: That is correct, and in terms of the process, well, practicing that process would be part of the basis of cosmopolitan education as well as a mandate for our schools. At the very least, this would be an education in deliberation and democratic dialogue. This education would assure that future participants had the skills to participate and that they would be familiar, if not comfortable, with the dialogical requirements and procedures. *(Pinzak paused, picked up his coffee, and sat back in his chair. He sipped casually as he read the screen. "Is my characterization too stilted for Emile? Am I capturing his phrasing?" He leaned forward, put down his cup, and resumed typing.)*

Me: There is another benefit to our cosmopolitan education and a vital one. Students who have experience in democratic dialogue will want, I think, to build on that experience and continue that practice. In other words, as they grow older and move out into the world, they'll apply pressure in whatever groups and organizations they are members of to institute democratic dialogue. As we've discussed before, this kind of pressure, from the bottom up, is the best way, and perhaps the only way, to move societies toward democratic dialogue. Examples in local politics like Porto Alegre and demands from civil-society networks, the private sector, and the grassroots might push the power brokers at the top to transform the decision-making apparatuses of national, regional and even global political structures. *(Pinzak stopped typing, took three sips of coffee, replaced*

the cup, and read over what he had written. After another minute's pause and a
quick scan around the patio, he resumed.)

Me: If we combine practicing democratic dialogue with "cosmopolitan"
content, then what would cosmopolitan education consist of, in your estimation?

Emile: Well, it should resonate *("Would Emile use that word?" Pinzak*
wondered) with what we have described as dialectical thinking and the other
ingredients *("Now, that is an Emile word," he thought with a smile)* essential to
democratic dialogue. It ought to be built of or around five mental capacities: the
ability to introspect; the ability to assess evidence and to compare and contrast
using that evidence; the ability to see, hear, and even appreciate multiple perspectives; the ability to see that worldviews are interpretive; the ability to understand and respect, though perhaps not yet embrace, ambiguity; and, finally, the
ability to push for breakthroughs or to find unity or ways to transcend conflicting positions.

Me: Such skills cannot possibly be attained by children of all ages.

Emile: Of course not. Schools must teach age-appropriate skills, based
largely on studies showing us children's developmental levels at each grade. We
ought not to transform identities before those identities have even been formed
and established. Remember, dialectical thinking is characteristic of mature
adults. We cannot expect and do not want the kinds of open dialogue in elementary and secondary schools that we have described as democratic dialogue for
adults. Nevertheless, schoolchildren are certainly ready for different kinds of
democratic dialogues within their classrooms and within their schools.[7]

Me: So you envision cosmopolitan education offered in different forms at
every grade level.

Emile: Yes, and if we are to offer true cosmopolitan education, then our
schools cannot simply serve as sites for citizenship preparation. Schools cannot
orient our future democratic participants to confront local and national problems
only. Students must be taught to expand their horizons to include global issues
and problems as well.

Me: And as we've been pointing out in our conversations, we can't pretend
that those orientations will not sometimes conflict. Such conflict itself would be
an educational opportunity for seeing various perspectives on these issues and
for trying to reconcile, or transcend (and thus integrate) those perspectives,
though we ought not to expect young students necessarily to do this often or
well. *(Here Pinzak stops typing and clicks on a couple of icons to open files on*
his computer screen.)

Emile: Still, keep in mind Ms. Gearhy's tenth-grade World History class.
Students may be expected to do a lot with the five mental capacities that I just
mentioned, as her class shows. Unfortunately, what her class achieved seems
anomalous, given the curricula in most schools today. Smith and Fairman point
out, citing numerous studies, that social studies curricula offer minimal focus, at
best, on dialogue or discussion skills on controversial topics.[8] "Most high school
social studies classes do not teach students to analyze multiple sources of conflict or to see conflict from multiple perspectives . . . or ask students to examine

alternative responses and evaluate their potential costs and benefits" (41-42). Failing to provide such a focus means that students do not have opportunities, or enough opportunities, to put themselves in the positions of others who hold perspectives different from their own. That is a push for understanding and honoring the perspectives of others, but it does not have to go so far as to undermine the formation of students' identities.

Me: Do you think that cosmopolitan education, with an emphasis on critical thinking and dialogue, would undercut education for citizenship? Would it undercut any civic focus on inculcating love of country? Is that your thought or worry?

Emile: No, because, as we said earlier, cosmopolitan education, an education to prepare novice participants for dialogical procedures, is not significantly different from democratic education. The active part of democratic citizenship is participation. Because we envision multiple levels of democratic dialogue going on all the time, from local to national to global levels, then preparing persons for participation in any one of them also prepares them for participation at every other level. That does not undercut one's sense of and pride in citizenship.

Me: I agree with that. It is difficult to imagine skepticism about, or hostility toward, the idea of asking young students to practice age-appropriate democratic dialogue and decision-making. But asking them to spend time studying world cultures and world events is a different matter. Some will see this either as taking time away from studying one's own country or as some insidious form of political indoctrination against the actions and values of one's country.

Emile: Philosopher of education Eamonn Callan agrees with that perspective. He wants to avoid a civic education, and the pursuit of justice that underlies it *(Pinzak cuts and pastes the quotations from his files)* "that gives pride of place to a cosmopolitan sensibility at the cost of particularistic affiliations."[9] In Callan's view, our civic education should be constructed ideally around the concept of "liberal patriotism." Although liberal patriotism is an "identification with a particular, historically located project of political self-rule"—that is, American liberal democracy—it nevertheless also "entails a sense of responsibility to outsiders and insiders alike" (198).

Me: Of course, the danger here is that a liberal patriot may well feel a sense of obligation or responsibility to outsiders *only* when her country is committing the injustice.

Emile: Callan points out exactly that idea. He writes that it is "precisely the thought that 'we Americans' have done these terrible things that gave impetus [during the Vietnam War] to their horror and rage" (198). This thought is to be contrasted with our feelings and sense of responsibility when, as Callan suggests, Soviet tanks rolled through Prague. Because, according to Callan, our political-moral identity was not implicated in the Soviet action, we somehow do not have to have a similar sense of horror and rage.

Me: Perhaps we do not have to, but should we? Nussbaum's point is that we certainly should. So what do we do? Where do you think that sentiments like

Callan's leave us? *(Pinzak pauses again and leans back in his chair. He lets out a sigh and again scans the patio. He picks up the notes that Emile had left for him. Emile's script, as before, is elegant. Pinzak notices that there are no mistakes, no cross-outs, no blots of ink. The lines are written straight across the page, not a dip or slant among them. He wonders, but without amazement, whether writing out these references was as effortless for Emile as its appearance was graceful. Putting down the notes and leaning forward, Pinzak places his fingers on the keyboard, hesitates, and then begins to type.)*

Emile: Callan provides us with two possibilities. First, should we "cultivate a civic identity in which patriotic affinities are muted or disappear altogether and a cosmopolitan ideal of 'world citizenship' is brought" to the forefront? Or, second, should we cultivate a kind of patriotism "in which identification with a particular project of democratic self-rule is yet attuned to the claims of justice that both civic outsiders and insiders" will make (198)?

Me: It would seem that Nussbaum would favor the first, while Callan would favor the second.

Emile: Perhaps these two are not the only options. Recall that in her metaphor of concentric identity circles, Martha Nussbaum argues that we ought to try to bring the outer circles of our relationships, the circle of all humanity, closer to the center, to our selves.[10] By doing so, we do not push away from our identities those particular relationships of significance to us. Instead, we need to take into consideration the effects that our moral and political decisions have on all of humanity. If our civic education helps us extend our sympathies, as Hume proposed, and if we could do so without muting or eliminating our local and national affinities, then could Nussbaum and Callan agree on such a civic education?

Additionally, we need to consider that patriotism itself seems to have its own version of concentric circles. For example, Theodore Roosevelt warned against "that overexaltation of the little community at the expense of the great nation."[11] Here is a nod toward Roosevelt's "New Nationalism" as opposed to what he called "the patriotism of the village." If we move from the village to the nation, then we move also, as we have been arguing, from the nation to the world. As Alexander Pope wrote in "An Essay on Man": "God loves from Whole to Parts; but human soul/Must rise from Individual to the Whole/ . . . Friend, parent, neighbor first it will embrace/His country next, and next all human race."

Me: No, civic education must consist exclusively either of world citizenship—a term that implies, at the least, a world state—or of love of one's community and a patriotic affiliation with one's country. There ought to be a composite that will work here. At the same time, a proper civic education should convey and instill in the young a love of one's nation and its ideals, to go along with knowledge about that country's history. Such knowledge ought to include how and when those ideals have been instantiated, vitiated, abandoned, or ignored.

Emile: The educational system in the United States, for example, requires knowledge about the country's history, but that history is not studied often enough, as Smith and Fairman point out, in a context of critical thinking. So it is difficult to get students thinking in terms of your last point. Additionally, missing almost totally from the curriculum is any focus on world history and the history of other countries, critically examined or not.

Me: What if we required every high school student to select one foreign country to focus on intensively during her four years of high school? Could that be construed as brainwashing or manipulation? No one would be telling the student what to think about that country; instead, the student would be given guidance on how to study the country. For example, in the first year, the student might study the country's history. In the second the student could concentrate on its political and economic systems; in the third, its cultural traditions; and in his fourth year, he could do a research project on some aspect(s) of that country. Such a study would certainly broaden his horizons.

Emile: And there would be knowledge and research overlap among students in the class studying other countries, as they share throughout the four years lessons, facts, and stories about their respective countries.

Me: The idea is not to try to instill in students a love of some kind of amorphous global community. It is, instead, to teach students how to study a topic—another country—and to respect another country, its history and development, its successes and failures, its rise and fall (if appropriate), and its people and their struggles and triumphs.

Emile: Perhaps the schools could create within them, rather than among them as they do now, a model of the United Nations. In other words, as much as possible, each member country of the UN would be represented. Because students in different grades and even in the same grades would be studying the same countries, they would form UN teams, just as the UN has now. And the younger students would be under the tutelage of the older students studying the same countries. In this way the older students would mentor the younger ones. Such interaction in itself would be educative, in that older students would learn to listen to and to be patient with younger ones.

Me: The model UN could serve as a framework for international competition and cooperation, as students would role-play the parts of ambassadors, diplomats, and heads of state.[12] At the same time, it could be used as a model for addressing global issues that require cooperation. Through operating within that framework, students would practice their dialogical skills and would have first-hand experience dealing with those who hold divergent views on these global issues.

Emile: Of vital importance would be ensuring that the skills developed in and through a cosmopolitan curriculum would be used outside of the classroom as well and, indeed, outside of the school. Thus, the neighborhoods in which those schools would exist, the communities that would send children to those schools, and the counties, states, and nations that would support such education would be settings for student involvement in democratic dialogue and conflict resolution. The sites of participation and action must therefore be expanded well beyond the classroom.

Pinzak paused again and flopped back against his seat. He was convinced, having engaged in this brief writing exercise, that he could, indeed, write a dialogue between himself and Emile, though he would need to do more research, certainly, on cosmopolitan education. He liked the idea of writing a dialogue and describing Emile. He didn't like the idea, however, of referring to himself as *"Me."* He thought to himself: "I sat back in my chair and sipped my coffee." Writing in the first person seemed pretentious, styled, even weird. Maybe he could refer to himself in the third person, as *"Pinzak,"* as if he were an impartial observer. Would that be even weirder? But how could he, Pinzak, be the author of a book in which he referred to himself in the third person, as if he were someone else? "Perhaps someone else should write this book," he mused. "It would be simpler," he thought, "if someone else could simply write the dialogue as Emile and I spoke." But there was no Emile; anyway, there was no Emile available now. Without Emile, only Pinzak could reconstruct the conversations. "So," he thought, "how about if I write the book as an impartial observer and ascribe the writing to someone else?" He thought immediately of his best friend among political theorists—Jack Crittenden. "He'd find the idea entertaining," mused Pinzak, "and, Lord knows, he could use another publication."

Pinzak laughed at the idea. As he did so, his glance fell on the pen. He picked it up with his right hand and felt a pang of sadness. He adored Emile. Now, and suddenly, he was gone. Pinzak rolled the pen between his palms. Writing about cosmopolitan education had made him think of Martha Nussbaum and her concentric circles of identity. That and Diogenes brought up memories of their first conversations. "Without Emile," Pinzak thought, "I would never have thought about cosmopolitan identity as a focus, and I would never have learned about dialectical thinking, dialogue, and the rest. I owe him a lot." Pinzak removed the cap from the pen and scribbled a sentence on the back of the note: "Cosmopolitan right shall be limited to universal hospitality." The quotation, Pinzak knew, was from Kant's "Third Definitive Article for Perpetual Peace."[13] Pinzak had not realized that he knew the quotation. He pondered that and thought: "Kant sees hospitality as a right of the stranger, and because every stranger has that right, it must be enforced by law. Is it really enforceable by law, if persons don't feel hospitable to strangers?"

Then, without thinking, Pinzak wrote the name *"Samaritan"* and stared at it. Then he doodled *"Good Samaritan,"* referring to the parable told by Jesus (Luke 10:29-37). And he began writing:

A lawyer—a Biblical scholar of Mosaic law, really—asks Jesus, "Who is my neighbor?" The question seems straightforward and easy enough to answer. But Jesus tells a story: A "certain man" goes to Jericho and is set upon by a band of thieves who steal his belongings, strip him naked, and beat him senseless. So the man, unidentified and, because naked and speechless, unidentifi-able, lies unconscious by the road. By chance "a certain priest" happens by, sees the man, crosses the road, and keeps moving. The priest is undoubtedly a rabbi. To aid the man if the man were a non-Jew would be to risk defilement; the priest does not check to ascertain whether the injured man is a non-Jew, but keeps moving by.

Next comes "a Levite." Levites, from the Hebrew tribe of Levi, helped the rabbis, the descendants of Aaron, in the temples. Presumably also worried about the risk of defilement, the Levite, too, crosses the road and keeps walking.

Then comes a Samaritan. Samaritans and Jews each believe the other to be vile, corrupt, and venal. Regardless, this Samaritan does not know whether the injured man is a Jew or not. He does not know where the man is from. It is a good bet, however, that this man is not his neighbor. Nevertheless, when the Samaritan sees the injured man, he feels compassion, caring not who the man might be. The Samaritan goes to the man, binds his wounds, places him on his own beast, and leads the man to an inn. The next day, the Samaritan gives money to the innkeeper, saying something like, "Take care of this stranger and, when I return, if I owe you more money for what it cost to care for him, I shall repay you."

At this point, Jesus turns to the lawyer and asks, "Now, which of the three is neighbor unto him that fell?"

The answer, of course, is all three. Jesus is pointing out that a neighbor cannot be defined by propinquity of place or relation. A neighbor is *anyone* who needs helps or assistance, regardless of status or circumstance. That Samaritan did not know the man lying on the road, other than to recognize him as a fellow being in need of aid. His "love" for this neighbor was not born of similarity of language, religion, history, proximity, or any other kind of relationship. It was born only of fellow feeling, born solely from compassion.

So do we owe "hospitality" or aid to anyone and everyone in need? We do, and the basis of that hospitality is not legality, but compassion. The basis is cosmopolitan compassion—the being-to-being connection. But how could the priest and the Levite, both ostensibly compassionate men, not provide aid? They did not feel the need to do so; their compassion could not override their concerns about ritual purity or whatever else stopped them from helping. The beginning and the end of cosmopolitanism is that everyone matters; how another person's life goes, and how the person says his life is going or how she wants it to go, matters to me.

Pinzak put down the pen, the beautiful ebony pen, and turned off his computer. "I was that man in need of aid; I was Emile's neighbor." Pinzak then wondered, as he packed his computer and Emile's reference notes into his bag, whether that "certain man" on his way to Jericho had felt as Pinzak was feeling right now. Just as the "certain man" had been given so much by the Samaritan, so Pinzak had been given so much by Emile. Emile had presented to Pinzak an approach to understanding cosmopolitanism that Pinzak could not have imagined, let alone come to, on his own.

For the Greeks, the foundation of the *polis* was *paideia,* the lifelong educational network that inculcated and reinforced Greek values and culture. In the modern era the foundation of the nation-state is the social contract. "What," Pinzak thought, "might be the foundation of an incipient global community? Could it be democratic dialogue? Isn't that a foundation for and a method of creating planetary consciousness and cosmopolitan identity that reflect a global conscience? How else might we embrace ambiguity, honor difference, and yet recognize and call forth enough commonality to pursue democratically constructed global policies and actions that reflect the will and consent of the people?"

Emile had opened up Pinzak to a world of psychological and political possibilities, or, rather, he had opened up Pinzak to the psychological and political possibilities for the world. Now there seemed no way to repay Emile for such a gift. Pinzak knew that aid had been given—to him—and, as the Samaritan had, Emile had gone away. Perhaps for good. Pinzak zipped his bag closed and then picked up the pen. Holding it in his left palm, he stared down at it, running the fingers of his right hand the length of the pen before placing it in the inside pocket of his jacket. He stood up, reached into his back pocket for his wallet, and placed a sizeable tip on the table for Bobby. He replaced his wallet, slipped his bag onto his right shoulder, and thought about payment and repayment. Could he talk to his students and colleagues, let alone strangers, as Emile had talked to him? Could he himself begin the process, the dialogical and introspective process, of opening his heart and mind to others to forge a cosmopolitan identity, an identity as wide as the world?

Notes

1. Nelson Noddings, ed., *Educating Citizens for Global Awareness* (New York: Teachers College Press, 2005), xiii.

2. Jean-Henri Dunant, *A Memory of Solferino* (Geneva: International Committee of the Red Cross, 1986).

3. Cited by David Markson, *The Last Novel* (Berkeley, Calif.: Shoemaker & Hoard (now Counterpoint Books, 2007), 138.

4. There are numerous organizations currently trying to engage persons in the United States and around the globe in different forms of dialogue on important social and political issues. There are far too many to list here, and so the following is a partial list, perhaps not even a representative list:

Conversation Café: www.conversationcafe.org

World Café: www.theworldcafe.org

National Issues Forum: www.nifi.org

Wisdom Councils: www.wisedemocracy.org

Citizen Juries—Jefferson Center: www.jefferson-center.org

Public Dialogue-Public Conversations Project: www.publicconversations.org

America Speaks: www.americaspeaks.org

International Institute for Sustained Dialogue: www.sustaineddialogue.org

National Coalition for Dialogue and Deliberation: www.thataway.org.

Study Circles: www.everydaydemocracy.org

Interactivity Foundation: www.interactivityfoundation.org.

5. John S. Partington, *Building Cosmopolitanism: The Political Thought of H. G. Wells* (Burlington, Vt.: Ashgate Publishing Co., 2003), 81.

6. As I stated in an earlier Encounter, being-to-being connection does not preclude such connections between humans and animals, though that subject is well beyond the scope of this work. An opening for such connection is made through Derrida's concept of singularity, which he describes as a bond related to the "incalculable singularity of every-one, before any 'subject' . . . beyond all citizenship, beyond every 'state,' every 'people,' indeed even beyond the current state of the definition of a living being as a living 'hu-man' being." In *Philosophy in a Time of Terror: Dialogues with Jurgen Habermas and Jacques Derrida*, ed. Giovanna Borradori (Chicago: University of Chicago Press, 2003), 120.

7. For a detailed discussion of age-appropriate participation in democratic dialogue, see Crittenden 2002, especially "Democratic Schools," 179-92.

8. Stacie Nicole Smith and David Fairman, "The Integration of Conflict Resolution into the High School Curriculum" in *Educating Citizens for Global Awareness*, ed. Nel Noddings (New York: Teachers College Press, 2005), 46.

9. Eamonn Callan, "A Note on Patriotism and Utopianism," in *Studies in Philosophy and Education* 18 (1999): 197.

10. Martha C. Nussbaum, "Cosmopolitanism and Patriotism," in *For Love of Country*, ed. J. Cohen (Boston: Beacon Press, 1996), 9.

11. Theodore Roosevelt, "Religion and the Public Schools," *Collected Works*, 15; in Stephen Macedo, *Diversity and Distrust* (Cambridge, Mass.: Harvard University Press, 2003), 93.

12. One of the key learning methods advocated by the Consensus Building Institute, a non-profit organization dedicated to improving resolution practices in public disputes, is role-playing. By taking on the perspectives and background of individuals and groups in conflict situations, students have an opportunity "to internalize concepts, principles, and ideas through lived experience and reflection, leading to changes in behaviors and actions." Smith and Fairman add: "In a study of our work with Israeli and Palestinian schools, Haifa University researchers found that after participating in *Workable Peace* [CBI's curriculum on conflict assessment, management, and resolution on contemporary and historical conflicts] role-playing on other historical conflicts, students demonstrated substantial changes in their ability to see the Israeli-Palestinian conflict from the point of view of the other side" (50). Students taking the pretest before the exercise could write little or nothing on the perspective of the other side. "At posttest, virtually all of the Workable Peace students were able to write with understanding and empathy from the other group's perspective" (50).

Another benefit of role-playing, according to Smith and Fairman, is that students learn to invent new options and to find acceptable trade-offs to reach agreement. Because of their experience seeing issues from the other's side, students become comfortable and accomplished at raising options that address the needs and interests of all parties. Creating options becomes collaborative and not adversarial (51). Indeed, brainstorming about options and possible outcomes is an excellent prelude to reaching agreement.

13. Immanuel Kant, *Kant's Political Writings*, ed. Hans Reiss. Cambridge, U.K.: Cambridge University Press, 1970).

Bibliography

Ackerman, Bruce. "Rooted Cosmopolitanism." In *Ethics* 104 (April 1994): 517-535.

Alexander, Charles N., and Ellen J. Langer, eds. *Higher Stages of Human Development.* New York: Oxford University Press, 1990.

————, J. L. Davies, C. A. Dixon, M. C. Dillbeck, S. M. Druker, R. M. Oetzel, J. M. Muehlman, and D.W. Orme-Johnson. "Growth of Higher Stages of Conciousness.: In *Higher Stages of Human Development,* eds. Charles N. Alexander and Ellen J. Langer. New York: Oxford University Press, 1990.

Alinsky, Saul. *Reveille for Radicals.* New York: Random House, 1946.

Anderson, Benedict. *Imagined Communities.* London: Verso, 1991.

Andresen, Jensine. "Meditation Meets Behavioral Medicine." In *Journal of Consciousness Studies* 7, nos. 11-12 (2000): 17-73.

Appiah, Kwame Anthony. *Cosmopolitanism: Ethics in a World of Strangers.* New York: W. W. Norton & Company, 2006.

Archibugi, Daniele. *The Global Commonwealth of Citizens.* Princeton, N.J.: Princeton University Press, 2008.

————, and David Held. *Cosmopolitan Democracy.* Cambridge, U.K.: Polity Press, 1995.

Arendt, Hannah. *Between Past and Future.* New York: Viking Press, 1968.

————. *Men in Dark Times.* London: Jonathan Cape, 1970.

Aristotle. *On Rhetoric.* Trans. George A. Kennedy. New York: Oxford University Press, 1991.

————. *The Nichomachean Ethics.* Trans. David Ross. Revised J. L. Ackrill and J. O. Urmson. New York: Oxford University Press, 1998.

Aurelius, Marcus. *Meditations.* London: Penguin Classics, 2006.

Ayer, A. J. *Language, Truth and Logic.* New York: Dover, 1952.

Bakke, Dennis W. *Joy at Work.* Seattle, Wash.: PVG, 2006.

Baldwin, James Mark. *The Individual and Society.* Boston, Mass.: R. G. Badger, 1911.

Barber, Benjamin. *Strong Democracy.* Berkeley, Calif.: University of California Press, 1984.

Barry, Brian. "Statism and Nationalism: A Cosmopolitan Critique." Pp. 12-66 in *NOMOS 61: Global Justice,* eds. Ian Shapiro and Lea Brilmayer. New York: New York University Press, 1999.

Basseches, Michael. *Dialectical Thinking and Adult Development.* Norwood, N.J.: Ablex, 1984.

Beauregard, Mario, and Denyse O'Leary. *The Spiritual Brain.* New York: Harper Collins, 2007.

Beck, Don Edward, and Christopher C. Cowan. *Spiral Dynamics.* Malden, Mass.: Blackwell Publishers, 1996.

Beck, Ulrich. *Cosmopolitan Vision.* Malden, Mass.: Polity Press, 2006.

Beitz, Charles. *Political Theory and International Relations.* Princeton, N J.: Princeton University Press, 1999.

Benack, Suzanne, and Michael A. Basseches. "Dialectical Thinking and Relativistic Epistemology." In *Adult Development, Volume 1: Comparisons and Applications of Developmental Models,* eds. Michael L. Commons et al. New York: Praeger, 1989.

Benhabib, Seyla. *The Claims of Culture: Equality and Diversity in the Global Era.* Princeton, N.J.: Princeton University Press, 2002.

———. *Another Cosmopolitanism.* New York: Oxford University Press, 2006.

Benson, Herbert. *The Relaxation Response.* New York: Harper Torch, 1976, 2000.

Berger, P. L., and T. Luckmann. *The Social Construction of Reality.* New York: Doubleday, 1967.

Bernstein, Richard. *Beyond Objectivism and Relativism.* Philadelphia, Penn.: University of Pennsylvania Press, 1983.

Berthoff, Ann E. *The Making of Meaning.* Montclair, N.J.: Boynton/Cook, 1981.

Biaocchi, Gianpaolo. "Participation, Activism, and Politics: the Porto Alegre Experiment and Deliberative Democratic Theory." In *Politics and Society* 29 (2001): 29, 43-72.

Bickford, Susan. *The Dissonance of Democracy.* Ithaca, N.Y.: Cornell University Press, 1996.

Blanchard-Fields, Fredda. "Postformal Reasoning in a Socioemotional Context." In *Adult Development, Volume 1: Comparisons and Applications of Developmental Models,* eds. Michael L. Commons et al. New York: Praeger, 1989.

Bohm, David. *Unfolding Meaning.* Mickleton, U. K.: Foundation House Publications, 1985.

———. *On Dialogue.* New York: Routledge, 2004.

Bohman, James, and William Rehg, eds. *Deliberative Democracy.* Cambridge, Mass.: MIT Press, 1997.

Borradori, Giovanna. *Philosophy in a Time of Terror: Dialogues with Jurgen Habermas and Jacques Derrida.* Chicago: The University of Chicago Press, 2003.

Boulding, Kenneth. *The Meaning of the Twentieth Century.* New York: Harper Collins, 1988.

Breckenridge, Carol A., Sheldon Pollock, Homi K. Bhabha, and Dipesh Chakra Barty, eds. *Cosmopolitanism.* Durham, N.C.: Duke University Press, 2002.

Brock, Gillian, and Harry Brighouse, eds. *The Political Philosophy of Cosmopolitanism.* New York: Cambridge University Press, 2005.

Button, Mark, and Kevin Mattson. "Deliberative Democracy in Practice: Challenges and Prospects for Civic Deliberation." In *Polity* 31, no. 4 (1999): 609-37.

Byatt, A. S. "What Is a European?" In *New York Times Magazine,* 13 October 2002.

Callan, Eamonn. "A Note on Patriotism and Utopianism." In *Studies in Philosophy and Education* 18 (1999): 197-201.

Cameron, Keith, ed. *National Identity.* Exeter, U.K.: Intellect Books, 1999.

Campbell, Debra Jane. "Taking Democracy Seriously: A Proposal for Citizen Lawmaking." Ph. D. dissertation, Arizona State University, 2004.

Carmichael, D. "Irony: A Developmental and Cognitive Study." Ph. D. dissertation, University of California, Berkeley, 1966.

Chickering, A. Lawrence, and James S. Turner. *Voice of the People: The Transpartisan Imperative in American Life.* Goleta, Calif.: da Vinci Press, 2008.

Childers, Erskine, and Brian Urquhart. *Renewing the United Nations System.* Uppsala, Sweden: Dag Hammarskjold Foundation, 1994.

Cochrane, Molly. "A Democratic Critique of Cosmopolitan Democracy: Pragmatism from the Bottom-Up." *European Journal of International Relations* 8, No. 4 (2002): 517-48.

Cohen, Joshua, ed. *For Love of Country?* Boston, Mass.: Beacon Press, 1996.

———. "Procedure and Substance in Deliberative Democracy." Pp. 407-37 in *Deliberative Democracy,* eds. James Bohman and William Rehg. Cambridge, Mass.: MIT Press, 1997.

———. "Deliberation and Democratic Legitimacy." Pp. 17-34 in *The Good Polity,* eds. Alan Hamlin and Philip Petit. Oxford: Blackwell, 1989.

Commons, Michael L., Francis A. Richards, and Cheryl Armon, eds. *Beyond Formal Operations.* New York: Praeger, 1984.

———, Jan D. Sinnott, Francis A. Richards, and Cheryl Armon, eds. *Adult Development, Volume 1: Comparisons and Applications of Developmental Models.* New York: Praeger, 1989a.

———, Cheryl Armon, Lawrence Kohlberg, Francis A. Richards, Tina A. Grotzer, Jan D. Sinnott, eds. *Adult Development, Volume 2: Models and Methods in the Study of Adolescent and Adult Thought.* New York: Praeger, 1989b.

Cook-Greuter, Susanne R. "Maps for Living: Ego-Development Stages from Symbiosis to Conscious Universal Embeddedness." In Commons, Michael L., et al., eds. *Adult Development, Volume 2: Models and Methods in the Study of Adolescent and Adult Thought.* New York: Praeger, 1989.

———. "Postautonomous Ego Development: A Study of Its Nature and Measurement." Ph.D. dissertation, Harvard University, 1999.

Crick, Bernard. *Essays on Citizenship.* London: Continuum, 2000.

Crittenden, Jack. "Veneration of Community." In *Communal Societies* 9 (1989): 105-22.

———. *Beyond Individualism.* New York: Oxford University Press. 1992.

———. "The Social Nature of Autonomy." In *Review of Politics* 55, no. 1 (1993).

———. *Democracy's Midwife.* Lanham, Md.: Lexington Books, 2002.

Dallmayr, Fred. *Achieving Our World.* Lanham, Md.: Rowman & Littlefield, 2001.

———, and Jose M. Rosales, eds. *Beyond Nationalism?* Lanham, Md.: Lexington Books, 2001.

Dannreuther, Roland. "Cosmopolitan Citizenship and the Middle East." Pp. 143-67 in *Cosmopolitan Citizenship,* eds. Kimberly Hutchins and Roland Dannreuther. New York: St. Martin's Press, 1999.

Derrida, Jacques. *Cosmopolitanism and Forgiveness.* New York: Routledge, 2001.

Doble, John, and Jean Johnson. *Science and the Public: A Report in Three Volumes.* New York: Public Agenda Foundation, 1990.

Dryzek, John. *Deliberative Democracy and Beyond.* New York: Oxford University Press, 2002.

Dunant, Jean-Henri. *A Memory of Solferino.* Geneva: International Committee of the Red Cross, 1986.

Ellinor, Linda, and Glenna Gerard. *Dialogue: Rediscover the Transforming Power of Conversation.* New York: John Wiley & Sons, 1998.

Elster, Jon. "Introduction." Pp. 1-18 in *Deliberative Democracy,* ed. Jon Elster. Cambridge, U.K.: Cambridge University Press, 1998.

Emerson, Ralph Waldo. "Politics." In *Essays: Second Series,* 1844. www.transcendentalists.com/emersonessays.htm.

Erikson, Erik. "The Problem of Ego Identity." In *Identity and Anxiety,* eds. M. R. Stein, A. J. Vidich, and D. M. White. New York: Simon and Schuster, 1960.

Euben, Roxanne L. "Killing (For) Politics." *Political Theory* 30, no. 1, (2002): 4-35.

Falk, Richard. "Revisioning Cosmopolitanism." In *For Love of Country?* Ed. Joshua Cohen. Boston, Mass.: Beacon Press, 1996.

Fishkin, James. *Democracy and Deliberation.* New Haven, Conn.: Yale University Press, 1993.

Follett, Mary Parker. *Creative Experience.* New York: Peter Smith, 1951/1924.

Forester, John. "Beyond Dialogue to Transformative Learning." In *Political Dialogue: Theories and Practices,* ed. Stephen Esquith. Atlanta, Ga.: Rodopi, 1996.

Fowler, James. *Stages of Faith.* San Francisco: Harper & Row, 1981.

Freud, Sigmund. *Civilization and Its Discontents.* New York: W.W. Norton, 1961.

Garfield, Charles, Cindy Spring, and Sedonia Cahill. *Wisdom Circles.* New York: Hyperion, 1998.

Gilligan, Carol, John Michael Murphy, and Mark B. Tappan. "Moral Development Beyond Adolescence." In *Higher Stages of Human Development.* Eds. Charles N. Alexander and Ellen J. Langer. New York: Oxford University Press, 1990.

Glazer, Nathan. "Limits of Loyalty." Pp. 61-65 in *For Love of Country?* Ed. Joshua Cohen. Boston, Mass.: Beacon Press, 1996.

Glover, Jonathan. *Humanity.* New Haven: Yale University Press, 1999.

Godwin, William. *Memoirs of the Author of a Vindication of the Rights of Women,* chapter vi, 90; quoted in Peter Singer, *One World* (New Haven, Conn.: Yale University Press, 2000), 159.

Goleman, Daniel. *Emotional Intelligence.* New York: Bantam Books, 1995.

Gutmann, Amy. "Democratic Citizenship." Pp. 66-71 in *For Love of Country?* ed. Joshua Cohen. Boston, Mass.: Beacon Press, 1996.

———, and Dennis Thompson. *Democracy and Disagreement.* Cambridge, Mass.: Harvard University Press, 1996.

Habermas, Jurgen. *Knowledge and Human Interests.* Boston, Mass.: Beacon Press, 1971.

———. *The Inclusion of the Other.* Cambridge, Mass.: The MIT Press, 1998.

———. *Time of Transitions.* Malden, Mass.: Polity Press, 2006a.

———. *The Divided West.* Malden, Mass.: Polity Press, 2006b.

Hamill, Pete. *New York Daily News,* July 20, 2002, www.deliberative-democracy.net/resources/, accessed July 2009.

Harris, Sam. *The End of Faith.* New York: W. W. Norton & Company, 2004.

Heater, Derek. *World Citizenship and Government.* New York: St. Martin's Press, 1996.

———. "Does Cosmopolitan Thinking Have a Future?" Pp. 179-98 in *How Might We Live? Global Ethics in a New Century,* eds. Ken Booth, Tim Dunne, and Michael Cox. New York: Cambridge University Press, 2001.

Hegel, G. W. F. *Phenomenology of Spirit,* trans. A. V. Miller. New York: Oxford University Press, 1979.

Held, David. *Democracy and the Global Order.* Stanford, Calif.: Stanford University Press, 1995.

————, Anthony McGrew, David Goldblatt, and Jonathan Perraton. *Global Transformations.* Stanford, Calif.: Stanford University Press, 1999.

————. "Reframing Global Governance: Apocalypse Soon or Reform!" In *Globalization Theory: Approaches and Controversies,* eds. David Held and Anthony McGrew. Malden, Mass.: Polity Press, 2007.

Hill, Jason D. *Becoming Cosmopolitan.* Lanham, Md.: Rowman & Littlefield, 2000.

Himmelfarb, Gertrude. "The Illusions of Cosmopolitanism." Pp. 72-77 in *For Love of Country?* ed. Joshua Cohen. Boston, Mass.: Beacon Press, 1996.

Hobbes, Thomas. *Leviathan.* Ed. Michael Oakeshott. New York: MacMillan Publishing Co., 1962.

Hoffe, Otfried. *Kant's Cosmopolitan Theory of Law and Peace.* New York: Cambridge University Press, 2006.

Hollinger, David A. *Postethnic America.* New York: Basic Books, 2000.

Hume, David. *Treatise of Human Nature.* Oxford: Clarendon Press, 1968.

Huntington, Samuel. "The Hispanic Challenge. In *Foreign Policy* (March/April 2004: 1-12.

Hutchings, Kimberly, and Roland Dannreuther, eds. *Cosmopolitan Citizenship.* New York: St. Martin's Press, 1999.

Hutchings, Kimberly. "Political Theory and Cosmopolitan Citizenship." Pp. 3-32 in *Cosmopolitan Citizenship,* eds. Kimberly Hutchings and Roland Dannreuther. New York: St. Martin's Press, 1999a.

————. "Feminist Politics and Cosmopolitan Citizenship." Pp. 120-42 in *Cosmopolitan Citizenship,* eds. Kimberly Hutchings and Roland Dannreuther. New York: St. Martin's Press, 1999b.

Hutchins, Robert M. "World Government Now." Pp. 411-24 in *Readings in World Politics,* edited by Robert Goldwin. New York: Oxford University Press, 1959.

Isaacs, William. *Dialogue and the Art of Thinking Together.* New York: Random House, 1999.

Irigaray, Luce. *Between East and West,* trans. Stephen Pluhacek. New York: Columbia University Press, 2002.

Jacobs, Didier. *Global Democracy.* Nashville, Tenn.: Vanderbilt University Press, 2007.

James, William. "A Suggestion About Mysticism." In *Understanding Mysticism,* ed. Richard Woods. Garden City, N.J.: Image Books, 1980.

————. *The Varieties of Religious Experience.* Cambridge, Mass.: Harvard University Press, 1985.

Jefferson, Thomas. *The Writings of Thomas Jefferson.* Twenty volumes ed. Albert Ellery Bergh. Washington, D.C.: Thomas Jefferson Memorial Association, 1905.

Johnson, Jean. *Science Policy Priorities and the Public.* New York: Public Agenda Foundation, 1989.

Jones, Charles. "Patriotism, Morality, and Global Justice." Pp. 125-70 in *NOMOS 61: Global Justice,* eds. Ian Shapiro and Lea Brilmayer. New York: New York University Press, 1999a.

————. *Global Justice.* New York: Oxford University Press, 1999b.

Jones, W. T. *A History of Western Philosophy: The Medieval Mind,* Volume 2. New York: Harcourt, Brace and World, 1969.

Kant, Immanuel. *Kant's Political Writings.* Ed. Hans Reiss. Cambridge, U.K.: Cambridge University Press, 1970.

Kaplan, Pascal. "Toward a Theology of Consciousness." Ph.D. diss., Harvard University, 1976.

Kegan, Robert. "Making Meaning: The Constructive-Developmental Approach to Persons and Practice." In *Personnel and Guidance Journal* (January 1980).

———. *The Evolving Self.* Cambridge, Mass.: Harvard University Press, 1982.

———. *In Over Our Heads.* Cambridge, Mass.: Harvard University Press, 1994.

Kelsen, Hans. *General Theory of Law and State.* Cambridge, Mass.: Harvard University Press, 1945.

Kleingeld, Pauline. "Kantian Patriotism." *Philosophy & Public Affairs* 29 (2000): 313-41.

Kohlberg, Lawrence. *Essays on Moral Development.* San Francisco: Harper & Row, 1981.

———, and Robert A. Ryncarz. "Beyond Justice Reasoning: Moral Development and Consideration of a Seventh Stage." In *Higher Stages of Human Development,* eds. Charles N. Alexander and Ellen J. Langer. New York: Oxford University Press, 1990.

Koplowitz, Herb. "Unitary Consciousness and the Highest Development of Mind." In *Adult Development, Volume 2: Models and Methods in the Study of Adolescent and Adult Thought,* eds. Michael L. Commons, Cheryl Armon, Lawrence Kohlberg, Francis A. Richards, Tina A. Grotzer, and Jan D. Sinnott. New York: Praeger, 1989b.

Kramer, Deirdre. "Post-Formal Operations? A Need for Further Conceptualization." In *Human Development* 26 (1983): 91-105.

———. "Development of an Awareness of Contradiction Across the Life Span and the Question of Postformal Operations." In *Adult Development, Volume 1: Comparisons and Applications of Developmental Models,* eds. Michael L. Commons, Jan D. Sinnott, Francis A. Richards, and Cheryl Armon. New York: Praeger, 1989.

———, and Diana S. Woodruff. "Relativistic and Dialectical Thought in Three Adult Age Groups." In *Human Development* 29 (1986): 280-90.

Krause, Sharon. *Civil Passions.* Princeton, N.J.: Princeton University Press, 2008.

Kuhn, David. *The Structure of Scientific Revolutions.* Chicago, Ill.: The University of Chicago Press, 1962, 1996.

Kuper, Andrew. "Reconstructing Global Governance: Eight Innovations." In *Globalization Theory: Approaches and Controversies,* eds. David Held and Anthony McGrew. Malden, Mass.: Polity Press, 2007.

Leighninger, Matt. *The Next Form of Democracy.* Nashville, Tenn.: Vanderbilt University Press, 2006.

Levi-Strauss, Claude. "Cosmopolitanism and Schizophrenia." Pp. 177-85 in *The View from Afar.* New York: Basic Books, 1985.

Lewit, David. "Porto Alegre's Budget Of, By, and For the People." www.yesmagazine.org. Posted December 31, 2002. Accessed June, 2009.

Linklater, Andrew. "Cosmopolitan Citizenship." Pp. 35-59 in *Cosmopolitan Citizenship,* eds. Kimberly Hutchings and Roland Dannreuther. New York: St. Martin's Press, 1999.

Loevinger, Jane. *Ego Development.* London: Jossey-Bass, 1976.

Louden, Robert B. *The World We Want.* New York: Oxford University Press, 2007.

Lu, Catherine. "The One and Many Faces of Cosmopolitanism." In *The Journal of Political Philosophy* 8, no. 2 (2000): 244-67.

Lukes, Steven. "Relativism in Its Place." Pp. 261-305 in *Rationality and Relativism.* Eds. Martin Hollis and Steven Lukes. Cambridge, Mass.: The MIT Press, 1982.

Maalouf, Amin. *In the Name of Identity.* Trans. Barbara Bray. New York: Arcade Publishing, 2000.

Macedo, Stephen. *Diversity and Distrust.* Cambridge, Mass.: Harvard University Press, 2003.

Manin, Bernard. "On Legitimacy and Political Deliberation." In *Political Theory* 15, no. 3 (1987): 338-68.

Mansbridge, Jane. *Beyond Adversary Democracy.* Chicago: University of Chicago Press, 1980.

Maslow, Abraham. *Toward a Psychology of Being.* New York: Van Nostrand Reinhold, 1982.

Mathews, David. *Politics for People.* Urbana, Ill.: University of Illinois Press, 1994.

Matilal, Bimal Krishna. "Ethical Relativism and Confrontation of Cultures." In *Relativism,* ed. Michael Krausz. Notre Dame, Ind.: University of Notre Dame Press, 1989.

Markson, David. *The Last Novel.* Berkeley, Calif.: Shoemaker & Hoard (now Counterpoint Books), 2007.

Marx, Karl. *A Contribution to the Critique of Political Economy.* New York: International Publishers, 1970.

———. *Capital,* Volume 1. New York: Penguin, 1976.

Marx, Karl, and Frederick Engels. *Economics and Philosophical Manuscript* in *Collected Works Volume Three.* New York: International Publishers, 1975.

———. "Critique on the Gotha Programme." Pp. 564-570 in *Selected Works,* ed. David McLellan. New York: International Publishers, 1975.

———. "Theses on Feuerbach." Pp. 3-8 in *Collected Works Volume Five.* New York: International Publishers, 1975.

———. "The German Ideology." Pp.159-191 in *Selected Works,* ed. David McLellan. New York: Oxford University Press, 1977.

McCoy, Martha, and Patrick L. Scully. "Deliberative Dialogue to Expand Civic Engagement: What Kind of Talk Does Democracy Need?" In *National Civic Review* 91 (2002).

McDonough, Kevin, and Walter Feinberg, eds. *Citizenship and Education in Liberal-Democratic States: Teaching for Cosmopolitan Values and Collective Identities.* New York: Oxford University Press, 2003.

McNamara, Patrick. *Where God and Science Meet: How Brain and Evolutionary Studies Alter Our Understanding of Religion* (forthcoming).

Mead, George Herbert. *Mind, Self & Society.* Chicago: University of Chicago Press, 1934.

Mill, John Stuart. *Utilitarianism, On Liberty, and Considerations on Representative Government.* London: Dent, 1972.

Miller, David. "The Ethical Significance of Nationality." *Ethics* 98 (July 1988): 647-62.

———. "In What Sense Must Socialism Be Communitarian?" *Social Philosophy & Policy* 7, No. 2 (1989): 51-73.

———. *On Nationality.* Oxford: Oxford University Press, 1995.

———. *Citizenship and National Identity.* Malden, Mass.: Polity Press/Blackwell, 2000.

———, and Michael Walzer. *Pluralism, Justice, and Equality.* Oxford: Oxford University Press, 1995.

Miller, Melvin E. "World Views, Ego Development, and Epistemological Changes from the Conventional to the Postformal." In *Transcendence and Mature Thought in Adulthood,* eds. Melvin E. Miller and Susanne R. Cook-Greuter. Lanham, Md.: Rowman & Littlefield, 1994.

———, and Susanne R. Cook-Greuter, eds. *Transcendence and Mature Thought in Adulthood.* Lanham, Md.: Rowman & Littlefield, 1994.

Miller, Richard W. "Cosmopolitan Respect and Patriotic Concern." In *Philosophy & Public Affairs* 27 (1998): 202-24.

Monastersky, Richard. "Religion on the Brain." In *The Chronicle of Higher Education* 52, no. 38 (May 27, 2006): A15-19.

Montesquieu, Charles de Secondat. *Pensées et Fragments Inedits de Montesquieu* 1. Ann Arbor, Mich.: University of Michigan Press, 1899.

Mutz, Diana. *Hearing the Other Side.* New York: Cambridge University Press, 2006.

Neff, Stephen C. "International Law and Cosmopolitan Citizenship." Pp. 105-19 in *Cosmopolitan Citizenship,* eds. Kimberly Hutchings and Roland Dannreuther. New York: St. Martin's Press, 1999.

Newberg, Andrew, and Mark Robert Waldman. *Born to Believe.* New York: Free Press, 2007.

———. *How God Changes Your Brain.* New York: Ballantine Books, 2009.

Newberg, Andrew, Eugene D'Aquili, and Vince Rause. *Why God Won't Go Away.* New York: Ballantine, 2001.

Niebuhr, Reinhold. *The Children of Light and the Children of Darkness.* New York: Charles Scribner's Sons, 1960.

Nielsen, Kai. "Cosmopolitan Nationalism." In *Nationalism and Ethnic Conflict: Philosophical Perspectives,* ed. Nenad Miscevic. Chicago, Ill.: Open Court, 2000.

Noddings, Nel, ed. *Educating Citizens for Global Awareness.* New York: Teachers College Press, 2005.

Nussbaum, Martha C. "Patriotism and Cosmopolitanism." In *For Love of Country?* ed. Joshua Cohen. Boston: Beacon Press, 1996.

———, and Amartya Sen. "Internal Criticism and Indian Rationalist Tradition." In *Relativism,* ed. Michael Krausz. Notre Dame, Ind.: University of Notre Dame Press, 1989.

Olssen, Mark. *Toward a Global Thin Community.* London: Paradigm Publishers, 2009.

O'Neill, Onora. "Bounded and Cosmopolitan Justice." Pp. 45-60 in *How Might We Live? Global Ethics in a New Century,* eds. Ken Booth, Tim Dunne, and Michael Cox. New York: Cambridge University Press, 2001.

Parekh, Bhikhu. "Cosmopolitanism and Global Citizenship." In *Review of International Studies* 29, (2003): 3-17.

Parkinson, John. *Deliberating in the Real World.* New York: Oxford University Press, 2006.

Partington, John S. *Building Cosmopolitanism: The Political Thought of H. G. Wells.* Burlington, Vt.: Ashgate Publishing Co., 2003.

Perry, William. *Forms of Intellectual and Ethical Development in the College Years.* New York: Holt, Rinehart & Winston. 1968.

Piaget, Jean. *The Language and Thought of the Child.* London: Routledge & K. Paul, 1952.

———. *The Construction of Reality in the Child.* New York: Basic Books, 1954.

Pinsky, Robert. "Eros Against Esperanto." In *For Love of Country?* ed. Joshua Cohen. Boston, Mass.: Beacon Press, 1996.

Plato. "Protagoras." In *Plato: The Complete Works,* trans. Stanley Lombardo and Karen Bell. Indianapolis: Hackett Publishing Co., 1997a.

———. "Seventh Letter." In *Plato: The Complete Works,* trans. Stanley Lombardo and Karen Bell. Indianapolis: Hackett Publishing Co., 1997b.

———. "The Republic." In *Plato: The Complete Works,* trans. Stanley Lombardo and Karen Bell. Indianapolis: Hackett Publishing Co., 1997c.

Plotinus. "The Fifth Ennead." In *Plotinus: The Enneads,* trans. Stephen MacKenna. London: Faber and Faber, 1969.

Polletta, Francesca. *It Was Like a Fever.* Chicago, Ill.: The University of Chicago Press, 2006.

Power, Samantha. *A Problem from Hell.* New York: Basic Books, 2002.

———. "A Hero of Our Time." In *New York Review of Books* 51, no. 18 (November, 2004): 10-28.

Pranis, Kay. *The Little Book of Circle Processes.* Intercourse, Penn.: Good Books, 2005.

———, Barry Stuart, and Mark Wedge. *Peacemaking Circles.* St. Paul, Minn.: Living Justice Press, 2003.

Rakove, Jack N. "The Structure of Politics at the Accession of George Washington." Pp. 261-94 in *Beyond Confederation,* edited by Richard Beeman, Stephen Botein, and Edward C. Carter, II. Chapel Hill, N.C.: University of North Carolina Press, 1987.

Rawls, John. "Kantian Constructivism in Moral Theory." In *Journal of Philosophy* 77 (September 1980): 515-72.

———. "Justice as Fairness: Political not Metaphysical." In *Philosophy and Public Affairs* 14, no. 3 (1985): 223-51.

———. *Political Liberalism.* New York: Columbia University Press, 1993.

Roche, Douglas. *Global Conscience.* Toronto: Novalis Press, 2007.

Rousseau, Jean-Jacques. *Social Contract with Geneva Manuscript and Political Economy.* Ed. Roger D. Masters, trans. Judith R. Masters. New York: St. Martin's Press, 1978.

———. *Emile.* Trans. Allan Bloom. New York: Basic Books, 1979.

———. *The Social Contract and Discourses.* London: J. M. Dent & Sons, 1983.

———. *Political Writings.* Ed. and trans. Frederick Watkins. Madison, Wis.: The University of Wisconsin Press, 1986.

Rubio-Carracedo, Jose. "Globalization and Differentiality in Human Rights." In *Beyond Nationalism?* Eds. Fred Dallmayr and Jose M. Rosales. Lanham, Md.: Lexington Books, 2001.

Ryan, Alan. "Cosmopolitans." *The New York Review of Books* 53, no. 11 (2006): 46-49.

Ryfe, David. "Does Deliberative Democracy Work?" In *Annual Review of Political Science,* no. 8 (2005): 48-71.

———. "Narrative and Deliberation in Small Group Forums." In *Journal of Applied Communication Research* 34, no. 1 (2006): 72-93.

Sachs, Jeffrey. *Common Wealth.* New York: Penguin Press, 2008.

Sanders, Lynn. "Against Deliberation." In *Political Theory* 25, no. 3 (1997): 347-76.

Satz, Debra. "Equality of What Among Whom?" Pp. 67-85 in *NOMOS 61: Global Justice,* eds. Ian Shapiro and Lea Brilmayer. New York: New York University Press, 1999.

Saunders, Harold H. *Politics Is About Relationship.* New York: Palgrave/Macmillan, 2005.

Schlereth, Thomas J. *The Cosmopolitan Ideal in Enlightenment Thought.* Notre Dame, Ind.: University of Notre Dame Press, 1997.

Schuon, Fritjof. *The Transcendent Unity of Religions.* New York: Harper & Row, 1975.

Shapiro, Ian, and Lea Brilmayer, eds. *NOMOS 61: Global Justice.* New York: New York University Press, 1999.

Shroder, Tom. *Old Souls.* New York: Simon & Schuster, 1999.

Shue, Henry. "Mediating Duties." In *Ethics,* vol. 98 (1988).

Sidgwick, Henry. *The Method of Ethics.* Chicago: University of Chicago Press, 1962.

Singer, Peter. *One World.* New Haven, Conn.: Yale University Press, 2002.

————. "Famine, Affluence, and Morality." Pp. 272-285 in *Applied Ethics: Critical Concepts in Philosophy,* eds. Ruth F. Chadwick and Doris Schroeder. New York: Routledge, 2002.

Sinnott, Jan D. "The Dance of the Transforming Self: Both Feelings of Connection and Complex Thought Are Needed for Learning." In *New Directions for Adult and Continuing Education,* no. 108 (2005): 27-37.

Smith, A. D. *National Identity.* Reno, Nev.: University of Nevada Press, 1991.

Smith, Stacie Nicole, and David Fairman. "The Integration of Conflict Resolution into the High School Curriculum." In *Educating Citizens for Global Awareness,* ed. Nel Noddings. New York: Teachers College Press, 2005.

Souvaine, Emily, Lisa L. Lahey, and Robert Kegan. "Life After Normal Operations." In *Higher Stages of Human Development,* eds. Charles N. Alexander and Ellen J. Langer. New York: Oxford University Press, 1990.

Stace, W. T. *The Teachings of the Mystics.* New York: New American Library, 1960.

————. *Mysticism and Philosophy.* London: MacMillan, 1973.

Stevenson, Ian. *Twenty Cases Suggestive of Reincarnation.* Charlottesville, Va.: University Press of Virginia, 1974.

————. *Unlearned Language: New Studies in Xenoglossy.* Charlottesville, Va.: University Press of Virginia, 1984.

————. *Where Reincarnation and Biology Intersect.* Westport, Conn.: Praeger, 1997,

Sunstein, Cass R. *Designing Democracy.* New York: Oxford University Press, 2001.

Swarns, Rachel L. "Role in Group Enhances Mbeki's Image." In *New York Times,* July 10, 2002.

Tallian, Laura. *Direct Democracy: A Historical Analysis of the Initiative, Referendum, and Recall Process.* Los Angeles, Calif.: People's Lobby, 1977.

Taylor, Charles. *Philosophical Papers 1: Human Agency and Language.* Cambridge: Cambridge University Press, 1985.

————. *Philosophical Papers 2: Philosophy and the Human Sciences.* Cambridge: Cambridge University Press, 1985.

————. *Sources of the Self.* Cambridge, Mass.: Harvard University Press, 1989.

Tocqueville, Alexis de. *Democracy in America.* Ed. J. P. Mayer and trans. George Lawrence. Garden City, New York: Doubleday, 1969.

Toulmin, Stephen. *Return to Reason.* Cambridge, Mass.: Harvard University Press, 2001.

Tuan, Yi-Fu. *Hearth & Cosmos.* Minneapolis, Minn.: University of Minnesota Press, 1996.

Turner, Bryan S. "National Identities and Cosmopolitan Virtues." In *Beyond Nationalism?* Eds. Fred Dallmayer and Jose M. Rosales. Lanham, Md.: Lexington Books, 2001.

Underhill, Evelyn. *Mysticism.* New York: E. P. Dutton, 1911.

Vertovec, Steven, and Robin Cohen, eds. *Conceiving Cosmopolitanism.* New York: Oxford University Press, 2002.

Wade, Jenny. *Changes of Mind.* Albany, New York: State University of New York Press, 1996.

Waldron, Jeremy. "What Is Cosmopolitan?" In *The Journal of Political Philosophy* 8, no. 2 (2000): 227-43.

————. "Cosmopolitan Norms." In *Another Cosmopolitanism,* by Seyla Benhabib. New York: Oxford University Press, 2006.

Walker, R. B. J. "Polis, Cosmopolis, Politics." In *Alternatives* 28 (2003): 267-86.

Walsh, Katherine Cramer. *Talking About Politics.* Chicago: The University of Chicago Press, 2004.

———. *Talking About Race.* Chicago: The University of Chicago Press, 2007.

Walzer, Michael, ed. *Toward a Global Civil Society.* Oxford, U.K.: Berghahn Books, 1995.

Wexler, Philip. *Mystical Society.* Boulder, Col.: Westview, 2000.

Wheatley, Margaret. *Turning to One Another.* San Francisco: Berrett-Koehler Publishers, 2002.

Wheatley, Shannon. "Everyday Cosmopolitical Practices in Contested Spaces: Moving Beyond the State of Cosmopolitanism." Ph.D. dissertation, Arizona State University, 2010.

Wilber, Ken. *Eye to Eye.* New York: Anchor Press/Doubleday, 1983.

———. *The Complete Works of Ken Wilber, Volume Six: Sex, Ecology, Spirituality.* Boston: Shambhala Publications, 2000a.

———. *Integral Psychology.* Boston: Shambhala Publications, 2000b.

———. *A Theory of Everything.* Boston: Shambhala Publications, 2000c.

———. *Boomeritis.* Boston: Shambhala Publications, 2002.

———, and Bill Ury. "Towards an Integral Theory of World Governance: The Importance of Stages of Development." http://in.integralinstitute.org/talk, December 6, 2004, accessed June, 2009.

———, and James Turner. "The Integral-Political Imperative, Part 3: A Trans-Partisan Vision for America." http://in.integralinstitute.org/contributor.aspx?id=180, April 18, 2008, accessed June, 2009.

Wilpert, Greg. "Integral Politics: A Spiritual Third Way." In *Tikkun* 17, no. 4 (2001).

Wolin, Sheldon. "The People's Two Bodies." In *democracy* 1, (1981): 9-24.

Wood, Gordon S. "Interests and Disinterestedness in the Making of the Constitution." Pp. 69-109 in *Beyond Confederation,* eds. Richard Beeman, Stephen Botein, and Edward D. Carter II. Chapel Hill, N.C.: University of North Carolina Press, 1987.

———. "Knowledge, Power, and the First Congress." In *Knowledge, Power, and Congress,* eds. William H. Robinson and Clay H. Wellborn. Washington, D.C.: Congressional Quarterly, Inc. (1991): 44-65.

Woodruff, Paul. *First Democracy.* New York: Oxford University Press, 2005.

Yankelovich, Daniel. *The Magic of Dialogue.* New York: Simon & Schuster, 1999.

Zimbardo, Philip. *The Lucifer Effect.* New York: Random House, 2007.

Index

agency, 69-71, 80; and autonomy, 80; and AQAL Model, 117
Alexander, Charles, 97
Alinsky, Saul, 103n27
analysis, 235
Anderson, Benedict, 25, 144n17
Anderson, Jensine, 189n2
Appiah, Anthony, 52, 161-62
AQAL Model, and Wilber, Ken, 2, 109, 112-127; and autonomy in community,141; and autonomy in pluralistic society, 141-42; and religion, 154; and behavior, 206
Arendt, Hannah, 18, 28, 35n20, 45
Aristotle, 138; and *phronesis,* 145n25; and *synesis,* 171, 209-10; and *sumbouleuesthai,* 193n44
Aufheben, 114-15, 143n2, 143n4
Aurelius, Marcus, 17; authentic person, 110-11; and Maslow, Abraham, 110-11
autonomy, 57; and formal operational level of self, 72, 79-80
Ayer, A.J., 173

Bakke, Dennis, 102n24
Baldwin, James Mark, 79
Barber, Benjamin, 59n13, 271
Basseches, Michael, 84, 112
Beauregard, Mario, 95, 104n37; and Paquette, Vincent, 155, 190n8
Beck, Donald, 82
Beck, Ulrich, 53
Benhabib, Seyla, 230-31, 244n49, 284, 292
Benson, Herbert, 94, 104n36
Bernstein, Richard, 187
Bickford, Susan, 225, 226, 243nn38-40, 227
Bohm, David, and dialogue, 226-28, 231, 243-44n41, 244n42, 244n43
Boulding, Kenneth, 2

Brahe, Tycho, 18, 33n5
Burke, Edmund, 67, 68
Button, Mark, 235-36, 246n60
Byatt, A. S., 59n12

Callan, Eamonn, 314-15
Cathedral at Chartres, 106; and labyrinth, 107-109
Chickering, A. Lawrence, 85, 103n26; and transpartisan dialogue, 85, 103n26; and storytelling, 222, 243n28
Christian Centering Prayer, 193n49
citizen juries, 263
citizenship and national identity. *See* Miller, David
Civil Society Assembly or Chamber, 277; and United Nations, 277
Cloots, "Anarchsis," 19, 33n7; and social contract theory, 19
communitarians, 52-53
consensus, 261; *consentire,* 261; in democratic dialogue, 261
Consensus Building Institute, 220-21
"Considerations on the Government of Poland," 33n4
contemplation, 173, 193n49; and Christian Centering Prayer, 193n49; and Plotinus, 175, 193n55; contemplatives, 181, 194n62
contextualism, 81, 102n23
Cook-Greuter, Susanne R., 82-83, 89, 93; and Maslow, Abraham, 111, 207
cosmopolitan constitution, 288
cosmopolitan education, 10, 309-19
cosmopolitan identity, 2-3; and Nussbaum, Martha, 6, 28-29; and dialectical thinking, 7, 83, 88-89, 90, 103nn31-32; and Gutmann, Amy, 29, 35n7; and moral obligation, 63, 67; autonomy and agency, 79-

national identity. *See* Miller, David
National Issues Forums, 10, 220, 233,
    242n21, 264; and Kettering
    Foundation, 264, 301n17
nationality, 44-49; and Miller, David,
    44-46; and pride of principle v.
    pride of place, 49; and Habermas,
    Jurgen, 49; and totalitarianism, 50
Native American Wisdom Councils, 10
natural law theory, 17
neuropsychology, 8
neuroscience of religion, 8
Newberg, Andrew, 95, 104n37; and
    cognitive neuroscience of religion,
    154, 189n3; and HMPAO-SPECT
    imaging, 154, 189nn3-4; and sur-
    vey of spiritual experiences,
    190n12
Nielsen, Kai, 51
Nietzsche, Friedrich, 14, 75, 101n18
Nussbaum, Martha, 6, 27; and cosmo-
    politan identity, 6, 31-32; "Patriot-
    ism and Cosmopolitanism," 24,
    34n16; and *For Love of Country?*
    24, 31, 38; and Stoics, 24-25;
    and allegiance to human beings,
    26, 39; and humanity, 53; and
    identification as cosmopolite, 43-
    44; and moral capacity, 52; and
    right to autonomy, 52; and Ap-
    piah, Anthony, 52; and Himmel-
    farb, Gertrude, 53; and national
    identity, 53; and Barber, Benja-
    min, 59n13; and Pinsky, Robert,
    59n15; and cosmopolitan educa-
    tion, 65, 315

"oceanic feeling," and Freud, 95
On Nationality, 58n4, 58-59n8. *See
    also* Miller, David

paideia, 319
Parkinson, John 223, 243n33, 272; and
    Electronic Town Hall, 272-73,
    301n31
Partington, John S., 302nn24-25
perspectivism, 171; or *synesis,* 209-10
phronesis, 187, 194n64

Piaget, Jean, 71; and formal operations,
    101n15
Pinsky, Robert, 59n15
planetary consciousness, 212
Plato, 15, and *Protagoras,* 16; and
    Socrates, 16; and integral politics,
    137-38; and power of dialectic,
    229-30, 244n47; and imagination,
    250
plebiscitary democracy, 201-202
Polletta, Francesca, 222, 242n24,
    242n26, 226, 244n42
Porto Alegre, 199-200, 240nn2-3
Power, Samantha, *A Problem from
    Hell,* 24; and Dallaire, Romeo, 64,
    99n1
Pranis, Kay, 223, 228, 243n31, 244n44,
    252-55, 300nn2-3, 300n6
principle of subsidiarity, 216
Protagoras, 16
public jury, 218-19
public (communal) validation, 172,
    193n47

"R2P," "responsibility to protect," 290,
    291, 304n48. *See also* United
    Nations
Rawls, John, 51, 172, 193n48
reason-giving, 170, 171, 192n41, 210
relativism, 81, 102n23
relaxation response, 94, 179, 194n61
Roche, Douglas, 1
Roosevelt, Theodore, 315
Rousseau, Jean-Jacques, 14; and *Social
    Contract with Geneva Manuscript
    and Political Economy,* 33n4;
    and *La Nouvelle Eloise,* 14; and
    Julie's Elysium, 14; and *Emile,*
    15, 33n4; and world city, 18; and
    cosmopolites, 18, 33n4; and "A
    Discourse on the Origins of In-
    equality," 33n4; and education,
    33n4; and "Considerations on the
    Government of Poland," 33n4;
    and "A Discourse on Political
    Economy," 33n4; and state of
    nature, 33n4; and justice, 33n4
Ryfe, David, 246n61

About the Author

Jack Crittenden is Associate Professor of Political Science in the School of Politics and Global Studies at Arizona State University. The author of *Beyond Individualism* (1992) and *Democracy's Midwife* (2002), he is currently working on a book on direct deliberative democracy, as well as a novel about the life and times of Pinzak. He also works with the Interactivity Foundation on promoting citizen and student discussions of important social and political issues.

Breinigsville, PA USA
07 March 2011
257081BV00001B/2/P